MAKING CONTACT

MAKING CONTACT

A SERIOUS HANDBOOK FOR LOCATING AND COMMUNICATING WITH EXTRATERRESTRIALS

Edited by Bill Fawcett

WILLIAM MORROW AND COMPANY, INC.
NEW YORK

Library of Congress Cataloging-in-Publication Data

Making contact : a serious handbook for locating and communicating
with extraterrestrials / edited by Bill Fawcett.—1st ed.
p.   cm.
ISBN 0-688-14486-1
1. Unidentified flying objects—Sightings and encounters.   2. Life
on other planets.   3. Human-alien encounters.   4. Interstellar
communication.   I. Fawcett, Bill, 1947–   .
TL789.M238   1997
001.942—dc21   97-1653
CIP

Printed in the United States of America

First Edition

1 2 3 4 5 6 7 8 9 10

BOOK DESIGN BY OKSANA KUSHNIR

CONTENTS

INTRODUCTION

There will be no more important event in our lifetime, perhaps in the history of the human being, than the first contact with an extraterrestrial civilization. The frightening part of this, aside from speculation in movies such as *Independence Day,* is that this contact appears most likely to be made by someone who simply happens to be in the right (or wrong) place at the time the contact is made. The purpose of this handbook is to prepare the reader to be this person. It began with the speculation, What would you need to have on hand to make such a contact successfully? After asking this question of numerous UFO experts, scientists from different fields, historians, and even science fiction authors, it became apparent that what you have to know, or to be able to find out quickly, was as important as what you have with you at the time. This led to an examination of past encounters and speculation on why such a contact has not already occurred. The result is *Making Contact.* Here you will find articles that range from a historical overview of past contact events and speculation on the biology and psychology of extraterrestrials to a list of names and contact information on individuals and agencies that are prepared help. This book deals with the nitty-gritty of establishing communications and what to carry in your pockets to a discussion of the morality needed to maintain a stable interstellar society. There are also a number of simple diagrams at the end of the book that may assist you after contact with extraterrestrials. It is possible that nothing could prepare anyone to be at the focus of such an event. Hopefully this book will at least leave you better prepared.

Included between the sections of this book are short case studies of actual incidents. For anyone who is a student of UFO phenomena, be he amateur or professional, the research of data from encounters with UFOs is usually a very frustrating experience. There are three basic types of events one must sift through, and the vast majority of these often lead to a dead end.

The first type of event is that someone has seen a natural phenomenon and misinterpreted it as being extraterrestrial in origin. Unfortunately, this sometimes becomes the rationalization for all unexplained observations, either by a dismissive media or by those who simply do not want to admit the possibility of alien contact. Yet we must remember that even if the phenomenon can be explained as natural or man-made, most observers at that instant believe that they are seeing *something else* and as a result might very well be frightened or elated, and thus within their own minds the data are distorted. In this way a meteor can sprout wings, Venus on the horizon at dawn will dart all over the sky, and a lenticular cloud will spin and flash lights—for at that moment the truthful observer will be so excited as to become convinced that that is what he or she saw. We see this type of event when examining records of experienced pilots who suddenly take on Jupiter in a dogfight, convinced that it is weaving and maneuvering.

The second type of event is the one that truly muddies the waters, the case of crackpots or paranoids who see aliens lurking behind every tree. Maybe they actually do see them there, maybe they were abducted and had needles poked in their bodies, but it is obvious that many who claim to have such experiences actually need an adjustment of their medication. This is the truly frustrating aspect of UFO research, for yet again it is such individuals that the media and detractors of serious research often seize upon. Unfortunately, maybe some of these individuals actually did have an experience that truly terrified them, but they come across as so unreliable or unbalanced that it is difficult to sift through the data and come to a clear conclusion.

The third type is the one this book will pay serious attention to, and yet even here there will be frustration. Focusing in on those phenomena that might very well be alien contacts, one quickly realizes that the information flow can become even more distorted. When the cases reported in this book are examined, one must truly try to imagine being in the position of those who observed the events described—in other words, imagine yourself scared out of your wits or darn near in a state of ecstasy because it's finally happened to you. Even when it comes to the myth of the dispassionate trained observer, there is still a level of excitement that will distort reaction and recall.

Therefore, when considering the cases cited in this study, it is easy for all of us to Monday-morning-quarterback how the situation was handled. That frustration is quite evident as well among those who have had encounters, the wish to be able to replay the event so that this time they get it right, just as we wish we could replay so many other events in our lives.

If you were to have the chance to prepare for an encounter, if you were given notice that exactly twenty-four hours from this moment you would meet aliens, what would you do? How would you prepare?

There is that greatly overworked statement that we study history in order to learn from it and to avoid repeating it. Perhaps that is the best point to consider when examining the case studies: What went right, what went wrong, and how could it have been handled differently? Taking that as a departure point, the next step is obvious and that is to prepare in your own mind what you will do if the chance comes your way and you experience a contact. For who knows? You could be next.

SECTION ONE

MAKING CONTACT

PREPARING
FOR THE UNKNOWN

by Richard F. Haines

Any contact of the third or fourth kind is
likely to be dangerous. This is, by definition,
the unknown. But this does not mean you
cannot prepare yourself physically and
emotionally for the experience.

AN ACTUAL SCENARIO[1]

A chill, low-moaning wind moved across the clearing, which was surrounded by spindly second- and third-growth pines. To the south and
west, less than a hundred yards away, lay the shore and a little farther
yet the dark expanse of Lake Champlain. To the north and east lay
Vermont's usually pungent green forests and gentle hills. The only people living within miles were Nancy and Jim, a newly married couple
who had found their dream house by the lake. Residents for barely two
months, now they were anticipating the advent of winter.

It was just after sundown in mid-November when they had their
visit, or whatever it might be called. The young couple was still at the
supper table enjoying a second cup of coffee. Both of them were mar-
veling at their luck in finding this idyllic spot. But it wasn't to remain
so for long.

At this moment neither of them could have seen or heard the even-
surfaced metallic disk with rows of slowly rotating multicolored lights
around its circumference that had smoothly descended through the
thick, dark overcast. Nearing the earth, the ninety-foot-wide object be-

---

[1]This story is based upon an actual event that occurred in a different part of the country
in the fall of 1988. The narrative illustrates a typical recollection of details without
hypnotic regression.

gan to move more irregularly with sudden starts and stops; only a low generator-like hum could be heard if one were near it. Finally it was in place, fixed solidly in the air.

Nancy was the first to see the glow through the picture window. Her first thought was "fire" because the ground appeared in a flickering, pulsating reddish-orange light. "Our roof is on fire," she cried.

Quickly Jim's gaze followed hers. Then he jumped up and raced down the hall and out through the front door in seconds. He didn't even turn the porch light on under the overhanging roof but ran down the steps onto the gravel path that led to the parking area. Then he stopped and, wheeling around, looked up at his roof. He thought to himself, *But we didn't even have a fire going in the fireplace.* His logic was sound. He was so intent on looking for flames, he was surprised and strangely unsettled to see nothing but darkness there. *What's going on?*

But as his eyes became accustomed to the night's darkness, he made out a small circle of very intense, flickering, orange-red light like a searchlight coming from a spot in the sky at least a hundred feet or more above him. It was clearly hanging below the bottom of the clouds. Soon he made out what looked like the outline of a huge circle of dull metal. Around its circumference were dim, pulsating colored lights all aiming outward like spokes on a wagon wheel.

The ground around him was brightly illuminated by the single, intense light centered in the bottom of the object. Within a circle about a hundred feet across, it was as bright as midday as far as he could tell.

"What is that thing?" he cried out loud. He was overwhelmed by the sight. *No, it just cannot be . . . something that huge just suspended there . . . totally silent!* Jim's mind was reeling in disbelief. He stood frozen to the spot, not sure whether he was physically paralyzed or only immobilized by the fear that was quickly displacing his amazement and awe.

Meanwhile Nancy had started to get up from the kitchen chair to follow her husband outside. But she hesitated and turned toward the phone on the counter only a few feet away. Her first thought was to call the fire department. *But,* she reasoned to herself, *I'd better wait until we know what's wrong for sure.* It was at that moment that she felt a tickling sensation at the crown of her skull and then a soothing warmth spread quickly in her neck and shoulder muscles and more slowly down her chest and back. Within ten seconds it was complete. Nancy felt very funny now, she could not hold her head upright, and her chin dropped to her neck involuntarily, abruptly. But she could still see all right.

For an unknown period of time strange, foreign ideas began to flood her mind, mathematical formulas she knew nothing about, scientific terms she had only heard in her Introduction to Physics class in college. Moments later the dizziness began, and she felt as if she was falling through space. Nancy has always been prone to seasickness and was afraid she was going to vomit. It was a terrible feeling and it came over her so quickly this time. *That's funny,* she thought, *why would I think it was quicker this time?*

Before she knew it, she felt herself slump down onto the kitchen floor like a sack of dried beans; all of her muscles were so relaxed that she couldn't stand up any longer. Finally her mind went blank. She could still see and hear, but she couldn't process anything. Nothing made any sense any longer.

It wasn't until some time later that Jim staggered back inside the house in a dazed state, his eyes glazed, his mind almost completely blank also. The sky was now completely dark. Not only had the object left but the clouds were a leaden pitch-black.

"Nan, honey, where are you?" he called out weakly. "Hon, it's me . . . it's all right now. It's gone."

Nancy heard her husband's footsteps in the hallway and they somehow broke the spell that had held her immobile on the floor for a long time.

He felt a tremendous relief when he heard her voice coming from the back of the house. "Oh . . . oh, is that you, Jim? I'm so glad you're okay." She paused a moment and then said, "What happened? I was so worried about you, you were gone so . . ." She didn't finish her statement, as her mind was still confused. "Where have you been?" she asked as she glanced at the wall clock. It read just past ten P.M.

He just held her close and repeated weakly, "It's all right. It's gone now."

INTRODUCTION

Statistically speaking, it is a fact that unidentified flying objects (UFOs), or whatever they are, can appear at any place on earth and at any time of day or night. No place or time is safe from their presence, nor immune from their influences—and there are many different kinds of influences on humans both good and bad.[2] UFOs do not respect any

[2]Research on various "behavioral" patterns of UFOs has been conducted over the years using various computerized databases, the largest of which is UFOCAT (for UFO Catalogue) maintained by the J. Allen Hynek Center for UFO Studies, in Chicago. Surprisingly consistent patterns have been found to characterize the phenomenon.

cultural boundaries, do not restrict their activities to people in particular language groups or to those who hold a certain pattern of beliefs. And they seem to display a kind of arrogant presence. What do I mean by this?

I have studied the subject of anomalous aerial phenomena for almost thirty years. Over this time I have noticed that these apparently metallic disks do not obey "established" laws of physics; in doing so they continue to confound scientists. Some of these vapor-shrouded objects can produce strong radar returns. Others are seen by multiple eyewitnesses but remain invisible to radar. They often fly "too close" to airplanes; indeed jet interceptor pilots seem to be taunted by them. Official U.S. government records have acknowledged that very bright unidentified balls of light incapacitated several electrical systems on board an American-built F-4 Phantom jet of the Imperial Iranian Air Force in September 1976 sent up to chase them. The lights clearly outperformed the jet aircraft. After their aerial game of cat and mouse was over, the lights accelerated out of sight to the west.

Other UFOs may hang silently in the night sky near a farm house blinking what look like anticollision beacons until someone comes outside with a shotgun. Seven cases have been reported where someone heard their bullet ricochet off the surface of the object, like "metal striking metal." The object sometimes emits a small object or a loud sound or a ray of light before quickly shooting upward out of sight. Still others progress majestically across the daytime sky in formations of ten, twenty, or more at a time.[3] It is as if they are toying with us, at least acting as if they are invincible.

Based upon these kinds of typical UFO responses reported from around the world, we should ask, What should you do if you are suddenly confronted by a UFO? This is the subject discussed here. I will suggest some practical things you should do, each of which is related to different ways UFOs manifest themselves. These UFO manifestations fall into several groups; one's response should vary depending upon which kind of event occurs. These groupings are I. distant sightings, II. close encounters, and III. direct bodily involvement.

---

[3]The interested reader may want to read *Project Delta: A Study of Multiple UFO* (1994) by the author, which documents 473 cases involving two or more UFOs seen at the same time and place.

I. DISTANT SIGHTINGS

An example of this kind of UFO experience would include a nighttime sighting of an anomalous light passing in zigzag fashion across the sky, an obviously distant grouping of multicolored objects cavorting like a military acrobatic team, a radar contact in an air traffic control center,[4] or a distant cloud that seems to coalesce into a smooth metallic object that then flies away. There are scores of other possibilities as well. In the suggestions that follow it is assumed that the person can see, hear, and/or feel the presence of the UFO but is not in any clear or present danger from it.

What to Do

First, do not panic. There is no reason to panic because it will do no good and only may increase the risk of personal injury. Just try to stay calm and in the same place throughout the entire sighting. *Second,* if you think you are perceiving something highly unusual in the sky (or under water), mark your present location in some way. Also take careful note of the direction you are looking in. Use all available visual landmarks and a compass if possible. This will greatly assist others later in studying the phenomenon. *Third,* if possible, try to find someone else to come see the phenomenon with you, but if you are successful, do not compare notes with him. Allow him to record his own experiences. Most UFO sightings last about five minutes or less, so this step may not be possible. *Fourth,* get a pencil and paper and write down exactly what happened. Record the time, date, and place, and make sketches. Try not to interpret what you experienced; leave that for others later. Write down only objective facts.

II. CLOSE ENCOUNTERS

The author of this now-familiar term, *close encounter,* Dr. J. Allen Hynek, was a professional astronomer and professor of astronomy at Northwestern University near Chicago. He was hired by the U.S. Air

---

[4]A radar sighting is so different a category from all the others that it will not be dealt with here. The radar operator is (a) safely inside a building; (b) surrounded by colleagues; and (c) highly constrained in how he or she can respond.

Force relatively early in his career to provide scientific analysis services to their Project Blue Book, a collection and analysis of anomalous atmospheric phenomena,[5] which many military personnel had been reporting since World War II. He once told me that when he first began this consulting work, he didn't believe UFOs existed. "This job probably couldn't amount to much," he once said. Little did he realize that he would be given access to such startling classified evidence positively supporting the existence of UFO phenomena that he would have to change his mind about them. Although initially skeptical that such objects could exist, or at least be visiting earth across the vast expanse of space that surrounds us, eventually Dr. Hynek did change his public position. When Project Blue Book was terminated (December 17, 1969), Hynek lost this consulting work and went on to found the private Center for UFO Studies near Chicago. He also developed the first useful taxonomy of sightings, which continues to be used today—a classification scheme that includes the idea of the "close encounter."

Dr. Hynek found it useful to group close (UFO) encounters into three separate categories, which are defined below. As before, I will provide suggestions on how to respond if you should find yourself in each kind of close encounter; my comments are based on working with many people over the years who claim to have had such an encounter as well as what happened to them afterward. Of course one cannot know in advance, or even during the experience, exactly what kind of close encounter one is having. For instance, in the opening story Nancy and Jim had only a vague idea what had taken place that night at their home. They had no way of knowing whether they had experienced a close encounter of the first, third, or fourth kind. But if you should find yourself in this situation and have a general understanding of these categories, it may help you to decide what is happening and what you can do about it.

CE-1: Close Encounter of the First Kind

According to Hynek's definition,[6] the first kind of encounter is one in which the unidentified flying object (UFO) is seen at close range but produces no permanent interaction with the environment (other than some possible psychological trauma to the observer). He defined "close"

---

[5]This effort was known by the names Project Sign, Project Grudge, and Project Blue Book. An interesting and detailed history of these efforts, which ended in 1969, are found in D. M. Jacobs, *The UFO Controversy in America* (1975).
[6]See J. A. Hynek, *The UFO Experience* (1972), p. 32.

as being within about several hundred feet of the object, craft, or phenomenon. If we ignore the element of missing time and mental confusion in our opening story, when Jim went outside and looked up, he was experiencing a close encounter of the first kind.

What to Do

First, do not panic! Such self-defeating behavior will only increase the risk of personal injury and lessen your ability to remember details accurately. *Second,* stay put. Don't run or try to hide except to protect yourself from debris or other objects that may be flying through the air. *Third,* try to concentrate mentally on as many details as possible. If you are having a "typical" CE-1, your senses may be literally filled to overflowing. Your mind may seem to be in a confused state, your adrenaline pumping. And you may feel like immediately running and hiding. But don't do it. It won't make any difference anyway to the phenomenon— intelligent or unintelligent, animate or inanimate. If what you are seeing is a craft under the guidance of highly intelligent beings and it is within a couple of hundred feet, "they" know of your presence and probably will carry out their objective anyway. And if "they" are only a natural phenomenon, such as a luminous plasma that is "riding" on a nearby electromagnetic field line, it probably won't matter very much whether you are close or far away. *Fourth,* after the encounter is over, mark the spot with a pile of stones, broken tree branches placed in a cross, a handkerchief tied to a twig, and so on. *Fifth,* go home and write down everything you can remember, including all seemingly unrelated events; make drawings. For example, if you come home later than you expected, note the times involved (when you left and when you returned), or if you suddenly notice some new scar or other skin blemish, note it in your journal. *Sixth,* try to find someone you trust and care for and tell him or her exactly what happened to you. It's okay to insist on confidentiality from her at this point. Such sharing will help you get the experience outside yourself and make it more objective. *Seventh,* telephone or write to one of these organizations to report your experience:

Mutual UFO Network
103 Oldtowne Road
Seguin, TX 78155

J. Allen Hynek Center for UFO Studies
2457 West Peterson Avenue
Chicago, IL 60659

They will treat you with respect and keep your information confidential if you so indicate. *Finally,* if you think you can tolerate the social ridicule and curiosity that usually accompany reporting a UFO sighting, you may want to contact the authorities. Call your local police, newspaper, radio station, sheriff's department, or the Federal Aviation Administration (FAA) to find out if others reported seeing the same thing. But then be prepared to be ridiculed. In spite of the fact that about one-half of America's adults now believe in the existence of UFOs, our society is not yet ready to respond with the compassion or acceptance that is needed toward those who have actually encountered one.

CE-2: Close Encounter of the Second Kind

A Close Encounter of the Second Kind refers to events similar to the first kind except that definite physical effects are noted on both animate and inanimate material. For example, vegetation is scorched or pressed down; tree branches or grass stems are bent or fractured; various-shaped impressions are made in the ground; soil may be affected in other ways (e.g., dehydrated, scorched, irradiated, covered with some residue); animals may act with fright. Inanimate objects such as automobiles and airplanes may be interfered with in different ways. For example, radios may suddenly change stations or experience static interference, car engines can stop altogether, compasses may rotate, and direction finders cease to operate. A broad spectrum of so-called electromagnetic effects have been reported.

Your response to a CE-2 should be little different from your response to a CE-1 or a distant sighting. Referring to the previous section, follow all eight of the steps listed[7] but add a *ninth,* which will help protect you from possible injury. If you should find some unknown artifact(s), materials, substances, or ground impressions, do not touch or disturb them in any way. Not only will you protect yourself from possible injury but you will help safeguard the evidence for others. If it is raining, try to locate a large plastic tarpaulin (or painting sheet) to cover the spot where the evidence is.

---

[7]One of the most important of these steps is the seventh: You should contact a research organization that is experienced in protecting and collecting this evidence in such a way that valid scientific measurements can be obtained.

CE-3: Close Encounter of the Third Kind

A Close Encounter of the Third Kind involves seeing a UFO at near range in which one or more humanlike creatures are seen or associated with the object in some way. Interestingly, while the literature contains many such stories, the human witness is seldom affected in any significant way. More commonly the creatures go about their business as if no one is present, even ignoring the humans altogether.

What to Do

First, do not panic, but instead try to remain calm and as observant as possible. *Second,* if you are approached by "them" and can walk or run away, do so. Don't wait. If at all possible, don't permit yourself to be captured by the beings. Unfortunately this may be less up to you and your response and more up to "them," as will be mentioned in the following section. Most likely they will leave you alone. *Third,* try to remember as many details as you can. You will probably be very excited or confused; try to use a mental-association technique to help you recall details later. Associate a visual detail with a letter of the alphabet, such as the following:

A = *a*liens (creatures seen, about five total, one taller)
B = *b*ees (they moved around in an irregular manner)
C = *c*ounterclockwise rotation, disk, flew away vertically
D = *d*ipped down as it approached
H = *h*umming sound
L = *l*ights, many colors, red and blue predominated
M = *m*etallic silver suits, worn by creatures
and so on

III. DIRECT BODILY INVOLVEMENT

CE-4: Close Encounter of the Fourth Kind

A CE-4 is still poorly understood and is shrouded in fear and skepticism in most Western societies. In a typical encounter in which someone claims to have been abducted, we will find a broad array of symptomatology: unexplained body marks, abnormal emotional reactions, an unusual altered state of consciousness, lucid dreams, out-of-body vision(s), obsessive-compulsive behavior, personality changes, reception of previously unknown information, and other responses. It is partially this breadth of symptoms that has confused investigators and inhibited most physical scientists and physicians from getting involved.

So how can you know whether you have been abducted? This is not a simple question, and its answer must be found in a comparison of the experiences of many others who claim it has happened to them. Importantly, a large majority of these people describe much the same set of events. It is this particular diagnostic "sign" of event-consistency that can be used to determine the likelihood that an abduction has taken place. Bullard (1995, p. 108) has said, "A depth of integration holds the themes of the abduction story together in a plausible whole. The experience lasts a lifetime, and shifts focus in keeping with changes in the life cycle, especially the reproductive cycle." In other words the high degree of consistency found between the details of the claimed abduction scenario and one's lifestyle changes are striking and suggest that an actual, physical event has taken place.

Thus, if you have experienced at least seven or eight of the following nine "episodes," as I call them, there is reasonable evidence to believe that you have had a close encounter of the fourth kind, sometimes called an alien abduction. These episodes are distilled from reading the literature and working with many people who claim to have had a CE-4. Other researchers offer other signs as well.

What are these general episodes? They include the following:

1. An *alerting-orienting stimulus*, which diverts your attention from some current, ongoing task to a new direction or event. Usually the stimulus consists of an unusual light, noise, vibration, or electrical-shock sensation. There is reason to believe that if one does not permit one's attention to remain diverted in the new direction, the other (abduction) events will not take place.

2. *Capture*; i.e., those events surrounding one's transport or abduction from the original environment to a new, unfamiliar environment, often a craft or relatively small enclosure. A currently debated issue is whether or not transport is physical or only mental. There is fascinating evidence on both sides.

3. *Communication* and *special messages* with/from the "beings." Any mental (telepathic), auditory, or written transfer of information to you qualifies here. Interestingly, there are documented cases where the person develops new talents, understandings, and "capabilities" suddenly following the claimed abduction.

4. A *tour* of the new place you find yourself in. Some abductees interpret this episode as being given to them in exchange for their cooperation. They are often shown highly advanced technology, architecture, displays and controls of some sort, as well as a host of other unfamiliar things.

5. A *personal examination* of some type; it could involve scrutiny of one's body, mind, or psyche. It is usually performed ruthlessly in comparison with terrestrial medical practice. The "visitors" do not seem to realize that human beings feel pain, nor do "they" appear to respond to our humor.

6. *Travel to and from a second, larger craft or enclosure;* this episode is interesting for several reasons. First, it is not a theme found in very many science fiction books or movies (and therefore probably does not originate in them), and second, very often this episode has a different thematic character from the abductee's preexisting lifestyle, interests, or belief system. The place where one is allegedly taken is sometimes described as mythological in character, with Greek-like statues and columns, giant animals, and vaporous beings. The larger environment itself is always completely enclosed and may appear less technological (e.g., a gardenlike valley with an artificial sky/roof) compared with the original craft or enclosure/cave.

7. A *tour of a second environment* is given. Here one may be escorted to different locations, during which time the beings may communicate telepathically. As before, the tour episode seems to be offered as an inducement to cooperate as much as to educate.

8. The *return* episode includes all events surrounding how you were brought back to your starting point. My work has shown that one is returned in the identical mode of transport that one was originally taken to the second (large) environment, almost like running a movie backward.

9. The *aftermath* episode includes all of the physical, psychological, physiological, psychic, and spiritual life changes that are experienced after the abduction. Of course some of these sequelae can serve as medical and scientific evidence for the occurrence of a traumatic event(s) and as such are very important to have been examined. As many hundreds, if not thousands, of people have discovered, their personal aftermath events can last a lifetime.

What to Do

It is difficult to provide a list of specific procedures to follow for several reasons. For one thing, each person's abduction experience is somewhat different, and for another, it is most likely that you will not remember very much of your encounter until much later. Some people begin to recall fragmented bits of details only after many years. It is common for some type of trigger event to occur to cause a memory to jump into consciousness. You are suddenly confronted with a bizarre recollection that seems to be based on a real event but that makes no sense by itself. You may simply experience a slowly growing awareness of some of the earlier abduction episode(s) at a conscious level. Lucid dreams and/or precognitive visions of future events may also occur. Because of the diversity of possible responses it is difficult to advise you exactly on the best course of action.

It is fair to say that you have two general courses of action in seeking help with your experiences. In one, which I call the *clinical course,* you would meet with a licensed psychologist or psychiatrist in order to work out the best stress-coping techniques for you. Your primary objective would focus on establishing your psychological health and well-being. In the second course of action, which I call the *research course,* you would work closely with a trained UFO investigator who understands what you have gone through and who also understands something about the rich diversity of UFO phenomena. Your mutual objective would be oriented more toward understanding the core identity of the phenomenon and its impact on yourself and mankind. To help keep from biasing you, the investigator would probably not tell you many details at first but would only gradually disclose relevant facts as your meetings continued. But whichever course you should follow, be prepared for a long and intense interaction, where your deepest beliefs and attitudes may be probed and challenged, where your personality may be tested and analyzed. Be prepared to become a new person.

Therefore, if you suspect that you may have been abducted, *first,* keep a personal diary as you begin to recall earlier experiences no matter how bizarre they may seem. Such records can be of great value to investigators, who can help you work through your traumatic aftermath. But don't expect everything to suddenly become clear. It may require months or years of living with turmoil inside yourself. Sometimes you may even come to think that you are losing your mind. But persevere in what you know to be a psychologically real and intensely personal experience.

Second, tell someone you trust and care for about your suspicions. Tell him as much as you can and ask for his support. Do not keep your experience to yourself.

Third, if you believe that the abduction occurred recently and you notice some bodily scar or other symptoms, for instance, persistent double vision, metallic taste, ringing sounds, disorientation, unsettling dreams, blood discharge, persistent or abnormal thirst, an oversensitivity to light, skin burns, abnormal cardiac responses, and so forth, you should seek assistance from a medical professional regardless of whether he or she believes in the reality of the C-4 or not. Unfortunately it is true that most physicians in America will jump to a psychiatric explanation for most of your claimed aftermath conditions. You should decide in advance how much you are willing to tell your doctor about your encounter. Fortunately there are some medical practitioners supportive of such claims who are also experienced in working with people who think that they have been abducted. Some practitioners are trained in the use of special methods and techniques to unlock your memory. You may want to contact one of the organizations listed Appendix D for such a referral in your area. You should recognize that use of hypnotic regression may or may not actually help in recovering these memories, depending upon many factors. If you think that the abduction took place a long time ago, it may not be as important to obtain an immediate medical examination or counseling. Remember that it is your physical well-being that needs to be safeguarded before documenting the possible reality of the event.

Fourth, don't try to deny the reality of your memories, no matter how strange and impossible they may seem to be. Denial will only embed them deeper into your subconscious. And if, somehow, you should discover that your abduction was only an imagined event with no possible basis in fact, your subconscious will be able to find suitable ways of catharting the associated emotional baggage you may have been carrying around. In other words, time will have a way of healing you of your scars.

PERSONAL OBSERVATIONS—SUMMARY AND CONCLUSIONS

After working with many people from all walks of life and from many different countries of the world who claim to have seen an anomalous aerial phenomenon or of being taken against their will to a very strange-appearing place, and after studying the reliable literature, I am convinced that they are describing a highly consistent phenomenon that has been with mankind for a very long time. I have little doubt that to be forewarned and educated about the things that can happen to you is a good thing, a useful thing. I hope that you may never need to apply these suggestions, but if you do, perhaps you will be better off for having considered them.

REFERENCES

Bullard, T. E. *The Sympathetic Ear: Investigators as Variables in UFO Abduction Reports*. Mt. Rainier, MD: Fund for UFO Research, 1995.

Haines, R. F. *Project Delta: A Study of Multiple UFO*. Los Altos, CA: LDA Press, 1994.

Hynek, J. A. *The UFO Experience*. New York: Ballantine Books, 1972.

Jacobs, D. M. *The UFO Controversy in America*. Bloomington, IN: Indiana University Press, 1975.

Story, R. D., ed. *The Encyclopedia of UFOs*. Garden City, NY: Doubleday & Co., 1980.

IIIIIII

THE PAPUA INCIDENT
by William R. Forstchen, Ph.D.

THIS SERIES OF SIGHTINGS, spanning a period of over a year, from 1958 to 1959, stands as one of the most remarkable and well-documented UFO cases known. If ever there was an event that clearly indicates that "something is happening," this one is it, yet due to the remoteness of the region, lack of photographic evidence, and the fact that the majority of witnesses were "natives," it seems that the Papua Incident has all but slipped through the cracks.

Papua, more commonly known as New Guinea, is one of the remotest regions on earth. The area where the sightings took place, in the Baniara Subdistrict, on the western tip of the island, is a region that was hotly contested by Allied and Japanese forces during World War II. It is an area administered by Australia and at the time of the sightings had a strong European presence due to the aftereffects of the war and extensive missionary work. Due to this impact on the area, many of the local residences and witnesses to the rash of UFO sightings had been west-ernized and were in fact fairly well educated.

The prequel to the 1958–59 sights happened in 1953 near Port Moresby to Mr. T. P. Drury, who was no less than the director of Civil Aviation for the Territory of Papua. Mr. Drury had flown over thirty different types of aircraft and had an extensive aeronautical background. He reported that while standing along a coastal road with his wife and children he noticed an unusual cloud starting to form in what was otherwise a clear blue late-morning sky.

The cloud, which started as a small wisp, rapidly built up into a large cumulus. Fortunately Mr. Drury had a movie camera with him, and he started to film the cloud. While filming the cloud a bullet-shaped metallic-looking craft shot out of it. The craft shot out at a 45-degree angle relative to the horizon, and Drury estimated that it was traveling at supersonic speeds as high as Mach 5. The craft continued upward and disappeared. There was no sound, nor was there a sonic boom.

Drury immediately drove to the airport and found that there was no reported aircraft in the area. A check with the Royal Australian Air Force came up blank as well regarding possible flights in the region. Drury submitted his film to the RAAF, and states that when the film was returned after being sent to America, many of the frames had been clipped, leaving him with nothing more than the image of the cloud.

Additional sightings were reported, from 1955 to 1957, of lights hovering and then moving rapidly off the coast, but these stand as simply a warm-up to the major events of the next two years.

The first "serious" sighting took place in February 1958, when a red light appeared over the Port Moresby airport, dropped to two hundred feet, and "buzzed" the airstrip. The incident was reported by several airport personnel who had years of experience in the field of aviation. All of them stated that what they saw was not an airplane or a helicopter.

Next there was a report from a Catholic missionary station of a bright light hovering over the station in the Milne Bay District. Throughout 1958 there were repeated sightings of bright lights crossing over Good-enough Bay. Dozens witnessed the events, including several missionaries, one of them being Reverend Norman Cruttwell, an Anglican priest, who reported the sightings to the *Flying Saucer Review* of London. After this first rash of sightings Reverend Cruttwell volunteered to record any additional sightings for the International UFO Observers Corps. No major events occurred until early 1959, when a rash of sightings broke out along the coast. A bright light, compared to a "Tilley lamp," which is a kerosene lamp similar to a propane lantern, was repeatedly observed along the coast. The first sighting was reported on March 19, 1959, by a Papuan priest, Reverend Albert Ririka, and a teacher, Augustine Bogino, who worked at Menapi, which is located on the north side of Goodenough Bay. They stated that they observed a bright white light hovering over the Stanley Mountain Range on the other side of the bay.

Eight days later the next sighting of a bright light was reported at Dogura, on the other side of Goodenough Bay, followed by numerous sightings along the bay during the month of April. All reports were similar, describing a bright light moving, usually in a straight line, over the bay.

At Boianai, where the most remarkable events of all would take place, the head missionary, Reverend William Booth Gill, who had served in Papua since 1946, reported his first sighting on April 9, 1959. Reverend Gill was completely unaware of the earlier sightings when he reported seeing a bright light hovering over the mountains behind his station.

During the month of May there were more sightings, but the nature of what was being observed now changed, from a brilliant white light to multicolored lights, one of the observers being the assistant district officer, Mr. Ronald Orwin, who reported watching an object move slowly across the sky, changing colors from bluish white, through green, to orange and bright orange-red. The light snapped off, and then reappeared several minutes later, going through the same cycle of color shifts yet again.

The events climaxed in June over Boianai in what stands as one of the most remarkable "events" ever recorded of UFO contacts. The main reporter was Reverend William Gill, from Boianai station. Though not a trained observer, Reverend Gill, in a very methodical manner, attempted to document the incredible series of sightings that occurred over his station.

The incident started on June 21 when Papuan teacher Stephen Moi came to Reverend Gill with a report of having seen a bright light descend from the mountains behind the station. The glow of light gradually decreased until Moi stated that he could discern an "inverted saucer" hovering in the sky, tilted upward so that the bottom was visible. The object then rose straight up and disappeared. Gill questioned Moi about his sighting, and Moi claimed never to have heard the term *flying saucers*. Gill asked him if it did not look more like a ball or a coin, but Moi insisted it had the appearance of an upside-down saucer. This point is important since Moi had no preconceived notions or understanding of what was being reported in the Western media about UFO contacts. Gill forwarded a report on the incident and rather interestingly closed off his note with the signature "Doubting William." Reverend Gill's opinions, however, were radically changed on the night of June 26, 1959.

At 6:45 in the evening Reverend Gill sighted a bright white light outside his house and called Stephen Moi and another assistant to join him. The object stopped, hovering at a height of three to four hundred feet above the ground. The object shifted colors, was circular in shape, and had an open upper deck.

Fortunately Reverend Gill had the presence of mind to start taking notes while the incident was going on, and thus we have a minute-by-minute account.

Members of the mission community came out to watch, and for the next four hours the Boianai mission station apparently was the focus of attention for a number of UFOs. Almost immediately after the first UFO stopped to hover over the station, Gill reports that four "men" appeared on what he believed was an upper-deck superstructure. The men were illuminated by a shaft of blue light emanating from the center of the ship and by a glow encircling the ship. The ship was too far away to make out any details other than the fact that they appeared to look like men, according to Reverend Gill. Several small ships were spotted as well over the next four hours, moving about, disappearing up into the clouds for a time and then descending again. Shortly before eleven P.M. the ships disappeared.

Reverend Gill gathered the witnesses and went so far as to separate them off and then asked for sketches of what they saw. All the independently drawn sketches proved to be remarkably similar. He then worked up a report, based upon his notes, and twenty-five of the thirty-eight witnesses signed it. The report included sketches of the objects, as well as hand-drawn maps indicating where the ships were sighted relative to the mountains and the coastline. The witnesses included Reverend Gill, five Papuan teachers, and three medical assistants.

In and of itself the June 26 incident is remarkable, but it pales when compared with what would happen the following night.

This incident started at 6:00 P.M. The sun had just set behind the mountains, but it would not be completely dark for another forty-five minutes. Reverend Gill noted that one of his medical assistants first sighted the UFO, and called him out to see it at 6:02 P.M. Gill called several others to join him, and he watched as the ship approached, and two smaller ships appeared, one over the mountains, the second one overhead.

On the larger ship four "men" again appeared on the upper deck. Gill stated that two of them seemed to be working on something in the middle of the upper deck. They would bend over and disappear behind the guard railing, then reappear, raising their arms as if adjusting something that he could not see. One of the men stood by the railing and looked down at the group of a dozen who were watching. Gill said it reminded him of how someone looked when leaning over the railing of a ship at sea to look at the ocean.

Gill then stated, "I stretched my arm above my head and waved. To our surprise the figure did the same. Ananias [a Papaun medical assistant] waved both arms over his head, then the two outside figures did the same. Ananias and self began waving our arms, and all four seemed to wave back. There *seemed* [italics in original report] to be no doubt that our movements were answered. All the mission boys made audible gasps, of either joy or surprise, perhaps both.

"As dark was beginning to close in, I sent Eric Kodawa for a torch and directed a series of long dashes toward the UFO. After a minute or two of this, the UFO apparently acknowledged by making several wavering motions back and forth in a sideways direction, like a pendulum."

Gill and his community shouted and waved, making motions for the ship to descend and land, but there was no further response. It's interesting to note that Gill actually went to dinner at 6:30, and at 7:00 the community went to church for evensong, with the UFOs still in sight. By the time evensong was over, at 7:45 P.M., the UFOs were gone.

The following night they were back again, but there were no more close approaches, though at 11:00 P.M. Gill notes that eight objects were all in view at the same time. There was a loud bang on the roof of the Mission House at 11:20 P.M. and Gill went outside to see four UFOs hovering in a circle. Gill described the noise as sounding as if something metallic had hit the roof, but there was no follow-up sound of something rolling off. Nothing was found on the roof or alongside the mission house the following morning. This ended the sightings at Boianai.

The three days of sightings at Boianai were corroborated by sightings from other stations along Goodenough Bay with a number of reports of UFOs, some of which were different from the ones seen at Boianai. Throughout July there were more sightings along the bay and in the mountains. Many of these incidents in and of themselves could stand out individually as interesting cases worthy of note, but they are over-shadowed by what happened at Boianai. The last major sighting was in October, thus ending the contacts which happened on dozens of occasions and were witnessed by hundreds, perhaps thousands.

ANALYSIS

If there is a frustration over the Papua sightings, it is that they were not accepted as significant enough to be presentable as all but conclusive proof that UFOs exist. Several factors are undoubtedly at play here. First and foremost is the remoteness of the region where the sightings occurred. To this day there are still Neolithic tribes on the island of New Guinea, some of which still practice cannibalism. During World War II the Goodenough Bay area was the scene of intense combat. Survivors on both sides reported it to be at war not only against the human enemy but also against some of the most difficult terrain and climate on the face of the earth. Perhaps it is this very remoteness that led the visitors to the region in the first place. There have also been suggestions that there might be a correlation between the prolonged combat in the region and the subsequent investigation by aliens. The western end of Papua is unique in that it experienced a brief period of significant contact with the higher technological societies of our world, then reverted to a backwater region. Except for Attu and Kiska in the Aleutians, there are few other spots on this planet that were so fiercely fought over and then later abandoned.

It took time for the reports from Papua to filter out to the rest of the world, and due to its remoteness it was not the type of event that would instantly have drawn the media. Do remember that this was 1959. The first airstrips had only been hacked out of the jungle less than twenty years before, and most of the mission stations did not even have radios, let alone telephones, televisions, or even electricity. Thus there was no media blitz regarding this incident, since by the time reports were circulated, it was pretty well over.

Another reason why this incident does not stand out as perhaps the most significant of UFO encounters may be that nearly all the observers were non-Europeans in a remote area. Though the word is overworked, there might very well be a hint of racism regarding the attitude concerning these reports. For, after all, disdainful reviewers claim, it is a remote region and most of the people are one step removed from the Stone Age, and so on.

Yet as Reverend Gill pointed out in his report, it is for precisely this reason that the reported sightings have a veracity to them. The observers were not "contaminated" by preconceived notions put out by the media, nor even by serious UFO studies regarding alien life or the fact that such things might exist. Reverend Gill was a good enough observer to not "coach out" answers, but instead let the witnesses tell what they saw in their own way. The remoteness works to another advantage as well, in that the multiple sightings along a coastline of thirty miles or more were noticed by individuals and groups *independent* of one another. In other words identical reports came in without any possibility of one sighting contaminating another, or in any way influencing another. In the weeks after the events, missionary contact with isolated groups up in the Stanley Mountains indicate that sightings were not confined to the missionary stations but were reported in the interior as well.

Perhaps the most important element missing in the series of sightings is photographic evidence. The one movie taken, six years before the major outbreak, was reported to have been altered after being submitted for evaluation. If only Father Gill had had a camera, his incident would most likely have been hailed as conclusive proof at last. Yet this shows, as well, a certain prejudice regarding the New Guinea sightings. We are, essentially, a visual society. The reports submitted by numerous witnesses, the sworn statements of Anglican priests and their parishioners, do not seem to really count when compared with one smudged photograph, and this is unfortunate.

It's interesting to note that many of us would never think to doubt the word of our parish priest here in the States, yet reports from a number of missionaries do not quite seem to draw the attention they truly deserve.

This case stands out, as well, as one of those incidents in which almost nothing should have been done differently by the human observers. Father Gill displayed a remarkably calm, disciplined approach to the entire affair. He stood, notepad in hand, taking minute-by-minute notes of what was taking place. He then called the witnesses together, had them independently note down what they saw, made out a statement, asked them to read it, and only sign it if they agreed. He was so matter-of-fact about the entire event that it did not disturb his evening meal, church services, or even going to sleep while the UFOs were still overhead.

Regarding his interaction with the "visitors," it could not have been better. He did not panic, no weapons were ever displayed, his parishioners were friendly and even continued with the daily church service while the UFOs were overhead. Most of all, he displayed a friendly attitude, waving, even gesturing for the visitors to land, and elicited a friendly wave in return. (It's an interesting point to speculate on that the gesture of waving was responded to in kind and most likely viewed as friendly. This raises a number of questions regarding the point of whether humanoid species have a universal "body language" displaying friendliness or hostility.) Reverend Gill's actions stand as an interesting model for consideration as to how to deal with a UFO encounter; he attempted to be scientific in his approach, took careful notes while the event was unfolding, displayed friendliness, and provided a clear and concise "after action" report.

If there is any regret over this entire series of events, it is that no photographs were taken. It's frustrating to consider what we might have been presented with if Father Gill had had in his possession a good camera with a telephoto lens and high-speed film. To have caught the wave back on film would have been remarkable, and most likely become one of the most famous photographs of the twentieth century. The gesture, instead, is now only a memory in the minds of those who, nearly forty years later, are still alive to remember it.

THE FOLKLORE OF
ET CONTACT

by Jerome Clark

The history of UFOs, by many names, goes
back to the Bible. In the eighteenth century
there was a spurt of sightings of "flying ships,"
complete with sails in some cases. The history
of modern UFO contact begins in 1947.
Perhaps one of the most amazing things about
UFO-related contacts is the wide variety of
forms these have taken.

In May 1979, writing in a now-defunct magazine called *Second Look,*
Victor Marchetti, a disaffected former CIA officer, took note of the
agency's interest in the UFO question. UFOs, he said, were not a "subject of common discussion" because they, in his words, "seemed to fall
into the category of 'very sensitive activities.'"

He went on, "There were, however, rumors at high levels of the CIA
... rumors of unexplained sightings by qualified observers, of strange
signals being received by the National Security Agency [the U.S. government's electronic intercept and communications intelligence collec-
tor], and even of little gray men whose ships had crashed, or had been
shot down, being kept 'on ice' by the Air Force ... at Wright-Patterson
Air Force Base in Dayton, Ohio. And there was the odd case of the
lady from Maine who, while in a hypnotic trance, had allegedly communicated with a starship."

This last reference is to an undeniably real event. The Maine woman's
name was Frances Swan, one of the hundreds of Americans who by
the early 1950s were claiming contacts with kindly beings from other
worlds. Though flamboyant figures such as George Adamski and Daniel
Fry were attracting the bulk of the attention with their tales of physical
interactions with space people and their productions of photographs

allegedly of spacecraft, most contactees were quiet, obscure, and sincere recipients of what they believed to be psychic messages that came through in dreams, visions, voices in the head, or automatic writing.

Mrs. Swan, an automatic writer with a lifelong interest in the occult, recorded messages from Affa, who communicated from a giant spaceship that had flown in from the planet Uranus. These communications, mostly platitudinous, should have been of interest to no one but Mrs. Swan, except that at one point she told her neighbor, retired Navy Admiral Herbert Knowles, about them. Knowles, who was impressed with her sincerity, urged the Office of Naval Intelligence (ONI) to investigate.

This brought a series of visitors from Washington to the Swan and Knowles residences. None was a high-ranking officer, and none was especially impressed. In 1959, five years after the events just described, an ONI officer who had dealings with the CIA's Photographic Intelligence Center in Washington found some memos on the affair and decided to fly up to Maine himself. This man, who was so impressionable that even Mrs. Swan deemed him something of a fool, became convinced that Affa had communicated to him via automatic writing. On his return to Washington he demonstrated his new powers to the CIA photo center director Arthur Lundahl and to Lundahl's assistant, Lieutenant Commander Robert Neasham. Supposedly Affa promised that a spaceship would show up, but nothing more exciting than a cloud passed by.

Nonetheless around this rather inconsequential incident grew a body of folklore, reported in several UFO books of the 1970s, which held that a UFO had appeared and even blocked out radar signals. It is more likely that Marchetti read this particular story in the UFO literature than that he heard it from CIA colleagues.

LEGENDS OF THE FALLS

Tales of saucer crashes have circulated since the late 1940s. They were, as a matter of fact, the subject of one of the very first UFO books, Frank Scully's 1950 best-seller *Behind the Flying Saucers,* based on what proved (to the surprise of few) to be hoaxed testimony about fallen Venusian and Martian spacecraft in the Arizona and New Mexico desert. Until the mid-1970s few conservative investigators were willing to pay any heed to such reports, to which the caustic phrase "little men in pickle jars" was attached early on. Typically most such accounts are dubious on their face, either because the claimant's credibility is suspect or because, even if he or she appears to be sane and sincere, the story seems unverifiable.

Still, when investigation is possible, the results can be intriguing. The first published crash case, which occurred in Lincoln County, New Mexico, in July 1947 and is now called the Roswell Incident, became the focus of a belated investigation. That investigation began in the late 1970s and has continued well into the 1990s. Hundreds of individuals who had a direct or indirect involvement in the episode have been interviewed, nearly all attesting to the occurrence of an extraordinary event that military authorities went to remarkable lengths to keep secret.

In 1994, at the request of New Mexico Representative Steven Schiff, the General Accounting Office—which conducts investigations for Congress—launched an official probe, which determined only that all official records of the event are missing and unaccounted for. The GAO investigation was still in progress when, in September 1994, the U.S. Air Force released a revised version of its original explanation, that the object at Roswell was a balloon, this time said to have been part of a classified project—an explanation that flew in the face of considerable witness testimony and could not be verified in contemporary records of balloon launchings. Unfortunately barring the sudden discovery and release of the relevant government documents, it appears unlikely at this late date that the truth about the Roswell event will ever be known with certainty.

Though the issue of alleged UFO crashes has generated attention and controversy in both UFO and mainstream media in recent years, another issue has come to the fore, albeit farther out on the fringes. What I will call the Dark-Side Hypothesis has its roots in a body of lore about secret government contacts with extraterrestrials. Marchetti, as we have seen, had heard those rumors from, so he says, CIA associates. Such lore goes back to the early days of UFO study and interest—in other words, back to the late 1940s.

The earliest such rumor I have been able to find is set in 1948, when a large spaceship is said to have landed near Juneau, Alaska. According to Tom Comella, an Ohio saucer enthusiast who chronicled the yarn a few years later, President Truman and his top aides met with the occupants "in an interplanetary parlay.... The earth members of the meeting could not understand some of the space people's humble beliefs and actions."

This story may be a tale that grew in the telling, based on a hoax perpetrated by a movie maker named Mikel Conrad, whose 1949 grade-Z picture *The Flying Saucer* was hyped as containing actual footage of a saucer captured in Alaska. Conrad subsequently confessed this was all a lie.

Another rumor circulating in the early days asserted that President Truman had met aliens not in Alaska but in the Australian bush.

Nineteen fifty-four saw the introduction of one of the most persistent of contact rumors. It continues to circulate even now. In this one President Eisenhower, while on what was billed as a California vacation trip, secretly went to Edwards Air Force Base to meet five saucers and their occupants. The rumor's immediate inspiration was something that really happened: Eisenhower's sudden disappearance from the Palm Springs ranch where he had been staying. A press wire story took note of a widespread belief that he had died. The President resurfaced shortly afterward, along with the explanation that he had suffered tooth problems and been treated by a local dentist.

As early as January 13, 1954, the allegation that saucer wreckage was being stored at a "West Coast military field" was noted by the well-known radio broadcaster and UFO enthusiast Frank Edwards. The story of Eisenhower's visit made it across the Atlantic Ocean by April, when British writer Harold T. Wilkins received a letter from an unnamed "friend in California." In *Flying Saucers Uncensored,* published the following year, Wilkins wrote, "I am assured that these five saucers actually did land *voluntarily* at this Edwards Air Force Base. They were discs of different types and their entities invited the technicians and scientists to inspect their aeroforms and witness a demonstration of their powers." Wilkins's informant claimed to have the story from three sources, none named. Nonetheless from some of the references it is clear that one source was Gerald Light, a mystic also known as Dr. Kappa.

On April 16, 1954, Light wrote N. Meade Layne, director of an occult organization called Borderland Sciences Research Associates, to claim that he and three prominent men had actually been at the base and seen "human beings in a state of complete collapse and confusion as they realized that their own world had indeed ended with such finality as to beggar description. The reality of 'otherplane' aeroforms is now and forever removed from the realms of speculation and made a rather painful part of the consciousness of every responsible scientific and political group. . . . It is my conviction [Eisenhower] will ignore the terrific conflict between the various 'authorities' and go directly to the people via radio and television."

Light's letter neglects to mention that he was claiming not to have visited the base in his physical body, as the reader would naturally assume, but to have manifested there in an out-of-body state.

In 1956 two magazines with the same name, *Flying Saucer Review,* one British, one American, reported two versions of the contact rumor.

In the American *Flying Saucer Review* an anonymous writer identified only as a radio executive said that in 1949 he participated in a South American archaeological expedition, in the company of unnamed prominent scientists who told him the U.S. government intended to release, gradually over a period of years, its knowledge of humanlike space visitors five thousand years in advance of us. Nothing is said here of direct contact between the government and the extraterrestrials, but it is certainly implied.

England's *Flying Saucer Review* also relied on an anonymous correspondent. Nine years later, after his death, he would be identified as Rolf Alexander, M.D. Alexander claimed to have spoken with a "highly placed American who was in touch with Air Force Intelligence and in a position to know the facts about flying saucers." This individual said the U.S. government had communicated with ETs, whom it found to be "completely friendly . . . undoubtedly trying to work out a method of remaining alive in our atmosphere before landing." When their ships had tried to land on three previous occasions, disastrous consequences followed immediately, according to Alexander's informant. "Breathing the heavily oxygenated atmosphere of this Earth had literally incinerated the visitors from within and had burned them to a crisp," Alexander wrote.

Nine years later *Flying Saucer Review* revealed that Alexander's source was the famous general and diplomat George C. Marshall. Unfortunately, as *Flying Saucer Review* did not note, Alexander was hardly a credible source. His real name was Allan Alexander Stirling, a New Zealand sailor who had jumped ship in 1920 and entered the United States illegally. For most of his life he maintained a career in which, flashing bogus medical credentials, he peddled dubious health cures which from time to time earned him prison time. He also boasted of vast psychokinetic powers that enabled him to break up clouds.

FRIENDS FROM TOPSIDE

It was in the contactee subculture, however, that tales of high-level contacts between earthly and unearthly powers flourished. George Hunt Williamson, who claimed psychic and radio contacts with a variety of ETs, wrote in his book *Other Tongues—Other Flesh* (1953), "Some people are wondering if our government is attempting contact with Saucers. They have already had contact, but they are still working at it as evidenced by the fact that at Edwards Air Force Base in California there is a highly secret operation known as Project NQ-707. This project and its personnel are concerned with nothing but radio-telegraphic contact with Saucers. They have been successful in their work and have attempted to get the Saucers to land at a rendezvous point near Salton Sea in Southern California."

Williamson, a fringe archaeologist, was an associate of the most influential contactee of the 1950s, George Adamski. Supposedly Williamson had observed, from a distance, Adamski's initial contact with a Venusian in the California desert on November 20, 1952. Subsequently Adamski would tell of boarding flying saucers piloted by Venusians, Martians, and Saturnians and being flown in them into outer space. To most people, including a great many ufologists, Adamski's story sounded like nothing so much as clumsy science fiction. Yet Adamski attracted an international following and a wide readership for his three books on his interplanetary adventures.

According to Adamski, no less than President Kennedy had met space people. In 1962, when Adamski flew to Saturn to attend a conference, he met the Saturnian spaceship that took him there at a U.S. Air Force base. Its occupants had been conferring there with government officials. On March 9, 1965, he told an Ohio newspaper reporter that before the end of April a "high government official"—apparently Vice President Hubert Humphrey—would confirm his story. All that happened at the end of April, ironically, was Adamski's death from natural causes.

Before all this, however, Adamski had been the recipient of a remarkable letter written on State Department stationery and mailed from Washington, D.C. The letter, impressed with the department seal and signed by R. E. Straith of the Cultural Exchange Committee, expressed support for Adamski's efforts. It also said that the "Department has on file a great deal of confirmatory evidence bearing out your own claims. . . . While certainly the Department cannot publicly confirm your experiences, it can, I believe, with propriety, encourage your work."

To Adamski's followers, of course, this was all the proof they needed of the authenticity of his space-contact stories. The "Straith letter," as it would be called, garnered enormous publicity; even *The Times* of London reported the department's denial on April 10, 1958. The believers saw the department's statement as a cover-up, and Adamski explained that no one had been able to find Straith or his committee because both operated under a high degree of secrecy. As late as 1983 two authors of an admiring biography of Adamski wrote of the Straith letter that "while much of the evidence is circumstantial . . . on balance there is even more in favor of the letter['s] being authentic."

Mainstream ufologists were as skeptical of the Straith letter as of Adamski's other claims. One of them, Lonzo Dove, studied the letter's typeface and concluded it had been composed on the typewriter of Gray Barker, a West Virginia saucer publisher known for his sense of humor. Dove prepared a manuscript and submitted it to Jim Moseley, editor of *Saucer News*. Moseley declined to publish it on the grounds that Dove's charges, which in fact were well argued and convincingly documented, lacked proof. Years later, after Barker's death in late 1984, Moseley confirmed long-standing rumors when he confessed that he and Barker had forged the Straith letter using real State Department stationery obtained from a young man whose father worked there.

An employee of the Canadian government's Department of Transport, Wilbert B. Smith, spoke and wrote openly, especially in later years, of his contacts with what he affectionately called the "boys from topside": space people to the rest of us. In the early 1950s Smith, a radio engineer, headed a tiny operation known as Project Magnet, through which the Canadian government sought to gather UFO information. Little came of it, and it was only minuscully funded, but its final report, which Smith drafted in 1953, stated that "we are forced to the conclusion that the vehicles are probably extraterrestrial."

Actually Smith was hardly "forced" to a conclusion he held even before he started. He was wholly sympathetic to contactee claims of all kinds and had relationships, both cordial and professional, with a number of contactees, including Frances Swan. In 1958 he said in a letter to ufologist Donald Keyhoe, who disdained contactees, "I have spent too many hours conversing with people from elsewhere to have any doubts about their reality or that they are what they claim to be. Those of us who have been fortunate enough to have made contact with these people have learned a great deal, and profited greatly through this knowledge."

It is not clear whether Smith meant he was conversing directly with "people from elsewhere" or communicating through psychic contactees who were channeling in his presence. In any case, as he would write, his methodology consisted of asking "innocuous but significant questions" such as "Do people live on the planet Mars? If so, what is the shape of their houses? Do people on Mars use money? If so, what does it look like?" After satisfying himself that he was dealing with true space people, he would press them for scientific and technical information. Of these efforts he reported, "[A]lien science was definitely alien, and possibly even forever beyond our comprehension. . . . Another approach was tried, the philosophical, and here the answer was found in all its grandeur. . . . I began for the first time in my life to realize the basic 'Oneness' of the Universe and all that is in it. Science, philosophy, religion, substance, and energy are all facets of the same jewel, and before any one facet can be appreciated the form of the jewel itself must be perceived."

As was not the case with the likes of Adamski and Williamson, no serious observer has ever doubted Smith's sincerity (he died in 1962), though his judgment in accepting channeled material as literally descriptive of alien life and knowledge is certainly open to question. It should be noted that at no time did he claim to be doing his contact work in any official capacity. When asked what his government thought, he would say his Department of Transport colleagues knew of it but had no interest in it. Probably they regarded it as a private religious matter that, so long as it did not affect his job performance, was of no concern to them.

Though the standard view of the contactees is that they offered an entirely sunny view of flying saucers and space visitation, in which friendly extraterrestrials had come here both to teach us and to save us from blowing ourselves up with nuclear weapons, there were also darker strains. Adamski and Williamson, for example, claimed that evil space people are here as well. The evil space people are allied with what they called the Silence Group. The Silence Group seeks to thwart the technological advances and moral reforms of the good ETs, known as the Space Brothers. The Silence Group consists of the "International Bankers"—traditionally a code word for Jewish financial interests. Adamski and Williamson were devotees of conspiracy theories ordinarily associated with anti-Semitism. Some of their critics have even argued— stretching a point to breaking—that the blond-haired, blue-eyed Venusians are akin to the Aryans of Nazi mythology. Only Adamski was consciously anti-Semitic, at least in private conversation, but his prejudices were more casual than virulent.

ENCOUNTERS IN THE DESERT

The ET-contact stories that came to prominence in later years had their roots in two events, one of which almost certainly occurred, the other of which may or may not have occurred, over a six-day period in late April 1964.

In the first of these the event that almost surely did take place, a Socorro, New Mexico, police officer named Lonnie Zamora reportedly encountered a landed egg-shaped object and glimpsed briefly two of its occupants, small figures dressed in white coverall outfits. On the side of the UFO, Zamora saw a distinct symbol, shaped like an arrow pointing vertically from a horizontal base toward an umbrellalike half-circle. Zamora's encounter, which occurred on April 24, is well known to every student of the UFO phenomenon, and even Project Blue Book investigators, ordinarily adept at finding explanations even when they had to be force-fit, conceded that this one defied their best efforts. Two years later, writing in *Studies in Intelligence* (February 1966), the classified CIA house bulletin, Blue Book head Lieutenant Colonel Hector Quintanilla characterized it as the most puzzling case he had ever dealt with.

There were other UFO sightings in the Southwest at the time of the Zamora incident, though the Socorro sighting attracted all the attention. Along with the documented reports was a fantastic albeit unsubstantiated rumor. It was reported in the July 1964 issue of the *Bulletin* of the Aerial Phenomena Research Organization (APRO), based in Tucson. According to the APRO story, on April 30 the pilot of a B-57 bomber from Holloman Air Force Base, Alamogordo, New Mexico, radioed the base control tower that he had under observation an "egg-shaped and white" UFO with markings "the same as the one at Socorro." Shortly thereafter the UFO landed on the base.

APRO directors Jim and Coral Lorenzen said they had their story from a "very reliable source." Others claimed to have heard the story, including a radio operator who supposedly had monitored the exchange between the pilot and the control tower. To a newspaper reporter who inquired about the alleged sighting, Holloman offered a flat denial; nothing had happened, a spokesman declared. The Lorenzens swore that they had a separate source for the report; thus, they wrote, "we had three entirely independent, unconnected sources of information."

Around this time an airman buying clothes in Alamogordo blurted out an incredible story. A UFO was parked in a hangar at Holloman, he said, and was under heavy guard. But a day or two later he returned to the store with an apology. He had made a "mistake," he told his listeners, and the story wasn't true. And that was the end of the matter—until nine years later.

In 1973 two well-connected California businessmen, Robert Emeneger and Allan Sandler, were invited to Norton AFB in California to discuss a possible documentary film on advanced research projects. A long, complex series of events followed, during which—so they would assert—they began work on a film that was to reveal what they were told were air force UFO secrets, chief among them a landing and contact at Holloman

AFB in May 1971. At six o'clock one morning that month, so the story went, a UFO landed, and military officers and government scientists met for an extended period of time—two or three days—with aliens. Cameras recorded the landing. According to Paul Shartle, Norton's audio-visual director, who told the story on national television in October 1988, the resulting 16mm film had shown "three disc-shaped craft. One of the craft landed, and two of them went away." A door opened on the landed vehicle, and three beings emerged. Shartle said, "They were human-sized. They had an odd, gray complexion and a pronounced nose. They wore tight-fitting jump suits and thin headdresses that appeared to be communication devices, and in their hands they held a 'translator.' A Holloman base commander went out to meet them."

At one point during his dealings with the air force, Emenegger claimed, he was even taken to Holloman and shown the alleged landing site and the building in which the spaceship had been stored as well as others (Buildings 383 and 1382, specifically) in which meetings between air force personnel and the ETs had been conducted. Though Emenegger's air force sources told him little of the content of those meetings, they assured him that he would be able to use the film in his documentary. At the last minute permission was withdrawn, but Emenegger did get independent confirmation of the film's existence from a colonel at Wright-Patterson AFB.

Emenegger's own film *UFOs Past, Present and Future* and a paperback book of the same title appeared in 1974. The Holloman incident, treated in three pages of the book's "Future" section, is depicted as something that "hypothetically" could happen. Elsewhere, in a section of photos and illustrations, is an artist's concept of what one of the Holloman entities looked like, though it, along with other alien figures, is described only as being "based on eyewitness descriptions." Emenegger's association with the military and intelligence people he had met while doing the film would allegedly continue for years. Once during the late 1980s, he says, his sources told him that he was about to be invited to film an interview with a live extraterrestrial in a southwestern state, but nothing came of it.

Except for the date, May 1971, one would link this alleged event with the supposed Holloman landing of April 1964. Later, however, ufologist William Moore, coauthor of the first book on the Roswell incident, would claim to have entered into a long-term relation with air force intelligence and counterintelligence officers who allegedly were cover-up insiders. They told him that the Holloman landing Emenegger described had really taken place on the April date. One of Moore's principal informants, Kirtland AFB Sergeant Richard Doty of the Air

Force Office of Special Investigations (AFOSI), said the same thing to Linda Howe. Howe was also promised footage of the Holloman landing, along with other extraordinary UFO-related films, but again, nothing came of this.

As Moore and his associate Jaime Shandera relate it, their air force informants tell of supersecret projects that communicate, electronically and physically, with several extraterrestrial races, at least one of which— the little gray men familiar to students of abduction lore—actively directed human evolution and helped shape our religious beliefs. Supposedly the climax to Steven Spielberg's 1977 film *Close Encounters of the Third Kind* is a slightly fictionalized version of the Holloman landing.

None of this is supported by any evidence, but the motives of the informants remain murky. If nothing else, though, they provided a framework for a new generation of tellers of tall tales, who would wed nightmarish conspiracy theories to UFO-cover-up stories.

The way Moore's sources told it, ET visitation does not threaten the well-being of the earth's inhabitants, and those government, military, and intelligence people who maintain the cover-up do so for honorable and patriotic motives, which are understandable even to those who do not agree with them. But in post-Vietnam, post-Watergate America it seemed impossible for some to believe the government would do anything for any but the most sinister of reasons. The seeds of the Dark-Side Hypothesis were about to sprout.

TALES FROM THE DARK SIDE

During the 1970s much of middle America was taken with reports of cattle mutilations said to be occurring in the tens of thousands. Speculation focused immediately on Satanic cults, the CIA, and extraterrestrials. In a couple of instances persons who had been hypnotized to "remember" abduction experiences related that they saw not only cattle mutilations but evidence of human mutilations. There is no certain way to judge whether these were true memories or mere confabulation (though the absence of persuasive evidence for a cattle-mutilation "phenomenon" makes the latter the more probable explanation). There is no doubt, however, that the mutilations had created a climate of anxiety in which it was widely feared that human beings would be the next victims.

In 1977, as part of an April Fool's Day joke, a British television network aired a mock documentary titled *Alternative Three,* which purported to expose a massive international conspiracy. According to the show, the world's leaders had secretly conspired to develop an advanced space program that years ago had led to the establishment of slave colonies on the Moon and Mars, to which they would flee once the greenhouse effect started to destroy the rest of the human race. Meanwhile, needless to say, the ruling class killed or in other ways neutralized all those who suspected the truth. Mutilated bodies were dumped in remote places.

While inherently absurd, the show was presented so straight-facedly that many impressionable viewers took it to be a *real* documentary. Publication of a paperback based on the show spread the story to the United States and wowed paranoid ufologists, who already had begun to suspect that maybe evil aliens and the U.S. government were working in cahoots to mutilate cattle and people. If we are to credit William Moore's account, some of his military sources at Kirtland AFB even encouraged the delusions of a civilian scientist who believed he was deciphering electronic signals between Kirtland and UFOs and who had incorporated abduction, mutilation, and *Alternative Three* scenarios into the terrifying fantasies that eventually led to his complete emotional collapse. According to Moore, the military's purpose was to drive the scientist crazy by filling him with fantastic disinformation. The signals he was monitoring were quite real and highly classified, though they had nothing to do with UFOs.

If this is so, this is a genuine case of egregious official misconduct. But it was nothing compared with the yarns that evolved over the 1980s. These yarns revived early contactee Silence Group ideas, sometimes in fairly blatantly anti-Semitic form, and wed them to more modern UFO ideas, such as crashed UFOs, cover-ups, abductions, and mutilations. They also brought in lock, stock, and barrel every lunatic political-conspiracy theory the far right had ever hallucinated.

By the late 1980s elements of American ufology were on the brink of hysteria. Puzzlement led to paranoia, frustration, and rage. The first major Dark Side figure, John Lear, the estranged son of aviation pioneer William P. Lear, startled ufologists with some of the wildest tales they had ever heard. According to Lear, years ago the secret government that controls the world (yes, *that* secret government) entered into an unholy alliance with man-eating aliens in exchange for access to ET technology. The ETs, from an ancient race near the end of its evolution, use materials from human and cattle body parts to rejuvenate themselves, and government and alien scientists are creating soulless android creatures in vast underground laboratories in the Southwest. Not only that, according to Lear, whose political views are far to the right of center; the evil secret government sought to enslave the world's population through drug addiction.

Milton William Cooper soon came along to pick up where Lear left off. According to Cooper, a former navy petty officer who claimed as sources classified documents he had seen while in service, the secret government runs drugs, launders money, and encourages massive street crime so that Americans will be receptive to gun-control legislation. It has also introduced AIDS and other deadly diseases as a method of population control. It plans to round up Americans soon and place them in concentration camps before shipping them off to the secret slave colonies on the Moon and Mars. This of course is right out of *Alternative Three*.

If the early contactees had a basically benevolent vision, which they presented to the impressionable with no supporting evidence, Lear, Cooper, and their clones did the same with a grim vision for which they had no verification whatever. But such are the vagaries of belief that many of their listeners never thought to question. They assumed that if somebody said it and it was awful enough, it must be true. It is unlikely, however, that before the traumas of the 1960s—the assassinations, the destructive and futile war in Vietnam, the agony of Watergate—the Dark Siders would have done as well. As already noted, the early contactees had their own version of a Dark-Side Hypothesis, but it was relatively tame next to Lear's and Cooper's, and it was a distinctly secondary theme in their preachments.

Americans emerged from the 1960s and the early 1970s in a state of profound disillusionment. Whereas in the 1950s a Senator Joe McCarthy could speak of a government riddled with subversives, he presumed that a basically decent society was under threat from outsiders, in this case Soviet agents and Communist sympathizers. After Vietnam and Watergate many Americans came to see their society and their institutions as fundamentally flawed, cynical, manipulative, even evil. That this view is as unrealistic as its opposite is beside the point. What matters is that some Americans could now imagine their government to be capable of *anything,* from complicity in the assassination of a president, as Oliver Stone's paranoia-laced (and hugely popular) movie *JFK* would have it, to the betrayal of the whole human race to malevolent extraterrestrial intelligences.

There is virtually no chance that any of these things are true, and there is virtually no chance that any of these beliefs are going to go away soon. In fact if societal stress in the form of racial tensions, employment insecurity, street crime, and other ills continues throughout the rest of the decade and into the early years of the next century, we will see even more of it. Paranoia is a sign of societal as much as of individual emotional disorder. And it is the ultimate unfalsifiable hypothesis: It explains *everything*.

In the real world, and that includes the real world of rational UFO research, much remains to be explained. The trivialization and exploitation of the cover-up issue ought not to blind us to the fact that we have good reason to believe officialdom has not been entirely forthcoming about its involvement with some interesting UFO cases. We have testimony from highly credible sources, not the least of them the former base commander of Wright-Patterson AFB, retired Brigadier General Arthur Exon, that the air force has run a top-secret UFO project and that something truly extraordinary did crash in New Mexico in July 1947.

THE THINGS THAT AREN'T HAPPENING NOW

If Moore's story is accurate, we also have a legitimate instance of official misconduct in the Kirtland AFB incident I have briefly described above. Even if events happened as alleged, no one will be brought to account for it. That is not because there is a lawless secret government but because counterintelligence operatives know they can act with relative impunity when they are dealing with individuals on society's fringes.

Several years ago the noted political journalist Murray Kempton wrote these wry and chilling words: "Domestic covert warfare has no existence as a current event. We never know about it until it is revealed to us as the history that government admits only after assuring us that it has stopped. When it is going on, it is noticed by no one who wants to be thought reasonable, and anyone who speaks of it is dismissed as irrational. Our secret wars at home are never said to happen as long as they are going on, and mightn't we wonder whether one is happening right now when all we know about it is that it isn't?"

In the wake of revelations that came out of congressional hearings and journalistic probing during and after the Watergate era, no one doubts anymore that the FBI, the CIA, and other police and intelligence agencies have engaged in illegal monitoring and even harassment of private citizens. Such activity, as Kempton notes, is said not to be occurring now—or is it? If it is happening to persons interested in UFOs, nothing will be done about it; indeed, those being victimized will have

an ever harder time being believed than, say, those Kempton was thinking of when he wrote his words: opponents of Reagan administration
policy in Central America. After all, as the conventional wisdom has it,
anybody who investigates UFO reports is a kook, and kooks are always
paranoids.

There are plenty of UFO kooks and paranoids, God knows. But
sometimes, as the saying goes, even paranoids have enemies. The scientist who intercepted electronic signals at Kirtland AFB was something
of a kook and a paranoid, but that did not make his victimization by
cynical counterintelligence operatives any less real or morally reprehen-
sible. Who, however, will ever believe him—who, that is, can see that
justice is done?

From the late 1970s on, official-looking documents that purport to
tell about crashed UFOs and classified projects such as the fabled "Ma-
jestic 12" have freely circulated. A number have been traced to the same
AFOSI office at Kirtland whose operatives victimized the scientists and
confided UFO "secrets" to Bill Moore, Linda Howe, and others. Besides
wasting everyone's time and throwing ufologists into confusion, such
disinformation serves to take investigators off the scent of potentially
authentic UFO secrets, such as those surrounding the Roswell incident.

It also encourages the freelance disinformers, those who spread absurd tales of treaties with aliens, concentration camps on Mars, and other
rubbish. Those who swallow this want to be fooled, and those who are
guarding possibly real secrets may be only too happy to oblige them.
There is no reason to believe that the major Dark Siders are government
agents, but it is reasonable to deduce that if they didn't exist, the agencies responsible for the cover-up would probably have to invent them.

Whatever their differences, the early contactees and today's Dark
Siders do have one major common element: an audience to which it
does not occur to ask the hard or obvious questions—for example,
Where's your evidence? I have learned through long experience that if
you ask questions like this, if you express the disbelief you would think
to be the only possible rational response, you are immediately suspect.
You may be an agent of the conspiracy. There is of course no way to
answer such accusations. If you deny them, you're assumed to be lying.
If you jocularly respond in the affirmative, you are assumed to be telling
the truth. If you refuse to answer, on the grounds that the question is
too absurd to merit a response, you are assumed to be conceding the
point. In the end you can only shrug and hope that your accuser is
harmless.

The most interesting part of the tiny signal that sounds amid the noise is the fact that over the past two decades active-duty air force personnel have made incredible claims about ET contacts. Unfortunately so far that fact is more interesting than the stories they tell. The stories are utterly without supporting evidence.

Nonetheless there apparently *is* a film that purports to depict a landing and contact at Holloman AFB. A number of persons who seem to be telling the truth say they have seen it. But the existence of a film hardly proves the existence of ETs. It is entirely conceivable—in fact highly likely—that the aliens are really actors wearing masks. I have interviewed a retired air force sergeant who was at Holloman in April 1964. He states flatly that no such landing occurred. If it had, he says, he would have known about it.

One could argue of course that maybe it didn't happen in April 1964, as some versions of the legend have it, but in May 1971, as Emenegger's air force informants said.

Or one could argue that we are all the victims of a bizarre psychological-warfare experiment. As early as September 1952 the CIA was expressing concern that the Soviets could use the UFO issue for psychological-warfare purposes. In January 1953 the CIA convened a panel, headed by physicist H. P. Robertson, to consider the issue. The Robertson panel agreed that the manipulation of UFO data could pose a national-security problem. The panel went on to urge a policy of official debunking of UFO reports. That recommendation was followed from then on until the closing of the air force's public UFO project in 1969.

With the contact stories we see the opposite: not the debunking but the *encouraging* of the most outlandish UFO rumors of all. What could the purpose be? If such an operation is in effect, and it is hard under the circumstances to resist such speculation, a good deal of time, money, and attention has gone into it—from the early 1970s at least to the present. Whatever it is seeking to accomplish, it is important to somebody.

A third interpretation combines the first two. There is hard evidence of ET visitation, presumably from the Roswell incident and perhaps from other, so far less-documented events. Possibly communication has been established. At the same time there is a psychological experiment going on. Rumors are being introduced into society to see how people respond to news of an extraterrestrial presence.

Certainly somebody knows which, if any, of these interpretations of these weirdly persistent rumors is correct. I am not that person. Neither, unless I am sorely mistaken, are you. All we have in our possession are some odd facts, a few other possible facts, and many likely or certain lies. In short, not a lot to go on, but enough to keep an intriguing question alive and the focus of paranoia, charlatanism, mystery, and wonder for years to come.

SECTION TWO

AFTER CONTACT

A HISTORICAL EVENT

by William R. Forstchen, Ph.D.

There's been a lot written as to what to do if you have an experience observing, or come into direct contact with, a UFO. The most important point, and most likely the toughest one to remember at the moment, is to stay calm. Your observations and later recall of events could be crucial to piecing together the puzzle of UFO contacts, and a calm approach is essential.

A little preparation beforehand could be important. First and foremost is the recording of evidence. If you have a camcorder in your house, do you know where it is at this moment, are the batteries fresh, do you have tape in it? A little simple preplanning in this area, making sure you have a blank tape in a convenient location and a freshly charged battery in place could very well make the difference.

If you don't own a camcorder, just having a camera handy is important. Disposable cameras can be picked up for less than ten dollars. Having one in the glove compartment of your car and another in an easily remembered location in your home is crucial.

If you are filming something with a camcorder, even if it is just a dot hovering in the distance, provide a running commentary. Keep talking, adding descriptions of what you are seeing, because film might not pick up some of the details. Try to provide reference points as well while filming, be sure to include nearby structures, or other objects close by to the UFO; this can help provide scale background later on. Slowly shifting from wide angle to zoom can provide important background information as well for later analysis, so don't just lock on your target with a close-up and hang there. If you don't have a camcorder but possess a tape recorder, this can be important as well. Many people report unusual sounds, but actual recordings of sound are rare. Talk calmly and again try to describe as many details as possible. If you are witnessing the event with someone else, ask them to provide commentary, but do so without prompting, let them describe it in their own words.

One of the real frustrations is that so many of these events happen without multiple witnesses. If you can reach a phone, call a neighbor or even call the police. Leave the phone off the hook and if possible describe what you are seeing. Yet again, the most important point in all of this is to attempt to stay calm. Take a few deep breaths, focus on what is happening, and make a conscious effort to try to remember as many details as possible. Can you estimate the distance to the object, how big do you think it is, what color and shape is it, are there any usual sounds and are you experiencing any unusual physical sensations? If you don't have a camera, camcorder, or tape recorder with you, try to find something to write on. Note the exact time and location of the object, along with your position relative to it. Try to sketch it as soon as possible, even if you've photographed it—remember, photographs don't always turn out.

It is important as well to note the names of other witnesses if any are with you. If you share this experience with someone else, as soon as it is over ask him to go to another room or just to step away from you and not to discuss what you've seen. Without prompting in any way ask him to record what he saw and to sketch it as well. If you can maintain a controlled manner like that, researchers will place greater stock in the evidence submitted, seeing less possibility of the experiences of one person contaminating the evidence submitted by another.

The key points to recall here are to prepare beforehand, try in some manner to record the event while it is happening, then immediately after the event record either on videotape or in writing what you saw. Even if you didn't have a camcorder with you, a videotaped interview afterward on a borrowed camcorder can be helpful in recording details that might be forgotten later. Even if you did manage to catch the object on tape, interviewing all witnesses on tape immediately afterward can be helpful. Remember, don't prompt anyone, simply let her tell the story in her own words. If there is any prompting, confine it to a request for details on size, shape, movements, direction of travel, and so on.

Be sure to try to clearly show the exact time your interview is taking place; an easy trick is to turn on your television at the end of the interview and turn to a channel that shows the time and date, thus verifying that you did not throw the interview together long after the event. Immediacy is important, researchers place greater stock in impressions stated right after an event, rather than a day, week, or month later.

If your contact is more direct, in other words if you are actually approached by an alien, the advice to remain calm might be difficult to remember, but it is even more crucial now. We are all familiar with the stories of abductions, and it seems that if such events are true, there is really little anyone can do to prevent it from happening. Staying calm will help you get through it, no matter how unpleasant it might be. Displaying an intelligent, rational approach can only play in your favor.

Several incidents indicate that aliens are aware of what we could call universal human gestures. Extending your arms, palms outward, or slowly raising your hands over your head, palms outward, is seen as a peaceful gesture. Pointing might be construed as aggressive, screaming could be misinterpreted as threatening. If you feel you can handle it, try to approach the visitor; talk in a slow, deliberate manner; don't make any quick moves; and underneath it all realize that whoever it is you are encountering is most likely in control of the situation. If they have the ability to cross interstellar distances, they also have the ability to nail you in the blink of an eye if that is their wish, so the fact that you are still alive is a fair indicator that there is no harmful intent. Most of all, don't get caught up in the idea that you can somehow restrain your visitor so that you can then turn him in as evidence; it is an idea that will guarantee a less-than-pleasant end to your encounter.

All the time this is going on, try to observe the details. Where did he walk, is there a chance of footprints being left, are there any unusual physical sensations, can you see details of his features? Even the most inconsequential point might be an important clue later on.

After your contact is finished, don't contaminate the area. Try to avoid walking where your visitor did. If you have a camera, photograph the site, and as in visual contacts, try to note down, as soon as possible, what happened and every possible detail you can remember.

Now might very well come the most difficult part of all: Whom do you tell? (See Appendix D.) If you feel a need to contact the police, go ahead, though it's suggested that if you personally know an officer in your local police force, contact him first and ask him to come over on his own. Having two strange officers come in, especially officers who've had a busy night dealing with some of the more disturbed elements of our society, might result in a negative report, which could taint your evidence. Try to avoid media contact—the situation there almost always gets out of hand and at best you'll be made out to look foolish. If there are other reports in the media about the same sighting, don't contact the other witnesses; doing so can be viewed as tainting your own evidence. Let properly trained investigators handle that. If you want to contact government officials, that is your decision, but the evidence suggests that in the end your report will get buried or destroyed. Above all else, look out for sensationalism. Friends will spread the story, it will get distorted, and trying to rectify it later on will prove to be nearly impossible, so be cautious at the start regarding whom you tell.

Regarding film, it's best to hold on to it and wait. Do not turn it over to any officials, news media, or friends. If you have a bank safety deposit box, put it in there without telling anyone where you have it. When the film is going to be developed, try to arrange to be present and make sure you immediately get the negatives back and then store them in a secure place—never allow the negatives out of your possession! If you've videotaped the event, make a copy but yet again, keep the original. Regarding notes, allow transcripts or photocopies to be made, but here again, keep the originals. One path to follow here is to photocopy your notes, then have the originals notarized and placed in a sealed envelope so there cannot be any suggestions later on that you changed them.

Realize from the very start that you will face skepticism, mockery, and at times outright harassment if you admit to your experience. You will also draw a certain fringe element who are somewhat over the edge regarding UFO contacts and will want to share their experiences regarding abduction, channeling, crystal therapy, and visits to Venus. If your report starts getting identified with that type of crowd in your community, your chance of getting a fair hearing is all but shot. Yet again, the crucial point here is to be organized beforehand, stay calm during the event, and report it accurately afterward. It is just such reports that will gradually turn the tide of public and official skepticism and hopefully create a path to a truly open and scientific study of the body of evidence that clearly indicates that we are not alone.

HOW TO TALK
TO AN EXTRATERRESTRIAL

by Jonathan Vos Post

INTRODUCTION

This is your first meeting with an un-Earthly nonhuman entity: an extraterrestrial (*ET*). If you handle it well, you will be the greatest hero alive and be able to make a fortune selling your story to the media. If you blow it, the repercussions could be unimaginably terrible, perhaps an interstellar war that could annihilate humanity. Feeling a little stressed out? Rule Number One: *Don't panic.* Just follow these simple guidelines, and all will be well. We hope.

FIRST CONTACT

A Handful of Coins, a Loop of String, a Flashlight, and Two Magnets

Hopefully the extraterrestrial you encounter is not injured from the crash of its UFO, poisoned by local chemicals or germs, irrationally terrified of you, nor irrationally intent on injuring you. Hopefully its senses will allow it to see the items you are carrying in your pocket right now—if you've read this handbook before this Close Encounter and had time to prepare.

If the ET has radically different senses, seems uncommunicative, or otherwise nonresponsive, then you will have to skip ahead to the time when teams of experts have been assembled to assist you in your task of contact.

But if these problems do not obstruct you, you will be initiating communications with a set of cheap, easily obtained communications tools, using the following:

- Eighteen specific coins, totaling $3.27, as detailed shortly
- A loop of string, at least 48 inches (but no more than 72 inches) in circumference
- A pocket flashlight
- Two small bar magnets
- A pad of paper and a couple of pens or pencils

This may not sound like much, but may work wonders. If you also have a camera, a videocam, and/or a cassette recorder, so much the better. Obviously the more rolls of film, blank cassettes, and extra batteries you have, the better. Practice using your equipment beforehand so that you may use it easily when under the unprecedented excitement and stress of First Contact. Photograph and tape everything that happens in your Close Encounter if you can. If not, then at least take quick and careful notes on what happens, using the paper and pen or pencil, until the experts can take the next steps.

Good luck!

Pocket Change Worth Billions

Now that you've bought *Making Contact,* make a further investment of $3.27. Get the following coins assembled and keep them in a little envelope or pocket, separate from your usual pocket change:

1	Susan B. Anthony dollar coin	$1.00
2	pennies	$0.02
2	nickles	$0.10
9	dimes	$0.90
3	quarters	$0.75
1	half-dollar coin	$0.50
18	miscellaneous coins totaling	$3.27

Practice arranging these coins on a flat surface. These coins represent the Sun, planets, and major moons based on their approximate relative sizes as follows:

SUN	Susan B. Anthony coin (a silver dollar is even better if possible)
MERCURY	a penny
VENUS	a nickel

EARTH	a nickel, circled by the MOON, a dime
MARS	a penny
JUPITER	the half-dollar, circled by the four giant Galilean moons: IO, EUROPA, GANYMEDE, and CALLISTO, represented by four dimes
SATURN	a quarter, with its giant moon TITAN, a dime
URANUS	a quarter
NEP- TUNE	a quarter, with its giant moon TRITON, a dime
PLUTO	a dime, with its moon CHARON, a dime

When you meet the extraterrestrial, locate a flat surface (sidewalk or bare dirt) between the two of you and lay out the coins as you have practiced.

If it is daytime, point to the dollar coin, then point to the Sun, and say, "Sun!" If you have your pocket flashlight, hold it close to the Sun-dollar so that the coin is brightly illuminated.

Then point to the second nickel, pat the ground, point at the ground all around you, and say, "Earth!" Pick up the Earth-nickel and, keeping it close to the ground, move it around the Sun-dollar, then put it back down where it was. If the Moon is visible, point to it, point to the dime next to the Earth-nickel, and say, "Moon!" Pick up the Moon-dime and, keeping it close to the ground, move it around the Earth-nickel, then put it back down where it was.

Then be silent for a minute, back away from the coins, and watch for a response.

If the ET knows the structure of our solar system, as observed by it or its companions from a remote location or by more immediate observation on the way in toward Earth, it will recognize the model of the solar system you have shown it. This will establish that you are an astronomically sophisticated being who knows his way around your own local part of the galaxy.

The ET now has the chance to show you something about that solar system model. It might, for example, place a few pebbles or sand grains in between the Mars-penny and the Jupiter-half-dollar to show you where most of the asteroids are concentrated. It might indicate planets or the Oort or Kuiper Belt of comets far beyond Pluto. It might convey some information about the Moon or some other planets if it made one or more stops on the way to Earth. It may construct a model of its own solar system. If it moves the coins into any new configuration, be sure to record that in your written or photographic notes.

You have gotten information that may be worth billions of times your original $3.27.

A Loop of String, Approximately
72 Inches in Circumference

Allied pilots, during World War II, who had to fly over certain remote and exotic areas such as Borneo (now called Kalimantan), were encouraged to carry a loop of string up to six feet long, the ends of which were tied together to make a single loop about three feet long. The idea was that if they crash-landed their plane in an area where non-English-speaking natives were likely to be present, the pilot should (when someone approached through the jungle), casually take the loop of string from his pocket and begin to make a cat's-cradle string figure and as many other string figures as he knew. It is said that, on more than one occasion, this was actually tried.

In each case, the story goes, the native watched with increasingly friendly interest and then politely borrowed the loop to demonstrate some string figures popular in his own tribe. It seems to me that such an anthropological First Contact technique might be useful in extraterrestrial First Contact as well. You will find out if and how the ET pays attention to your activity, have something to talk about, and—after you've handed the loop to the ET—learn something about how dexterously the ET manipulates at least one kind of object.

If you're very lucky, the ET will show you patterns of its own culture. After all, the string figure has been (sometimes independently) discovered and perfected by members of the following tribes, areas, or nations: Apache, Australia, Austria, Borneo, Chaco, Cherokee, China, Chippewa, Clayoquaht, Denmark, England, Eskimo, France, Germany, Hawaii, India, Ireland, Japan, Kabyles, Kiwai, Klamath, Korea, Kwakiutl, Lifu, Melanesia, Natik, Nauru, Navaho, the Netherlands, New Guinea, New Zealand, Omaha, Onandaga, Osage, Pawnee, the Philippines, Polynesia, Pueblo, Pygmy, Salish, Scotland, Switzerland, Tannas, Tewas, Tlingit, Tsimshian, Uap, Ulungu, Wajiji, and Zuni.

The best reference on how to weave with both hands a hundred intricate patterns supposed to represent natural and artificial objects is *String Figures and How to Make Them.*

Perhaps the most important anthropologist ever, Dr. Franz Boas, was the first to publish a careful description of how a so-called primitive people (Eskimo) make string figures, in 1888. Other cultures use "a thong of skin . . . a cord of cocoanut fibre . . . [or] of human hair finely plaited. A woven cord which does not kink as easily as a twisted cord will prove most satisfactory; unfortunately, it cannot be spliced, the ends therefore must be knotted in a small square knot or laid together and bound round with thread."

We describe below how to make the common cat's cradle. Following are illustrations of some common patterns.

Cat's Cradle

The first thing to do is to make the familiar cat's cradle as described below. It is known in many parts of the world. In southern China it is called *Kang Sok* ("well rope"); in Korea it is called *Ssi-teu-ki* ("woof-taking"); in Japan it is called *Aya ito tori* ("woof pattern string-taking"); in Germany it is variously called *Aheben* ("taking off"), *Faden-aheben* ("taking-off strings"), *Fadenspiel* ("string game"), and *Hexenspiel* ("Witch's game").

Step 1. Take the untwisted loop of string and pass the four fingers of each hand through the loop, then separate the hands, keeping the palms facing each other. You are now holding the loop taut so that each end of it passes across the backs of your hands and one side of the loop rests on the webs of flesh between thumb and forefinger.

Step 2. With the thumb and index finger of the left hand, turn the left near string away from you across your left palm, and then toward you across the back of the left hand, bringing the string to the right between the thumb and index finger. Separate the hands, keeping the palms facing each other and holding the loop taut. You now have two strings across the back of your left hand (a little loop around your left hand) and one string across the back of your right hand.

Step 3. With the thumb and index finger of the right hand, turn the right near string away from you across your right palm, and then toward you across the back of the right hand, bringing the string to the left between the thumb and index finger. Separate the hands, keeping the palms facing each other, and holding the loop taut. You now have two strings across the back of each hand and a single string across each palm.

Step 4. Bring the hands together and put the right middle finger up under the string that crosses the left palm. Draw the loop out on the back of the finger by separating the hands (palms still facing each other).

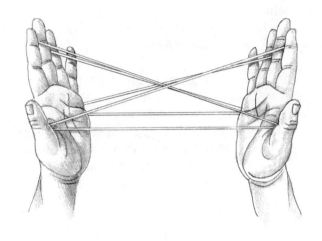

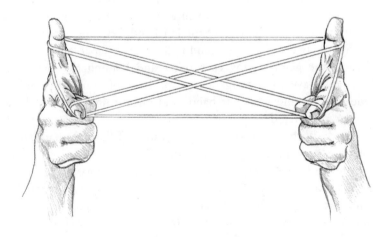

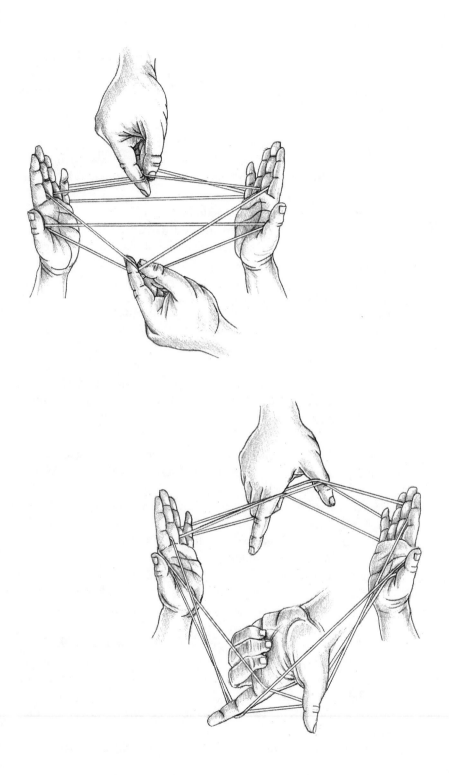

Step 5. Bring the hands together, and put the left middle finger up under the string that crosses the right palm. Draw the loop out on the back of the finger by separating the hands (palms still facing each other).

There is now a loop on each middle finger and two strings across the back of each hand; the "cradle" being formed by a straight near string, a straight far string, and the crossed strings of the middle finger loops.

Show this to the ET. Note its reaction.

If there are two people involved in the First Contact, then you are in good shape. First of all, this means that one of you can be doing the talking, motioning, and demonstrating while the other keeps notes, takes photographs, or narrates into a cassette recorder.

If there are two of you, you can now play cat's cradle by first having one of you make the cat's cradle according to the above five steps and then taking turns transforming it through a series of different configurations as follows.

Soldier's Bed = Church Window = Fish Pond

The next step in the game of cat's cradle has three different English names, and in Korea is called *Pa-tok-hpan* ("chess board"); and in Japan *Nekomata* ("mountain cat").

By *near, far, left,* and *right* we describe the position of the strings as seen by the person from whose hands the figure is being taken away.

Step 1. Person A makes the cat's cradle as above.

Step 2. Person B puts his left thumb away from A under the right near middle-finger string and his left index finger away from A under the left near middle-finger string.

Step 3. Person B brings the thumb and index finger together and picks up between their tips the two near middle-finger strings just where they cross at the near side of the figure.

Steps 4 and 5. In the same way person B picks up the two far middle-finger strings by putting the right thumb toward A under the right far middle-finger string, and the right index finger toward A under the left far middle-finger string, then bringing the right index finger and right thumb together and picking up between their tips the two far middle-finger strings just where they cross at the far side of the figure.

Step 6. Now separating his hands, B draws the right hand away from A and the left hand toward A and carries the thumb and index finger of each hand, still holding the strings, around the corresponding side string of the figure and up into the center of the figure.

Step 7. Then, by drawing his hands apart and separating the index fingers widely from the thumbs, he removes the figure from A's hands and extends the "Soldier's Bed." There is now a loop on each thumb, a loop on each index finger, and a string passing across the backs of the thumbs and index fingers of each hand. The figure is formed of the four finger loops crossing in the middle, a straight near string and a straight far string.

There are a series of other transformations that will end up passing the figures back and forth between the two players through at least eight configurations total, the other six of which are called in English "candles," Manager, Diamonds, Cat's Eye, Fish in a Dish, and Clock.

Consult the reference book listed, or a bunch of children, to learn the other positions. You may be challenged to learn more complicated string figures too. Practice makes perfect.

You can now not only play with children and other UFO enthusiasts but have a chance to do something peaceful, interesting, and revealing when you make First Contact.

When I first wrote this, I thought that I was the first to contemplate it for human-ET First Contact. But in further researching this chapter I found a science fiction author, the anthropologist Chad Oliver, had beaten me to the punch by some thirty-six years. In the novel *Unearthly Neighbors*, I was stunned to read this paragraph [p. 73, revised edition]:

Tom Stein maneuvered two of the [ET] kids, both boys, down the trail that led to the stream [on Sirius Nine]. He took a length of cord from his pocket and made a skillful cat's cradle on his fingers. The boys were intrigued, and watched him closely. Tom went through his whole bag of string tricks—the anthropologist's ace in the hole—and tried his level best to make friends.

So give Chad Oliver credit, not me, when you play cat's cradle with an ET and make friends. Assuming, of course, that anthropologists and science fiction writers are on the right track at all.

A Pocket Flashlight

A small pocket flashlight (with as many extra batteries as you like to carry) is a good thing to have in any case, as you know if you drop your keys in the dark on a moonless night. It may be very valuable during extraterrestrial First Contact. This surely applies if the First Contact begins in, or continues into, the night. If the ET communicates with light, then it is absolutely necessary.

The flashlight helps to demonstrate that you are a technological being. Don't point it first at the ET; that might appear hostile, rude, or weaponlike.

The flashlight gives you a chance to point at various things and speak their names: "ground, tree, foot, human, ET, coins, string. . . . and what is that thing in your third claw?"

Even parrots can be taught to learn the names of things repeatedly pointed to or held up: "This is a grape. I'm holding a grape. Do you want the grape?"

The flashlight can be used to illuminate the pad of paper and writings done with pen or pencil. It can be used to illuminate the coin in the center of the coin-model solar system, to make it shine like the Sun. If you wear eyeglasses, or carry a magnifying glass or other lens, you can use it to demonstrate simple concepts of optics. You can cast shadows with it. If you have sunglasses or use the plastic of your car taillight, then you can project different colors and name those colors.

The use of the flashlight can be occasionally contrasted with, amplified by, or accompanied by the flash of your camera, if you are carrying one.

Two Small Bar Magnets

If you have two little bar magnets, the kind often glued to the back of a decorative refrigerator magnet, then there are some things you can demonstrate and test.

The purposes of these experiments are four:

1. To show to the ET that you are a representative of a technologically sophisticated scientific civilization
2. To provide specific scientific items and phenomena to talk about and to develop a common vocabulary if possible

3. To see how the ET reacts to demonstrations of scientific principles
4. To begin testing the properties of UFO or ET-related substances

You should have at least the two small bar magnets suggested here. You can enhance your demonstrations to the ET if you also have

1. A pocket compass
2. A long steel knitting needle
3. A few iron tacks
4. A long iron nail
5. A sewing needle
6. A cork
7. Thread or string beyond that used for your cat's-cradle demonstration

Before you meet the ET, mark your bar magnets to show which are the north poles (the poles that attract the north-seeking end of a compass needle) and which are the south poles (the poles that attract the south-seeking end of a compass needle).

What kind of magnets are the two that you are carrying in your ET communications kit? They are *permanent* magnets, as opposed to electromagnets that only work when electricity is flowing through wires. Permanent magnets have been known for thousands of years (at least since the ancient Greeks investigated the mineral lodestone, today called magnetite), but have become much more sophisticated in the twentieth century. Two Japanese physicists, Honda and Takei (no, not the car company or the actor who played Sulu on *Star Trek*) in 1917 first added cobalt to tungsten steel to make powerful permanent magnets. In 1932 another Japanese team created even stronger magnets from alloys of iron, nickel, and aluminum. Many such materials are available under trade names such as Alcomax, Alnico, Hycomax, and Iconal. Other magnets are made today from ceramic materials. The poles of the magnets may be near the ends or the faces of the magnets. Magnetic rubber strips are often used on refrigerator doors, and rolls of this strip are available in hardware stores.

Experiment 1: Magnet and Compass

It is believed by some historians that the Chinese may have discovered the magnetic compass. The Chinese Emperor Huang-Di is said to have had a magnetic (lodestone) compass in his chariot, approximately 2,050 years ago. We are certain that the French crusader Petrus Peregrinus, in A.D. 1269, gave detailed written descriptions of a floating compass and a pocket compass much like the kind we use today. Nearly 450 years ago Queen Elizabeth I's physician, William Gilbert, first hypothesized that the Earth itself acts like a giant magnet. He built a spherical model of the Earth out of lodestone and showed that it had a magnetic field around it similar to the field of the Earth. We think that the Earth's magnetic field is caused by a molten iron-nickel-sulfur material swirling in the Earth's core—the so-called dynamo effect. The much more powerful magnetic fields of Jupiter and Saturn are believed to be caused by dynamos of metallic hydrogen, a substance first created on Earth (at the Lawrence Livermore Laboratory) in early 1996. Most likely the ET comes from a planet that has a magnetic field and therefore has some chance of recognizing the behavior of a pocket compass.

Show the pocket compass to the ET. Say, "Compass." Place it on the ground. Point to the needle that's pointing north, point with your arm and finger in that same direction, and say, "North." Point in the opposite direction and say, "South." Observe if the ET looks at the compass, in the directions that you have pointed, and write down or dictate into a cassette recorder what the response is.

Move one of your bar magnets near the compass so that the needle points away from north. Hold up the magnet and say, "Magnet." Show how the bar magnet can pick up tacks or the long nail. Write down what the ET says or does. If there are any pieces of UFO material or other substances nearby that seem related to the ET, pick them up and prepare to use them in the next experiment/demonstration.

If possible, float one of the bar magnets on top of a cork in a puddle or open container of water. It should also point north/south, like the needle of a pocket compass.

Finally, if you and the ET are still interested, you can show that the magnetic north pole and the geographic North Pole are not in the same place. This is very important to people who use the compass to actually navigate. You can show the angle between *true north* (that is, geographic north) and *magnetic north* (as shown by the pocket compass) in your First Contact location.

When the sun is at the highest point in the sky (noon, unless modified by daylight savings time), then hold a plumb line (a string or thread with any weight tied to the end) so that it casts a shadow on a piece of paper lying on the ground. This shadow will lie in a north-south direction pointing toward true north (geographic north). Now place your pocket compass on the shadow and draw a line showing the direction in which it points. The angle between this line and the shadow is called the *declination*. Some planets have a very large declination, such as Uranus in our solar system. The ET has a chance to show whether or not it understands this, if the ET has given meaningful responses to other experiments/demonstrations so far.

Experiment 2: Testing UFO Material

You know from ordinary experience that some materials can be picked up by magnets and some cannot. Instead of merely classifying materials into two categories, magnetic and nonmagnetic, we need to be more scientific if we are going to analyze materials relating to an ET.

Two centuries ago Michael Faraday discovered that all the materials he tested were influenced in one way or another by a magnetic field. Some were attracted by a magnet and some were repelled, although they weren't themselves magnets. We call the kind of material that is strongly attracted *ferromagnetic* because it behaves like iron (Latin: *ferrum*). This includes iron, nickel, and cobalt. If you have a Canadian nickel, it is ferromagnetic because it is mostly nickel and will cling to a magnet the same way iron does. The kind of material that is very weakly attracted to a magnet (so that under ordinary conditions it seems that it is not attracted) is called *paramagnetic*. The kind of material that is weakly repelled by a magnet is called *diamagnetic*. Diamagnetic materials include bismuth, copper, glass, water, and mercury. These weak repulsions typically take a strong electromagnet to discover. Another category of material that has been rapidly developed since World War II is the *ferrimagnetic*, which has magnetic properties although it is an electrical insulator (nonmetal). Examples of this type are the *ferrites*. A ferrite rod is used as the aerial of many transistor radios.

If there are pieces of the material of the UFO available, or pieces of material near the ET, test them with your magnets and make a first rough attempt to classify them as *ferromagnetic, paramagnetic, ferrimagnetic*, or *diamagnetic.*

If the compass needle moves when you hold a piece of ET material near it, then that material is itself a magnet. If the material does not appear to be a magnet, but is strongly attracted to and sticks to one of your bar magnets, it is *ferromagnetic*. If that material is not shiny and metallic in appearance, then it may be *ferrimagnetic,* although this needs to be validated by showing that it is not an electrical conductor (which would require a battery and wires, or a continuity tester). If the material does not seem to respond to the magnet at all, it may be either *paramagnetic* or *diamagnetic*. If it is clearly repelled by your bar magnet, then it is *diamagnetic*. Maybe the ET has materials that are more powerful diamagnets than anything we have. It is worth investigating.

To test for *diamagnetism*, you may need to suspend a piece of the material by a thread and dangle it right between the north pole of one bar magnet and the south pole of the other. If the ET material twists on the thread to line up with the line connecting the two magnets, it is *ferromagnetic* or *ferrimagnetic*. If the ET material twists on the thread so that it is perpendicular to the line connecting the two magnets, it is *diamagnetic*.

Experiment 3: Magnetization,
Magnetic Induction, and Curie Point

Take an unmagnetized knitting needle. Hold your pocket compass (if you have one) to show that both ends of the knitting needle attract the same pole of the compass. Now magnetize the knitting needle with the bar magnet. Hold the knitting needle immobile on the ground, touch the north pole of one bar magnet (the end that attracts the "North"-pointing pole of the compass) and drag the magnet along the length of the knitting needle to its end, then (keeping the knitting needle in place) pull away the magnet and repeat exactly a few times. The knitting needle should now be magnetized. Show this to the ET by demonstrating that one end of the knitting needle attracts a different pole of the compass than the other end does.

Attach a chain of tacks to the end of one of your bar magnets. Strongly heat one of the tacks with a match flame or (better) pocket cigarette lighter until that tack and the tacks beneath it fall off. When a ferromagnetic material (like the tack) is heated above its "Curie point," it stops being ferromagnetic.

Hang a long nail (if you have one) suspended from the south pole of one of your bar magnets, The X end of the nail has now become, by magnetic induction, a north pole, and the Y end a south pole. Bring the north pole of the other bar magnet near the Y end of the hanging nail. It should be attracted and swing to point toward the north pole of the second bar magnet. Now bring the south pole of the other bar magnet near the Y end of the hanging nail. It should be repelled and swing away from the south pole.

When a magnet is brought close to a ferromagnetic material such as iron, some of the "magnetic domains" in the material change so that the material becomes a magnet. This process is called *magnetic induction*. When the magnet is removed, most of the domains change back to the way they were before so that the material is no longer a magnet. Materials that act this way are called *nonretentive* or magnetically *soft*. Magnetically soft materials, like your iron nail, mumetal, and Permalloy C, are used in the cores of electromagnets and transformers. They stop being magnets as soon as the electricity is switched off.

Other materials, including steel, have microscopic magnetic domains that stay in place once changed by a magnet, so that the steel continues to be a magnet after being in contact with the magnet that touched it. Your knitting needle is an example of that.

Take a piece of any ferromagnetic material you have identified from the UFO or ET. Stroke it with one of the bar magnets and then see if it has been induced to become a magnet or not. Now you can determine if the ET material is magnetically *hard* or *soft*.

A Pad of Paper and a Couple of Pens or Pencils

Speech Lessons, Informants, and Two or More Extraterrestrials

Your best chance to start learning the extraterrestrial language is if there are two or more of them and they are speaking to each other. If so, the following steps are recommended, based in part on *How to Learn an Unwritten Language*:

(1) Determine what your best approach is to language learning. Some people learn best by merely hearing and mimicry (imitation), the way children learn, leaving the pattern making to their unconscious minds. A few people are natural mimics, who apprehend, react to, and remember new language patterns almost at once. If you are such a person, it is good luck for planet Earth, as you will not have to consciously analyze the extraterrestrial language in order to speak to the ET or ETs in a way they will at least recognize as language. You should correct your natural bias by being particularly careful to record every ET speech act, and not be distracted by your own involvement in mimicry. You should make a concerted effort to use whatever analytical approaches are recommended in this handbook, in addition to your own talent.

Other people learn best by memorizing rules and vocabulary, then practicing speech patterns as examples of those rules. If you are such a person, then you will be virtually unable to use language patterns until you have explicit conscious insight and awareness of the relationships of sounds and system. To compensate for your bias, you must force yourself to make a social contact with the ET or ETs, thus avoiding the danger of an overly elaborate written analysis, which does not contribute to the possibility of some small degree of conversation with the ET.

(2) Make and effort to listen carefully, while recording, normal conversation between the two or more ETs (or at least any soliloquizing by a single ET). The ability to catch even a hint of the "drift of a conversation" will be a great success. At first, look and listen for the ETs' culturally acceptable indications of continued attention, or the YES of agreement. These are prerequisites for you to contribute to any dialogue or group conversation. The most likely opportunity for observing conversation between the ETs is when they are sharing a work task, such as trying to repair their UFO or collecting samples or tending to the medical needs of an injured ET. In case of such apparent injury, it is recommended that you don't do anything. The Hippocratic Oath of doctors says that first of all you must do no harm. In the case of the ET, anything you do—changing the position of the body, or wiping away fluid, or pouring water into a mouth—may be a fatal mistake.

(3) Make many attempts to engage in conversations with individual ETs, using the coins, string, flashlight, and so forth as something to talk about. You should seek out chances for conversation and should make a point of talking to every ET with whom you have direct contact. Make a particular effort with any ET that intuitively or analytically seems to be a child, based on body size or playfulness. You might well be wrong—for example, a "dimorphic" species is one in which two sexes (if they have two sexes) may differ greatly in size or appearance—but as we will explain in the section "What Is the Meaning of Meaning?" children, especially babies, have a superior ability to learn new languages quickly.

(4) Spend several brief periods, within view of the ET or ETs, listening intensively to materials recorded on your audiocassettes and mimicking them as best you can. These materials should include both connected texts and word lists. The texts that you will repeatedly try to mimic should be short enough to be repeated several times in a single listening and rehearsal period. The purpose of doing this is that the cassette accurately records such things as rhythm and intonation pattern, and if you listen often enough, you may pick up enough "feel" to be able to mimic, albeit crudely at first. This is not likely to be possible in "free conversation," where patterns may shift too quickly for you to follow. In addition, by using the cassette recorder, you can concentrate your attention on hearing and mimicry without being confused by trying to understand the meaningful content of the sounds or by planning to say something.

Listen to recorded lists of words to try to distinguish tone, stress, and length patterns. Listening for these things should alternate between lists in which one feature is identical, and lists with contrasts between items (as discussed in our section on "By Way of Contrast"). For example, if the ET language has syllables, practice with one list of ET words that have stress on the first syllable, one with stress on the second syllable, and one with stress on the third syllable.

(5) Gather new data whenever possible. There are three ways to do this: (a) Record and make written notes on any ET utterance you hear, and write down or photograph the context in which it occurred; (b) if one of the ETs volunteers a special role in trying to communicate—the "informant"—then use the coins, string, flashlight, and so forth to provoke or elicit language data from the informant; (c) record conversations between ETs on cassette.

The unelicited data (a and c) are the ones most likely to be smooth and accurate; elicited data are likely to be "wooden" and "foreign," contaminated with the flavor of the English language you are using in your speech. Conversely, some ET language details can be studied and understood more quickly if the crucial examples are elicited in a patterned way, such as by moving through the list of numbers, planet names, objects that you point to, or the Periodic Table of the Elements.

(6) Processing of data. When the top scientific experts begin to arrive, they will take over this important task. It is vital that each day's collection of audio, video, photographic, and written noted data be processed almost at once. A backlog of material that has not been analyzed becomes a source of frustration and a roadblock in the way of further activity. This means that all audio-recorded data should be transcribed as soon as possible (and soon after, computerized). Each ET utterance elicited from the informant should be planned to illuminate some particular problem or an example of a particular pattern.

(7) Organize the Contact episodes. At least the nucleus of what you learn every couple of hours should be a planned lesson, including drilling on the sound system (4 and 9), one or more grammatical patterns to be practiced until you develop some ET language habits, and some vocabulary items (the ET name, the name for "Earth," the words for "one, two, three") to be memorized within the grammatical context. You are both student, trying to learn a bit of the ET language, and teacher, trying to get the ET to get a little English.

(8) Drill and memorize what you learn from each session. Review old sessions. Each session you should hope to learn something new, have the ET learn something new, and have a shared experience of mutual

satisfaction with progress. What you learn should be reviewed often and not counted as learned until you and/or the ET can use that material in "free conversation" at normal speech speed.

(9) Drill on the sound system with the informant. Each session have several intensive minutes of contrastive listening and mimicry, especially by you of ET sounds that are different from English sounds, and by the ET of English sounds that are different from ET sounds. Your recorded cassette may not be up to the task, as only high-fidelity sound equipment can accurately record fine differences between phonetic sounds (such as *sss* versus *fff*, or *t* versus a glottal stop). Contrastive listening means listening for particular sounds, and especially listening to pairs of words in which similar but contrastively different sounds occur. In such a drill you and the ET are doing intentionally and consciously what a child does unconsciously in its hours of repetitive babble.

There is a possibility that would help you very much, if you are lucky. That is, the ETs may have intentionally simplified their language and made it more logical. They might communicate through not an ancient "natural" language but a more modern, deliberately designed "artificial" language. After all, humans have proposed or created over five hundred such languages since the seventeenth century, such as Basic English, OPA, Loglan, Interglossa, and Esperanto. If the ETs have created such a language, presumably to eliminate the threat of war, to aid in complex enterprises between beings of different birthplace, and to aid in international, interplanetary, and/or interstellar communications, then they have made your job vastly more simple. But don't count on it.

PROTOCOL AND PROTAGORAS: THE EMPIRICAL APPROACH

In this handbook we assume that the evidence of the ET is so overwhelming that nobody on the scene can dispute the fact that humans and aliens must now communicate. We assume that the survival and comfort of the ET is not in immediate jeopardy, so that you may concentrate on careful communications while a team is brought to bear on solving longer-term problems. We also assume that your being in the right place at the right time makes you the focus of all activity for some time to come and gives you access to an essentially unlimited line of credit from the local government and banking institutions. If these conditions are not met, you must simply do your best to apply the lessons of this handbook as best you can with the more limited resources at your immediate disposal.

Let's say, though, that all is well at the outset. The first step is to be sure that you can concentrate on communicating and not be tied up in local politics. Appoint someone you trust to be Political Liaison, and issue him or her this order:

"Your job is to keep the politicians off my back while I talk to the ET. Issue a communiqué at once, citing this handbook's Appendix C, 'Declaration of Principles Following the Detection of Extraterrestrial Intelligence,' the First Soviet-American Conference on Communication with Extraterrestrial Intelligence (CETI), U.S. President Jimmy Carter's and Secretary General of the United Nations Kurt Waldheim's statements recorded on the *Voyager* spacecraft record, and the International SETI Petition by Carl Sagan and friends. Invite the delegations of all nations, as well as local, county, state, and federal authorities, to convene a council to agree on a political modality. That will keep them too busy to bother me."

The 1982 film by Steven Spielberg *E.T.*, one of the most successful box office draws of all time, showed us a lovable extraterrestrial, but also gave the worst possible advice for you in your own Close Encounter. In *E.T.* the plot hinges on well-intentioned children hiding the abandoned extraterrestrial from government authorities on the grounds that scientists would just want to kill and dissect it. Nonsense! Your job is to make sure that the proper authorities are notified, but that you have assembled such a winning team of experts that the government can't take the lead away from you.

The second step therefore is to get the proper technical assistance. Appoint a second trusted friend as Technical Liaison and issue him or her this order:

"I need the following people and their staffs here immediately [then get him a copy of Appendix D, "People to Contact for First Contact," which can be found at the end of this book]. Never mind, for now, who they are. Trust me, they are all influential enthusiasts for and/or experts on Communications with Extraterrestrial Intelligence (CETI). Tell them that they all work for me, and if they don't follow my orders, I won't give them access to data or list them as coauthors of anything. Go get them!"

The third step is to secure local infrastructure. Appoint a third trusted friend as Logistics Commander. Tell him or her the following: "(1) Reserve every hotel room, motel room, bed and breakfast, student dormitory room, and rental car or truck in a twenty-mile radius; (2) phone the Regional Sales Director of AT&T, MCI, and Sprint and demand a dedicated T-3 phone line from each of them, being sure to tell each who else you asked; (3) call the PR Director of Apple, IBM, Sun, and Hewlett-Packard, tell them each that you need a hundred top-of-the-line workstations and their fastest Internet server, fifty thousand giga-bytes of hard disks, emergency power generators, and tell each which competitors you talked to; (4) call every restaurant and fast-food outlet within twenty miles and tell them that you'll list their names and num-bers on press releases if they provide free food for the duration; (5) call the nearest major hospital and tell them you have over one hundred top scientists arriving from all over the world who are already over-excited and need stand-by medical observation and support. And get me a couple of aspirin."

Theory is of little consequence right now. You need to tap the brains of masters of the field of communications and analyze how they actually work. The first man to do this was the fifth-century B.C. Greek sophist Protagoras. He is credited with being the first to distinguish sentence types: narration, question, answer, command, report, prayer, and invi-tation. Today we classify more forms of what Firth calls "speech functions," such as: commands, requests, invitations, suggestions, advice, offers of assistance, gratitude, agreement and disagreement, greeting, leave-taking, encouragement, permission, promising, apology, threats, warning, insulting, pleadings, and so forth. "There are very many such terms in the everyday language (one might compare, on a different plane, G. W. Allport's collection of 18,000 terms in English referring to personality characteristics)."

Aristotle also said that Protagoras was the first to call attention to the distinctions of gender and tense. Your job is like his, except a million times harder.

WHAT KIND OF LANGUAGE?

We assume that the ET is not a superlinguist who already knows En-glish or can learn it while you are still getting a grip on the situation. We assume that he does not carry the equivalent of a Universal Trans-lator (a probably impossible gadget) or *The Klingon Dictionary: The Of-ficial Guide to Klingon Words and Phrases* by Marc Okrand. No, we must think long and hard about what language is, and how our experience with human languages might extend to ET languages (*Xenolinguistics*).

Francis P. Dineen, Georgetown University Institute of Languages and Linguistics, says that there are eleven characteristics of language. He was thinking of human languages, so we will need to make a few adjustments. He lists:

1. Language is **sound**
2. Language is **linear**
3. Language is **systematic**
4. Language is a **system of systems**
5. Language is **meaningful**
6. Language is **arbitrary**
7. Language is **conventional**
8. Language is a **system of contrasts**
9. Language is **creative**
10. Languages are **unique**
11. Languages are **similar**

Let's take these one at a time, and reconsider them in the UFO context.

Sound, Light, Viruses, and Neutrinos

Language is **sound**. Or is it? Most humans speak and listen to language, using the same fleshy articulatory equipment to produce speech sounds and to hear them. The sounds may appear strange to you, but they may be accurately described in terms of the movements of organs such as vocal cords, tongue, lips, and teeth. But the primacy of speech is not absolute, given the importance of writing and the use of various sign languages. We have no evidence yet that the ET uses sound, or writing, or sign language, so we must immediately find out what *medium* is used for language signals in the ET.

Your science team, since they arrived, have been observing the ET with every scientific instrument imaginable. Ask them which medium the ET seems to be emitting the most complex signals in:

(a) *Light*. Aliens may be emitting electromagnetic radiation, such as radio waves (see "The Waveries" for a story of ETs that *are* radio waves), microwaves, infrared, visible light, ultraviolet, X rays, or gamma rays. Deploy any additional sensors needed in each frequency range, record everything, digitize those into the computer system, and tell the scientists to set up software-controlled gadgets to emit coded radiation in whatever frequency or frequencies the ET is emitting. Examples in science fiction of light-communicating ETs include the novel *VOR* (which stands for Violet Orange Red), and Steven Spielberg's 1977 film *Close Encounters of the Third Kind.*

Even on Earth, quite a variety of life-forms generate light. As one essay puts it, "Many insects, fish, crustaceans, squids, fungi, bacteria, and protozoa bioluminesce: They throb with light. The angler fish even hangs a glowing lure from its mouth, which attracts prey. A male firefly flashes its cool, yellow-green semaphores of desire, and the female, too, is randy, she flashes back her consent." The legend of the fall of Troy includes mention that the news of ultimate victory was flashed from Asia Minor to Greece by a sequence of signal fires, a technique that led to the rise of the heliograph (relaying signals by reflecting sunlight by mirrors spaced far apart).

Try to determine if the ET is emitting light by natural, biological means or by the use of some hardware. Use your pocket flashlight and/or camera flash to copy whatever light patterns you can see.

(b) *Sound.* The ET may be producing subsonics, too low in frequency for humans to hear, as blue whales, alligators, and elephants do; or sounds that we can hear; or sounds too high in pitch for our ears, as dolphins, praying mantises, and bats can do. Bats "echolocate" by responding to the echoes of the fifty-thousand clicks per second that they can produce (more than twice the frequency we can hear). The frequency range may be narrow, or it may cover many more octaves than human speech, as with dolphins. Record everything, and get it digitized for the computers.

The microphone arrays set up by the science team will reveal this pretty quickly. Have them set up a computerized frequency-transponder system to stretch or squeeze the sound into a human-audible range for the Linguistics subteam to hear. Have your Tech Liaison bring John Lilly, or Michael Hyson, and any dolphins they can bring and keep comfortable. Dolphins might be better at sonic communication than humans, and might be useful ambassador-translators.

A special case of sound is music, again invoking *Close Encounters of the Third Kind.* As one poet observed, "A single chord is a calling card and, at that, a mighty simple chord, based on universally shared mathematics. This is an old idea, going back to the Greeks and the music of the spheres. There has always been a connection between music and mathematics, which is why scientists have often been inordinately fond of music. . . . Science fiction argues that if music is mathematical, it must be universal. For interstellar space, don't bother with verbal messages;

send a fugue. To be safe, send both," and indeed *Voyager 1* and *Voyager 2* were launched in 1977 carrying a digital record of miscellaneous sounds of earth, including music. A popular joke (in NASA and SETI circles) is that the ETs land and demand, "Send more Chuck Berry!"

George Rochberg, a composer, says that "music is a secondary 'language' system whose logic is closely related to the primary alpha logic of the human body. If I'm right, then it follows that the perception of music is simply the process reversed, i.e. we listen with our bodies, with our nervous systems and their primary parallel/serial memory functions." The problem with this theory is that, while every single human society has music, the music in each culture is different.

Philosophy professor and science fiction pioneer Olaf Stapledon agrees: "Man himself, at the very least, is music, a brave theme that makes music also of its vast accompaniment, its matrix of storms and stars."

Observe whether the ET produces patterns of sound with an object—it might be a musical instrument. If you can, imitate its sound with a harmonica, guitar, violin, or any other instrument you happen to have on hand and with which you are familiar. But don't expect full emotional communication. As Victor Zuckercandl says in *The Sense of Music*, "We can translate from any language into any other language; yet the mere idea of translating, say, Chinese music into the Western tonal idiom is obvious nonsense." Music, like primary language, is arbitrary, in the sense of our section entitled "Arbitrary Is as Arbitrary Does."

In the novella *The Moon Moth* the protagonist reads in the *Journal of Universal Anthropology* the following:

> The population of the Titanic littoral is highly individualistic, possibly in response to a bountiful environment which puts no premium upon group activity. The language, expressing this trait, expresses the individual's mood, his emotional attitude toward a given situation. Factual information is regarded as a secondary concomitant. Moreover, the language is sung, characteristically to the accompaniment of a small instrument. As a result, there is great difficulty in ascertaining fact from a native of Fan, or the forbidden city of Zundar. One will be regaled with elegant arias and demonstrations of astonishing virtuosity upon one or another of the numerous musical instruments. The visitor to this fascinating world, unless he cares to be treated with the most consummate contempt, must therefore learn to express himself after the approved local fashion.

This includes instruments such as

Stimic: three flute-like tubes equipped with plungers. Thumb and forefinger squeeze a bag to force air across the mouth-pieces; the second, third, and fourth little fingers manipulate the slide. The *stimic* is an instrument well-adapted to the sentiments of cool withdrawal, or even disapproval. *Krodatch*: a small square soundbox strung with resined gut. The musician scratches the strings with his fingernail, or strokes them with his fingertips, to produce a variety of quietly formal sounds. The *krodatch* is also used as an instrument of insult.

(c) *Smell*. Smell is the most ancient and the most emotionally evocative sense you have. When you sniff an odor, molecules of the scent are absorbed by the mucous membrane of the fatty, moist, yellow tissue in your nasal cavity, behind the bridge of your nose, stimulating microscopic cilia on special olfactory nerve cells, which are replaced every month or so. The nerve cells send messages to your brain. In fact the "olfactory bulb" in the brains of fishes is the evolutionary ancestor of your entire cerebrum—the thinking part of your brain.

You have, according to the popular "stereochemical" theory of J. E. Amoore (first suggested by the poet Lucretius in about 60 B.C.!), seven basic smell-receptors (shaped and sensitive molecules) on those nerve cilia, and therefore everything you smell is a combination of seven basic smells. They are: pepperminty, floral, ethereal (alcohol, or pears), musky, camphoraceous (moth balls), pungent (vinegar), and putrid (rotten eggs). Something smells pepperminty to you if it has wedge-shaped molecules that fit into a V-shaped receptor site on your nerve cilia, and floral if it has a molecule shaped like a disk with a straight handle, which fits into a bowl-and-groove-shaped receptor site. Putrid molecules are negatively charged, and couple to positively charged receptors; while pungent molecules have a positive charge that links to a negatively charged receptor.

In all likelihood the ET will have a completely different set of basic smells. Your receptors are locks, designed to fit particular key molecules. The ET will have different locks and different keys. Still, it might be informative to present to the ET a series of smells that are basic to you and to smell if it replies with any smells that you can recognize. On the down side, you might be poisoning the ET.

A specially important type of smell communication is that of "pheromones"—from the Greek words *pherein* ("to carry"), and *horman* ("to excite"). Precise scent molecules trigger some creatures to ovulate, to begin courtship behavior, to take a dominant or submissive role, to mark territory, to identify family, to designate egg-laying places, or to make a trail back to home. Pheromones are important to insects and to mammals. Martha McClintock demonstrated that a group of women living together synchronize their menstrual cycles because of some pheromone in their sweat.

One way of telling if the ET has evolved as a smell-priority creature is where its smell receptors are located. If the ET, for instance, is snake-like, with a head close to the ground, it is more likely to smell odors that cling to the ground. If the ET has feathery antennae, like moths or butterflies, it may have the supersensitive pheromone receptors on these antennae. If the ET has four or six legs and a head dropping close to the ground, then it may be somewhat like a bloodhound or truffle-hunting pig. But this is only a hint, not a certainty. After all, how can we tell whether or not the ET is smelling with its feet? Well, maybe if it wears no shoes. . . .

The chemistry and biochemistry experts on the Science Team have been running samples of exhaled and secreted gas and liquid from the ET through mass spectrometers and other analysis devices. They are coding that data for the computer system and will now tell you if the molecular output from the ET is varying quickly over time.

If the ET is like terrestrial insects in its use of pheromones and other chemicals as a medium of communication, we need to track the changes in smell and be able to make stinky signals in return. Have the Chemical Synthesis subteam make stocks of every chemical the ET produces, and set up a smell-o-vision gadget that will puff software-controlled coded smells at the the ET. Call in the top perfume designers and "noses" from London, New York, Tokyo, and Paris, just to be sure.

(d) *Taste.* Follow the instructions for Smell, except based on samples from the surface of whatever part of the ET seems involved, such as mouth (as in people), antennae (as in insects), or carapace (as in lobsters). Pay attention to your master chef, but don't feed anything to the ET yet, for fear of poisoning.

Our word *taste* comes from the Middle English *tasten* ("to sample, touch, examine"), which in turn derives from the Latin *taxare* ("to sharply touch"). Taste is important to mammals, who evolve a love for the flavor of their mother's milk; and later to tell good food from bad. Observe carefully to see if, how, when, and in what context the ETs eat, drink, and touch objects to the organs of eating and/or drinking. Observe whether they eat what appears to be meat or plant matter— taste has different significance for hunting carnivores than for grazing herbivores.

You have roughly ten thousand tastebuds on your tongue, as first noted by Georg Meissner and Rudolf Wagner in the last century, with specific areas of your tongue devoted to the four basic tastes—sweet (tip), bitter (back), sour, and salty. Your taste of food and drink is really a combination of taste and smell.

The ETs may be cannibals, by the way, in the sense of eating one another, but unlike shlocky sci-fi movies, they will not want to eat humans. We are guaranteed to be extremely poisonous to them if they have anything like an immune system responsive to foreign proteins. For a dissenting view, however, see *Anything You Can Do*.

(e) *Touch*. The ET may communicate through vibrations, squeezes, scratchings, or other tactile modalities. We are most sensitive to touch on certain hairless areas of skin: fingertips, palm, foot sole, tongue, nipple, and sexual organs. Many mammals are most sensitive with whiskers near the mouth. Look for what body parts the ET uses to delicately touch objects in its surrounding environment. These are probably among the more touch-sensitive places on its body. There may be social barriers to touch in specific places or in particular contexts. You don't want to accidentally be guilty of extraterrestrial sexual harassment! The legal phrase *noli me tangere* means "don't interfere," but literally means "don't touch me."

Your sense of touch comes from tiny encapsulated nerves called Meissner's corpuscles, buried between the top layer of skin (epidermis) and the second layer (dermis). You have almost ten thousand such touch nerves on each square inch of fingertip.

You also have deep pressure-touch sensors, called Pacinian corpuscles, near joints, and in mammary glands and genitals, that signal to your brain what is pressing on your body, how your organs are shifting position, and what position your limbs, fingers, and toes are in (proprioception). These Pacinian corpuscles are also sensitive to vibration. In addition, you have Merkel's disks (which sense and signal about steady, constant pressure below the surface of your skin) and Ruffini endings, deep beneath skin, which respond to pressure, and special nerves for sensing temperature, and the sensitivity to touch at the base (follicle) of your hairs. Maybe, but not surely, the ET has touch sensors of similar kinds. Observe carefully if the ET has hairs, vibrissae (stiff catlike whiskers), snouts, bristles, cerci (vibration-sensors on the bellies of cockroaches), antennae, tongues, bills, fingers, tentacles, or other parts likely to be touch related.

Look for how the ETs (if there are more than one) touch one another. Try to note which touches look like caressing, kissing, biting, sucking, scratching, patting, nudging, massaging, kneading, fumbling, wiping, tickling, fondling, grooming, brushing, stroking, prodding, banging, hugging, or licking. You may be way off base, but photograph, sketch, video, or note in writing whatever you can about such behaviors. If the ET reaches out to touch you, be very careful not to jerk away or to overreact. Try to touch it back in the same way.

Gather some musicians (who can make precise motions with fingers or tongues), safecrackers (with ultrasensitive fingertips), chiropractors (good at bending, twisting, pulling, and squeezing), doctors, chiropodists, manicurists, barbers, and masseuses. And have the Science Team set up tactile-transponders for computer input-ouput that can translate touch into software and the reverse.

(f) *Posture.* The ET may communicate by wiggling its limbs or other body parts in a visual language. Your Science Team has been watching, recording, and computerizing its motions. Enhance that analysis with a top American Sign Language expert, Marcel Marceau, or other available master mime, modern dancers, dance instructors, choreographers, semaphore signalers, and Labanotation folks, who can translate choreography into computer notation and vice versa. Tell Robin Williams that you've got a sequel to *Mork and Mindy* in production, and fly him here.

There are conventionalized symbolic gestures to convey narration and emotion in the dances of Indonesia, Indochina, Korea, China, and Japan. "It would seem as if kinesthesia, or the sensing of muscular movement, although arising before language, should be made more highly conscious by linguistic use of imaginary space and metaphorical images of motion," says Whorf.

> Kinesthesia is marked in two facets of European culture: art and sport. European sculpture . . . is strongly kinesthetic, conveying great sense of the body's motions; European painting likewise. The dance in our culture expresses delight in motion rather than symbolism or ceremonial, and our music is greatly influenced by our dance forms. Our sports are strongly imbued with the element of the "poetry of motion." Hopi [Native American] races and games seem to emphasize rather the virtues of endurance and sustained intensity. Hopi dancing is highly symbolic and is performed with great intensity and earnestness, but has not much movement or swing.

Watch carefully for signs that the ET sometimes moves in dancelike or gamelike ways, but expect that the differences in the nature of those motions may be greater than the differences between European and Hopi dance.

Weston La Barre gives a referenced list of human gestural, or allelo-languages, including:

> the sign languages of Australian aborigines; the silent gestural lan-
> guage of European monks, designed to avoid interrupting the med-
> itations of others, an allegedly international language of traveling
> medieval monks, reliably dated from, at the latest, the fourth century
> A.D. onward; the hand-language of deaf-mutes and those who would
> communicate with them; the gestural argots or kinesic trade-jargons
> of truck drivers, Hindu merchants, Persians, gypsies, carnival folk,
> burglars, street urchins, tobacco auctioneers, and others; the elaborate
> gestural language of the Hindu *natya* dance-dramas; the ritual hand-
> poses or *mudras* of Buddhist and Hindu priests in Bali; the drum
> languages of West Africa and Central Africa, the Jivaros, Melanesians,
> Polynesians, and Javanese; the "whistling language" of the Canary
> Islanders and some West Africans; the special camphor-gathering lan-
> guage of the Jakun, and the allusive communications of Patani fish-
> erman and many hunting peoples.

In modern American and international life, think of railroad semaphores, naval flags, and the universal code of weather maps, military
salutes, and thumbs up or down. As scientist/science fiction author
Gregory Benford warns, rules of thumb might be different for beings
with different thumbs.

R. L. Birdwistell lists the basic assumptions of *Kinesics* (the systematic
study of the communicational aspects of body motion) as measured in
interpersonal contexts, in a way that we believe might also apply to
extraterrestrials:

> 1. Like other events in nature, no body movement or expression
> is without meaning in the context in which it appears.
> 2. Like other aspects of human behavior, body posture, move-
> ment, and facial expression are patterned, and thus subject to sys-
> tematic analysis.
> 3. While recognizing the possible limitations imposed by partic-
> ular biological substrata, unless otherwise demonstrated, the sys-
> tematic body motion of the members of a community is considered
> a function of the social system to which the group belongs.
> 4. Visible body activity like audible acoustic activity systemati-
> cally influences behavior of other members of any particular group.

5. Until otherwise demonstrated, such behavior will be considered to have an investigable communicational function.

6. The meanings derived therefrom are functions both of the behavior and of the operations by which it is investigated.

7. The particular biological system and the special life experience of any individual will contribute idiosyncratic elements to his kinesic system, but the individual or symptomatic quality of these elements can only be assessed following the analysis of the larger system of which his is part.

(g) *Biomorphic writing.* The ET may have evolved (or been modified for) direct production of writings of some sort. For example, in the story "Help, I Am Dr. Morris Goldpepper," aliens have specially shaped teeth for chewing sequences of symbols onto sticks that they pass back and forth for visual inspection and rechewing. The ET may write on paper with self-made ink (like squid ink), or carve marks onto stone with diamond claws. Give it copies of any bits of material found on or near its person or from its vehicle.

Look for variations of the "writing" methods devised by early human cultures: the knotted ropes and notched sticks of ancient China, South American Indians, and West African and Australian natives. The *quipu* (knots) used by Incas in old Peru included yellow ropes to symbolize gold, white ropes for silver, red ropes for soldiers, green ropes for grain, a single knot for "10," two knots for "20," a double knot for "100," and so on. The messages conveyed by these knotted cords evolved to such complexity that *quipucamayocuna* (official keepers of the knot) were apointed to interpret them. It is possible that extraterrestrials have evolved some such nonpictorial nonwritten pseudowriting and may even have evolved special variations of their ancestral manipulatory organs to produce them rapidly and efficiently.

(h) *Biological vectors.* The ET may use other living things as the medium of communication. For instance it may produce and analyze coded DNA (or its equivalent), encapsulated in linguistic viruses. In such a case, add to the Science Team Dr. Leroy Hood, formerly from Cal Tech, now at the University of Washington in a chair endowed by Microsoft's Bill Gates, to build a computerized genetics-to-computer-to-genetics translator. And put the Centers for Disease Control on alert.

(i) *Direct nerve contact.* The ETs may directly join their nervous systems together and speak brain-to-brain. If so, get the top neurologists and microneuroanatomists to modify their squid axon voltage clamps into devices for reading and writing the electrochemical impulses of the

ET nerves. Start the Science Team working on a neural interface to fit in between the ET nerves and a human volunteer's nerves. Note that our nerves use a particular pulse-frequency code, sodium-potassium ion transport scheme, and neurotransmitter menu likely to be quite different from the ET's nervous infrastructure. That's why the neural interface is a must-have.

We may not have such a technology yet, but might evolve one in the future. This is suggested by the short story "Crisis" by Edward Grendon in 1951:

> By 1980 the balance had shifted. The progress of the physical sciences had by no means stopped, but had slowed considerably. The social sciences, on the other hand, had moved ahead with unexpected speed. The integration between academic and therapeutic psychology had been the first step; the rest followed quickly. When the final *rapprochement* between psychoanalysis and neurology was made, there existed, for the first time, a comprehensive theory of behavior, not only of human beings and animals but of other—so far theoretical—nervous systems as well. Just as the mathematicians were able to postulate geometries that existed in no known Universe when they were first devised, the psychologists were now able to postulate non-Terran behavior systems.

(j) *Exotic radiations.* Outside the electromagnetic spectrum of (a), there are other forms of radiation that may be used by beings or civilizations. These include ions, electrons, neutrons, mesons, neutrinos, and gravity waves. Unless the ET is the size of a moon, it is unlikely to produce significant gravity waves, and unless it has a fission or fusion reactor in its belly, it is unlikely to emit neutrons, mesons, or neutrinos. Still, it never hurts to have the Science Team look for such emissions and be prepared to produce similar ones, perhaps piped in through magnet-guided vacuum pipe from the nearest atom smasher. Neutrinos or gravity waves may, on the other hand, be the way to detect the ET civilization in the first place, but that discussion belongs in another chapter.

(k) *Telepathy.* While there is no clear evidence that people can ever "read" each other's minds, we are socially familiar with the notion of telepathy, and many cultures have such a notion. There are South American natives who believe that the drug Yage allows people to read minds in religious ceremonies, and J. B. Rhine and others at Duke University have performed experiments that tantalized some scientists for decades. It may be that telepathy would give such a Darwinian advantage to any creature that evolves it that the very lack of such creatures on Earth means that telepathy is impossible. But we can't be sure.

After all, in one of the few science fiction novels written by a Nobel Prize winner, William Golding's *The Inheritors*, telepathic Neanderthals are displaced by nontelepathic *Homo sapiens,* who, without the mental advantage of telepathy, are forced to develop language and technology. The suggestion here is that telepathy is actually an evolutionary *dis*advantage.

If the ET is telepathic, there are several possibilities. Maybe we can "hear" its thoughts, and it can't hear ours. This gives our Science Team an advantage to exploit. Maybe it can "hear" our thoughts but cannot project messages back into our minds. If so, it has the responsibility to let us know, which puts us back to square one. Maybe we can sense its emotions, or it can sense ours. This is of limited value, since we may not have the same emotions, and even human emotional communications (i.e., music) produce at best ambiguous results.

If clear signals can go from ET to human and back by telepathy, we need a very disciplined human thinker to communicate. I suggest an expert in meditation, with a sense of humor and a delight in technology, such as the Dalai Lama. Whatever you do, keep everyone else out of telepathy range, or else the ET may tap into unspoken violence, prejudice, or the chaotic human unconsciousness.

(l) *Combinations.* The ET may use two or more of the above modalities in combination. The "waggle dance" of the honeybee combines direction (with respect to the position of the Sun), touch, and smell. As an example of (c) and (f), Kurt Vonnegut has written about aliens who communicate by farting and tap dancing, who are all beaten to death by irritated rednecks.

Linear or Nonlinear?

Language is **linear**. That means, for humans, that language sounds are produced by a series of movements of the speech organs, one after the other. We can represent human language by using distinct symbols for each individual sound, and by putting them in order from first to last in the same order as the sounds are emitted. The order of the symbols (left-to-right as in English, right-to-left as in Hebrew, or top-to-bottom as in Chinese) doesn't matter, as long as we are consistent.

There is no guarantee that this is true for the ET. If the ET has a different perception of the flow of time, that is difficult, but does not produce an absolute barrier to communication. What if the ET has a different perception of linguistic space?

The alien might produce multiple sequences of sounds (or whatever) simultaneously, in counterpoint. For instance it might make a series of eight noises in a row, each of which has eight frequencies simultaneously. The message would not be coded as a string or line of symbols but rather as an eight-by-eight square of symbols, like pieces arranged on a chessboard. Musical composers and conductors may be said to think in two dimensions, which is why a musical score is written with multiple instruments from top to bottom as well as melodies written from left to right. An ET of this type might be speaking in crossword puzzles rather than in words.

So long as we can detect, record, and computerize everything the alien does, we will be able to solve the crossword puzzle or to detect the pattern of linguistic chess pieces. It will be painstakingly slow, but we can proceed.

Similarly, the alien linguistic units may be connected to one another not in sequence or in fixed two-dimensional array but as a network of connected language atoms that point to, connect to, or refer to one another in a pattern that is different every time. This would be a spoken version of what Theodore Nelson calls *hypertext*. It took Ted Nelson some twenty years to convince the world that hypertext made sense at all. I know, because I was one of the two computer programmers who first put his idea into practice in the mid-1970s. Now it is a commonplace on computers through software such as *HyperCard* on the Macintosh, or more astonishingly, the World Wide Web on the Internet. An ET that could speak hypertext would be hard for us to keep up with, but the computer provides the essential interface. Eventually an alien on the World Wide Web would provide a kind of intersociety communications the likes of which we could not have imagined a decade ago.

Another possibility is that the ET communicates in three dimensions or more at once. The ET might, for example, emit not just a sequence of sounds but a phased array of sounds in frequency space to produce an acoustic hologram. Some people think that dolphins can send acoustic holograms to one another, which are like three-dimensional diagrams of the perceived or imagined world. We humans do not know how to think in holograms, but we can produce them and analyze them by computer. John Lilly and some dolphins in a tank would again be a useful translation team. Coincidentally, one of Ted Nelson's first jobs was as a documentary filmmaker for John Lilly's dolphin communication labs, and my mother, Patricia Frances Vos, worked for Haskins Laboratories, which analyzed recordings of dolphin speech.

As Ted Nelson puts it, inventing a Lewis Carroll–like portmanteau word from *interconnected, twisted,* and *tangled,* "Everything is profoundly intertwingled."

Systematic, We Hope

Language is **systematic**. That means that in every human language on Earth the number of symbols needed to write speech in that language as a linear sequence is definite in number. As few as a dozen letters might be needed (as in Hawaiian), or as many as fifty or so. But not every combination of sounds and symbols is possible in any given language. That is, there are only a finite number of units that have only a limited number of ways to be combined.

If this is not so for the ET, we are in trouble. If the ET language has an infinite number of units, we could never learn more than an infinitesimal part of that language. But we cannot conceive of aliens being able to handle that either. We suspect that this is a universal law of language, applicable throughout the universe. Only infinite beings could use infinite languages. They would be as gods to us.

The combination of linearity and systematic restriction on combinations lets us describe and compare languages, both in terms of sounds and grammar. To take an example from Dineen, *table* and *stable* are both common words in English, and each can be made into other English words by adding a single sound at the end (suffixing). We can now have *tables* and *stables*. But there is no sound that we can put at the start of (prefix to) *stable* that would make an acceptable English word, nor any sound that can be suffixed to *tables* or *stables* to make an acceptable English word.

If there are no systematic limits to combining units of ET language, our linguistic experience will be of little use, and we can only hope that our Science Team will be provoked into making an unpredictable breakthrough.

I Never Metasystem I Didn't Like

Language is a **system of systems**, or a **metasystem**. The *table* and *stable* example above is usually explained in terms of two kinds of linguistic reasoning. We would say that *phonologically* (in terms of sound system) there is no such word as *jtable* or *ztable*. We would say that *grammatically* there is no way to suffix a sound after the *-s* at the end of *tables*.

That is, there is a system of sounds (phonology) and a system of grammar. Both systems are in force all the time, and both systems restrict the combinations and the order within combinations. There are also systems of style (stylistics) and meaning (semantics) that limit combinations and sequences.

If the ET language is not this kind of metasystem, or system of systems, each with its units and rules of combination of units, then our current scientific method of analyzing a language into each system, one at a time, is doomed to failure. Again, though, this is the kind of fruitful failure that could spur our Science Team to a great leap forward. But that would scarcely happen overnight.

What Is the Meaning of Meaning?

Language is **meaningful**. The reason you are in charge of studying the ET language is that we assume the language is connected to almost every aspect of the ET's life and culture. On Earth there is a stable relationship between the group of sounds spoken by people of one language and the civilized environment in which the speakers of that language live. We assume that the same is true of the ET.

A child becomes a functioning part of his or her community primarily by acquiring language. The leaders of each society become leaders and exert their leadership primarily through their ability to communicate with their constituency through language. Let's look at each of these two sentences more carefully.

A baby is not an adult, not only because the baby is small, weak, and unable to care for itself. The baby cannot fully understand what we say to it, nor tell us precisely what it wants. True, a mother may be able to recognize her baby's cry from that of another baby. True, the baby can recognize mommy and daddy and very quickly learn to respond to a few special voices and words. But it takes a couple of years of almost constant linguistic experimentation and play before the baby becomes a toddler able to speak and understand sentences. The baby also acquires its parents' language in the context of interacting with toys, foods, parents, furniture, and the patterns of daily home life.

Three times in history experiments were performed to see if children raised in an environment with no language would speak a common protolanguage or create a language of their own. First, Psammetichos, king of Egypt, had this tried; then Frederick II, king of Sicily, in roughly A.D. 200; and finally King James IV of Scotland, approximately A.D. 1500 (using deaf-mute nurses, cooks, and servants in a remote castle). These experiments would be considered unethical today of course. Unfortunately, as the people of those times did not exercise what we would call controlled scientific methods, the results were uncertain.

How, then, can we communicate with an ET, since neither of us is a baby acquiring language for the first time? Babies have *linguistic plasticity*: an extraordinary ability to almost effortlessly learn any language or combination of languages spoken consistently in their environment. This seems to be due to a *neural plasticity* in which the baby's brain has an unusual ability to create, compare, and extend language patterns. Once the brain becomes less plastic, as we grow up, it becomes harder and harder for us to learn languages.

The obvious solution is to have a human baby grow up while interacting with the ET, or an ET baby grow up in a human environment. It is in this way that we intuitively accept Tarzan learning the language of apes while still a baby, or Michael Valentine Smith learning Martian by growing up on Mars. There would be legal problems in allowing a baby to grow up around our ET, but perhaps there will be no faster way to truly acquire its language.

Secondly, we said that linguistic power yields leadership. If our ET is a leader, perhaps we can count on its having special linguistic plasticity or discipline. But if it is just an ordinary crew member or passenger, it would indeed want to ask us humbly to "take me to your leader."

Arbitrary Is as Arbitrary Does

Language is **arbitrary**. The reason that speech alone does not suffice for people to communicate if they speak different languages seems obvious. There is no particular connection between the sounds used in each language and the message being expressed in those languages. That is precisely why there are many languages on Earth—5,445 different languages by one recent count.

If there were a one-to-one relationship between things and the words for those things, there could fundamentally be only one language, with one-to-one conversion rules to account for different sounds for the same basic words. There are a few words that do relate directly to what they represent, such as *murmur, buzz, hiss, bang, whisper, hum, chirp, screech, slither, plop, babble, thump*—but these imitations of the sounds of their referents (*onomatopoeia*) is a very small part of human languages, which in any case render the imitations differently. For instance, the English "cock-a-doodle-doo" imitation of a rooster crowing is expressed as "co-corico" in French and "chicchirichi" in Italian.

We should not expect the ET language to be very different in this concern.

Conventions: Pay at the Door

Language is **conventional**. Although we have just established that there is no predictable relationship between the expressions we use to represent things and those things themselves, we may not deduce that language is totally unpredictable.

When we consider a single item of language in isolation, it is certainly arbitrary. But no piece of language really exists in isolation; it is (as we have seen) part of a system of systems. This means that there are regular and accurately specifiable relationships between different units of the same language. When humans speak to one another, the formation and use of language units is so regular that it almost seems to be that there is an agreement between the speakers.

This virtual agreement is what we mean by language being conventional. The idea that language is conventional goes back at least to Democritus, Aristotle, and the Epicureans. The agreement is not explicit; it is an implicit agreement of facts and actions. Speakers in the same linguistic community use very similar expressions to designate the same things, and use the same set of conventions to deal with similar situations. This is what creates linguistic systems and keeps them stable.

Because language is conventional in this way, we can be reasonably certain that an accurate analysis of the speech of one person will apply to the speaking habits of another person from the same community.

We believe that the same applies to extraterrestrials. Therefore as you lead the Science Team in learning to understand the ET's language, you can rest assured that this will make it very much easier to communicate with the second ET from the same outer-space community.

There is a small but nonzero possibility that the ET language is not stable and conventional in this way. If so, we are in serious trouble. As Robert Sheckley has suggested in "Shall We Have a Little Talk," ETs with a sufficiently fast-changing language and ability to adapt to the continuous change in language systems will be beyond our ability to communicate with them for more than a short and increasingly frustrating period:

I have learned an exceptional number of exceptions. Indeed, an impartial observer might think that this language is composed of nothing *but* exceptions. But that is damned well impossible, unthinkable, and unacceptable. A language is by God and by definition *systematic,* which means it's gotta follow some kind of *rules.* Otherwise, nobody can't understand *nobody.* That's the way it works and that's the way it's gotta be.

In Sheckley's profound yet funny story, the brilliant human linguist has struggled to learn a language, falls in love with an alien, and then is horrified as the language changes overnight into what he first suspects is a joke on him, then realizes is

...a true language. This language was made up at present of the single sound "mun." This sound could carry an extensive repertoire of meanings through variations in pitch and pattern, changes in stress and quantity, alteration of rhythm and repetition, and through accompanying gestures and facial expressions. A language consisting of infinite variations on a single word!.... He could learn this language, of course. But by the time he learned it, what would it have changed into?.... All languages change. But on Earth and the few dozen worlds she had contacted, the languages changed with relative slowness. On Na, the rate of change was faster. Quite a bit faster... It changed endlessly and incessantly, in accordance with unknown rules and invisible principles. It changed its form as an avalanche changes its shape. Compared with it, English was like a glacier.... An observer could never hope to fix or isolate even one term out of the dynamic shifting network of terms that composed the Na language. For the observer's action would be gross enough to disrupt and alter the system, causing it to change unpredictably.... By the fact of its change, the language was rendered impervious to codification and control. Through indeterminacy, the Na tongue resisted all attempts to conquer it.

By Way of Contrast

Language is a **system of contrasts.** The main reason a single speaker's language habits are valid for others of his or her community is that language can be considered a system of differences. How those differences are manifest is not very significant. For example, parrots cannot produce exactly the same sounds as humans do because they do not have human vocal cords or nasal sinuses or tongues. Yet parrots can produce sounds that differ from one another in a way analogous to humans', so we understand their imitations of our speech as if it were human speech.

We don't care if the ET makes humanlike sounds by vibrating a membrane, rubbing its legs together like a cricket, or directly stimulating air molecules. If it can make sound, we can analyze its language as if (within limits) it were spoken sound, as in the "Sound, Light, Viruses, and Neutrinos" section, part (a).

You're So Creative!

Language is **creative**. As a system of contrasts, as discussed above, language is a pattern that is common to an indefinite number of speaking acts that refer to completely different referents. This pattern explains why we can, at any time, speak a sentence that no human being has ever spoken before and immediately understand a sentence that we've never heard before. By using our imaginations to manipulate the phonological, grammatical, lexical, and semantic systems of our language, we can act as fiction writers or poets in extending human awareness of possible connections between things in a creative way. In a sense, poets create a whole new world through language. This is so important that we will conclude our chapter with an examination of the importance of poetry to extraterrestrial communications.

First Contact with extraterrestrials will be very important in getting ourselves out of our parochial limitations of understanding. As Whorf suggests, "Science . . . following these well-worn cultural grooves, gives back to culture an ever-growing store of applications, habits, and values, with which culture again directs science. But what lies outside this spiral? Science is beginning to find that there is something in the Cosmos that is not in accord with the concepts we have formed in mounting the spiral. It is trying to frame a *new language* by which to adjust itself to a wider universe."

Unique in All the Universe

Languages are **unique**. Because languages are arbitrary, systematic networks of contrasts (as we have shown above), each human language deserves to be considered unique, one of a kind in all the universe. Even among the 5,445 or so languages on Earth, each has something that no other has. It may be a sound never used meaningfully (as a *phoneme*) as part of a word by other people, or a unique number of parts of speech, or a special way of combining those parts. Part of the challenge of learning a foreign language is to discover and master such individual patterns.

All human beings descend from the same ancestors. Current research on the mitochondrial DNA suggests that all living humans descend from a particular woman who lived roughly 200,000 years ago in Africa. Other research on the X chromosome suggests that we are all descended from a particular man who lived perhaps 280,000 years ago, but almost surely no more than 800,000 years ago. It will be awkward to explain if "Adam" and "Eve" lived tens of thousands of years apart.

Just as we have common biological descent, our languages all evolved (we think) from the same original language. So as different and unique as each language is, they are all cousins in the same family. Our ET does not have an ancestor in common with us. The ET language, similarly, did not descend from a prehistoric Earth language.

The challenge for your team is that there are things—we don't know in advance which things—common to all Earth languages that might not apply to the ET. We must start out assuming that its language is "more unique" than any we have ever encountered before.

Similarity

Languages are **similar**. As we have found, historically related languages such as the Romance languages have many features in common. All human languages, more broadly speaking, have features in common. All humans encounter and experience the physical world through the same senses (even if one or more is missing in an individual through birth, disease, or accident), and all of us experience in essentially the same way.

In the early eighteenth century Leibniz first suggested that all human languages derive not from an historical origin but from a common protospeech. The twentieth-century Italian linguist Trombetti argued that the Tower of Babel story is figuratively true, in that all human languages have a common origin.

As James Beattie said over two centuries ago, in 1788,

Languages, therefore, resemble men in this respect, that, though each has peculiarities, whereby it is distinguished from every other, yet all have certain qualities in common. The peculiarities of individual tongues are explained in their respective grammars and dictionaries. Those things, that all languages have in common, or that are necessary to every language, are treated of in a science, which some have called *Universal* or *Philosophical* grammar.

The differences in linguistic systems reflect the "social organization of speech." Arbitrary selection of significant features of experience makes it hard to learn an unrelated language. It is easier for an English speaker to learn French or German than to learn Iroquois or Bantu. Because of the pervasive similarities between all human languages, it is possible to learn new languages at all.

Since the ET may have a radically different social organization, a radically different set of senses, and a radically different way of experiencing the physical world, we must resign ourselves to the ET language having far fewer similarities to human languages than do any human languages to each other.

This leads us to ponder a key question: What are bedrock, fundamental, inherent similarities between our view of the world and the ET view of the world by which we can find *some* similarity, however slim, between its language and ours?

We will look closely at this question and then explore the answers in terms of the linguistic analysis that we must use to exploit those answers.

ESSENTIAL EQUIPMENT

by the Reverend Charles Woland
in conversation with Michael Scott, Ph.D.

"The most essential piece of equipment for any UFO hunter is a good pair of boots."

The Reverend Charles Woland had his first encounter with a UFO when he was a police officer serving with the Royal Canadian Mounted Police in 1959. He never reported the elongated silver object he had seen moving northward at unnatural speeds, though he later learned that many of his brother officers had seen similar objects. It has been almost forty years since his first sighting. Since then he has had numerous sightings of unidentified flying objects, and investigated several landing sites across the world, particularly in the British Isles. Now in his early seventies and living in retirement in the picturesque south of Ireland, the Reverend Woland shares his practical experience of half a lifetime of UFO investigation.

Although he has lived in Ireland for the past eight years, he still retains his Canadian accent. Standing at over six feet tall, with a shock of snow-white hair, Charles Woland became a minister of the Anglican Church when he left the RCMP in the early 1970s. (Therefore he has asked that a pseudonym be used to protect his identity. We have naturally honored this request.)

According to Woland . . .

If you're serious about this business, you need a good pair of boots. You will spend so much of your time on your feet; either standing in damp fields watching the skies or wading through muddy fields, crossing rivers and marshes to landing sites.

Originally, I used to wear army-issue jungle boots, or commercial Vietnam jungle boots, but the early patterns burned and blistered your feet pretty bad. I'd always get them a size too big and wear extra-thick socks. Nowadays I wear waterproof Magnum boots over a pair of Gore-Tex socks. They'll keep your feet wonderfully warm and dry, and you'll be able to stand on your feet for hours and trek across the wettest or most inhospitable terrain. I've seen people come out to skywatch in sneakers. They get tired very quickly, and if there is any condensation or dew on the grass, it will soak through the shoes and you can catch a chill fairly quickly.

I've known people to recommend steel-toe-cap tanker boots or field boots, but if you're lucky—or unlucky—enough to get to a landing site, some of them can be pretty hot, and the last thing you need to be wearing is steel-toed boots in a radioactive zone, no matter how low the rads. And while I'm on the subject, equip yourself with a good Geiger counter, and be sure you know how to use it. It could save your life!

So much of this business is done at night that warm clothing is essential. I'm always astonished to see people out in the lightest of jackets and trousers. Standing still for any length of time means you're going to get cold. When I was an officer with the RCMP, I learned the value of layering clothing, and also of always bringing more than I anticipated using. An oiled knitted woolen jumper is essential, as are heavy twill or tweed trousers. If it's winter, I'll wear thick cotton underwear and either silk or polypropylene long johns in the spring and fall. You may smile now, but at three o'clock in the morning, even in the warmest of climates, you'll be mighty glad if you do the same. There are some commercially available military outfits that are very usable—a one-piece flightsuit or quilted nylon flight jacket, for example, and a good leather jacket that will cut the wind. For particularly cold weather I recommend a parka jacket, either N-3B or N-2B weight. Even if you're wearing a parka with a hood, get yourself a hat and a good pair of gloves, preferably something fleece-lined, like Kenai or Windstopper. The only other clothing consideration you have is color—bright colors or dark. I prefer dark colors, something that will blend in to approach a landed craft unobserved, so I always wore dark colors.

Over the years I've been lucky enough to encounter most of the classic sightings. I've seen nocturnal lights and disks and also daylight disks; I have also had what are now called Close Encounters of the First and Second Kind, though never of the Third Kind. When I'm asked how I managed to see so many sightings over the years, I reply that it is simply a matter of being in the right place at the right time. It stands to reason that one has a greater chance of seeing a nocturnal light in the darkened skies of the countryside, than in the light-bleached skies over a major city.

Many of my most satisfying sightings have taken place on camping trips. So I always recommend that the serious ufologists equip themselves with a tent. I currently use the Easy Going Tent, a two-man waterproof nylon tent that only weighs three pounds. However, you can get away without a tent if you have a good sleeping bag. I'm now using an Aspen down bag; it's a little heavy at five pounds, but it's got a temperature rating of 0 degrees Fahrenheit. There are new bags on the market now, and I'm thinking about getting one of the new black mummy bags; they weigh an extra pound, but they're good right down to minus 25 degrees Fahrenheit. At my age you need a little comfort. To carry all this stuff, get yourself a good backpack; I'd recommend the Pioneer backpack.

When you're in the field, an essential piece of equipment is a good knife. I take two with me wherever I go: a Swiss Army knife which has everything but the kitchen sink, and a larger all-purpose knife for cutting and hacking. I've used a standard Bowie pattern knife that I brought back with me from Canada. I never succumbed to the temptation to buy one of the survival knives—always seemed as if you'd need a degree in astrophysics to get at all the stuff in the handle, and once you took it out, I could never work out how you were going to get it back in again.

Bring food and drink. A sturdy canteen that doesn't leak is an essential—what you put into it is up to you. I was once on skywatch with a fellow UFO researcher in the Mojave Desert when he missed a spectacular sighting of three nocturnal lights because he had gone back to the camper to make himself some coffee. Once your eyes have adjusted to the night sky, it is extraordinary the detail you can pick out. You will see more detail if you do not look straight at stars, and over the years I've come to depend on my instincts. If you see something moving from the corner of your eye but turn to look at it and it seems to have stopped moving, then turn your head slightly and look away from the object. You may find it starts to move again. Many of the UFOs I've sighted have been seen with the naked eye, but naturally you're going to need a good pair of binoculars. And here it is worthwhile spending a little money. I'm always amused by people who go out skywatching with a cheap pair of binoculars. Even if they do spot something when they look at it through the pieces of cheap plastic, all they'll see is rainbow-hued fuzzy spots. A good pair of field binoculars in at least 10×50 is essential. Avoid some of the monoculars or telescopes; you'll need a tripod to get a stable picture—and most of the objects you'll be looking at, or looking for, will simply not stay still enough.

A couple of years ago I got myself a Data Scope, which I've come to depend on. This is a combination range finder, compass, and chronometer. It's got a 5×30mm monocular lens, and a single button pops up the time, distance, and direction of the object you're looking at over the image. It's quicker and far more accurate than a compass.

Remember that most sightings take place at night or twilight, so you might consider a night-vision scope. I bought an NV-100 Night Vision Scope two years ago, and it has more than paid for its cost in the number of sightings I've made. It looks a little like a camcorder and is used very much like one, but it magnifies any available light by a factor of ten thousand. I used it to watch a doughnut-shaped craft fly low over Galway Bay in the west of Ireland. The image was so clear I could actually see the lightly oiled rainbow pattern on the surface of the craft.

In all the years I've been watching, I've only ever managed to get a handful of good photographs of UFOs. I have hundreds of shots of landing sites, naturally, but the serious researcher should be aware of the difficulty of capturing an object flying at high speed in an erratic pattern on film. There are many excellent cameras available—I use a Nikon F—but a good fast film is essential. I never use anything less than 400 ASA, and always, always bring more film than you think you will need. One of the most frustrating experiences of my career was running out of film at a landing site in Alberta.

And finally, make notes. Bring a small voice-activated tape recorder, or a notebook and a pen that will write at any angle in any conditions. Note everything you see.

And the final piece of essential equipment is patience—lots of patience. Sooner or later it will be rewarded.

TAKE ME TO YOUR LEADER:
THE UPS AND DOWNS OF CONTACT

by Chris A. Rutkowski

Although contact with extraterrestrials is
most often portrayed within ufology as a benign
or positive experience, there is a possibility
that aliens' intentions may be somewhat more
malevolent. The implications of contact—both
positive and negative—are explored through an
examination of media, ufological literature,
and relevant UFO cases, including a review of
abductees' and contactees' experiences.

As the flying saucer craze began to flourish in the 1950s, a classic image emerged from within the "doubting Thomas" subculture. In a typical scenario, an alien spaceship would land near a group of awestruck humans, who would scurry for cover from underneath the flashing lights and buzzing noises emanating from the craft as it extended tripod landing gear and settled to Earth. After a few pensive moments, a portal would open, a staircase would extend, and a green Martian would plod slowly down the steps toward the cowering terrans. It would walk determinedly forward, select its addressee, and then, with the best broken English its universal translator could muster, say: "Take me to your leader!"

The Earthlings, of course, would instinctively take the alien to the mayor of the town, who would welcome the creature and extend greetings to it and its kin. Life on our blue planet would never be the same.

But that would never happen in reality. The actual consequences of alien First Contact would be much more complex and probably more onerous. Pity the Martian who would try to adopt a simple contact scenario. This is *Earth*, after all.

WHO SPEAKS FOR EARTH?

When the Federation starship *Enterprise* enters the orbit of a newly discovered planet, Lieutenant Uhura simply makes her console emit a few *bleeping* noises and the visage of the planet's ruler appears on the forward view screen. If an alien federation exploration craft were to arrive at Earth, who would be our alien liaison?

This is not an easy question. The Earth does not yet have a global government, and may never have one. As ufologist Stanton Friedman observes about the lack of unified scientific and military efforts: "Nationalism is the only game in town." Despite the emaciated efforts of the United Nations, provinciality is the norm on our planet. Citizens seem to be encouraged to owe their allegiance to the monarch, military leader, premier, or prime minister of their individual countries. Democracy, communism, or dictatorship—all political systems are founded in a narrow nationalism that precludes anything resembling true altruism.

No one speaks for the planet.

Not that this has not been discussed in any forum. On the Internet, this very topic has been hashed and rehashed from time to time, with no definite consensus. There have been many individuals suggested: the president of the United States, the director-general of the United Nations, the pope, Deng Xiaoping, Walter Cronkite, Carl Sagan, Arthur C. Clarke, Ted Turner, and so forth.

The problem is not necessarily who *speaks* for Earth, but who *should speak* for Earth. There is a good argument to be made for the leader of the most powerful nation on the Earth, since that person can be considered the most powerful and influential on the planet. But another argument could be made for the leader of the most populous nation on the Earth, who would represent the most people. Similarly, one could hear proposals for the spiritual leader of the majority of Earth-dwellers (not the pope, obviously).

What about the scientists? Perhaps the true spokesperson should be a scientist who has shown a compassionate and sincere concern for the population of Earth. Perhaps a philosopher, then, would make a better choice. Certainly not an astronomer, who would be suitable for astronomical matters but not diplomatic ones.

A true military leader, perhaps? (But not necessarily a chief of staff!) Undoubtedly, the arrival of an alien race would constitute some obvious threats to our society. A strong front might be advisable, though a bit bold and heavy-handed. However, if the aliens are self-proclaimed conquerors, this might not be a bad idea. Aliens could be Kzinti or Klingons as easily as Mork or Alf.

The dilemma faced by an alien emissary, then, would be quite significant. There does not appear to be any one individual who would speak for the entire planet. (It is very possible that the *Star Trek* scenario is unlikely, and that no planet would be globally unified.)

Well, then, if not one individual, perhaps a select group or committee.

BUREAUCRACY AND BEMS

A number of years ago, a delightful cartoon in the magazine *New Scientist* contained an interesting twist to the contact theme. It depicted a landed saucer and a line of aliens exiting via a gangway. Each of the aliens was dressed in a black suit with a bowler hat and carried a briefcase. The startled Earthling witnesses stood aghast, but one person was saying, "Frankly, I'm disappointed."

The cartoon upturned our typical notion of benevolent aliens or conquering space creatures and exposed our intense need for salvation. What do we *expect* aliens to be like, anyway?

Fans of *The X Files* will know one popular theory: that a secret committee within the government has been in contact with aliens for many years and is somehow in cahoots with them. This secret society operates entirely outside of the law, but uses government and military resources as it sees fit. It is such a theory that was expounded by the sensational *Krill Papers* and other texts, which were circulated among ufologists in the eighties. Paranoid stories of underground alien bases and wars between rival alien groups flowed freely from computer bulletin boards and into the minds of many UFO buffs.

Aside from the fact that there can never be incontrovertible proof of such a society because of its very nature, this scenario is generally discounted by most serious ufologists because it involves two major factors: intelligence and total secrecy. Neither of these is regarded as probable in corrupt/incompetent military/political environments, and the possibility of both existing concurrently is debatable.

It seems reasonable, however, to expect that a group of top-level "movers and shakers" would have been selected at one point by a government as a kind of "emergency response team" in the event of alien contact. After all, even devout skeptics and science fiction writers such as Asimov and Clarke once predicted contact with extraterrestrials within the foreseeable future. It is precisely this concern that makes the existence of a group such as the infamous MJ-12 committee (whose alleged work it was to cover up government interest in flying saucers) very possible, and drives its pursuit.

As has been pointed out elsewhere, each of the individuals on the MJ-12 list would have been ideal candidates for such a project, bringing skills and knowledge that would assist in understanding alien contact. One trouble with the MJ-12 list is that it is not international. The intent would have been, supposedly, to protect American interests by having an all-American team to meet with the aliens to the betterment of American interests. It would be easy to say at this point that MJ-12 would share its information with other governments, but this *was* the time of the Cold War after all.

Given that situation, it would also have been logical that a Soviet version of MJ-12 would had to have existed, as well as one in China. If anything, this argument seems to support the existence of a truly international group of some kind (perhaps Sufi or Illuminati) that would have surmounted the nationalistic MJ groups on a more global scale.

Or, perhaps, there is no such group, and there never has been.

THE DREYFUSS DELUSION

In the movie *Close Encounters of the Third Kind,* the character played by Richard Dreyfuss experiences profound delusions and dissociative events as a result of his UFO experience. Ultimately, his contact drives him to seek the aliens at their selected landing site. Along the way, he meets other contactees/abductees and stumbles on an elaborate government-run contact operation that has certainly inspired later paranoid stories. In the final moment, it is not the select group of highly trained diplomats who are invited on board the ship, but the UFO experiencer himself.

It is this one scene that subconsciously must inspire many UFO believers and enthusiasts to remain immersed in the UFO subculture. Surely the aliens will see that it is *they* and not the clandestine agencies who are the *true* emissaries of Earth. Contactees often go one step farther and proclaim that they *already* have been chosen to be ambassadors by the Space Brothers.

But, really, who will be the first person to contact aliens? A ufologist? An astronomer? A contactee? (This entire article is void, of course, if we are to accept the claims of the various contactees, who already claim contact with the space beings.)

Stanton Friedman, a ufologist specializing in document retrieval and a popular lecturer at colleges throughout North America, has two anecdotes to illustrate how closed-minded professionals fail to realize their own folly. The first concerns astronomer Donald Menzel, noted debunker and allegedly a secret member of MJ-12. Menzel made a number of officious presentations to public inquiries into flying saucers, each time pointing out that all sightings could be explained by scientists. Menzel's public opinion was that aliens would seek to have an audience with scientists who were most involved in astronomy and space travel. Asked about the consequences of aliens visiting Earth, Menzel replied, "When they arrived, they would make themselves known to the [American] National Academy of Science, and they would certainly have to meet with me." In Friedman's opinion, this definitely typifies the ethnocentric stance taken by scientists who take the time to consider alien contact. Clearly, if contact has occurred, the general academic and scientific communities would know about it; since they do not, such contact has not taken place.

The second story concerns a newspaper editor who had not assigned a reporter to cover one of Friedman's lectures. Friedman often does his own publicity as he moves from community to community, and it is common for him to contact local media in advance of his arrival. When he came to this particular city, he noted that although most other media were covering the event, this one large newspaper had not bothered to respond. Friedman called the editor and asked why the newspaper was noticeably absent among the others. The editor replied by displaying his own opinion about aliens and UFOs: "If aliens had landed, they would have invited me to their press conference."

HOW TO INITIATE CONTACT: A STEP-BY-STEP GUIDE

Such an egocentric view goes completely against any rational plan of contact proposed by terrestrial scientists. It would seem more logical and cautious to first make clandestine contact with an anonymous denizen— to "test the waters," so to speak.

Anthropologists know that the first step toward contact with another civilization is that of observation. One can learn essentially all there is to know about a society through a passive study of its projected image.

In the case of aliens visiting Earth, they would gain a tremendous amount of knowledge of us through the monitoring of our radio, television, and written communications. It is interesting to speculate on what they might have learned from the first transmissions they might have picked up from Earth, such as an early radio episode of *Amos 'n' Andy*. (If they were analyzing our culture in any detail, they would note that we were in possession of significant technology but were essentially still barbaric and that our most common pastime was murder of our own and other species on the planet, often for food.)

Once they had completed a survey of our culture (if they were still interested in contacting us), they might want to examine our planet (and us) physically. A physical landing might not be at all necessary, since radar and infrared imagery can tell much about a planet's surface from an orbiting spacecraft. But, if required, there would need to be some precautions. Since their presence still would be a secret, they would have to ensure no one detected their entry or exit. Landings could be done at night and in isolated areas, perhaps to gather some soil and vegetation. And, if an examination of a higher life-form was needed, it could be done in such a way as to prevent the general population from being aware that they were under scientific study. This scenario would be particularly true if the visiting race was superior to its subjects. We can only refer to our own studies of other terrestrial life-forms, such as chimpanzees and fish, to see how contact with an inferior species is best achieved to the benefit of the superior race.

It needs to be said that the reported actions of UFOs and their operators are consistent with this scientific contact scenario. Of course, this is how *human* scientists likely would proceed. This, too, displays a certain amount of terrestrial egocentricity. How alien scientists would proceed is impossible to predict, since their procedures and methodology would be, by definition, *alien*. To employ this or any other argument to illustrate the reality or nonreality of extraterrestrial visitation is entirely unjustified.

THE BEM PROBLEM

The previous discussion makes sense only if the aliens are friendly and/or benevolent. If we apply other human characteristics of greed, personal gratification, and psychopathology to the aliens, we're in big trouble. Such was the case in the early fifties cinematic versions of bug-eyed monsters, who were bent on conquering Earth, raping its resources and stealing its women. (Or something like that.)

Even in our imaginations, aliens are often portrayed as the "bad guys" or with a casual attitude toward us. Marvin the Martian is irritated by earthlings (especially rabbits), although it is interesting that his evil intentions are caricatured in much the same way that *Hogan's Heroes* painted German Gestapo as buffoons. This is probably done in an appealing manner to completely remove any fear of invading aliens; after all, if they're as stupid as we are, what is there to worry about?

One can never rule out the possibility that the first contact with an alien race might be dangerous, risking complete annihilation of our civilization. Would we trust a harmless-looking alien, perhaps with the outward appearance of the large-eyed, cute E.T.?

This is not an easy question, since our natural xenophobia has caused us to reject anything looking slightly unlike us. Many people have an abject fear of spiders and snakes; imagine human-sized ones, wishing to shake our hands! This was the core of the SF drama, *V*, which pitted terran rebels against lizards who fooled Earth bureaucrats into thinking that all was well.

Given that we might not trust an alien at first contact, how could we make any progress toward fostering a relationship? We might expect that "they" would feel the same way toward us, and we could be in a serious quandary.

The one possible saving grace is that visiting aliens would come to Earth only through a mastery of advanced technology, far beyond our present capabilities. In other words, *they* would be in a position to call the shots, not us. They would clearly be in the position to make the first moves and determine how our interaction would proceed. (Alternatively, assuming we were of about equal technologies, a delightful SF story, *First Contact,* written by Murray Leinster in 1945, proposes a very clever solution to the trust problem.)

There are many theories about why the aliens are here at all. After a rather unremarkable daylight disk sighting in Canada in 1985, the witness wrote,

> I've given this matter a lot of thought, and I have heard an interesting theory about why these beings are visiting us, and why they don't bother communicating with us. We are from another planet in the galaxy. About two million years ago, around the time of the "missing link," we were criminals, nonconformists, and artists [sic]. Rather than try to exterminate us, they shipped us off to the planet Earth, and

pretended we never existed. They wiped out our memories with powerful drugs.

From time to time now they check up on us. They know far more about us than we know about them. (Cameron, 1995, p. 108)

THE DOWNSIDE OF CONTACT

A now-classic book on UFOs presented the negative aspects of contact when it was published almost thirty years ago. *Flying Saucers Are Hostile* (New York: Award Books, 1967), written by Brad Steiger and Joan Whritenour, offered a contrary view to the prevailing notion that saucer pilots had the best of intentions. Its message was simple:

> There is a wealth of well-documented evidence that UFOs have been responsible for murders, assaults, burnings with direct-ray focus, radiation sickness, kidnappings . . .

This is all the more remarkable because one of these authors later published a series of books dealing with spiritual salvation based on information channeled from benevolent space entities (e.g., *Revelation: The Divine Fire* [New York: Berkley, 1973]). However, in recent years, Steiger has again focused on the negative aspects of contact [*The Rainbow Conspiracy*, [New York: Pinnacle, 1994]).

The basic trouble with this caution is that many of the incidents are *not* "well documented" and exist primarily as anecdotes, often from second- or third-hand sources. Nevertheless, there are several cases on record where witnesses appear to have been injured during their UFO experiences.

The most significant of these may be the Thomas Mantell crash of 1948. In January of that year, Mantell was leading a flight of four P-51 Mustangs near Godman AFB in Kentucky when he was asked to investigate an unidentified object near the base. All four planes flew up to 22,000 feet in chase of the object, but Mantell alone climbed higher to attempt an intercept. Unfortunately, none of the planes were equipped with oxygen, so when Mantell went higher, it appears he blacked out. When the wreckage of his plane was found, much was made of the incident as being due to an alien ray-gun blasting a pursuing terrestrial craft out of the sky. It was later revealed that the navy had been testing a secret Skyhook balloon in the area and had not shared its information with the National Guard, for whom Mantell had been flying. To this day, some UFO buffs insist the balloon story is a white-wash and point out that Mantell was an experienced pilot who was unlikely to mistake a balloon for a giant spaceship, whereas debunkers dismiss it with ease.

NEVER MESS WITH THE SPACE BROTHERS

Although relatively few contactees claimed their mentors had malevolent intentions, some aliens clearly came from the pulp-fiction molds of the 1950s. A case in point was a woman who shall be referred to here as "Vonda."

In 1977 this author had been interviewed on a local television show about a series of UFO reports in southern Manitoba that he had investigated. That evening, a telephone call came in from a woman in a northern Manitoba community. This person, Vonda, explained that she had intimate knowledge of aliens and their spacecraft and that she spoke to the Space Brothers twice a week. She wanted to know if UFO researchers in Winnipeg would be interesting in having her present an illustrated lecture about her experiences.

Although there was no formal group in existence at that time, there were enough independent investigators and researchers in contact with each other that an emergency meeting was arranged in the author's small downtown apartment. Regardless of what she might have to say, a lecture by a full-fledged contactee was rare at the time, so it seemed a perfect opportunity to have a group meeting. In fact, Vonda was so anxious to speak with us, she stated that she would leave the next morning on the long journey south to Winnipeg and lecture to us that evening.

About twenty interested and slightly disinterested people gathered in the small apartment. Vonda arrived with her husband in tow, and they brought in pamphlets, books, photographs, and a small movie projector. Her husband elected to sit on the steps of the apartment block rather than go inside (because he had "heard it all before," he explained). And Vonda began her soliloquy.

"I died when I was six years old," she began, "but I rose up again on the third day. I soon found that I could talk to the insects and animals."

Vonda went on to describe how she felt she was psychically gifted, and she began her contact with benevolent space beings at an early age. The Space Brothers took her to other planets, and even inside the Earth through holes in the North and South Poles. Her station wagon was "teleported" while she was on a long road trip, and she proudly showed off the "burn marks" on her car (although to the untrained eye they looked remarkably like rust).

She lived part of the year in maritime Canada, where she had a large following in the form of a churchlike congregation. She would often hold religious ceremonies in fields where "scout ships" had landed, encouraging others to tune in to the spiritual guidance of the Space Brothers. Her group built a pyramid in the middle of a field, and would sit inside so that spiritual energy could be better focused upon themselves in meditation. At one point, Vonda told us that she had been given a vision by these entities that she should strike the ground with a wooden rod at a certain location (slightly reminiscent of a biblical story), and a well would be created. According to her testimony, she did so, and water did spring forth. This water was used by her to heal the sick and cause the blind to see and the lame to walk.

At this point, it would have appeared that the Space Brothers (for it would be unkind to call them aliens) were benevolent and were interested only in helping Vonda bring humans to galactic salvation. Alas, there was one incident that raised some doubts in this regard. It was easy to see the undercurrents of emotional reaction to her "teachings." Vonda told the gathered listeners that she and some others had watched a "scout ship" land on a hilltop, and the next morning, a cross-shaped patch of burned grass was visible. She declared the site "holy," and it was immediately roped off. Soon, pilgrimages were made to the venerated landing pad.

However, a few unenlightened local residents thought the whole thing was rather silly, and procured a bulldozer to erase any sign of the shrine and drive the worshipers out of the area. Perhaps expectedly, Vonda's faithful protested by lying down in front of the bulldozer, and the attempt was halted. A few days later, however, Vonda gravely explained that the bodies of those trying to demolish the sacred site were found in a lake with their bones broken, as evidence that we must not tamper with the will of the Space Brothers.

Even in the realm of contactees, apparently there is inherent danger in the contact.

BURNED BY A UFO?

Perhaps the most intensely investigated and best-documented UFO incident on record in North America is also one that is largely unknown to the public and the majority of UFO buffs. It had the distinction of being investigated by military officials of two countries and literally dozens of government departments and civilian organizations.

The witness to this incident claimed that he had been burned as a result of an encounter with a metallic craft, which left behind other traces of its landing. He was examined by more than one dozen physicians in the United States and Canada. Site investigations were made by members of the RCMP, RCAF, other government officials and numerous civilians.

The spectrum of officials who were involved in this case included representatives of the Royal Canadian Air Force Training Command Headquarters; Canadian Forces Base Winnipeg; RCMP Criminal Investigations Division; the Canadian Department of Health and Welfare; and the provincial Department of Health and Welfare. In addition, the USAF Condon Committee investigated, *Life* magazine had been out, and two connected but separate civilian groups, APRO and CAPRO (Canadian APRO) had become involved. Furthermore, the federal Department of Mines and Natural Resources became involved, as did the Whiteshell Nuclear Research Establishment, the Manitoba Cancer Institute, the Mayo Clinic, and other medical establishments. Even more remarkable, diligent researchers have uncovered hundreds of official documents related to the case.

On May 20, 1967, at 5:30 A.M., Stefan Michalak left his motel in the quiet resort town of Falcon Lake, Manitoba, intending to do some prospecting. After a few hours, he found a quartz vein and spent some time examining it. Around noon, he had just finished lunch when he noticed two cigar-shaped objects with "bumps" on them, at about forty-five degrees in elevation, descending toward him and glowing red. As they approached, they appeared to be more oval and then disk-shaped. The farthest one of the pair stopped in midflight while the other drew nearer and appeared to land on a large, flat rock, which was later determined to be about one hundred fifty feet away. It was the color of "hot stainless steel," surrounded by a golden-hued glow. A brilliant purple light flooded out of openings in the upper part of the craft. For the next half hour, Michalak stayed near the rock, making a sketch of the object and noting various peculiarities. He became aware of waves of warm air radiating from the craft, accompanied by the "smell of sulfur." He also heard the whirring of a fast electric motor, and a hissing, as if air were being expelled or taken in by the craft.

A door opened in the side of the craft, revealing some lights inside. Michalak approached to within sixty feet of the craft and heard two humanlike voices, one with a higher pitch than the other. He was now convinced that the craft was an American experimental craft, and walked closer to it. In what may have been the finest example of a diplomatic *faux pas,* he claims he called out, "Okay, Yankee boys, having trouble? Come on out and we'll see what we can do about it." Getting no response (the voices ceased abruptly with his invocation), but being a little flustered, he asked in Russian, "Do you speak Russian?" (Having grown up in Europe, Michalak knew several languages.) There was still no answer, so he gave greetings in German, Italian, French, and Ukrainian, then once again in English.

He boldly walked closer to the craft and poked his head into the open doorway. He saw a "maze" of lights on what appeared to be a panel, and beams of lighting running in horizontal and diagonal patterns. Michalak stepped away from the craft, and three panels slid over the opening, sealing it totally to the outside. Examining its outer surface, he touched the side of it with his gloved hand. Drawing his glove back, he saw that it had burned and melted.

Unexpectedly, the craft shifted position, and he now faced a gridlike exhaust vent. A blast of hot air shot suddenly onto his chest, setting his shirt and undershirt on fire and causing severe pain. He tore off his burning garments, and threw them to the ground. He then looked up in time to see the craft depart like the first, and felt a rush of air as it ascended.

When it had left, there was a strong smell of burning electrical circuits mixed with the original smell of sulfur. Looking down, he saw that some moss had been set burning by his shirts, so he stamped it out. He walked over to where he had left his things, and noticed that his compass was behaving very erratically; after a few minutes, it became still. He went back over to the landing site, and immediately felt nausea and a surge of pain from a headache. The landing spot looked as if it had been swept clean (no twigs, stones, etc.), but piled up in a circle fifteen feet in diameter was a collection of pine needles, dirt, and leaves. As he looked around, his headache became worse, he felt more nauseous, and broke out in a cold sweat. Feeling very weak, he vomited.

He decided to head back to the motel. On the way back, he vomited several more times, and had to stop to regain his strength.

After walking for a few more minutes, Michalak reached to his motel, but thinking he was "contaminated," he remained outside in a clump of trees nearby. But he eventually entered the motel coffee shop to inquire whether or not a doctor was available, as his pain had become considerably worse. He was told that the nearest doctor was in Kenora, Ontario, forty-five miles east of Falcon Lake. Michalak decided to return home. He went to his room, where he waited until the next bus to Winnipeg arrived at around 8:45 P.M. He called his wife, telling her that he had had an "accident" and not to worry, but to send their son to meet him at the bus terminal. When he arrived back in Winnipeg around 10:15 P.M., his son immediately took him to a hospital.

When his physician examined him, he found first-degree burns on his abdomen that were not considered serious. He prescribed 292s for the pain and seasickness tablets for the nausea. On the twenty-third, Michalak went to a radiologist, who found no evidence of radiation trauma. A whole-body count taken a week later at the Whiteshell Nuclear Research Establishment also showed no radiation above normal background. The curious geometric pattern of burns on Michalak's abdomen was diagnosed as thermal in origin.

Over the next few days, Michalak reported that he lost 22 pounds from his normal weight of 180. However, his physician could not verify this weight loss, since he had not seen him for over a year. But since Michalak and his family reported he was unable to hold food down for several days, his weight loss could have been considerable.

Also reported was a drop in his blood lymphocyte count from 25 to 16 percent, returning to normal after a period of four weeks. These two counts were six days apart, but were associated with normal platelet counts on both occasions. This contributes to the argument against the theory of radiation exposure.

There is some evidence to indicate that the red "welts" or burns went through periods of fading and recurrence, a most unusual medical situation. Because of the possibility of radiation at the site, it was quickly suggested that the welts were radiation burns. However, this is quite incorrect.

Radiation was also blamed for an "awful stench" that seemed to "come from within" Michalak's body. It was suggested that a quick dose of gamma rays may have deteriorated the food he had just eaten, giving him a vile odor and causing him to vomit "green bile." Individuals consulted on this, however, say that such a strong burst of gammas would have deteriorated *Michalak,* not just his digested food!

Yet another physiological effect was the "insect bites" rash that appeared on Michalak's upper torso. The medical reports show that Michalak had "skin infections," "having hivelike areas with impetiginous centers." Later, he had "generalized urticaria" (hives) and felt weak, dizzy, and nauseated on several occasions. Several times over the next several months, he was examined for "numbness" and swelling of the joints. However, the Condon Committee reported that the rash was "the result of insect bites and was not connected with the alleged UFO experience." Also, an RCAF officer stated that he had been bitten by black flies when he was with Michalak searching for the site.

A hematologist's report showed that Michalak's blood had "no abnormal physical findings," but had "some atypical lymphoid cells in the marrow plus a moderate increase in the number of plasma cells." This is in some contradiction to several published sources that claimed that there were "impurities" in Michalak's blood. However, the reported irregularities in his blood would not in themselves be the cause of his condition.

The swelling of his body, though, strongly suggests an allergic reaction of some sort. At work one day Michalak felt "a burning sensation" around his neck and chest. Then he had a "burning" in his throat, and his body "turned violet." His hands swelled "like a balloon," his vision failed, and he lapsed into unconsciousness. Doctors diagnosed his affliction as "the result of some allergy." Later Michalak described how sometimes his wrists swelled so much that they filled his shirt cuffs. What sort of allergy did he have?

HOLD THE MAYO

In August 1968, Michalak went to the Mayo Clinic in Rochester, Minnesota. The purpose of his visit was to undergo tests to determine exactly what was ailing him, as the doctors in Winnipeg appeared to be unhelpful. (It is worthy of note that Michalak paid for the Mayo tests entirely on his own, as Canadian medical insurance would not cover such a trip.)

Michalak had been found to be in good health but with neurodematitis and simple syncope (fainting spells due to sudden cerebral blood pressure losses). The syncope was suggested to be related to hyperventilation or impaired cardiac output. This is interesting, as Michalak indeed has had heart problems within the past few years.

The psychiatric report showed that despite the usual generalizations normally assigned to individuals giving a detailed UFO encounter story, there was no other evidence of delusions, hallucinations, or other emotional disorders. It seems that there was nothing wrong with Michalak. He had no ailment *directly* related to an encounter with a UFO.

What really happened at Falcon Lake? In addition to Michalak's physiological effects, an elevated level of radiation was detected at the site where he had his experience. He did exhibit some very unusual ailments, including a reported weight loss, peculiar "burn" marks on his chest and stomach, charred hair, an odd rash, and recurrent dizziness. Some UFO investigators have said he met alien beings; some say he stumbled upon a secret government or military craft. Skeptics have proposed the only other explanation that would explain many of the facts: a hoax.

Yet, Michalak *was* extremely ill after his encounter. He spent a great deal of his own money traveling to the Mayo Clinic and was exposed to a lot of ridicule. The results of the tests were negative; the physicians could find no explanation for Michalak's symptoms, and the psychiatrists could find nothing in his background that would account for such a bizarre tale. If it was a hoax, it is the most contrived on record, involving radiation, "contaminated" soil, medical examinations, and a flurry of interrogation by government officials at many levels.

In the report of the Condon Committee, Michalak's experience was described as "unknown." Their concluding remarks were impressive: "If [the case] were physically real, it would show the existence of alien flying vehicles in our environment."

At the very least, Michalak's experience is a warning for anyone to think twice before getting too close to a landed saucer.

CANCER: THE NUMBER-ONE OCCUPATIONAL HAZARD OF UFOLOGY

When considering dangers of UFO contact, the work of Dr. Michael Persinger must be referenced. Persinger is physiological psychologist at Laurentian University in Sudbury, Ontario, Canada. He received international attention recently when Dr. Susan Blackmore, a psychical-researcher-turned-debunker and CSICOP member, visited his laboratory and willingly offered herself as a test subject for his studies concerning electromagnetic (EM) effects on the temporal lobe of the human brain. She reported that while wearing a special helmet with electrodes that emitted EM radiation, she was able to feel vague sensations of a "presence" nearby and as if someone was touching her leg. This, of course, proved to debunkers that alien abductions are actually caused by EM fields in abductees' bedrooms.

Whether or not abduction experiences may be even partly induced by EM effects is still a matter of debate. However, Persinger's previous research suggested that UFOs are a hazard not only to UFO witnesses but to UFO investigators as well.

Persinger proposed many years ago that UFO experiences might be caused by EM radiation produced by natural processes such as strain beneath the Earth's crust. He called this the tectonic strain theory of UFOs (or TST). Papers dealing with certain aspects of the TST have been published in several journals, covering various disciplines. The proposed mechanism is interdisciplinary in nature, and carries with it some necessary qualifications to enable it to cope with a poorly understood, mysterious phenomenon in terms of a better-known, mysterious phenomenon. In the words of its proponent,

> Whereas earthquake-related luminosities appear contingent upon large releases of structural strain (seismic activities), the luminosities and electromagnetic correlates of alleged close encounters with UFOs are associated with highly localized, less intense changes in crustal structures not necessarily involving major seismic activity. (Persinger, 1979)

In layman's terms, the energy created when layers of rock press upon or slide past one another is either converted into light that is mistaken for UFOs or zaps human brains and makes people *think* they are having UFO experiences. Persinger arrived at this theory by comparing times and dates of UFO sightings with times and dates of earthquakes. Because he found some statistically good matches, he deduced that this meant the two were related.

It was pointed out by critics of the TST that the UFO sightings Persinger used as data were nearly all explained as aircraft, balloons, and stars, but he was undaunted and developed his theory further. He realized that human exposure to electromagnetic energy is very dangerous, so he noted that close encounters with such radiation would cause the severe "physical and biological consequences" to which he had alluded in his earlier research.

Basically, when an EM-created UFO is seen by a witness, that person would be exposed to a certain level of radiation that might or might not have an effect on the witness's body. If the witness encountered the UFO within a short distance, the radiation might cause him or her to hallucinate a detailed meeting with aliens. In closer proximity, a full-blown abduction experience might be detailed, hence the interest in Persinger's EM studies of the temporal lobe. Alternatively, if the witness was not predisposed to aliens, he or she might experience a "visitation" by the Virgin Mary, or even a ghostly apparition. In effect, Persinger's TST explains *all* paranormal and Fortean phenomena.

DEATH BY UFO

It's the "biological consequences" that are most relevant for our purposes here. Persinger realized that both prolonged exposure to such radiation and short-duration exposure to intense radiation would be very detrimental to one's health. In the latter situation, Persinger suggested that intense EM effects could include epileptic fits and even death by electrocution. This would certainly be the most severe possible consequence of a UFO experience, and a good reason to stay away from a landed UFO.

But Persinger's altruism allowed him to give a warning to UFO investigators and researchers. He warned that since on-site investigators of a UFO incident would be exposing themselves to areas with abnormally high EM fields, they, too, would be risking their health. He cautioned that such prolonged exposure to this radiation might lead to a higher incidence of cancer among UFO investigators. It can be assumed that UFO abductees with a long history of contacts would be at risk as well.

Medical experts, however, are not fully supportive of this suggestion. One neurosurgeon noted,

Before it can be suggested that luminous aerial phenomena are evidence that seismic radiation will raise the incidence of cancer in the geographic vicinity of the phenomena, the physical mechanism to produce such effects should be at least partially understood. Despite the large number of papers describing the tectonic strain theory, the evidence that it reflects a real phenomenon is not convincing. (Rutkowski and Del Bigio, 1989)

But, even if only a *few* UFOs are explained as translocated seismic energy, the logic of the theory suggests that if they *are* caused by natural EM radiation, humans had better beware!

CIRCULAR REASONING

Parallel to the physiological TST effects related to UFOs, a note about inherent dangers associated with crop circles was disseminated on the Internet in early 1996. Basically, the "earth energy" *or* the "alien irradiation" that is considered by ardent believers to be the cause of the mysterious formations (ignoring the overwhelming evidence of simple human hoaxers) is detrimental to cereologists' health.

Simon Burton, writing in the *CNI News*, noted,

> Reports of negative effects have ranged from the psychological—feelings of panic, oppressiveness, general unease—through to the physiological—aches, pains, headaches, nausea, etc. My own reaction to a "bad" circle is usually a lingering ache in one leg, although I have twice now had the alarming experience of waking up "the morning after" to find a square grid of clearly defined circular welts caused by broken blood vessels on my back. Fortunately such physical symptoms seem to be rare. Most physical effects seem to be limited to equipment malfunctions, "gremlins" etc. (Burton, 1995)

Although Burton implied that physiological effects of crop circles upon humans is common, it is in fact very rare and appears to be dependent on unknown variables, as there are no effects noted by other frequent visitors to crop formations.

However, in Alberta, Canada, in 1991, some crop circles were said to cause headaches, equipment malfunctions, and give rise to "eerie" sensations and noises. For example, Canadian crop-circle researcher Chad Deetken reported experiencing profound effects while sleeping one night in a crop circle. He was visiting some circles in Saskatchewan in 1990, and decided to camp overnight inside one formation. He reported that during the night, a "feeling of terror" overcame him, and he bolted from the site immediately. He had earlier documented how the area was permeated with some kind of "energy." And when he decided to sleep overnight in a circle the next year, he and his companions reported experiencing "tension" and "dizziness" during the night.

Similarly, later circles found in Alberta were thought by some researchers to be the sites of powerful energy and would cause severe headaches. But another researcher who investigated the same sites, Gord Kijek, reported *no* such physiological effects, even though he is very prone to migraine headaches from environmental stresses. Furthermore, although equipment malfunctions are often cited when listing the physical effects of crop circles, Kijek often made calls on his cellular telephone while standing *inside* crop circles, with no interference whatsoever. Such contradictory information suggests that the claimed physical effects might depend rather strongly upon the individual reporting them.

Burton noted that the claimed injurious effects of crop circles seemed to be identical to those experienced by the controversial psychologist Wilhelm Reich in his quest to understand orgone energy, a mysterious force that, he said, could control weather, neutralize nuclear radiation, and knock flying saucers out of the sky.

Burton is quick to suggest that this supports the contention that crop circles are related somehow to orgone energy:

> Much of the above has a familiar ring to it. Some, perhaps all, of the symptoms of Oranur sickness seem similar to "Circle Sickness." The description of trees bending over like rubber hoses must also strike a chord of familiarity. Indeed Wilhelm Reich's son Peter in his autobiographical *Book of Dreams* describes once finding on his father's ranch "a big place in the grass we hadn't mowed where it was all matted down." When giving the explanation that that must be where a deer had been sleeping, his companion comments, "She must have been a pretty big one."

However, another crop-circle researcher, Paul Fuller, who is viewed as a bit of a killjoy by some cereology proponents, has offered some evidence that despite Levengood's analyses, the material found in the pictogram is nothing more than common iron filings. The composition of the material is in some doubt, and a debate about the claims and analyses has waged for many months on the Internet.

As for the danger posed to cereologists, Burton noted,

> So, should we avoid crop circles? I think we should at least treat them respectfully as potentially harmful to health.

Finally, popular ufologist/cereolgist Linda Moulton Howe was quoted as stating,

The crop circle sickness issue has come up periodically since at least 1990 or 1991 when several people complained. Four of us inside Cherhill [see above] all developed the same tight band of very dull headache at the same time in 1993. Dr. Levengood is convinced that microwaves are part of the energy [that forms crop circles], combined with a plasma. Would such an energy have a residual effect on us after it created the formation? I don't think anyone has a clear answer yet.

This is certainly an understatement.

In support of the reality of "circle sickness," the CNI editor noted,

Amid widespread claims of crop circle fakery, there are also claims that some people experience strange, sometimes painful physiological effects upon entering a crop circle, effects that seem highly unlikely if the circle were made by human pranksters.

However, it could also be said that since so few people report effects, "circle sickness" may be more of a psychological illness than a physiological one.

THE "NOT READY FOR CONTACT" HUMANS

One of the common arguments given at one time in favor of the government withholding the "truth" about UFOs was that the American people were simply not prepared for the knowledge. Scenarios of angst-filled citizens jumping off bridges and tall buildings because of the "awful truth" were proposed by cynics who felt that the general populace could not deal with the concept of an invasion, no matter how benign or passive.

To counter such arguments, it could be pointed out that we now live in a world in which *Babylon 5* aliens grace our television screens, Scully and Mulder have met aliens in darkened corridors, and *Star Wars* is undergoing a revival. Aliens and UFOs are hardly foreign concepts anymore. They are used by advertising agencies to sell chocolate bars, camera film, diet soft drinks, and computers. (It should be noted that the author sometimes wears a tie emblazoned with images of Marvin the Martian.) How could it be said that humans would be afraid of cute, cuddly extraterrestrials?

The answer is that, for the most part, people know that Hollywood aliens are *not* real. With the exception of those who equate the "aliens are here" scenarios with their own reality, terrans understand that media aliens belong in the realm of fantasy. Therefore, there is no need to worry. The *Invasion of the Body Snatchers* is not factual, and there are no pods reproducing us underneath our beds. (Readers are advised to check their own homes at this point, just to be sure.)

Jacques Vallee once offered the possibility that we are somehow slowly being "conditioned" by external forces to accept the coming of the ultraterrestrials. There could be a kind of "cosmic thermostat" that is causing us to become more introspective and also be receptive of mystical and extraterrestrial influences. For example, if we strayed from the spiritual path, our belief systems could be shaken by encounters with paranormal phenomena, or we might encounter otherworldly entities in our houses or backyards.

But the reality instead might be that humans live in a very narrow set of parameters throughout their everyday existences. A sensitivity or a devotion to mystical matters is hardly commonplace among the masses. Major religious denominations are reporting dwindling attendance as secularity appears to dominate society. In the present general state of consciousness (or lack therein), it is more likely that meaningful encounters with the unknown would be very shocking to the percipient.

It is this writer's opinion that the general populace is *not* prepared for the shift in its worldview that would be precipitated by open visitation by extraterrestrials. While the panic displayed by the *War of the Worlds* audience might not be repeated, it is probable that the shattering of the ethnocentric universe would be highly disruptive. Evidence for this position comes from the growing numbers of abductees who are presenting themselves to counselors, therapists, and psychologists.

THE ABDUCTEE PROBLEM

One of the strongest arguments against abductees "really" being in receipt of direct (and often physical) alien contact is the greatly conflicting nature of the experiences they recall. In very few cases are the aliens described exactly alike (with identical planets of origin, identical spacecraft, identical medical instruments, identical relayed intent, etc.). Admittedly, some abductee researchers are attempting to identify matching symbols observed by some abductees on board the ships, and there are some cases that have some similar characteristics, but for the most part, each abductee case possesses some unique facets. This may be partly explainable due to differing recollections by disparate abductees and deliberate interference by the aliens themselves, but these could be considered arm-waving exercises. (One ufologist even has suggested that, because the abduction stories are so bizarre and incredible, abductions are proof that aliens have their own warped sense of humor.)

Although most abductees seek help from ufologists, it is increasingly apparent that ufology is ill prepared to deal with them. An abductee case is far more complicated than an ordinary sighting of a UFO. Even though abductions are often considered the fourth category of close encounters, they are extremely different from the lesser three categories and should be placed in a category or series of categories of their own.

It is usually recognized that UFO investigators do not investigate UFOs, but the reports made by the witnesses themselves. Already, ufology is once removed from pure scientific investigation and could be considered more analogous to memorative studies by anthropologists. Abduction cases are even more humanistic; there is often no definite "time" of an event, and it might not "take place" in a precise location. They are extremely subjective and may represent something beyond our investigation.

This is why psychologists are more suited to abduction studies. Researchers often have found that abductees have emotional and psychological problems that may or may not be directly related to their experiences. Some appear to have a history of sexual or domestic abuse, and others exhibit symptoms of stresses within their lives. (It is possible that it is *because* of such backgrounds that they are "chosen" or are otherwise sensitive to abductionlike encounters. It is even possible that lifelong abductions are the *cause* of the psychosocial problems.) Regardless of the cause and effect, however, an abductee seeking help from a UFO buff is asking for trouble. Simply put, few ufologists have the therapeutic tools and expertise required to properly unravel an abductee's experiences within a framework of personal problems.

CODE NAME *ADAM*

Charles is an abductee-contactee who has self-published a booklet about his experiences. Charles was originally from Ottawa but was raised by foster parents in rural Quebec. He described his childhood in rather grim detail:

I remember that my stepmother was always helpful with my learning. She would take the spelling book and question me on how to spell certain words. If I were having trouble, she would offer me the whip as encouragement.

In his late teens, he took a number of different jobs throughout Ontario and Quebec, and eventually ended up in northern Manitoba mining towns. Still, things didn't work out well, and after many more false starts, he became a spot-welder at a firm in Winnipeg. In about 1976, he began his contact with what he believed to be an extraterrestrial being. "I started hearing beep noises [sic] in my right ear," he wrote. As a result or consequence of the beeps, he began being interested in a variety of subjects that had never attracted him before. He began writing about his life in poetry and narrative prose. He believed that his body was "a storage battery for a good amount of electromagnetism," and that his brain somehow was able to decode the beeps into new information about the Earth and space.

Among the information decoded by Charles is the "fact" that a convoy of spaceships with the code name *Adam* came to Earth in 5602 B.C. According to his writings, they came because of a great galactic war in which an evil villain named Lucifer managed to escape the catastrophe. Peace reigned on the newly civilized Earth for 1,656 years, until a planetary alignment destroyed the Solarium Magneto Magnesium Crystalline Power Stations. Charles noted, "All technology was wiped out and millions died." Since then, we've been on our own, but a Civilization Star Ship came to Earth in 1947, and will land before the year A.D. 2000. However, Lucifer has found us as well, and we are apparently in danger of playing into his hands once again.

Charles's book goes into some detail about his insight into the coming endtime. Like the Raelians, another contactee group based in France but with representatives around the world, he believes that humans are the result of interbreeding experiments between highly intelligent aliens and early terrestrial species. It is apparent that the experiments were unsuccessful.

DAVE KOWAL'S ENCOUNTERS

Another case possibly representative of the abductee problem is that of Dave Kowal (a pseudonym), who presented himself to this writer in 1988.

On January 26 of that year, Stanton Friedman gave a talk at the University of Manitoba on the subject of UFOs. His evening lecture was well attended (he had earlier been interviewed on both radio and TV), and the crowd of about three hundred people was enraptured by his presentation. At the close of his talk, he asked this writer to stand and be recognized as the principal UFO researcher in the province, and suggested that if any in the audience wanted to talk privately about their local experiences, they could arrange some time afterward.

As the crowd dispersed, one man hesitantly edged his way toward me. When he had finally wound his way through the empty rows of chairs, he shyly asked if he could speak with me at another time.

His nervousness suggested he probably had had a UFO experience of some sort and that he was very reluctant to tell anyone about it. This is quite understandable, since the "ridicule curtain" (defined by Dr. J. Allen Hynek) is very much in existence today, and many people tend to heckle UFO witnesses in a mistaken belief that they are "crazy" and not representative of the general population. (Indeed, polls have shown that approximately 8 percent of all North Americans have seen a UFO.)

We agreed to meet at a restaurant several days later. There, Dave described his experience.

The most vivid of his memories is one that originated from a night during the middle of November 1987. He was in his bedroom, preparing to go to sleep. He had been thinking about the day's events and had been meditating. He got into bed with the lights out, lay on his back, and started drifting off to sleep.

After a while, he became aware of a "presence" in his room, which seemed to be in the vicinity of his closet. Almost simultaneously, he felt a peculiar tingling sensation in his body. He was surprised to realize that he was paralyzed and unable to move in any way except the rotation of his eyes. He felt that the "presence" was somehow responsible and that it was approaching his bed.

Although he couldn't recall seeing the entity in its entirety, he did have the distinct recollection of seeing a "face" not more than a foot in front of his eyes. He could remember and draw this face without much difficulty, depicting a cherubic character with skin folds, slitlike eyes, a thin mouth, and wearing some sort of tight-fitting "helmet" on its head. Dave also felt that something had entered his mind, and that images of things he had seen in his life were brought to the surface of his mind and "taken" from him. He remembers "feeling" or "sensing" that whatever was doing this to him was also reassuring him that it meant no harm and that it only wanted certain things from his memory.

After a while, the flashes of his past life ceased, the entity seemed to withdraw, and sensation once again returned to his body. He told us that he was extremely disturbed by this incident. By itself, the incident was not as interesting as it could be. But Dave related it had been only the most recent of a series of strange events throughout his life. He had experienced similar paralytic episodes before, each associated with some out-of-body flight, and on one occasion had seen a UFO radiating pulses of light as if it was signaling to him. And in 1987, he and other members of his family had witnessed some nocturnal light UFOs moving over fields near their rural home.

Dave recounted his experiences in as much detail as he could remember. But beyond simple interviews, there was little that could be done to alleviate his concerns and find out what had really happened. It was decided to get some outside help.

Common to many of the published accounts of alleged UFO abductions is the hypnosis of the abductees, by which they are regressed to the time of the incident in order to uncover suppressed or hidden facts. Sometimes details of medical examinations on board the spacecraft are revealed, or trips with beings from other planets. From a psychological standpoint, hypnotic regressions are sometimes useful as therapy to uncover suppressed feelings or remove mental blocks. Some ufologists use hypnotic regressions to penetrate witnesses' memories of their experiences, which may have been deliberately clouded by their antagonists. Debunkers note that hypnosis cannot determine the "truth" of any memory, but instead allow a person's own beliefs to come through, whether they are "true" or not. That is, if a person believes he or she has been on board a UFO, even if that did not occur, that event will still be related under hypnosis. Hypnosis *cannot* be used to accurately distinguish between "fact" and "fantasy."

Knowing this, it was still felt that if Dave was willing, hypnosis might aid in evaluating the incident, and there would be the added bonus of the opinion of a professional psychologist. The hiring of a storefront therapist or hypnotist was rejected because the ethics and abilities of some of these have been called into question by debunkers, and as scientific an evaluation as possible was desired. A clinical hypnotist was located who was hesitant but willing to meet with Dave. Interviews were set up, and a session was arranged. The results were interesting.

Under hypnosis, Dave described his experience of the previous November. Some (but not many) details were added to the account. He now recalled seeing the entire body of the entity that had visited him in his bedroom and expressed a great deal of anxiety as it progressed toward him. In its hand was a "rod with a light on the end." The observers and the practitioner were unprepared for what happened next. When the lighted end touched Dave's forehead, he relived an acutely painful or otherwise traumatic sensation, even while hypnotized, to the point where the clinician had some difficulty in regaining control of his subject.

Apparently Dave had had what is now termed a "classic" visitation by some sort of entity in his home. There is of course no physical evidence to support his claims, but he is sure that it did happen, and we must at least accept the position that something happened to Dave to create a memory of the event. As with many UFO abductees, Dave appears to have a history of such experiences throughout his life. He has rarely talked with his friends or family about the incidents, and has been worried about their reactions should he reveal his experiences to them. Indeed, he has threatened legal action against this writer should his identity become known.

But the events of more recent years are a cause for concern. Following the hypnosis session, Dave declined further meetings with the psychologist under the auspices of "treatment" and tried to continue with his life. Unfortunately, his sense of being under observation by "them" and his perceived lack of self-direction without their control became a great strain on his psyche. Within a short while, Dave attempted suicide and was placed in the care of a counselor at a hospital. Unfortunately, the counselor had not had any experience in treating abductees and viewed Dave only as a mildly paranoid schizophrenic. It is difficult to say whether or not Dave has been rehabilitated or aided by his encounters with the professional community.

Today, Dave still feels he is under direct observation by aliens, although he no longer exhibits anxiety about their intent. He still feels that he has been contacted by extraterrestrials. At the urging and under the guidance of a local UFO buff, he became *animateur* for a local abductee support group.

The big question is whether or not Dave's contact is benevolent in nature. It could be that the aliens do not intend to make Dave anxious and that the reasons for their actions are entirely benign. On the other hand, would they not know the damage they are doing? Would Dave's death have justified the means of their experimentation (if that's what it is)?

Did Dave have a visit from an extraterrestrial entity or did he simply have a vivid dream? Without physical proof, a contact by UFO entities is extremely difficult to prove. Debunkers dismiss such claims, but we can recall that selective observation and sampling is a logical method of contact with new civilizations by anthropologists. We can ask, Which is the easiest explanation?

TAKING THE GOOD WITH THE BAD

Sometimes what may appear to be a positive contact may have other consequences that negate the good effects. In 1980, a UFO researcher in Ontario received a letter from a man in northern Manitoba. This person, whom we shall call Jacques, had lived most of his life in Quebec, but had moved to Manitoba in 1978. Jacques wrote about how he had lived a relatively uneventful and normal life until about 1971, when he suddenly became obsessed with the subject of space, space beings, and the meaning or purpose of man's life on Earth. He felt that he "wanted to go back there among the stars, because my place was in the stars, not on the Earth."

After a few months of his obsession, Jacques wrote that one night he was on his bed, thinking about his revelation, when he was "contacted" by something. He heard a sound "like an electric razor" inside his head, and this sound appeared to be communicating with him.

> We were communicating by sounds, acute sounds, and for him [sic] it was maybe the only way, so when I ask questions, if the answer is "yes," that's a long, acute sound, when it's "no," that's two short acute sounds. (Rutkowski, 1989, p. 35)

Jacques felt that this being in touch with him was altering his mind "like cleaning a house of all the garbage." He began seeing UFOs regularly and believed that his "unknown friend" was watching out for him and guiding him toward a higher level of ability and consciousness.

However, his "friend" was not pleased when Jacques met a woman and got married. The being caused them to fight frequently, and, according to Jacques, even gave them a "terrible disease" which made them itch constantly. Jacques knew that his friend was responsible, so he "had a long talk" with his "friend," explaining his displeasure, and "everything went just fine after that." He added in his letter, "That's rather incredible, isn't it?"

Jacques appealed to the researcher for help, "to find out the meaning of this unknown phenomenon." He wanted him to send him an IQ test and then meet to undergo hypnosis. Jacques wanted to converse with someone who was sympathetic to the idea of contact with extraterrestrial beings, rather than being treated as a psychotic individual by a therapist. However, because of the distance between them, the researcher and Jacques were never able to meet. Jacques's present whereabouts and condition are unknown.

OBSESSED

An obsession with reading books about space and UFOs is often encountered in cases of possible abductees. Again, we can ask whether it is the obsession that brings about the experiences or it is real experiences that create the obsession. Another case involved a professor at a Canadian university who for no apparent reason was overcome with an obsession to read and talk about UFOs. His particular discipline was not even remotely related to UFOs or space travel, yet he found himself speaking with other faculty members and even students *during* his classes about publicized UFO sightings.

His addiction became so bad that his marriage, too, was suffering, and his wife eventually forbade him to read UFO material at home. He went to hear Stanton Friedman, a noted Canadian ufologist, speak at his university one day, and this only served to heighten his interest in the subject. Now, whereas some abduction researchers might read into this that the man had been contacted by aliens and that his subconscious was dealing with the experiences, this case took a different turn.

After many months of self-examination and talks with friends, the professor "rehabilitated" himself to the point where he still had an interest in the phenomenon but was no longer obsessed. Researchers found him to be quite rational, and there was no reason to suspect anything was "wrong" with him, yet it remains curious that the obsession appeared so rapidly, without precedent, and persisted for as many months as it did. What is perhaps more remarkable is that he was able to consciously check his progress toward further obsessive behavior. In effect, his early stages of abduction were "cured." This suggests one of two things: Either his contact experiences really had ceased, or there never were any such experiences and his obsession was the result of a psychological aberration.

GIMME THAT NEW AGE RELIGION

When one considers obsessive behavior as it relates to UFOs, the parallel experience of religious ecstasy must also be mentioned. How would alien contact be interpreted within a context of religious fervor? The following case can perhaps give us some idea.

On Sunday, May 2, 1976, Mr. and Mrs. Fehr and their four children were traveling near Carman, Manitoba, Canada, which happened to be the center of a major UFO flap at the time. A deeply religious man, Fehr was pondering some grave concerns as he drove. He later published a tract about his and his family's experience, and this gives some insight into what actually transpired. He wrote that as he drove near Carman, he thought, "What is this world coming to? Why is everybody after money so much and so few have time to read and study the Bible; instead, they have to be with the worldly lusts. How long can this go on?" (Rutkowski, 1989, p. 38).

Something gave him the impression that they would see something as they traveled farther, something that would help him answer his questions. Approximately three-quarters of a mile north of Carman, Fehr noted that "a small cloud appeared in the sky west of us, very bright and strange." He drew his family's attention to the cloud, and as he drove, one of his children commented that the cloud appeared to have rainbow-colored stripes. When he next looked up, the "cloud" "opened up" with a noiseless explosion. Fehr pulled the car off the road, and together they gazed upward. A "big, colorful war" was taking place, with armored horses running to battle in the west, and in the east "quite a few white Angles [sic], each surrounded by pillars of fire." After a few minutes, the tableau disappeared and they got back in the car and continued home. But suddenly, their ten-year-old boy said that a big, red dragon was in the sky, and Mr. Fehr stopped the car again to look up.

He saw "a very bright, colorful funnel up side [sic] down over the whole car, two great big hands coming down underneath the car and felt as if we were lifted up into the Heavens."

He went on to describe his impressions:

While we were lifted up our feelings disappeared, our weight was gone and our flesh had disappeared, felt as though a little gust of wind could blow us anywhere ... I looked up again and saw an Angel up above as if it were the sun, two hands saying, 'COME, COME, COME' . . . Sitting and watching the Heavens, very bright and colorful [sic] pillars of fire still burning around us, a very bright star started falling from right above us, falling towards the north and as it came to the pillars of fire, they opened up. There was no flame over the path of the falling star. The star fell to the black horizon and disappeared. We still sitting [sic] and watching the Heavens, seen another star come from the north with terrible speed, going south.

At one point, Mr. Fehr looked over his shoulder to see if his family were alongside him, and found that they were still there. One of his children cried in alarm that the car was dangerously careening toward the ditch, and he had to take some evasive action. His other children, joining in his excitement, repeatedly called out that they could also see images in the sky, but of a somewhat more secular nature: a lion, a deer, an eagle, and a witch.

Fehr published his tract shortly after his experience, and he expounded his belief that he and his family had witnessed a vision of God's power and glory. He wrote, "Without the LORD, we are nothing. HIS power is way beyond mankind." He explained that the visions could be found in Revelation, chapters 4, 10, and 12.

What is most interesting is that he describes how other traffic on the road seemed to ignore the wondrous sight, failing to stop and watch the event with them. It did not occur to Mr. Fehr that the vision was personal and probably could not have been observed by anyone else not suitably "tuned in." Indeed, there is some evidence in his tract that others in the car did not share his experience at all, but were concerned at his rapture.

The experience of religious ecstasy has been documented by many writers. Historians recording the lives of various saints often cite their having episodes of spiritual ecstasy during periods of deep meditation. The experiences of Saint Bernadette, during which she spoke with the Virgin Mary, are examples of similar incidents. It must be noted that some researchers consider apparitions of the Virgin Mary to be analogous to UFO sightings, and while a literal definition of the term *UFO* might allow for such categorization, the two phenomena appear to be quite different on other levels. Nevertheless, it would be difficult not to classify the experience of Mr. Fehr as something other than a religious vision. The "falling stars" seen after the main experience were possibly just that, though they could also have been aircraft. Shortly after their experience, the Fehrs went to live as missionaries in South America. It is not known if they have had any further UFO experiences.

CONCLUSION

In summary, we can note that while the media may seem to portray extraterrestrials most often as "nice guys," there is a wide body of literature that cautions against the universal acceptance of this premise. Not only are there reasonable scenarios in which aliens might very well be our antagonists, ufological literature abounds with a much darker view of otherworldly visitors. It would seem that some ufologists are already prepared for the worst.

REFERENCES

Burton, Simon. " 'Circle Sickness' or 'Where Angels Fear to Tread': Does Wilhelm Reich's 'Oranur' Disaster Help Explain Mystery?" *CNI News* 13.7 (December 28, 1995).

Cameron, Vicki. *Don't Tell Anyone, but . . . UFO Experiences in Canada*. Burnstown, Ontario: General Store Publishing House, 1995.

Leinster, Murray. "First Contact." In *First Contact,* ed. Damon Knight. Los Angeles: Pinnacle Books, 1971.

Persinger, Michael A. "Possible Infrequent Geophysical Sources of Close UFO Encounters: Expected Clinical and Behavioral-Biological Effects." In *UFO Phenomena and the Behavioral Scientist,* ed. R. F. Haines. Metuchen, NJ: Scarecrow Press, 1979, pp. 396–433.

———. "Geophysical Variables and Behavior: IX. Expected Clinical Consequences of Close Proximity to UFO-Related Luminosities." *Perceptual and Motor Skills* 56 (1983): 259–265.

Rutkowski, Chris A. *Visitations?* Winnipeg, Manitoba: Winter Press, 1989.

———. "The Canadian Connection." *Swamp Gas Journal* 6, no. 1 (1992): 1–2.

———. "The Falcon Lake Case: Too Close an Encounter." *Journal of UFO Studies* 5 (1994): 1–34.

Rutkowski, Chris, and Marc R. Del Bigio. "UFOs and Cancer?" *Canadian Medical Association Journal* 140 (1989): 1258–59.

Steiger, Brad. *Revelation: The Divine Fire.* New York: Berkley Books, 1981.

Steiger, Brad, and Sherry Hansen Steiger. *The Rainbow Conspiracy.* New York: Pinnacle Books, 1994.

Steiger, Brad, and Joan Whritenour. *Flying Saucers Are Hostile.* New York: Award Books, 1967.

Strainic, Michael. "Once Upon a Time in the Wheat." *MUFON UFO Journal,* no. 284 (1991): 3–9.

ALIEN TYPES

If you are fortunate enough to actually encounter an alien, even to just glimpse one, then it is very important that you note as many details as possible about its physical form and attire. Such details as the number of fingers, color of skin and eyes, and hair or its lack add credibility to your account and provide fuel for UFO researchers.

Be sure to write down every detail and/or use a pen or pencil to modify the following sketches. Provided here are images based upon descriptions given from prior encounters of the Third or Fourth Kind. When observing an alien, try to mark its height compared with an object you can examine later, such as a tree limb or any man-made item. Also sketch and/or list any unusual objects it may use or carry, giving its effect if observed. Memory fades, and when you are experiencing something as unusual, and occasionally traumatic, as a UFO encounter, details will change as your mind tries to fit the memory in with the other parts of your life. So create this record as soon as possible after the encounter. Then send copies to the Center for UFO Studies, but don't let the original drawings or notes out of your possession.

LITTLE GRAY MEN

There are large numbers of reports, and a purported videotape of the dissection, of "little gray men." All seem to share the common characteristics of a small stature, large dark eyes, and tiny mouth. Some researchers regard these LGMs as bioconstructs whose job is to run the ships. Others see them as highly evolved individuals. Most contacts with them are friendly, excepting abduction reports. Many cases of encounters with these shorter aliens report them to be wearing a shiny, metallic bodysuit.

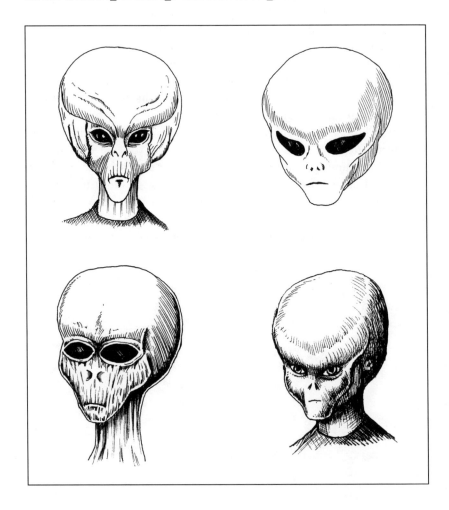

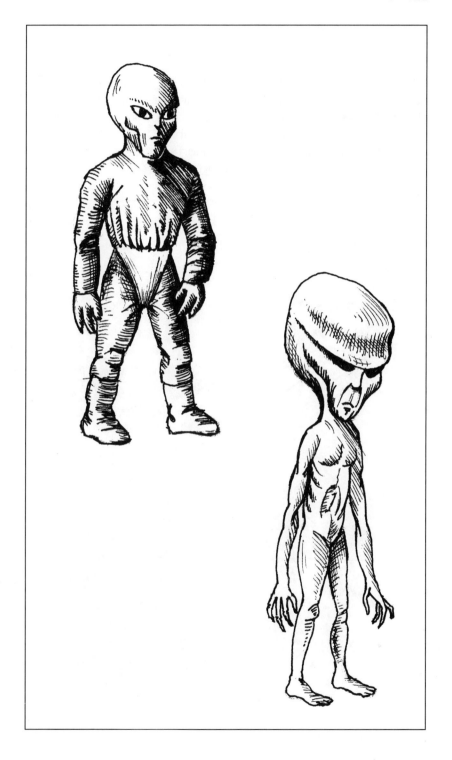

HUMANOIDS

Throughout the history of UFOs there have been a number of very human, often stunningly handsome, aliens. These range from "Aryans" to those in high-tech uniforms. The range of their behavior is just as great, mandating caution. Many abduction survivors describe their captors as humanoid, often tall and thin.

OTHER

The range of other types of reported aliens runs from reptilian to giants. Most seem to follow the convention of two arms, two legs, and a head. That is not to say that what is on that head conforms to anything that can be described as a face or that those arms and legs aren't covered by thick gray skin, fur, scales, or any color of skin. Aliens have been reported to vary from three to four feet to as much as twelve feet. Their attire also ranges from suits that completely cover them to barely more than a loincloth.

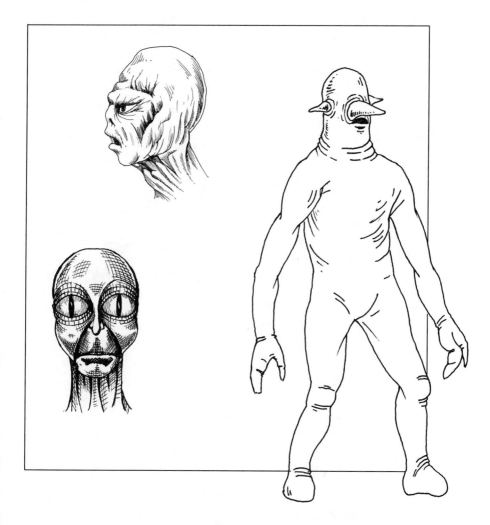

SPACECRAFT

These are four types of commonly viewed spacecraft as seen from different perspectives.

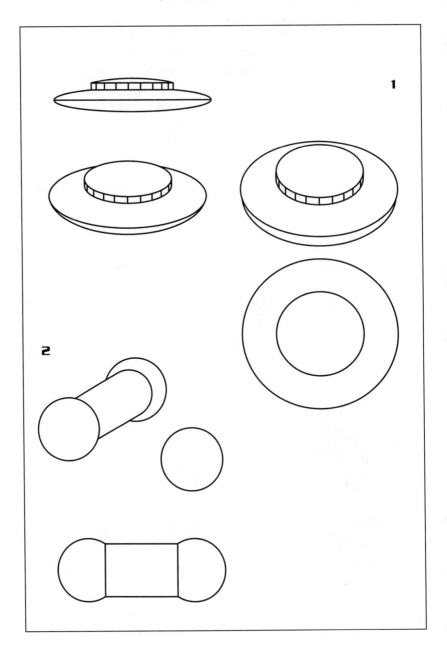

AIRLINE INCIDENTS
by William R. Forstchen, Ph.D.

THERE HAVE BEEN NUMEROUS sightings by airline pilots and passengers of "strange lights" or objects approaching their planes while in flight. There has been a general tendency, however, for pilots and especially commercial airline pilots, not to report such incidents unless they are a clearly identifiable near-miss situation, which the FAA requires to be reported (under the assumption, of course, that the other object is a terrestrial-based aircraft). The reason for this reticence is obvious: Pilots are worried about job security and have no desire to start arousing questions about their mental stability or competence.

On April 8, 1956, an American Airlines flight on a run through upstate New York had just lifted off from Albany when the captain, Raymond Ryan, reported seeing a very bright light, which he first assumed was an aircraft approaching with its landing lights on. He moved out of the way of what he thought was an incoming plane and then noticed that it appeared to be standing still, hovering above Schenectady. Ryan called the stewardess forward to witness what they were seeing in the cockpit as they passed Schenectady. As they passed near Griffiss Air Force Base, the pilot called the tower. Controllers in the tower asked the American Airlines flight to turn on its lights, then turn them off, so that they could get a precise fix on them. As soon as they turned their lights back off, the controller announced that he could clearly see a silhouette to the south of the airfield. Air traffic controllers in Watertown and Albany also made visual sightings of the object as well.

The air traffic controller at Griffiss asked Captain Ryan to abort his intended landing at Syracuse and to continue running parallel to the object until they could scramble some jets up. Ryan therefore passed up his landing and continued to fly out over Oswego while waiting for the jets to scramble from Griffiss. He was finally forced, however, to turn about, for after all he was on a commercial flight, and simply skipping a landing would have caused some serious consequences for both him and the airlines. More than fifteen minutes had elapsed since he had been informed that Griffiss was scrambling, but no fighters ever seemed to get up.

As he turned away, the object headed out over Lake Ontario and finally disappeared. Ryan later stated that the object had, at times, made some arcing turns at speeds he estimated to be in excess of a thousand miles an hour.

There were no subsequent reports by Griffiss or acknowledgment by them that there had been a move under way to scramble fighters or that any fighters had been sent up to investigate. Unfortunately the name of the traffic controller at Griffiss is not listed either.

Second Incident

On February 24, 1959, Captain Killian and First Officer James Dee were flying an American Airlines DC-6 on a flight from Newark, New Jersey, to Detroit, Michigan. The sky was clear and there was no moon. While passing near Williamsport, Pennsylvania, Captain Killian observed three bright lights off his left wing. He first thought they were the three stars of Orion's belt but then realized that Orion was clearly visible but in a different location of the sky.

The object, or objects, started to pull ahead. As Killian approached Erie, he contacted two other American Airlines flights in the vicinity. One of the planes was over Lake Erie and reported seeing the lights to the south, while the second plane, near Sandusky, Ohio, reported seeing the object off to the northeast. The three sightings clearly triangulated the object or objects in northeast Ohio, passing near Cleveland. The brilliance of the object continued to change, with Captain Killian stating that it flared up brighter than any star, then would fade out completely, only to flare back up again; the colors shifted as well from yellow-orange to a sharp blue-white.

As they started their final approach into Detroit, they lost sight of the object. Additional sightings were reported by at least two other airline crews, one of them with United Airlines. George Popowitch, who was working with the UFO Research Committee, and lived in Akron, stated that he received nine phone calls from observers on the ground who claimed to have seen the three lights shortly after nine P.M., the time that Killian was flying alongside the object.

ANALYSIS

There are literally hundreds of reported incidents of pilots, crews, and passengers on commercial, private, and military flights reporting encounters with UFOs. Unfortunately, clear daytime sightings are almost nonexistent.

Undoubtedly many of these can be explained. Even the most experienced of pilots will, on occasion, become disoriented while flying at night. Venus, low on the horizon in the morning sky, will often appear to bounce and move about, flaring and then dimming in intensity, but this is usually a phenomenon that appears just as it clears the horizon. Once it has risen five to ten degrees, the atmospheric distortion diminishes and it tends to then clearly resolve itself as a planet. Meteors, satellites, unusual lighting on the ground, and even other aircraft can, at times, be mistaken for a UFO. The two incidents cited above, however, obviously don't fall into this category. Both were in the early evening, while Venus tends to be mistaken when it is a morning star, in other words when it rises an hour or two before sunrise. Meteors and satellites can be ruled out because of the prolonged time involved in the sighting. The multiplicity of observers and the fact that so many of them were trained pilots, who all thought that the object was unusual enough to report a sighting, tends to rule out the response that it was one or two pilots who became excited and let their imaginations run. Everyone who sighted the objects in both incidents felt they were unusual and were willing to later make comments about them.

There is little if anything the witnesses could have done differently, except the folks at Griffiss. Why didn't they scramble in a timely manner? The Cold War was on in full force back in 1956, and bases like Griffiss were suppose to be able to scramble within minutes to intercept Soviet bombers. Nothing has ever been reported, however, regarding why Griffiss did not respond, or if it did, what they encountered.

THE AIR FORCE WAY

In 1959 the U.S. Air Force established a regulation for "the responsibility and procedure for reporting information and evidence on unidentified flying objects (UFO) and for releasing pertinent information to the general public." If you can wade through the bureaucratic language in spots, you will find this fascinating reading. More so since the Air Force has gone to such efforts to convince us that no UFOs are of extraterrestrial origin. You'll find Section B, paragraph 9, particularly clear and informative.

DEPARTMENT OF THE AIR FORCE

Washington, 14 September 1959

Intelligence

UNIDENTIFIED FLYING OBJECTS (UFO)

This regulation establishes the responsibility and procedure for reporting information and evidence on unidentified flying objects (UFO) and for releasing pertinent information to the general public.

SECTION A—GENERAL

SECTION A—GENERAL

1. Background Information. The Air Force investigation and analysis of UFO's over the United States are directly related to its responsibility for the defense of the United States. Because prompt reporting and rapid identification are necessary to carry out the second of the four phases of air defense—detection, identification, interception, and destruction, the Air Force maintains the Unidentified Flying Object Program. Successful implementation of the program requires strict compliance with this regulation by all commanders.

2. Definitions. To insure proper and uniform usage in UFO screenings, investigations, and reportings, the objects are defined as follows:

a. *Familiar or Known Objects.* Aircraft, birds, balloons, kites, searchlights, and astronomical bodies (meteors, planets, stars).

b. *Unidentified Aircraft:*

(1) Flying objects determined to be aircraft. These generally appear as a result of ADIZ violations and often prompt the UFO reports submitted by the general public. They are readily identifiable as, or known to be, aircraft, but their type, purpose, origin, and destination are unknown. Air Defense Command is responsible for reports of "unknown" aircraft and they should not be reported as UFO's under this regulation.

(2) Aircraft flares, jet exhausts, condensation trails, blinking or steady lights observed at night, lights circling or near airports and airways, and other similar phenomena known to be emanating

from, or to be indications of aircraft. These should not be reported under this regulation as they do not fall within the definition of a UFO.

(3) Pilotless aircraft and missiles.

c. *Unidentified Flying Objects.* Any airborne object which, by performance, aerodynamic characteristics, or unusual features, does not conform to known aircraft or missiles, or which does not correspond to definitions in a and b above.

3. Objectives. Air Force interest in UFO's is three-fold: First, as a possible threat to the security of the United States and its forces; second, to determine the technical or scientific characteristics of any such UFO's; third, to explain or identify all UFO sightings as defined in paragraph 2c.

a. *Air Defense.* The great majority of flying objects reported have been found to be conventional, familiar things of no great threat to the security of the United States and its possessions. However, since the possibility cannot be ignored that UFO's reported may be hostile or new foreign air vehicles of unconventional design, it is imperative that sightings be reported rapidly, factually, and as completely as possible.

b. *Technical and Scientific.* The Air Force will continue to collect and analyze reports of UFO's until all can be scientifically or technically explained or until such time as it is de-

termined that the full potential of a sighting has been exploited. In performance of this task the following factors should be kept in mind:

(1) To measure scientific advances, the Air Force must have the latest experimental and developmental information on new or unique air vehicles or weapons.

(2) The possibility exists that foreign air vehicles of revolutionary configuration or propulsion may be developed.

(3) There is a need for further scientific knowledge in such fields as geophysics, astronomy, and the upper atmosphere which the study and analysis of UFO's and similar aerial phenomena may provide.

(4) The reporting of all pertinent factors will have a direct bearing on scientific analyses and conclusions of UFO sightings.

c. *Reduction of Percentage of UFO "Unidentifieds."* Air Force activities must reduce the percentage of unidentifieds to the minimum. Analysis thus far has provided explanation for all but a few of the sightings reported. These unexplained sightings are carried statistically as unidentifieds. If more immediate, detailed objective data on the unknowns had been available, probably these too could have been explained. However, due to the human factors involved, and the fact that analyses of UFO sightings are based primarily on the personal impressions and interpretations of the observers, rather than on accurate scientific data or facts obtained under controlled conditions, it is improbable that all of the unidentifieds can be eliminated.

4. Responsibilities:

a. *Reporting.* Base commanders will report all information and evidence of UFO sightings, including information and evidence received from other services, Government agencies, and civilian sources. Investigators will be authorized to make telephone calls from the investigation area direct to the Air Technical Intelligence Center (ATIC), Wright-Patterson Air Force Base, Ohio (CLearwater 3-7111, ext. 69216). The purpose of the calls is to report high priority findings. (See section C.)

b. *Investigation.* The commander of the Air Force base nearest the location of the reported UFO sighting will conduct all investigative action necessary to submit a complete initial report of a UFO sighting. Every effort will be made to resolve the sighting in the initial investigation. A UFO sighting reported to an Air Force base other than that closest to the scene of such sighting will be referred immediately to the commander of the nearest Air Force base for appropriate action. (See paragraph 6.)

c. *Analysis.* The ATIC will analyze and evaluate:

(1) Information and evidence reported within the United States after the investigators of the responsible Air Force base nearest the sighting have exhausted their efforts to identify the UFO.

(2) Information and evidence collected in oversea areas.

Note. Exceptions: The ATIC, independently or in participation with pertinent Air Force activities, may conduct any additional investigations necessary to further or conclude its analyses or findings.

d. *Public Relations and Information Services.* The Office of Information Services, Office of the Secretary of the Air Force, will be responsible for releasing information on sightings, and, in coordination with ATIC, for answering correspondence from the public regarding UFO's. (See paragraphs 7 and 8.)

e. *Congressional Inquiries.* The Office of Legislative Liaison will:

(1) In coordination with the ATIC and/or the Office of Information Services, when necessary, answer all congressional mail regarding UFO's addressed to the Secretary of the Air Force and Headquarters USAF.

(2) Forward those inquiries which are scientific and technical to the ATIC for information on which to base a reply. The ATIC will return this information to the Office of Legislative Liaison for reply to the inquiry.

(3) Process requests from congressional sources in accordance with AFR 11–7.

f. *Cooperation.* All Air Force activities will cooperate with Air Force UFO investigators to insure the economical and prompt success of investigations and analyses. When feasible, this cooperation will include furnishing air or ground transportation and other assistance.

5. Guidance. The thoroughness and quality of a report or investigation of UFO's are limited only by the skill and resourcesfulness of the person who receives the initial information and/or prepares the report. The usefulness and value of any report or investigation depend on the accuracy and timeliness of its contents. Following are aids for screening, evaluating, and reporting sightings:

a. Careful study of the logic, consistency, and coherence of the observer's report. An interview with the observer by personnel preparing the report is especially valuable in determining the source's reliability and the validity of the information given. Particular attention should be given to the observer's age, occupation, and education and whether his occupation involves observation reporting or technical knowledge. When reporting that a witness is completely familiar with certain aspects of a sighting, his or her specific qualifications should be indicated.

b. Theodolite measurements of changes of azimuth, and elevation and angular size.

c. Interception, identification, or air search if appropriate and within the scope of air defense regulations.

d. When feasible, contact with local aircraft control and warning (ACW) units, pilots, and crews of aircraft aloft at the time and place of sighting. Also, contact with any other persons or organizations that may have factual data on the UFO or can offer corroborating evidence—visual, electronic, or other.

e. Consultation with military or civilian weather forecasters for data on tracks of weather balloons released in the area and any unusual meteorological activity which may have a bearing on the UFO.

f. Consultation with navigators and astronomers in the area to determine whether any astronomical body or phenomenon would account for the sighting.

g. Contact with military and civilian tower operators, air operations units, and airlines to determine whether the sighting could have been an aircraft. Local units of the Federal Aviation Agency (FAA) are often of assistance in this regard.

h. Contact with persons who may know of experimental aircraft of unusual configuration, rocket and guided missile firings, or aerial tests in the area.

i. Contact with photographic units or laboratories. Usually, these installations have several cameras available for specialized intelligence or investigative work. Photography is an invaluable tool and, where possible, should be used in investigating and analyzing UFO sightings. (See paragraph 19.)

j. Whenever possible, selecting as a UFO sighting investigator an individual with a scientific or technical background as well as experience as an investigator.

6. Reporting UFO Information. Both the Assistant Chief of Staff Intelligence, Headquarters USAF, and the Air Defense Command have a direct and immediate interest in the facts pertaining to UFO's reported within the United States.

a. All Air Force activities will conduct UFO investigations to the extent necessary for their required reporting action (see paragraphs 15, 16, and 17). However, investigations should not be carried beyond this point, unless such action is directed by Assistant Chief of Staff, Intelligence, Headquarters USAF, or the preparing officer believes the magnitude (intelligence significance or public relations) of the case warrants full scale investigation. Telephone contact should be made with the ATIC (CLearwater 3-7111, ext. 69216) at Wright-Patterson Air Force Base, Ohio, to obtain verbal authority for continued investigation. This should be so noted in the preliminary report. (Foreign activities will proceed on their own judgment and so advise the ATIC in the preliminary message.)

b. After initial reports are submitted, the ATIC may require additional data, such as narrative statements, sketches, marked maps and charts, and other required data, which can be supplied more quickly and economically by the Air Force activity that made the initial report. Therefore, ATIC is authorized to contact the appropriate Air Force activity.

c. Direct communication is authorized between ATIC and other Air Force activities in matters pertaining to UFO investigations. Specifically, the ATIC may call upon the Commander, 1137th Field Activities Group, Fort Belvoir, Virginia, to conduct further field investigation if review of the initial report indicates such a requirement. In this event, the AISS investigating will prepare the final report. (See paragraph 4b.)

SECTION B—PUBLIC RELATIONS, INFORMATION, CONTACTS AND RELEASES

7. Maintaining Public Relations. The Office of Information Services is responsible for:

a. In coordination with the ATIC when necessary, maintaining contact with the public and the press on all aspects of the UFO program and its related activities.

b. Releasing information on UFO sightings and results of investigations.

c. Periodically releasing information on this subject to the general public.

d. Processing, answering, and taking action on correspondence received from the general public, pertaining to the public relations, interest, and informational aspects of the subject. (See paragraph 9.) This office will forward correspondence and queries which are purely technical and scientific to ATIC for information on which to base a reply.

8. Releasing Information. All information or releases concerning UFO's, regardless of origin or nature, will be released to the public or unofficial persons or organizations by the Office of Information Services, Office of the Secretary of the Air Force. This includes replies to correspondence (except congressional inquiries) submitted direct to ATIC, and other Air Force activities by private individuals requesting comments or results or analysis and investigations of sightings.

9. Exceptions. In response to local inquiries resulting from any UFO reported in the vicinity of an Air Force base, information regarding a sighting may be released to the press or the general public by the commander of the Air Force base concerned only if it has been *positively identified as a familiar or known object.* Care should be exercised not to reveal any classified aspects of the sighting or names of persons making reports. (See paragraph 18.) If the sighting is unexplainable or difficult to identify, because of insufficient information or inconsistencies, the only statement to be released is the fact that the sighting is being investigated and information regarding it will be released at a later date. If investigative action has been completed, the fact that the results of the investigation will be

submitted to the ATIC for review and analysis may be released. Further inquiries should be referred to the local Office of Information Services.

10. Release by Non–Air Force Sources. If newsmen, writers, publishers, or private individuals desire to release unofficial information concerning a UFO sighting, every effort will be made to assure that the statements, theories, opinions, and allegations of these individuals or groups will not be associated with or represented as being official information.

11. Contacts. Private individuals or organizations requesting Air Force interviews, briefings, lectures, or private discussions on UFO's will be referred to the Office of Information Services, Office of the Secretary of the Air Force. Air Force personnel, other than those of the Office of Information Services, will not contact private individuals on UFO cases nor will they discuss their operations and functions with unauthorized persons unless so directed, and then only on a "need-to-know" basis.

SECTION C—PREPARING AND
SUBMITTING REPORTS

12. General Information:

a. Paragraphs 2 and 5 will be used as an aid and guidance to screenings, investigations, and reportings. The format will be as outlined in paragraph 15. Activities initially receiving reports of aerial objects and phenomena will screen the information to determine if the report concerns a valid UFO within the definition of paragraph 2c. Reports not within that definition will not be considered for further action under the provisions of this regulation.

b. To assist activities and personnel responsible for handling, screening, and processing initial, incoming UFO information, the general sources and types of reports are given here:

(1) Generally, initial UFO reports are received from two sources:

    (a) Civilian (airline, private and professional pilots, tower operators, technical personnel, casual observers, and the public in general), by correspondence, telephone, or personal interview:

    (b) Military units and personnel (pilots, observers, radar operators, aircraft control and warning units, etc.), by telephone, electrical message, or personal interview;

(2) Generally, UFO reports received from civilian sources are of two types:

    (a) Those referring strictly to an observed UFO, containing either detailed or meager information;

    (b) Those referring only in part to an observed UFO, but primarily requesting information on some aspect of the UFO program.

c. Reports considered to fall primarily in a public relations or information service category (see paragraphs 4d, 7, 8, 9, and b(2) above) should be referred to the Office of Information Services. UFO data sufficient for investigation and/or analysis may be extracted before referral to that office.

13. Methods for Transmitting Reports:

a. Together with any necessary screenings and investigations that must be performed preparatory to reporting, all information on UFO's will be reported promptly. Reports under 3 days from date of sighting will be electrically transmitted with a "Priority" precedence. Electrically transmitted reports over 3 days old should carry a "Routine" precedence.

b. Written reports of sightings over 3 days old may be submitted on AF Form 112, Air Intelligence Information Report (AIIR) and AF Form 112A, supplement to AF Form 112 (see paragraphs 14 and 15); however, their use should be kept to a minimum in reporting initial sightings. The delays often involved in processing and transmitting AF Forms 112 through channels may make followup investigations difficult, producing only limited usable information. This factor must be considered in cases where an immediate investigation or study of a reported sighting is considered necessary. Reporting by electrical means will eliminate delays. If requested by ATIC, a followup and/or complete report of all sightings initially reported electrically will be submitted on AF Form 112.

14. Where to Submit Reports:

a. *Electrical Reports.* Submit multiple addressed electrical reports to:

(1) Air Defense Command, Ent AFB, Colorado

(2) Nearest Air Division (Defense). (For United States only.)

(3) Air Technical Intelligence Center, Wright-Patterson AFB, Ohio

(4) HQ USAF (AFCIN), Wash. 25, D.C.

(5) Secretary of the Air Force (SAFIS), Wash. 25, D.C.

b. *Written Reports:* (Basic letters and AF Forms 112.)

(1) Within the United States, submit all reports direct to ATIC. ATIC will reproduce each report and distribute it to interested intelligence activities in the United States and to Office of Information Services, if such action is considered necessary.

(2) Outside the United States, submit reports as prescribed in "Intelligence Collection Instruction" (ICI) June 1954, direct to:

Hq USAF (AFCIN) Wash 25, D.C.

c. *Reports from Civilians.* Where possible, civilian sources contemplating reporting UFO's should be advised to submit the report, for processing and transmission, to the nearest Air Force base, other than ATIC.

15. Basic Reporting Data and Format.

Show the abbreviation "UFO" at the beginning of the text of all electrical reports and in the subject of written reports. Include in all reports the data required, in the order shown below:

a. *Description of the Object(s):*

(1) Shape.

(2) Size compared to a known object (use one of the following terms: Head of a pin, pea, dime, nickel, quarter, half dollar, silver dollar, baseball, grapefruit, or basketball) held in the hand at about arm's length.

(3) Color.

(4) Number.

(5) Formation, if more than one.

(6) Any discernible features or details.

(7) Tail, trail, or exhaust, including size of same compared to size of object(s).

(8) Sound. If heard, describe sound.

(9) Other pertinent or unusual features.

b. *Description of Course of Object(s):*

(1) What first called the attention of observer(s) to the object(s)?

(2) Angle or elevation and azimuth of object(s) when first observed.

(3) Angle or elevation and azi-

muth of object(s) upon disappearance.

(4) Description of flight path and maneuvers of object(s).

(5) How did the object(s) disappear? (Instantaneously to the North, etc.)

(6) How long was the object(s) visible? (Be specific, 5 minutes, 1 hour, etc.)

c. *Manner of Observation:*

(1) Use one or any combination of the following items: Ground-visual, ground-electronic, air electronic. (If electronic, specify type of radar.)

(2) Statement as to optical aids (telescopes, binoculars, etc.) used and description thereof.

(3) If the sighting is made while airborne, give type of aircraft, identification number, altitude, heading, speed, and home station.

d. *Time and Date of Sighting:*

(1) Zulu time-date group of sighting.

(2) Light conditions. (Use one of the following terms: Night, day, dawn, dusk.)

e. *Location of Observer(s).* Exact latitude and longitude of each observer, and/or geographical position. A position with reference to a known landmark also should be given in electrical reports, such as "2mi N of Deeville;" "3mi SW of Blue Lake." Typographical errors or "garbing" often result in electrically transmitted messages, making location plots difficult or impossible.

Example: 89 45N, 192 71W for 39 45N, 102 21W.

f. *Identifying Information on Observer(s):*

(1) Civilian—Name, age, mailing address, occupation, and estimate of reliability.

(2) Military—Name, grade, organization, duty, and estimate of reliability.

g. *Weather and Winds—Aloft Conditions at Time and Place of Sightings:*

(1) Observer(s) account of weather conditions.

(2) Report from nearest AWS or U.S. Weather Bureau Office of wind direction and velocity in degrees and knots at surface, 6,000', 10,000', 16,000', 20,000', 30,000', 50,000', and 80,000' if available.

(3) Ceiling.

(4) Visibility.

(5) Amount of cloud cover.

(6) Thunderstorms in area and quadrant in which located.

(7) Temperature gradient.

h. Any other unusual activity or condition, meteorological, astronomical, or otherwise, which might account for the sighting.

i. Interception or identification action taken (such action may be taken whenever feasible, complying with existing air defense directives).

j. Location, approximate altitude, and general direction of flight of any air traffic or balloon releases in the area which could possibly account for the sighting.

k. Position title and comments of the preparing officer, including his preliminary analysis of the possible cause of the sighting(s). (See paragraph 17.)

l. Existence of physical evidence, such as materials and photographs.

16. Negative or Inapplicable Data. Even though the source does not provide or has not been asked for specific information by an interviewer, do not use the words "negative" or "unidentified" until all logical leads to obtain the information outlined under paragraph 15 have been exhausted. For example, information on weather conditions in the area, as requested in paragraph 15g may be obtained from the local military or civilian weather facility. Use the phrase "not applicable" (N/A) only when the question does not apply to the particular sighting being investigated.

17. Comments of Preparing Officer. The preparing officer will make a preliminary analysis and a comment on the possible cause or identity of the object being reported, together with a statement supporting his comment and analysis. Every effort will be made to obtain pertinent items of information and to test all possible leads, clues, and hypotheses concerning the identity or explanation of the sighting. (See paragraph 5.) The preparing officer receiving the report initially is in a much better position to conduct an "on-the-spot" survey or followup than subsequent investigative personnel and analysts who may be far removed from the area, and who may arrive too late to obtain vital data or the missing information necessary for firm conclusions.

18. Classification. Do not classify reports unless data requested in paragraph 15 require classification. Classify reports primarily to protect:

a. Names of sources reporting UFO's and other principals involved, if so requested by these persons or considered necessary;

b. Intelligence, investigative, intercept, or analytical methods or procedures;

c. Location of radar and other classified sites, units, and equipment;

d. Information on certain types, characteristics, and capabilities of classified aircraft, missiles, or devices that may be involved in the sighting.

19. Reporting Physical Evidence. Report promptly the existence of physical evidence (photographic or material). All physical evidence forwarded to the ATIC should be marked for the attention of AFCIN–4E4g.

a. *Photographic:*

   (1) *Still Photographs.* Forward the negative and two prints. Title the prints and the negatives, or indicate the place, time, and date of the incident.

   (2) *Motion Pictures.* Obtain the original film. Examine the film strip for apparent cuts, alterations, obliterations, or defects. In the report comment on any irregularities, particularly if received from other than official sources.

(3) *Supplemental Photographic Information.* Negatives and prints often are insufficient to provide certain valid data or to permit firm conclusions. (See AFM 200–9—a classified document receiving limited distribution.) Information that will aid in plotting or in estimating distances, apparent size and nature of object, probable velocity, and movements includes:

(a) Type and make of camera,

(b) Type, focal length, and make of lens,

(c) Brand and type of film,

(d) Shutter speed used,

(e) Lens opening used, that is, "f" stop,

(f) Filters used,

(g) Was tripod or solid stand used,

(h) Was "panning" used,

(i) Exact direction camera was pointing with relation to true north, and its angle with respect to the ground.

(4) *Other Camera Data.* If supplemental information cannot be obtained, the minimum camera data required are the type of camera, and the smallest and largest "f " stop and shutter-speed readings of the camera.

(5) *Radar.* Forward two copies of each still-camera photographic print. Title radarscope photographic prints in accordance with AFR 95–7. Classify radarscope photographs in accordance with section XII, AFR 205–1, 1 April 1959.

Note: If possible, develop photographic film before forwarding. If undeveloped film is forwarded, mark it conspicuously to indicate this fact. Undeveloped film often has been destroyed by exposure during examinations made while en route through mail channels to final addresses.

b. *Material.* Each Air Force echelon receiving suspected or actual UFO material will safeguard it in a manner to prevent any defacing or alterations which might reduce its value for intelligence examination and analysis.

c. *Photographs, Motion Pictures, and Negatives Submitted by Individuals.* Individuals often submit photographic and motion picture material as part of their UFO reports. All original material submitted, will be returned to the individual upon completion of necessary studies, analyses, and duplication by the Air Force.

BY ORDER OF THE SECRETARY OF THE AIR FORCE:

OFFICIAL:

J.L. TARR
Colonel, USAF
Director of Administrative Services

THOMAS D. WHITE
Chief of Staff

DEPARTMENT OF THE AIR FORCE
Washington, 2 February 1960

Intelligence

UNIDENTIFIED FLYING OBJECTS (UFO)

AFR 200–2, 14 September 1959, is changed as follows:

6c. Direct communication is authorized between ATIC and other Air Force activities in matters pertaining to UFO investigation. Specifically, the ATIC may call upon the Commander, 1127th Field Activity Group, Fort Belvoir, Virginia, to conduct further field investigations if review of the initial report indicates such a requirement. In this event, the Headquarters 1127th USAF Field Activity Group will prepare the final report.

BY ORDER OF THE SECRETARY OF THE AIR FORCE:

OFFICIAL:

J.L. TARR
Colonel, USAF
Director of Administrative Services

THOMAS D. WHITE
Chief of Staff

U. S. AIR FORCE TECHNICAL INFORMATION SHEET

This questionnaire has been prepared so that you can give the U. S. Air Force as much information as possible concerning the unidentified aerial phenomenon that you have observed. Please try to answer as many questions as you possibly can. The information that you give will be used for research purposes, and will be regarded as confidential material. Your name will *not* be used in connection with any statements, conclusions, or publications without your permission. We request this personal information so that, if it is deemed necessary, we may contact you for further details.

1. When did you see the object?	2. Time of day: _____ _____

			Hour	Minutes
_____	_____	_____		
Day	Month	Year	*(Circle One):* A.M. or P.M.	

3. Time zone:
    (Circle One): a. Eastern
                   b. Central
                   c. Mountain
                   d. Pacific
                   e. Other _____

(Circle One): a. Daylight Saving
                    b. Standard

4. Where were you when you saw the object?

_____   _____   _____
    Nearest Postal Address   City or Town   State or Country

Additional remarks: _____

_____

_____

5. Estimate how long you saw the object. _____ _____ _____
                                      Hours   Minutes   Seconds

    5.1 *Circle One* of the following to indicate how certain you are of your answer to Question 5.
                      a. Certain   c. Not very sure
                      b. Fairly certain   d. Just a guess

6. What was the condition of the sky?
    (Circle One): a. Bright daylight   d. Just a trace of daylight
                     b. Dull daylight   e. No trace of daylight
                     c. Bright twilight   f. Don't remember

7. IF you saw the object during DAYLIGHT, TWILIGHT, or DAWN, where was the SUN located as you looked at the object?
    (Circle One): a. In front of you   d. To your left
                     b. In back of you   e. Overhead
                     c. To your right   f. Don't remember

8. IF you saw the object at NIGHT, TWILIGHT, or DAWN, what did you notice concerning the STARS and MOON?

8.1 STARS *(Circle One):*
a. None
b. A few
c. Many
d. Don't remember

8.2 MOON *(Circle One):*
a. Bright moonlight
b. Dull moonlight
c. No moonlight—pitch dark
d. Don't remember

9. Was the object brighter than the background of the sky?

(Circle One):   a. Yes   b. No   c. Don't remember

10. IF it was BRIGHTER THAN the sky background, was the brightness like that of an automobile headlight?:

(Circle One): a. A mile or more away (a distant car)?
b. Several blocks away?
c. A block away?
d. Several yards away?
e. Other

11. Did the object: *(Circle One for each question)*

a. Appear to stand still at any time?	Yes	No	Don't Know
b. Suddenly speed up and rush away at any time?	Yes	No	Don't Know
c. Break up into parts or explode?	Yes	No	Don't Know
d. Give off smoke?	Yes	No	Don't Know
e. Change brightness?	Yes	No	Don't Know
f. Change shape?	Yes	No	Don't Know
g. Flicker, throb, or pulsate?	Yes	No	Don't Know

12. Did the object move behind something at any time, particularly a cloud?

(Circle One):   Yes   No   Don't Know.   IF you answered YES, then tell what

it moved behind: _____

_____

13. Did the object move in front of something at any time, particularly a cloud?

(Circle One):   Yes   No   Don't Know.   IF you answered YES, then tell what

it moved in front of: _____

_____

14. Did the object appear: *(Circle One):*   a. Solid?   b. Transparent?   c. Don't know.

15. Did you observe the object through any of the following?

a. Eyeglasses	Yes	No		e. Binoculars	Yes	No
b. Sunglasses	Yes	No		f. Telescope	Yes	No
c. Windshield	Yes	No		g. Theodolite	Yes	No
d. Window glass	Yes	No		h. Other _____		

16. Tell in a few words the following things about the object.

 a. Sound _____

 b. Color _____

17. Draw a picture that will show the shape of the object or objects. Label and include in your sketch any details of the object that you saw such as wings, protrusions, etc., and especially exhaust trails or vapor trails. Place an arrow beside the drawing to show the direction the object was moving.

18. The edges of the object were:

 (Circle One): a. Fuzzy or blurred   e. Other _____
         b. Like a bright star
         c. Sharply outlined   _____
         d. Don't remember
                    _____

19. IF there was MORE THAN ONE object, then how many were there? _____
 Draw a picture of how they were arranged, and put an arrow to show the direction that they were traveling.

20. Draw a picture that will show the motion that the object or objects made. Place an "A" at the beginning of the path, a "B" at the end of the path, and show any changes in direction during the course.

21. IF POSSIBLE, try to guess or estimate what the real size of the object was in its longest dimension. _____ feet.

22. How large did the object or objects appear as compared with one of the following objects *held in the hand* and at about arm's length?

    (*Circle One*):
    - a. Head of a pin
    - b. Pea
    - c. Dime
    - d. Nickel
    - e. Quarter
    - f. Half dollar
    - g. Silver dollar
    - h. Baseball
    - i. Grapefruit
    - j. Basketball
    - k. Other _____

    22.1 *Circle One* of the following to indicate how certain you are of your answer to Question 22.
    - a. Certain
    - b. Fairly certain
    - c. Not very sure
    - d. Uncertain

23. How did the object or objects disappear from view? _____

    _____

    _____

24. In order that you can give as clear a picture of what you saw, we would like for you to imagine that you could construct the object that you saw. Of what type material would you make it? How large would it be, and what shape would it have? Describe in your own words a common object or objects which when placed up in the sky would give the same appearance as the object which you saw.

25. Where were you located when you saw the object? *(Circle One)*:
    a. Inside a building
    b. In a car
    c. Outdoors
    d. In an airplane
    e. At sea
    f. Other _____

26. Were you *(Circle One)*:
    a. In the business section of a city?
    b. In the residential section of a city?
    c. In open countryside?
    d. Flying near an airfield?
    e. Flying over a city?
    f. Flying over open country?
    g. Other _____

27. What were you doing at the time you saw the object, and how did you happen to notice it?

    _____

    _____

    _____

28. IF you were MOVING IN AN AUTOMOBILE or other vehicle at the time, then complete the following questions:

    28.1 What direction were moving? *(Circle One)*:

a. North	c. East	e. South	g. West
b. Northeast	d. Southeast	f. Southwest	h. Northwest

    28.2 How fast were you moving? _____ miles per hour.

    28.3 Did you stop at any time while you were looking at the object?
        (Circle One):   Yes   No

29. What direction were you looking when you first saw the object? *(Circle One)*:

a. North	c. East	e. South	g. West
b. Northeast	d. Southeast	f. Southwest	h. Northwest

30. What direction were you looking when you last saw the object? *(Circle One)*:

a. North	c. East	e. South	g. West
b. Northeast	d. Southeast	f. Southwest	h. Northwest

31. If you are familiar with bearing terms (angular direction), try to estimate the number of degrees the object was from the North and also the number of degrees it was upward from the horizon (elevation).

    31.1 When it first appeared:
        a. From true North _____ degrees.
        b. From horizon _____ degrees.

    31.2 When it disappeared:
        a. From true North _____ degrees.
        b. From horizon _____ degrees.

32. In the following sketch, imagine that you are at the point shown. Place an "A" on the curved line to show how high the object was above the horizon (skyline) when you *first* saw it. Place a "B" on the *same* curved line to show how high the object was above the horizon (skyline) when you *last* saw it.

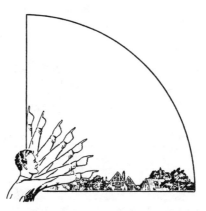

33. In the following larger sketch place an "A" at the position the object was when you *first* saw it, and a "B" at its position when you *last* saw it. Refer to smaller sketch as an example of how to complete the larger sketch.

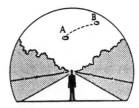

34. What were the weather conditions at the time you saw the object?

34.1 CLOUDS *(Circle One):*
   a. Clear sky
   b. Hazy
   c. Scattered clouds
   d. Thick or heavy clouds
   e. Don't remember

34.2 WIND *(Circle One):*
   a. No wind
   b. Slight breeze
   c. Strong wind
   d. Don't remember

34.3 WEATHER *(Circle One):*
   a. Dry
   b. Fog, mist, or light rain
   c. Moderate or heavy rain
   d. Snow
   e. Don't remember

34.4 TEMPERATURE *(Circle One):*
   a. Cold
   b. Cool
   c. Warm
   d. Hot
   e. Don't remember

35. When did you report to some official that you had seen the object?

_____ _____ _____
Day   Month   Year

36. Was anyone else with you at the time you saw the object?

   (Circle One):   Yes   No

36.1 IF you answered YES, did they see the object too?

   (Circle One):   Yes   No

36.2 Please list their names and addresses:

37. Was this the first time that you had seen an object or objects like this?

   (Circle One):   Yes   No

37.1 IF you answered NO, then when, where, and under what circumstances did you see other ones?

_____

_____

_____

_____

38. In your opinion what do you think the object was and what might have caused it?

39. Do you think you can estimate the *speed* of the object?

    (Circle One):   Yes   No

If you answered YES, then what speed would you estimate?   _____ m.p.h.

40. Do you think you can estimate how far away from you the object was?

    (Circle One):   Yes   No

If you answered YES, then how far away would you say it was?   _____ feet.

41. Please give the following information about yourself:

NAME _____
             Last Name   First Name   Middle Name

ADDRESS _____
             Street   City   Zone   State

TELEPHONE NUMBER _____

What is your present job? _____

Age _____   Sex _____

Please indicate any special educational training that you have had.

a. Grade school _____   e. Technical school _____

b. High school _____   (Type) _____

c. College _____   f. Other special training _____

d. Postgraduate _____   _____

42. Date you completed this questionnaire: _____ _____ _____
                                                Day   Month   Year

U. S. AIR FORCE TECHNICAL INFORMATION SHEET

[SUMMARY DATA]

In order that your information may be filed and coded as accurately as possible, please use the following space to write out a short description of the event you observed. You may repeat information that you have already given in the questionnaire, and add any further comments, statements, or sketches that you believe are important. Try to present the details of the observation in the order in which they occurred. Additional pages of the same size paper may be attached if they are needed.

NAME _____

(Please Print)

SIGNATURE _____

DATE _____

(Do Not Write in This Space)

CODE:

UFO OBSERVERS INSTRUCTION SHEET
(Sky Diagram)

1. GENERAL:

a. The diagram [on page 158] represents all of the sky normally visible to the observer, who is pictured standing under the center of the "dome" of the sky. It is designed to show a three-dimensional view of the area centered around the observer at the time of the UFO sighting.

b. The position of any object in the sky can be described by giving its *elevation*, or angle *upward* from the horizon, and its *bearing* or angle *along* the horizon, eastward from north.

   (1) *Illustrations*:

      (a) Elevation is 0 degrees for an object on the horizon, and 90 degrees for the point directly over the observer (zenith). Thus, an object half-way up from the horizon to the zenith has an elevation of 45 degrees.

      (b) Bearing (or "azimuth") is the angle along the horizon, starting from north and moving clockwise eastward. Thus, an object directly toward the east, no matter what its elevation is above the horizon, has a bearing of 90 degrees, an object in the south has a bearing of 180 degrees; toward the west, 270 degrees and so on. North is, of course, zero.

      EXAMPLE: An object is seen in the northeast and one-third of the way up from horizon to overhead. Thus, the object has a bearing of 45 degrees, and elevation of 30 degrees. Similarly, an object having a bearing of 180 degrees and an elevation of 60 degrees would be seen directly south and two-thirds of the way up from the horizon.

2. PLOTTING THE COURSE OF AN OBJECT ON THE SKY DIAGRAM:

a. The path of an object across the sky can be shown completely on this diagram simply by connecting with a curved or straight line the various positions the object successively occupies (see example sheet). To aid visualization, the path on the western side of the sky is represented by broken lines; the eastern side in solid lines. Direction of the object is indicated by arrows. The duration of the sighting can be shown by indicating the time at the positions where the object was *first* and *last* observed. Where possible, the time at various intermediate positions occupied by the object should also be shown.

b. The diagram can be made a more effective investigative and analytical tool by making the lines (showing the path of the object) thicker or thinner to indicate any varying brightness of the object observed. This is especially valuable when the object appeared only as a moving light at night. Thus, if a light becomes brighter and then gradually fades, it can be represented by a line becoming increasingly thicker and then gradually thinning out to nothing.

c. Use of colored pencils is especially recommended if the object changes color or hue during the sighting.

3. EXAMPLE OF DIAGRAM USE:

a. *Verbal Description of Example Sighting:* Object was first sighted in the southeast, about half-way up from the horizon to overhead, at 10:45 PM local time. Its shape or outline was hazy, but appeared round and about the size of a pea (at arm's length) from where observed. It was dim at first but brightened considerably as it got higher in the sky. Its color at this point was bluish white. After about two minutes it crossed to the western part of the sky a little to the north of overhead (zenith) and continued its flight toward the west. At this point its color appeared yellowish white. The light went dim when it got two-thirds of the way to the horizon. It then stopped and hovered for about one minute and then climbed rapidly, going toward the southwest and getting brighter. In less than thirty seconds, it had climbed to an elevation of approximately 60 degrees, and then the light went out abruptly.

b. *Pictorial Description of the Sighting:* By referring to the example sheet, notice how simply the above sighting can be portrayed and described, without words, on the example diagram attached here. Note the starting point at bearing 135 degrees (southeast) and elevation 45 degrees (half-way up from the horizon) at 10:45 PM (military time, 2245), and the arrow marking direction of flight. Note also the varying thickness of the line to denote changes in brightness, and the use of the dotted line to indicate its path in the western part of the sky. The "time indications" along the path—2 minutes to get to the meridian (the north-south overhead line), the hovering for 1 minute, and the ascent in 30 seconds to its complete disappearance—are all shown with a few lines. Thus, the entire sighting can be represented easily on one diagram.

4. FURTHER INSTRUCTIONS AND INFORMATION:

a. Relatively complex trajectories can easily be shown on a diagram of this type. A number of objects sighted can also be indicated, as can any changing formation. The apparent size and shape of the object should be drawn in, preferably by the observer. In the case of an object changing shape or color, this likewise can be drawn in. As previously pointed out, the use of colored pencils to indicate change of color is very desirable.

b. The landscaping in the sky diagram is placed there to help visualization. If any prominent landmarks such as known mountains, buildings, water towers, or specific installations, trees, etc., are part of the sighting area, they should be incorporated into the drawing. These landmarks may later prove to be invaluable as location, plotting or reference points.

c. If you are familiar with the constellations or other heavenly bodies, indicate, if possible, the relationship (and movements) of the object with respect to these bodies. This can be sketched on either page 6, item 33 or pages 9–10 of "Summary Data" sheet. Typical examples that can be easily illustrated: " . . . The object seemed to pass very slowly between the two bottom stars on the handle of the Big Dipper, which was in a vertical position, with the handle pointing down," or " . . . Object was about the size of a tennis ball—and remained slightly below and about 15 degrees to the left of the moon."

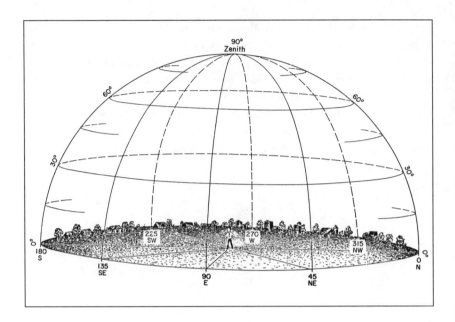

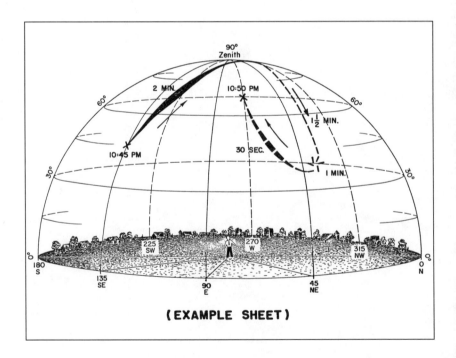

(EXAMPLE SHEET)

SECTION THREE

THE DANGERS OF CONTACT

UFOS, EXTRATERRESTRIALS, AND SCIENCE

A belief in UFOs is more than just a matter of opinion, or faith. A look at the science involved shows that there is not only a possibility, but the strong probability that there is intelligent life out there, and the equal probability that it is visiting here. The ideas in this article involve a range of the sciences. Many of the ideas were first presented in the *Journal for UFO Studies* by a noted scholar and UFO author, who could not take the time from his many pursuits to rewrite them himself. He has our thanks for permission to rewrite them in a format suitable for this book. We begin with an answer to the question, How likely is there to be other intelligent life in our galaxy?

THE QUESTION ARISES

Over the past few decades, many theorists and researchers in the scientific community have been reluctant to discuss the idea that extraterrestrial visitation could explain some sightings of UFOs. The pertinent question is, Why? Science has not shied away from discussing UFO phenomena, nor the possible existence of extraterrestrial intelligence (ETI). Still a reluctance remains to connect the two fields. Again one must ask, Why? Given that many scientists believe in the existence of ETI *elsewhere* in the galaxy, the prejudice against believing that ETI is visiting Earth is peculiar.

It is time to consider a connection, time to take seriously the ET hypothesis: Some sightings of unidentified flying objects might be phenomena produced by visitation from intelligent extraterrestrials.

LAYING THE GROUNDWORK FOR DISCUSSION

Since the 1960s, scientists have increasingly considered, discussed, and written about the question of ETI. They have debated the existence of intelligent extraterrestrials, the possibility of their traveling between stars, and the means of contact between them and ourselves. Carl Sagan and Frank Drake, among others, propose that our galaxy is teeming with intelligent life and technologically advanced civilizations.

Despite the intelligence and prominence of such scientists, for many years their vision had lacked concrete evidence, and many colleagues disregarded their position as unfocused speculation. Conservative scientists believed the field of ETI study could not be considered a scientific field at all.

In response, Frank Drake developed a major tool in the advance of the ETI discussion. The "Drake Equation" has provided a concrete approach to discussions of ETI, and has thus sparked much debate. The Drake Equation, in slightly simplified form, is as follows:

- the **Number of ET civilizations** in the Milky Way equals
- the **Rate of Sun-like Starbirths** per year, times
- the **Fraction of Suns with Planets,** times
- the **Number of Earth-like Planets per Sun,** times
- the **Fraction of Earths That Form Life,** times
- the **Fraction of Ecologies That Form Intelligence and Civilization,** times
- the **Average Duration of Civilizations**

This outline splits an unanswerable question (Do ET civilizations exist?) into six questions that scientists can answer, or at least discuss.

The many discussions inspired by the Drake Equation have led to a series of other questions:

- How could interstellar travel be achieved?
- What would motivate interstellar travel?
- Would extraterrestrial cultures colonize, and why?
- How could problems of time scale be addressed?
- What would such societies want from Earth, if anything?

Though conclusions from the Drake Equation vary widely, as do answers to other questions raised by it, a general consensus is arising from ETI literature: **Extraterrestrial intelligence occurs in many places in our galaxy and probably has the motive and means for some degree of exploration and communication.**

Of course, some scientists disagree, concluding that ETI, if it exists at all, is disinterested, paranoiac, or rare.

The heated debates on these issues, though, are too fascinating and varied to sum up so quickly. Using the Drake Equation as a starting point, let's review the main issues of the debate, as have so many before us in the past decade. Once we have them firmly in hand, we can turn to the question of a connection between ETI and UFO phenomena.

The Rate of Sun-like Starbirths

The universe is vast, old, and loaded with galaxies and stars. Nothing in astronomy is more obvious. Given these facts and the scientific intuition that nature is uniform—that the physical laws at work in one's bathtub are at work in the red spot on Jupiter—it would be hard to imagine that the Earth is the sole store of life in all of time and space.

Simply take a good look at the night sky. What average person, when confronted with the starry splendor of our universe, is not moved by the intuition that we are not alone? The methods and attitudes of science are, however, slower and surer than intuition. When scientists take a good look at the night sky, they are moved to ask questions such as, How many of those stars are like our own sun? And how often do new suns come into being? To put it another way, What is the **Rate of Sun-like Starbirths** in our galaxy?

First, we must find the general rate of starbirths—Sun-like or no—and then consider what we mean by "Sun-like" stars.

There is very little debate about the Milky Way's rate of starbirths. By looking at stellar nurseries—nebulas and other locations where stars are being formed—we can make direct estimates. Conversely, by estimating the age of the Milky Way and how many stars it holds, we can divide stars by time and get another estimate. Either way, the results are the same: our galaxy has averaged about twenty-five starbirths per year, perhaps slowing to between one and ten per year in its current, mature state.

But many of those stars are not the least bit Sun-like. Surely blue supergiants (one hundred thousand times brighter than our Sun) and red dwarfs (a thousand times dimmer than our Sun) could not be considered Sun-like.

"Sun-like," for the purposes of this article, means a star that, like our Sun, has a life span, metallic makeup, luminosity, stability, and general environment that favors the development of life.

We can turn the definition around. What stellar conditions favor the development of life? Most scientists agree on a few key factors:

- Advanced life-forms develop slowly, taking between two and six billion years. **To be Sun-like, therefore, a star must exist for at least two to six billion years.**
- Advanced life-forms need a planet to develop on. **A Sun-like star must be rich in the heavy elements that form planets.**
- Life-forms of any type require a relatively stable environment. **A Sun-like star must have planets in stable orbits and beyond the reach of solar flares.**

The first factor eliminates stars that burn too quickly—ultrahot blue supergiants and their kin. The second factor eliminates first-generation stars, which are made mostly of hydrogen and helium. Without heavier elements, planets don't form.

The third factor eliminates a number of star types.

Stars in the core of the Milky Way are subject to violent fluxes of radiation, which would routinely scour away any life. Our solar system and others in the spiral arms of the galaxy, however, are far enough out to be spared such bursts. For the purposes of this discussion, we will focus on stars in the spiral arms of the Milky Way.

Some stars don't provide enough radiation to produce a stable environment for life. Small, cool, red dwarf stars and their kin are so dim that their planets would have to orbit within range of deadly solar flares. Such planets would also be gravitationally locked, with one side always facing the sun. (Our own Moon is gravitationally locked with the Earth, thus creating the so-called dark side of the Moon.) On such planets one side would bake and the other side freeze.

The third factor also calls into question solar systems with two or more stars. The presence of a second or third sun in a system makes for erratic radiation patterns. Imagine our cycle of seasons, and nights and days, if Jupiter were a second sun. Even so, multiple solar systems can have stable close-in planetary orbits, and experts argue that between 10 and 90 percent of such systems could still evolve life.

It's time for some calculations. The Milky Way is estimated to contain about 250 billion stars. If we eliminate stars at the galactic core, and rim stars that couldn't have formed planets, we have about 100 billion left. Then, by cutting out stars that burn up too quickly (blue supergiants and their ilk), those that are too dim (red dwarfs and their ilk), and about half of the multiple-star systems, we have between six and fifteen billion Sun-like stars in the Milky Way.

The median of this range is just over ten billion, which happens to be roughly the number of years the Milky Way has existed. Crudely speaking, then, our galaxy has formed, on average, one Sun-like star for every year it has existed. In other words, the **Rate of Sun-like Starbirths** per year in our galaxy equals one.

This is a conservative estimate. Systems with suitable planets could not have formed early in the life of the Milky Way, since planet-building heavy elements did not yet exist. (Such elements are made through nuclear fusion at the cores of stars, then dispersed when the stars explode in novas.) The current **Rate of Sun-like Starbirths** would likely be greater than one. But let's be conservative. In building a proof for the probability of extraterrestrial intelligence, it behooves us to be conservative.

So our **Rate of Sun-like Starbirths** equals one, with the number of Sun-like stars in the Milky Way being between six and fifteen billion.

On to the next item on Drake's ETI grocery list.

The Fraction of Suns with Planets

For a long while, astrophysicists have believed that planets were commonplace in our galaxy, marshaling convincing models of star formation to support their beliefs. Direct evidence, however, was scant.

Of course, the recent discovery of three planets in three separate nearby systems (51 Pegasi, 47 Ursa Majoris, and 70 Virginis) is changing all that. By using the telescope at California's Lick Observatory and generating complex computer programs for analyzing the information from the telescope, Geoffrey Marcy and Paul Butler, astronomers from San Francisco State University, discovered gas giants orbiting the latter two stars. Their finds followed on the heels of a Swiss team's discovery of the first planet outside our system, a brown dwarf that orbits 51 Pegasi in extraordinarily tight quarters (the radius of the orbit is less than a quarter that of Mercury's). Marcy ventured, "We are going to find, between us and the Swiss, ten more [extrasolar] planets in the next two years."

The discovery of planets outside our system is now limited not so

much by technology as by time-sharing demands on observatory telescopes and supercomputers, as well as access to such new technologies
as Hubble. In a timely announcement, NASA has revealed plans to set
up arrays of space telescopes for the specific purpose of searching for
new worlds.

The mounting direct evidence only supports what theorists have long
suspected, that planetary systems are the rule rather than the exception.
Other research, too, supports this belief:

> • Though it is hard to detect a planet orbiting a star, it is easy
> to detect a star orbiting another star. Such secondary stars condense
> just as planets do, except that they have enough mass to trigger
> nuclear fusion at their cores. They become self-luminous planets,
> or, more conventionally, stars. Given that about half of the Milky
> Way's disk stars are in such multiple systems, it is reasonable to
> assume that a like number of the disk stars have planets.
> • Our own solar system contains several planetary systems, in-
> cluding the sixteen moons of Jupiter, the seventeen of Saturn, and
> even the one of Earth. Large rotating centers of mass seem natu-
> rally to acquire secondary bodies revolving about them.
> • Given that the chemistry and physics of our solar system match
> those of the rest of the Milky Way's disk, the forces that formed
> planets here should also form them elsewhere.
> • Many nearby stars act as though they have planets: They wob-
> ble, as though tugged by unseen gravitational forces. They rotate
> too slowly, having shifted some of their momentum outward (to
> planets), much as a spinning ice-skater slows as he or she spreads
> hands outward. They have dust disks, which are linked to planet
> formation.
> • Measurements of stellar speeds using Doppler shifts have sup-
> ported the idea that planets are common among nearby stars.

These indirect observations, coupled with the mounting evidence
from teams of star-finders, lead most planetary theorists and astronomers to the conclusion that planets are a natural, ordinary feature of
the cosmos. In fact many, including myself, would venture to say that
probably *all* the Sun-like stars in the galactic disk will have planetary
systems.

So in terms of the Drake Equation, the **Fraction of Suns with Planets**
is nearly a one-to-one ratio. This fraction means that the disk of the

Milky Way contains at least as many planetary systems as it does Sun-like stars—six to fifteen billion.

The Number of Earth-like Planets per Sun

Not all planets are earths. In our own solar system, with over forty major planetary bodies (when moons are included), only one is Earth. Venus is too close to the Sun, its greenhouse atmosphere entirely sterile. Mars is too far from the Sun, and is slightly too small to hold an atmosphere that would support life. Titan, a satellite of Saturn, is the only planet other than Earth with a nitrogen-dominated atmosphere, but it, too, is barren. As the saying goes, there's no place like home.

Or is there? Before we jump to such conclusions, let's determine what we mean by "like home."

A planet must satisfy a number of criteria to be considered Earth-like:

- It must be a rocky, terrestrial planet. We cannot comment on evolution in gas giants or other bodies, since we have only a terrestrial model to go by.
- It must have a stable orbit about its sun. Widely elliptical orbits like that of Pluto would not provide a consistency of temperature necessary for life.
- It must orbit at a distance that allows the solvent of life, water, to be in its liquid state. Planets too close to the sun (Venus) will have only water vapor, and planets too far (Mars) will have only ice.

Perhaps the best model for combining these different factors was proposed by Michael Hart in the late 1970s. He devised the concept of a continually habitable zone (CHZ) around Sun-like planets. The CHZ is a relatively narrow orbital band where a terrestrial planet would have a stable orbit that maintains liquid water.

Sounds simple, but there is a little more to the model than forming a summertime California. To understand the CHZ completely, we need to review how solar systems are born.

From a gas cloud of hydrogen and helium (peppered with heavier elements) a lump of sorts begins to condense. Not just one lump, but many, some larger than others and the protostar (or stars) largest of all. The gas cloud begins to spin as it condenses, and flattens into a disk that holds the nascent sun and its satellites. The star reaches an early, superbright phase, blasting the cloud away from the forming planets. This gale-force solar wind leaves only rocky cores near the sun (terrestrial planets) and hydrogen/helium-rich gas giants farther out.

The terrestrial cores continue to condense, and in doing so, heat up. Heavier elements melt and sink, while lighter ones rise, making a crust. The crust fractures, and gases such as carbon dioxide, oxygen, water vapor, and nitrogen escape to form a primordial Earth-like atmosphere.

The planet cools. This is a critical phase. Will the planet cool enough to rain out vapor and form oceans? If it is too near the sun, it won't. Without liquid water—which, among its other wonders, dissolves the greenhouse gas carbon dioxide—the planet's atmosphere will continue to heat up until the surface is too hot for any life-form. Thus we get Venus.

On the other hand, a planet too far from the sun will cool enough to make all the water rain out, dissolving too much carbon dioxide. Things seem fine for a few million years, and perhaps life begins, but the planet keeps cooling until it freezes. Primitive life-forms, if any exist, are snuffed out. This was the fate of Mars.

If the planet is in the right position and has the right range of mass (i.e., between one-half and two-and-a-half times the mass of Earth; Mars is a bit too small), a nitrogen-dominated atmosphere will form. Though amounts of oxygen will vary, concentrations will eventually stabilize within a certain range. Below 50 percent of Earth's current sea-level density of oxygen, fires will not start, and therefore technology would not develop. Above 120 percent of Earth's oxygen density, fires would rage out of control, routinely scouring the land.

Each Sun-like star, therefore, has an orbital life zone around it, a strip in which a planet must form to be considered Earth-like. How likely is such a happy accident? The original models indicated that this slot was so narrow, it was nearly impossible for a planet to end up in it. Earth was, likely, unique.

Several later developments have forced a revision of this view:

- Hart's atmospheric models have proven overly simplistic and sometimes directly inaccurate.
- Hart's models ignore the effect of primitive life-forms in stabilizing atmospheres.
- Revised models, more complex and likely more accurate than Hart's, predict a much wider life zone.
- Earth has maintained a steady surface temperature despite

marked fluctuations in solar radiation, a stability that Hart's models cannot explain.

The newly calculated life zones are six to seven times wider than Hart estimated. The new band extends from the Earth halfway to Venus on one side, and halfway to Mars on the other. What are the odds of a planet being placed in this region?

It's not just dumb luck. The planets in our own solar system orbit in a surprisingly orderly sequence. They waltz at respectful distances from each other, the lanes gradually widening the farther planets are from the sun. There are many theories about what causes this regularity:

- Planets forming too close to each other would either merge early on or collide later.
- As a planet condenses from a hydrogen cloud, it naturally sweeps clean a band of the disk affected by its gravitational field. Other planets would be "discouraged" from forming too close, and "encouraged" to form in the remaining lanes of cloud.
- Certain resonances of a star's gravitational and electromagnetic fields—and those of planets themselves—might provide favorable bands for planet formation.

By devising computer programs that incorporate our understanding of star and planet formation, we can run simulations that create planets around Sun-like stars. With a keystroke, we can make alternate planetary systems.

These systems look familiar, with terrestrial planets up close and gas giants farther out, the lanes widening in a pattern away from the star.

Interestingly, the width of the life zone turns out to be almost exactly the same as the width of planetary spacing in the area of the life zone. In other words, the distance from Venus to Earth (or from Earth to Mars) is roughly the same as the width of Earth's life zone. They match up nearly one-to-one. As a consequence, after many iterations of computer modeling, planets have appeared in life zones about 90 percent of the time. Nearly 10 percent of these systems had two Earth-like planets.

So there is someplace like home, after all.

But how many someplaces? Well, estimates vary. Even though a planet may fall in the life zone just about every time, some of those planets are too big or too small to produce the right atmospheric conditions, some rotate too slowly or too quickly, some wobble. Also, given that most of what we call Sun-like stars are smaller than our Sun, with perhaps generally smaller planets as well, the odds may drop. In other words, when shopping for a new home world, caveat emptor.

By averaging the outcomes of the various models used, we find that Earth-like planets appear in life zones around Sun-like stars about 50 percent of the time. So the **Number of Earth-like Planets per Sun** is a ratio of one per every two. In our galactic disk, with an estimated ten billion Sun-like stars, therefore, we should find five billion Earth-like planets.

Similar estimates were roughly summarized by Sebastian von Hoerner of the National Radio Astronomy Observatory:

> Some astronomical estimates show that probably about 2 percent of *all stars* have a planet fulfilling all known conditions needed to develop life similar to ours. If we are average, then on half of these planets intelligence has developed earlier and farther, while the other half are barren or underdeveloped [italics mine].

The Fraction of Earths That Form Life

Will the right sort of planet revolving at the right sort of distance around the right sort of star produce life? Apparently yes, if it has the right sort of starting materials. And how likely is that? Actually quite likely. Models and studies to date suggest that the right starting materials are automatically there.

As previously mentioned, elements heavier than hydrogen and helium are produced through nuclear fusion in the cores of stars and dispersed when these stars explode in supernovas. Using spectroscopy (light from distant stars is split into the visible spectrum and bands appear—the identifiable signatures of different elements), astronomers know that the elements present in our own solar system are also present in the galaxy at large, and in the same proportions. Once the galaxy had gone through its initial stage of building and dispersing elements, the building blocks of life were everywhere.

Not only do the elemental blocks exist everywhere, they readily begin to mortar themselves together into molecular structures that are the basis for all life. Amino acids and other organic molecules form very quickly, and should lead in time to polypeptides, and they in time to proteins and nucleic acids, and they to primitive life-forms.

Exploratory spacecraft report that Halley's Comet contains many of the organic molecules necessary for life. So, too, do meteorites and trails of comet dust. The basic components of life might, in fact, have been carried to Earth four billion years ago by such celestial messengers as shooting stars.

Our picture of planet formation, therefore, is modified as follows:

- Organic molecules such as amino acids exist in the very gas clouds from which stars and planets form.
- These materials are packed into the early cores of planets.
- Even after planet formation is complete, more of these materials rain down upon the planet surface in meteor showers.

Not only are there billions of earths out there, but they have each been showered by the materials needed to form life. Is the sheer presence of all this life-potential enough to ensure the development of life?

Experimenters seem to think so. Once science had written a recipe for the primordial soup of life, it was only a matter of time before evolutionary chefs got out their beakers. The recipe goes something like this: Fill one large beaker with primordial gases in their correct proportions, heat to the temperature of early Earth, let simmer under ultraviolet lights to simulate the radiations from a young sun, and add lightning to taste. What such experimenters cooked up was a batch of biochemicals, the specific biochemicals that make up all life on Earth. They brewed up the stuff of life.

That's the *stuff* of life, not life itself. To link biochemicals together to form proteins or nucleic acids (such as deoxyribonucleic acid, or DNA) is not currently possible in labs in short time frames. Still, strong arguments suggest that these links are formed in a quick, orderly fashion on Earth-like worlds:

- High-energy sources (such as ultraviolet radiation, lightning, and volcanic heat) and high surface area (such as the bubbles of sea foam) speed such linkages. What Earth-like world would not have volcanoes, lightning, sunlight, and sea foam?
- Even by artificially combining the simple molecules of life, scientists have come up with only a limited selection of biochemicals, many of which are the specific components of life on Earth. Not just any compound is possible.
- According to calculations, the most stable molecules—those best able to survive in the environment of primitive Earth—would be combinations of proteins and nucleic acids. This very alliance is the basis for all of Earth's life.

• Some proteins spontaneously combine to form microspheres, which look like tiny, double-layered bubbles. Though not living, these spheres act like cell membranes, not only creating and sustaining different electrical charges but also dividing like cells.

• Whatever route the biochemicals took to form proteins and eventually simple life-forms, it happened easily and quickly. Life first appeared on Earth just after the planet had cooled enough to form seas.

The progression from simple hydrogen and helium to complex living things is perhaps best summed up by Donald DeVincenci, of the NASA Ames Research Center:

The elements required for life—carbon, nitrogen, hydrogen, oxygen, phosphorus, and sulfur—originate in the formation of stars. Then they evolve into larger organic (carbon-based) molecules in space between the stars. In primitive planetary environments they combine into the building blocks of life, evolve into enzymes and the genetic code, organize into complex and stable cell-like structures, develop self-replication processes, and grow from simple to complex living things.

In short, given the right stuff (which is available throughout the galaxy) in the right place (an Earth-like planet around a Sun-like star), life will spontaneously and rapidly form. Life does it every time, and quickly. It is the basic biochemistry of the universe. Therefore, in the Drake Equation, the **Fraction of Earths That Form Life** is a one-to-one ratio, or, more simply, one.

The Fraction of Ecologies That Form Intelligence and Civilization

Intelligence and civilization are two somewhat arbitrary milestones of the progress of a species. Both achievements, however, are necessary to equip extraterrestrials for space travel, so these milestones are as good as any others.

While the rest of the universe is dissipating due to entropy, life-forms resist dissolution. Rather than becoming simpler and more inert, they inevitably advance in complexity and activity. This is a paradox. How could a physics of entropy give birth to a biology of order?

The great twentieth-century thinker Ilya Prigogine proposed a straightforward proof that explains how a universe that tends toward inert simplicity could produce creatures that tend toward living complexity. Paraphrased, the proof runs as follows:

> When a system is both adaptable and self-organizing, and that system is challenged, altered, stressed, or damaged, the system will reorganize itself, maintaining its former functions while adding new ones to deal with the perturbation. The system will become "more clever" in existing.

Prigogine's proof describes inanimate systems as well as life-forms. Even so, life-forms are quintessential adaptable, self-organizing systems. They evolve. They become stronger. Sometimes life-forms experience severe or even irrevocable setbacks, including extinction, though the general thrust of biology is toward improvement and advancement. Put simply, what doesn't kill you makes you stronger.

The natural history of Earth is the story of systems being stressed, challenged, or damaged, and reorganizing themselves, evolving. Despite numerous errors in countless trials, creatures have, in general, advanced. Rather than being the gradual, patient change of good traits toward better, evolution has more often been a story of dramatic and (relatively) rapid change, of sudden adaptation necessitated by environmental crisis.

For example, some current theories of human evolution involve the geologic catastrophe that formed the Great Rift Valley in Africa and turned eastern Africa from forest into savannah. Hominids trapped in a land with dwindling forests evolved into upright-walking ground-dwellers, and eventually, into us. They were challenged, stressed, perhaps even damaged, and bipedal locomotion resulted.

Some scientists warn against speculating about life elsewhere in our galaxy using the "single case" of evolution on Earth. Perhaps they are right, but to consider the natural history of Earth a single case is to sell our planet short. Billions of years of evolution on Earth have seen many billions of cases of evolutionary experimentation, in millions of distinct environments, thousands of which are still extant.

Through all these trials, organisms have discovered what works. The patterns of biological design and the basic structures of life are not random. Skeletons, for example, work, and demonstrate that they do work in thousands of species from many diverse environments. Every advanced creature on the planet has a skeleton, no matter how early its ancestors split from the common tree of life.

Nor are biological patterns inflexibly linked to a set of physical laws peculiar to Earth. By definition, an Earth-like planet would have the same physical laws—gravitation, electromagnetism, pressure, temperature, inertia, and so forth—that Earth has. And, after all, we've already seen how many Earth-like worlds there are out there.

On our own Earth, across completely isolated environments, creatures that occupy similar niches have separately evolved the same survival strategies. This is called convergent evolution. Similar sizes, shapes, structures, and even behaviors arise in creatures completely cut off from one another. Life finds what works, finds the most dependable path to success, and does so over and over again. Convergent evolution, which occurs everywhere across our world, demonstrates that biologically "getting it right" may involve billions of independent trials, but inevitably results in a quite limited number of biological solutions.

Bats evolved convergently in two separate areas. Opossums and other marsupials, in size and shape and structure, are very much like rodents and other placentals. Dolphins came from land-dwelling stock, but they have evolved many of the same structures and survival strategies as sharks (fish), and mosasaurs (reptiles). Everybody from wasps to waitresses have eyes, but there are over twenty distinct varieties, each developed separately.

Some things work, and some don't. Some, like eyes, work so well that they have separately evolved many times over. Like it or not, biology is part physics, and physics dictates that legs—in their infinite varieties—work best on land, and fins in water, and wings in air. Will creatures from other planets with Earth-like land, water, and air have not discovered legs, fins, wings . . . eyes, ears, noses, mouth . . . ?

Scientists who discuss extraterrestrial intelligence generally agree about the inevitable stages of evolution. Among them are multicellularity, complex body structure, large size, well-developed brains, and eventually intelligence and civilization.

But we needn't even venture from our own beloved planet to conjecture about the inevitable stages of evolution. Thinkers such as David Attenborough argue that if humans became extinct on Earth, some "unobtrusive" creature would rise to the occasion—and perhaps exceed us in intelligence, proving smart enough to avoid extinction.

And so the consensus is that once life-forms develop on an Earth-like planet, they will inevitably evolve intelligence, tool use, language, abstract symbolic thought, technology, and the other fruits of advanced civilization. In other words, the **Fraction of Ecologies That Form Intelligence and Civilization** is a ratio of one-to-one, or, simply, one.

Carl Sagan summed it up well:

> Something like the processes that on Earth led to man must have happened billions of other times in the history of the galaxy. There must be other starfolk . . . these nonhuman creatures of great learning have doubtlessly been sending explorative expeditions through interstellar space for countless millenniums.

The Average Duration of Civilizations

Our work with the Drake Equation is almost finished. We have only the final factor with which to contend: how long, on average, a civilization lasts. Though astronomical observations, lab tests, debates, models, computer imaging, and interdisciplinary research have done much to address the former factors in the Drake Equation, this last parameter remains a mystery. Regarding the life span of civilizations, Earth is, as far as we know, only a single case. To judge the life span of all galactic civilizations upon the single case of human civilization (which has existed for some fifty-five centuries since the invention of writing) would be, in the words of Carl Sagan, "planetary chauvinism."

Bereft of conclusions, the best science can offer so far is a starting point—a guideline or two.

The extremes of a civilization's possible life span are easy enough to determine. One can hardly imagine a civilization lasting less than a year or two. Most achievements that mark the beginning of civilization—writing; development of complex social hierarchy; rise in population density; construction of palaces, temples, tombs; and so forth—take hundreds of years to bring into being. By applying a geometric acceleration to the natural processes of evolution, we can predict that if it takes billions of years to form multiccllular organisms, hundreds of millions more to form complex creatures, and millions more to form beings with enough intelligence to develop civilizations, it will take thousands of years for those civilizations to take shape. Even after such time, most civilizations wouldn't have the means to completely extinct themselves and would have to rely on nature to do it for them.

Even so, let us postulate the existence of a race of intelligent mayflies, for whom a twenty-four-hour day is a lifetime. Sometime around the seven-hundredth generation of these transient creatures, a mayfly invents nuclear weaponry. On day seven hundred thirty (exactly two Earth years), a nuclear blast destroys all of mayfly civilization and every last mayfly. They are wiped out—the mayfly palaces crumble, the mayfly libraries burn, the mayfly creatures are extincted. If such extraterrestrial civilizations are the norm rather than the exception in our galaxy, the average life span for a civilization would be two years.

Perhaps . . . after all, it's a tough universe out there.

But surely civilizations would last longer. Let's face it, even our own erratic selves have managed to hang on for fifty-five centuries—1 percent of which has been lived in the ominous shadow of atomic weaponry.

Taking this fact as a justification for extreme optimism, we can argue (equally absurdly) that advanced civilizations such as ours will never die. Even though pharaohs, emperors, kings, and presidents come and go, civilization, once begun, carries on. Should global catastrophe strike, we will colonize Mars or the asteroid belt. Should stellar catastrophe strike, we will flee to Barnard's star. Should galactic catastrophe strike, there's always Andromeda. Only the death of the entire universe can snuff us (or any other technologically advanced race) out of existence. If such a scenario is the case, then the average life span of a civilization would be the life span of the universe at large.

Those are the best answers we have so far. Thus the **Average Duration of Civilizations** is, on the short end, a couple of years, and on the long end, the life span of the universe. That narrows it down, doesn't it?

In the final analysis all we have to go on is intuition, which tells us that some civilizations survive and some do not. Given the geometric acceleration of our own technologies, if any of the surviving civilizations began one or two billion years before ours, their current technology base would likely allow them movement among the stars.

Summary of the Drake Debate

At last, we've assembled at least approximate guesses for each factor in the Drake Equation. Let's review:

- On average, one Sun-like star is produced in our galaxy each year, for a grand total of ten billion Sun-like stars.
- Most if not all of these suns have planets.
- About half of these suns have Earth-like planets, which comes out to five billion earths.
- On average, every Earth-like planet will evolve life.
- Life, once begun, will always progress toward intelligence and civilization.
- The average duration of a civilization is between a couple of

years and the life span of the universe; though, more practically speaking, some civilizations make it and some don't.

Now let's see how these conclusions logically play themselves out in the discussion of the existence of extraterrestrial intelligence.

Our galaxy formed about ten billion years ago. At that time it was composed primarily of helium and hydrogen, with no heavier elements, and therefore no planets and no life. For about three billion years, first-generation stars coalesced and burned brightly and quickly, creating the heavier elements in their cores. Then, exploding in supernovas, the stars spread heavy elements throughout the galaxy. The first few "Sun-like" stars then began to form on the galaxy's outer rim, bringing along the first few "Earth-like" planets. That was seven billion years ago. Suns and earths were forming, then, for about two billion years before our own system came into being, five billion years ago.

Two billion years of planet formation occurred before Earth was formed. If one Earth-like planet comes into being every other year (a ten-billion-year-old galaxy contains five billion Earth-like planets), and every earth develops life, and every ecology develops intelligence and civilization, then perhaps one billion intelligent civilizations have evolved in the history of our galaxy. If those civilizations last, on average, two years, then one of them still remains. If those civilizations last, on average, until the universe collapses, there should be about one billion extraterrestrial civilizations out there.

And in two years (on average), there will be another. In another century there will be fifty more. The supposition is that fifty-five centuries ago, when humans developed writing, ours was the galactic marker that slid over to the side of civilization. There have been, perhaps, over twenty-seven hundred civilizations that have developed since then, in the Milky Way alone.

Think of all the other galaxies, and all the clusters of galaxies, and the superclusters of galaxies. . . . On the other hand, don't. According to our calculations, there is plenty of life only hundreds and thousands of light-years distant—rather than trillions.

OBJECTIONS BASED ON BODY FORMS

Our review of ETI discussions shows us that, based upon probability, scientists believe our galaxy to be teeming with extraterrestrials. Still, many of those same scientists are unwilling to consider a link between ETs and UFO phenomena. Again, we wonder, Why?

The question of appearance is one reason. Many learned commentators object that extraterrestrials described in UFO sightings are often reported to be humanlike in appearance. Creatures from other planets would have a completely different morphology, they argue, derived from their otherworldly home planets. To perhaps put too fine a point on it, ETs should look a lot more . . . well, alien.

On the surface, such an objection seems sure. One way of dismissing it is to speculate that ETs are somehow genetically connected to us— that we are their children, or vice versa. Such theories are rubbish, and I'll tell you why in my other article. In order not to get sidetracked here, let's say good riddance to bad rubbish, dismiss that particular dismissal, and move on to arguments based upon separate evolutions.

Why is it a mistake to think ETs should look completely alien?

What we have already seen indicates that the places extraterrestrial life would develop are Earth-like in size, temperature, composition, rotation, and location—places likely to have oceans like ours and dry land like ours and skies like ours, crossed by a Sun-like star. These worlds don't sound that alien. Would the life-forms that evolve on them not have tried legs for terrestrial locomotion, or fins for aquatic locomotion, or wings for the air?

The similarities, of course, go deeper than sandy beaches and wind-swept hills. The places will have the same mix of primary elements and compounds, the same solvent (water), the same basic chemistry. From this chemistry, amino acids and nucleic acids will form, and join to create basic life-forms, driven, as we are, by phosphate energy systems. In short the basic biology of the planets will be the same.

What about that biology, then? In my other article in this collection, "Modern Biology and Extraterrestrials," I go into greater depth on a subject that I summarize here.

Judging by the apparently required sequence of evolution, an intelligent extraterrestrial life-form would be an animal (not a plant), multicellular, oxygen-using, sexually reproductive, large in size (for a large brain), mobile, and land-dwelling (to allow the use of fire and development of appendages for manipulative tool use). The size of the beast necessitates certain similarities to our structures.

In order to feed all the cells in a large, complex, multicellular organism, the creature needs a nutrient absorption system more powerful than osmosis and other passive means. It needs a digestive tract, a disassembly line that runs from one end of its body to the other. Digestive tracts are one-way tubes, with a mouth at one end and an anus at the other, not to be confused. The distinct nature of these two features means that the mouth end of the creature has become its head, and the other end its tail.

Some nutrients aren't eaten, though, but drawn out of the air. Since gases are not as densely packed with nutrients as are foods, and since it would be impractical to trap enough gas in an hours-long one-way tube, gas exchange would need to take place fairly constantly and quickly, and in a bidirectional system. Gases would need to be forcefully drawn in and expelled, not acquired passively or through overall loco-motion (as with some fish). The gas-exchange system would likely share some tubes with the digestive system, too, to cut down on redundancy.

A powerful digestive tract and a strong gas-exchange system must be matched by an equally powerful circulatory system. Otherwise the nu-trients absorbed cannot be transported to the rest of the body, and wastes from the cells cannot be carried away. Again, we need a one-way mech-anism, a pump that forces nutrients to all points of the body and uses separate pipes to return waste materials to the digestive and gas-exchange systems.

The best way to get lots of the best kinds of food into the mouth end of a digestive tract is to have the major sensory organs located in proximity to the mouth. Creatures need to see and—perhaps more im-portantly—smell what they are about to eat. Given that the most nu-tritionally dense foodstuffs are animal proteins, and that most edible animal proteins are attached to animals that aren't yet finished with them, our ET might find itself needing to hunt. Sight, sound, and smell become vitally linked to the mouth. A hunter's eyes are best located to the front to allow binocular vision and depth perception. Ears are best located to the outside and high to allow maximum hearing and trian-gulation of sound. Noses are best located above mouths to allow food one last check before it enters the body.

To process all the information from these senses, and to do so in "real time," we need a brain situated as closely as possible to the main organs of sense. Brains, at least in any form that they take on Earth, are in-famously soft and vulnerable, and so need some kind of hard protection around them. A skull of some sort would do nicely.

Speaking of some sort of shell to protect the brain, there should also be hard material protecting the soft internal organs of the digestive, respiratory, and circulatory systems. But protection is not enough. A large terrestrial body requires mobility and flexibility, and to achieve these ends in anything larger than a slug, we need a skeleton. Exoskeletons are too inflexible; we'll have to go endo.

The creature will be bilaterally symmetrical (for the argument that establishes this, see my other article). It will have a head that contains a brain, eyes closely linked to the brain and in front, a nose directly above a mouth, and ears high and wide. The head, likely, will be on a pivoting neck so that the various senses can be turned without torquing the whole body.

Does this sound like a familiar package?

In fact such traits are observable in all large land-dwelling (and most large water-dwelling) creatures on Earth. The configuration results not from some planetary accident but from physics and chemistry—which would be similar if not identical on Earth-like worlds—as well as from predator-prey relationships.

Biologists are beginning to recognize the power of certain structures and packages of characteristics. As is the case with eyes, some structures are so important, they will be independently evolved, even dozens of times on the same planet.

The application of physics to biological design is still a new concept, but it has produced some interesting results. Fluid transport systems, as they occur in all organisms on our planet, are based on only five design principles. Five. Billions of genetic experiments produce millions of species but only five useful principles for fluid transport.

A particularly convincing case study of such convergent designs focuses on the most common skeletal unit on our planet, the fiber-wound cylinder (think of the threads crisscrossing the outside of your garden hose). It appears in plants, lower animal forms, and swimming mammals. It allows bending from side to side as well as minor torquing, while preventing the tube from being compressed. It is flexible, mobile, and strong—and it evolved several separate times, each time with *exactly the same angle of fibers.*

Mathematics and physics apply everywhere in the galaxy, and so, most likely, the fiber-wound cylinder, with its precisely best angle of fibers, will appear on every Earth-like planet of every Sun-like star.

Physics, geometry, and material strength limit the number of structural possibilities. Within these limits, a dynamic ecology will inevitably fill each useful structural niche, usually many times over.

Research into the strength of animal bones and the stresses habitually placed on those bones has provided another amazing case study. From hamsters to hippos, gerbils to giraffes, bones can withstand exactly three times the force habitually applied to them. Exactly. Natural selection has built the same safety factor into the bones of all terrestrial bony creatures. Stronger bones would be excessively heavy and would require too much of the system's energy to build and maintain. Weaker bones would debilitate the creature too often to be evolutionarily advantageous. Similar mathematical relationships exist for structures like tentacles, tongues, and trunks. Surely mathematics and physics aren't just playing favorites with Earth creatures.

So, we've got ETs with heads and faces and skulls, with skeletons that can withstand certain forces. But what would possibly cause them to have exactly two arms and two legs, like us? Why not four arms and three legs? Isn't more better? Where did we get our four limbs from?

From fish. Life on Earth evolved first in the sea and then moved to land. It had to. When life began in the seas, the atmosphere above was still too caustic and volatile to allow life on land. By the time the skies had settled down, ocean life had become pretty advanced. Of all the things that lived in the sea, only bony skeletal vertebrates had the size, mobility, and potential intelligence to become big-time successes on land.

Fish have fins, or, we might say with specist prejudice, fish have protolegs. Not all fins make good legs. Dorsal fins, for instance, stick straight up into empty air. Similarly, fins that stick straight down would not be able to support a creature, only dragging painfully over the rocky ground. Therefore a fish that becomes amphibious and eventually terrestrial will lose any fin along the midline of its body (except, of course, for the ever-useful tail). Only bilateral pairs of fins—pectoral and pelvic fins, specifically—would be effective as legs. They would, consequently, evolve.

Okay, that tells us why land animals have an even number of limbs. But why not six or eight, or any other number? Surely, the more legs, the more stable, mobile, and dexterous a creature could be, right? More is better, right?

Maybe land-dwellers on Earth have only four limbs because the first fish that crawled up on land happened to have four fins. Well, the truth is that in the great wash of time, nature experimented with any number of fins, from zero on upward. Eventually, fish with four fins outsurvived the rest. Somehow, four was advantageous, was enough without being too much.

How so? We can't answer for our oceanic ancestors, though we can for land creatures like us.

Two legs is too few. With two limbs, not only does a creature have a serious stability problem, but it also can do only one thing at a time.

Mostly what it ends up doing is running away from things with more legs.

But using that argument, six or eight or twenty-eight would be better than four. Most of us have wished at one time or another that we had eight limbs. Why don't we?

In a word, cost. Limbs are expensive—in terms of the nutrition required to keep them going, the mental capacity needed to utilize them, and the genetic code required to create them in the first place. Worse yet, limbs are vulnerable to injury and infection, conditions that might end the life of their owner. It's the very reason that fighting dogs like Doberman pinschers have their tails and ears docked—in a predatory world like ours, extra appendages are only liabilities.

Another analogy might make the problem all too clear. The cost of having extra limbs is like the cost of having extra cars. A household with one driver needs only one car. Having two cars won't make the driver more mobile, only make him or her pay two car loans, two insurance accounts, two licensing fees, and twice the cost for maintenance and repair. Add another driver to the household, and two cars makes sense. But three? Not really. A household with an extra car has extra expenses and no gain in mobility.

Similarly, limbs are expensive. They cost a lot to acquire (genetic coding), a lot to run (oxygen and nutrient supply and waste removal), a lot to maintain (repair and replacement of tissues and bone), and a lot to protect (immunity, hygiene, care, and conditioning). They also require a driver (an allotment of brain space). One driver can't drive two cars at once, and similarly limbs can be used simultaneously and independently only if they each have separate brain space and time. An extra limb, therefore, is a severe liability—creatures with spare limbs have not survived into the current crop of Earth's life-forms.

What about insects? spiders? millipedes? They aren't brainy, have lots of limbs, and are among the most successful creatures on Earth. True enough, but are their limbs capable of independent movement and fine motor skill? To program limbs for simple repetitive motions is very different from using them for the literally millions of tasks that human limbs perform (and that human brains must learn to make human limbs perform). The six-legged world of insects uses a nonindependent, three-up and three-down tripod walking pattern. Very little independent control is possible for the tiny limbs of these relatively simple creatures. Larger and more complex beasts need to get much more use out of a limb to justify its cost.

For that matter, many lower life-forms deal with the problem of injury by shedding the limb and growing a new one. That, too, is a luxury unavailable to creatures more complex than salamanders. Humans may be able to trade in their cars for newer models, but limbs are for life. If one of them gets totaled, it stays totaled.

Let's take one last stab at defending the "more is better" philosophy. What about octopi? They are smart, invertebrate, and have eight legs. Yes, they are, but the use of their legs is almost exclusively limited to unconscious, robotic control rather than focused intentionality. The brain cost of even unconscious control of these limbs is so high that, despite the intelligence of octopi, they cannot learn to navigate mazes.

After considering all these cases of limbs and the neural cost of running them, researchers have begun to suspect that there is a brain-dependent barrier ruling out six or more limbs for higher life-forms. Four limbs and a prehensile tail—or, in the case of elephants, four limbs and a dexterous trunk—is the most we get. Apparently, some as-yet-unidentified limitation of our central nervous systems prevents more.

For that matter, even when burdened with only four limbs, brains develop strategies for further minimizing their workload. The fact that the vast majority of humans have a dominant hand, which is used for precision tool use (e.g., drawing, writing, tinkering), means the brain doesn't have to learn such costly skills twice.

In the foregoing arguments, we have not proved that all extraterrestrials look like us, only that some probably do. Physics, geometry, materials, survival costs, predator-prey relationships, and the limitations of central nervous systems make certain body shapes and structures effective, and others not. It's that simple.

On the other hand, no one would be more shocked than I if extraterrestrials turned out to be Herbert Hoover look-alikes. Even given certain successful structural designs, there is much room for variation: mass, size, dimensions, colors, textures, traits of aging, consciousness cycles, and so forth. Identical duplication of the human form is not only unrealistic but highly improbable. On the other hand, absolute dissimilarity is equally improbable. Reports of extraterrestrials that have large-scale structural similarities to us with small-scale variations in pattern, in fact, would be the most believable sorts of reports. As Robert Bieri of Antioch College stated,

If we ever succeed in communicating with conceptualizing beings in outer space, they won't be spheres, pyramids, cubes, or pancakes. In all probability, they will look an awful lot like us.

OBJECTIONS BASED ON TRAVEL
AND MOTIVATION

Despite rigorous critiques, two other knee-jerk objections to the ET hypothesis still plague the popular mind. The first is that routine space travel could never be achieved, given the insurmountable extremes of distance and time. The second is the so-called Fermi Paradox: If ETs were so commonplace, we would have seen them by now, and since we haven't, they don't exist. The weaknesses of such positions do not prevent them from being restated. Let the counterarguments, too, be restated.

Impossibility of Space Travel

Given the problems of traveling at near light-speed (e.g., one's head weighing as much as the Sears Tower, and a thirty-second dish-soap commercial lasting for three centuries), some theorists believe travel across light-years, let alone light-decades, to be impractical, if not impossible.

Given the problems of breaking the sound barrier (e.g., the airplane entering an uncontrollable dive just before its wings rip off and the cockpit shakes apart), some aeronautical engineers believed that faster-than-sound travel was impractical, if not impossible. In the first half of the century, that is.

If the lessons of the past are not enough to convince us not to trust "absolute technological limits," perhaps the lessons of the present will suffice. Thinkers such as Robert Forward have proposed extensions of today's technology that would make travel to our nearest stellar neighbors a matter of decades rather than centuries. Nuclear fusion engines, lightsails, antimatter engines, and other propulsive means are currently designable, if not economically feasible. Certainly time will produce only better, more achievable designs, and even if it doesn't, current levels of technology make space travel possible, if not practical.

As stated earlier in this article, given the exponential acceleration of technologies on our own world, it is likely that an intelligent civilization that predates ours by millions if not billions of years has overcome barriers we consider to be impossible. Imagine modern technologies on display in the court of Charlemagne, only a thousand years back, and you begin to have an idea.

The Fermi Paradox

The conviction that there is little technologically to prevent ETI from traveling to the stars has inspired a bizarre back-door argument against the existence of ETI. This argument, allegedly (and casually) formulated by Enrico Fermi, goes like this:

- If lots of intelligent, advanced extraterrestrials exist, and
- If they can travel from star to star, then,
- Given the ample time ETs have had to reach us, and
- Given that we have no evidence of their visiting Earth,
- Either travel is not possible from star to star or
- Intelligent, advanced extraterrestrials don't exist.

Because travel from star to star has been shown to be possible, the apparent answer to this conundrum is that ETI doesn't exist. Summed up simply, the argument is If there are so many aliens out there, how come we haven't seen any?

The flaws in this argument are obvious. To begin with, the second "given" statement—that we have no evidence of ETs visiting Earth—demonstrates a profound prejudice. To say that nothing in our recent, or even distant, history might be interpreted to point toward extraterrestrial intelligence is tantamount to closing one's eyes. Though there may be no *conclusive* evidence, the allegation that all UFO phenomena have been satisfactorily explained without reference to extraterrestrials is simply false.

A second problem is the notion that extraterrestrial visitations would be obvious, if not overwhelming. The notion is that ETs would come to Earth only to colonize it, arriving as celestial conquistadors and blasting away at the natives.

It is dangerous enough to guess at the motivations of other humans; it is perhaps impossible to guess at those of extraterrestrials. Even so, such guesses include far more possibilities than merely colonization, any one of which, or all of which, might be motivating factors.

The seven most frequently discussed possible ETI motivations (a brief portion of what is, likely, an infinite list) follow:

- Colonization
- Material gain and power
- Threat at home

- Threat from Earth
- Galactic kinship
- Religious conversion
- Curiosity and exploration

Colonization

The first motivation, colonization, is typically discussed as a product of population pressure. There are much better reasons to colonize, such as establishing scientific or military outposts, but ETI literature more often touches on expansionism.

If, as most feel, the moving of craft from star to star would require a major investment of resources and technology, such travel would be done neither casually nor on a massive scale. A culture seeking relief from population pressures will not find it by sending three hundred citizens to the nearest star while three hundred billion remain behind. Condoms are cheaper than space capsules. Even we humans have spotted the dangers of overpopulation, not just for the planet as a whole but for individual nations in particular (e.g., China, India). Surely extraterrestrials that would qualify as intelligent would already have dealt with the problems of overpopulation.

Those objections aside, even if ETs did desire to colonize other planets in order to ease population pressures, they wouldn't head straight for other suns and earths. First, they would saturate their own system. In doing so, they would learn to live efficiently in space colonies or cities. By the time such folk would launch toward the stars and eventually reach our system, they would likely choose a convenient home in space, where solar energy and asteroidal minerals are abundant. The alternative is not so pleasant: to drop into a deep gravity well (Earth) teeming with unknown and potentially deadly microorganisms (diseases) and a violent primitive species (us).

In other words, ETs might have visited Earth many times (perhaps on study expeditions, perhaps on holiday) and might even now be living in our solar system, but might never have set up housekeeping on our planet. At our crude level of solar system exploration, it would be many years before we'd even notice they were around.

Earth may be an interesting planet to visit, but...

Michael Papagiannis from the University of Boston has speculated thus:

> Following life's innate tendency to expand into every available space, technological civilizations will inevitably colonize the entire galaxy,

establishing space habitats around all its well-behaved stars. The most reasonable place in our solar system to test this possibility is the asteroid belt, which is an ideal source of raw materials for space colonies.

Material Gain and Power

This motivation is really an analogue to the population problem. If it is truly difficult and expensive to travel among the stars, this possibility makes less sense than the first one. The constituents of the galaxy are abundant everywhere. Mass freighting of materials between systems would thus be pointless. Even rare commodities such as humans or genes would have to be considered nearly priceless to make the trip worth it. We ourselves will be able to entirely engineer genes before we will be able to travel to other stars. Why would we spend the trillions of dollars and long decades to harvest from Sirius something we could build right here at home?

But perhaps there are celestial Caesars who want to go, see, and conquer, just for the kick of it. Perhaps there are whole power-hungry races that will assume any risk, any cost, merely to dominate (we are, sadly, not so far from that mark). Well, if there are, none of them have gotten to us yet (and we haven't gotten to anyone else yet, either). If such conquerors arrive on Earth, they will find a very intractable native people, and likely will treat us the way the Romans treated the Scots—they'd give up trying to conquer us and build a barrier to keep us from roaming into the more civilized spaces of the galaxy. But I get ahead of myself. That is the fourth motivation.

Threat at Home

A home-world threat, whether to the whole system or to a small group, might motivate ETs to head for the stars. Hi-tech pilgrims in fusion-powered *Mayflowers* might leave the stifling repression of home worlds, intent on freer space. Such speculations are reasonable. The effect of this migration, however, would be piecemeal and would not saturate the galaxy. And, like the other colonists we had discussed, such refugees might prefer space colonies to digs on the surface of the sultry, crowded planet Earth.

What about an advanced civilization whose star is dying? Though such a catastrophe is inevitable for any civilization that lasts long enough, it would still be exceedingly rare. Suns last a heck of a long time. Even so, it might happen. Surely a people facing such annihilation would marshal all their resources—would literally move heaven and earth—to make escape. But an escape is just what such a journey would be. Travelers of this sort would flee to the nearest suitable spot and stay there. If that spot wasn't our system, we'd never know about the refugees.

And, thank goodness, no nearby stars have gone supernova in the last few million years.

Threat from Earth

Our current technology, not to mention bureaucracy, makes us a threat to no one but ourselves, but it is conceivable that we might be galactically troublesome in a few centuries.

After all, we are competitive, xenophobic, violent, curious, inventive, risk-taking, and irrational. We specialize in warfare, and some of our most peace-loving geniuses (e.g., da Vinci, Nobel, Einstein) have given us some of our most deadly weaponry. Some of our best thinkers are currently discussing with glee things such as relativistic rockets, devices that approach the speed of light. Such planet crackers could put us in an interstellar arms race before we even knew we had neighbors.

Wise neighbors would monitor us to see if we were learning to behave. Paranoid neighbors would monitor us to see if we should be destroyed. Curious neighbors would monitor us to see if we had come up with anything they themselves could use. Moral neighbors would monitor us to make sure we don't burn the house down with those matches we've found. Any of these motives would call for one thing: ultrasecrecy. The last thing a worried civilization would want to do is give itself away.

Galactic Kinship

There's nothing more satisfying than watching (and helping) a lower lifeform evolve. Advanced extraterrestrials might do so altruistically, stepping in as a *deus ex machina* when we draw near to self-destruction, or selfishly, breeding us to be slaves or pets. They might do so secretively, working behind the scenes to shape human history, or overtly, placing one of their own into a position of command (Carter? Reagan? Bush? Clinton?—you be the judge). The point is that, for whatever reason, ETs might take an interest in how things turn out on our planet, and might manipulate events on Earth without being detected doing so.

Religious Conversion

If stellar travel is as difficult as it seems to be, only severe survival pressures and "matters of the spirit" would motivate ETI to do it. Religion has certainly been a driving force on our planet, and perhaps such heavenly desires would drive ETs to Earth.

But wouldn't missionary hopes bring overt contact? Conversion by stealth would seem all too slow. Perhaps, though, creatures that have practiced patience and devotion on their long flight over could put up with a very gradual evangelism.

Curiosity and Exploration

This is perhaps the most likely and likable motivation discussed. It is difficult to imagine a technologically advanced race that is not curious. What race would experiment, would look for a better way, would develop technology, if it weren't curious? Curiosity and exploration are what have brought us this far and what have caused us to venture out into space. The motivation of curiosity, for us, amounts to a powerful "matter of the spirit," inspiring us to disregard economics, security, and practicality in our plunge forward.

But would curiosity occur in ETs?

In the most basic terms, a creature has three possible actions: to remain where it is, to move toward something, or to move away from something. These broad categories—which might be retitled *stasis, desire,* and *avoidance*—cover all behaviors. Though it has been said that alien intelligence would share nothing with human intelligence, how could ETI not partake in these three universal instincts? One of these three, moving toward something with desire, is closely related to, if not identical with, curiosity.

This is not mere supposition. These instincts are rooted firmly in neurobiology. A trio of hormones controls the three states. Desire—which includes impulsive and exploratory activity—is driven by the hormone dopamine. Avoidance—which includes caution and shyness—is driven by the sleep-state hormone, serotonin. Stasis—which includes dependency and conservatism—is inversely driven by the main energizing hormone, norepinephrine.

These three neurotransmitters are critical to behavioral stability. Imbalances produce schizophrenia, depression, hyperactivity, and neurosis. The balance of these chemicals is the root of human behavior.

Just human behavior? All life-forms must seek novelty, avoid harm, and conserve what is good. A creature, even an extraterrestrial creature, incapable of curiosity would be behaviorally crippled.

Would ET curiosity be enough to bring travelers to our world? No one can say. But if they do come, ETs will most certainly bring, among their other instincts, curiosity and a sense of exploration.

UFOLOGY AND SCIENCE

Let's review the conclusions we have reached so far:

- Our galaxy contains billions of Sun-like stars with Earth-like, life-bearing worlds.
- Most likely, many of these earths developed intelligent life, some much earlier than our Earth.
- Most likely, some of these civilizations still exist, and perhaps all of them do.
- Most likely, some of these advanced life-forms have bodies similar (but not identical) to our own.
- Almost certainly, these advanced life-forms have several instinctual motivations in common with us, curiosity being one of them.
- Most likely, some of these advanced life-forms can (with difficulty) travel from star to star.

None of these conclusions is forbidden by scientific information as we know it. Even those who disagree with one conclusion or another must admit that these positions are at least possible.

Whatever their form, conclusions are both an end and a beginning for science. From conclusions come new hypotheses, such as the following: Advanced extraterrestrial visitors have reached our solar system and may still be here; though not identical to us, they have many physical and psychological similarities; and they are motivated by curiosity and exploration. Such a hypothesis—the classical ET hypothesis—is a perfectly congenial scientific basis for further research.

Then why has it been so often dismissed out of hand or, worse, derided openly?

In posing that question for the fourth (or is it the fifth?) time, I realize that we have already given too much air time to detractors. They will exist for any new area of science. And given that we have already shown their dismissals to be, at best, the result of innocent ignorance—and at worst, of calculated prejudice—it is time for us to dismiss the dismissers.

Instead, let's focus on the growing number of eminent theorists who not only accept the hypothesis as valid but pursue its scientific validation. The Drake-Sagan school of explorers, for one, actively seeks ETI by means of radiotelescopy. Other astronomers have suggested extensive exploration of the asteroid belt, looking for colonies. Another researcher has scanned gravity-well points on the Moon, looking for traces of visitation.

No true scientist disapproves of such investigations as being outrageous, laughable, or beneath scientific dignity. The acceptable circle of research has tightened from nearby stars to the asteroid belt, to Mars, and to our own Moon. Surely it is time to allow the search for ETs to touch ground on our own planet.

Clearly, the ET hypothesis is an acceptable one, to be weighed alongside other possible explanations of UFO phenomena. We must next ask, Is this research being pursued properly?

Ufology, as a fledgling science, has for decades been engaged in gathering data—which means, of course, reports of sightings—clarifying the data, and searching for patterns. Many patterns have been found (e.g., times of sightings, population densities, witness numbers, witness types). Some investigations have turned up known phenomena (e.g., swamp gas, migratory birds); others have discovered known but unsuspected causes (e.g., the atmospheric reentry of rocket boosters); still others have pointed to rare or new natural phenomena (e.g., lightning that strikes toward space rather than toward Earth); and some have led to intriguing unsolved puzzles (e.g., engine interferences, ground markings).

After the pattern-finding step, science requires testing, or at least active observation. Conventional laboratory science, though, has only limited application in ufology (e.g., the analysis of photographs), because the phenomena are often not reproducible. In such cases, variables cannot truly be controlled.

Even so, for any given case all the possible hypotheses (including the ETI hypothesis, confabulation, hoax, misperception, psychosis, natural phenomenon, etc.) are falsifiable, and on any solved case all but one is falsified. Good investigators consider all such hypotheses, and have explained the vast majority of UFO phenomena using them. This piecemeal testing, and the results it produces, are significant achievements for any fledgling science.

Some cases, though, resist explanation by any but the ET hypothesis. They do not *prove* the hypothesis. As yet, no lab-testable evidence provides sufficient data to do so. But a vast number of cases defy mundane explanations. That alone is justification for further research and consideration of less mundane explanations.

Ufology is a difficult field, no doubt. In addition to the barriers encountered by any young science, ufology must also deal with sporadic and diverse phenomena, the analysis of which requires familiarity with many disciplines. Most investigations involve knowledge of general fields such as astronomy, meteorology, chemistry, physics, geology, biology, psychology, and sociology, and some require familiarity with such diverse fields as ornithology, entomology, electromagnetism, neurology, and zoology. Given, too, that researchers are most often secondary observers, always one step behind the phenomena witnessed by other (untrained) eyes, the teasing out of fact from fantasy is sometimes a most trying enterprise. These complexities are reasons to approach ufology with extra care and humility, not to dismiss it or oppose the already difficult labors of those who legitimately pursue it.

After all, what is the soul of science but honest curiosity about that which is unexplained? To so lightly dismiss the open-minded pursuit of answers to UFO phenomena is to listen to dogma, not science.

SUMMARY

Consideration of all these points leads to a few final conclusions regarding ufology and the ET hypothesis:

• UFO experiences caused by ETs would not be controlled or easily predicted by Earth scientists.

• If ETs are concerned with secrecy, UFO experiences caused by them would be rare, buried in a multitude of cases with mundane causes.

• If ETs are concerned with secrecy, UFO experiences caused by them might be made to be intentionally confusing.

• If ETs are concerned with secrecy, some UFO experiences caused by them might appear staged, as a means of hiding in plain sight.

• If ETs are concerned with secrecy, their visitations would leave little or no concrete physical evidence.

• Improbable or impossible characteristics of some UFO reports might be manifestations of ultra-advanced technology.

These last conclusions remind us not to reject some UFO reports—or the whole field of study—due to apparently absurd or confusing content. When astronomy was a relatively new field of study and Copernicus confronted the absurd and confusing phenomenon of the retrograde motion of planets, his conclusion that the Earth revolved around the Sun was met with equal dismissal, if not outright furor.

In conclusion, ufology needs room to grow, as does any new science. In the words of J. Allen Hynek:

I cannot presume to describe...what UFOs are, because I don't know; but I can establish beyond reasonable doubt that they are not all misperceptions or hoaxes.

||||||||

THE SCHIRMER INCIDENT
by William R. Forstchen, Ph.D.

Ashland, Nebraska, Policeman Herbert Schirmer, 12-3-67

A NEBRASKA STATE TROOPER, Herbert Schirmer, on duty since 5:00 P.M., reported that at 2:30 A.M., on the morning of December 3, 1967, he observed a saucerlike object hovering over the highway forty feet in front of him near Ashland, Nebraska. The object departed straight up at high speed.

The trooper, when he approached the object in his patrol car, which he estimated to be 40 feet away (later measured to be 150 feet), observed a red light flashing from windows or portholes in a saucer-shaped object. The object glowed brightly and started rising, emitting a sirenlike sound, with a flame-colored material coming from its underside. The trooper remained in his vehicle, leaning out to watch as the UFO ascended and then disappeared. The trooper immediately returned to his barracks, where he reported the incident.

He reported feeling a sense of paralysis, was sick and nervous, and also stated that he felt a sense of time distortion, that he believed the incident could not have lasted more than ten minutes, yet later checking showed that thirty minutes had elapsed. The area was checked the following morning by his superior officer, and nothing that could be substantially claimed as physical evidence was discovered.

Trooper Schirmer was described by his superior officer as reliable and truthful. At the trooper's request he underwent a polygraph test, which indicated that his description was truthful. With the trooper's approval he underwent a series of psychological-assessment tests administered at the University of Colorado, which indicated no anomalies in the trooper's personality. He also underwent a session of hypnosis, which resulted in additional information related to the belief that during the unaccounted-for twenty minutes he was bathed with a peculiar light from the UFO. There was, however, no clear evidence to back this information up, though the testing indicated a firm belief on the trooper's part in the validity of his experience. Unfortunately, without any physical evidence or significant collaborating reports from others, the case could not be considered to be conclusive.

It is interesting to note that local newspapers, commenting on the Schirmer Incident, reported that a similar sighting occurred near the same area in 1897, and was reported by a group returning from a church meeting.

ANALYSIS

The first question that should be raised regarding the Schirmer case is the argument, Why would he report it? Schirmer, twenty-two years old, was new to the force with only seven months of service. Given the nature of skeptical responses to UFO sightings, the possibility of Schirmer creating a hoax is nil. Hoaxes are usually attended with some crude attempts at creating physical evidence, but Schirmer made no claims to have seen any artifacts or to have even seen the UFO landing, nor was anything substantial recovered from the site of the incident. If Schirmer were truly a cool, pragmatic person, he might very well have never reported the incident, fearing that it could have a negative impact on his career. In the Schirmer case there was absolutely nothing to be gained, and much to be lost, by stepping forward to describe what happened.

The frustrating part of this case, of course, is that it was a lone sighting. It occurred on a fairly deserted stretch of road in western Nebraska at two-thirty in the morning. No one else later came forward to corroborate the incident. Regarding the missing twenty minutes, Schirmer, under hypnosis, later filled in the event with a number of details. Unfortunately evidence-gathering under hypnosis is suspect and can be prone to the internal creation of details that might not necessarily be true to the events that happened. The additional evidence Schirmer reported under hypnosis, that he mentally communicated with aliens who reported they were from Venus or Jupiter, that they would be back to visit him again, and that he was struck by a beam of light, might very well have happened to him. Yet, on the other side of the ledger,

Schirmer might simply have thought they happened when, in the weeks after the event, he attempted to come to terms with his experience and undoubtedly tried to force out additional memories or details.

Though the Schirmer incident stands as a fairly common encounter in the realm of UFO sightings, the key element here is that Schirmer was a young police officer who had no reason whatsoever to make the incident up, and in fact a number of logical reasons for not discussing it at all. Evaluation by his superiors indicates he was considered to be a reliable and truthful officer, so much so that his chief stated to the press he believed Schirmer's report to be true. The curious additional point is the statement in the local paper claiming that an identical sighting had happened in the same area at the end of the nineteenth century.

Was there anything Schirmer could have done differently? Under hypnosis he claimed that he had tried to make radio contact with his dispatcher but that the aliens had prevented him from doing so. In fact, short of having a camera in the car, this was about the only thing Schirmer could have done differently. It would have been helpful as well for him to have jotted some quick notes during the event or to have immediately sketched the UFO. Though the action would have required some nerve, it might have been interesting for him to have gotten out of the car and approached the object; however, he later stated under hypnosis that he had been paralyzed by the ray of light. Was he stopped or not? Not even Schirmer, most likely, knows for sure.

MAKING CONTACT:
MEDICAL IMPLICATIONS

by Mickey Zucker Reichert, M.D.

The Martians in H. G. Wells's novel *War of the Worlds*
were destroyed by earthly bacteria. Smallpox
and other diseases depopulated most of the
Mississippi Valley before the European settlers
ever arrived. Could you be facing the same fate
if you are involved in a contact with an alien?
Just how deadly is Centauri flu likely to be?

Since the days we first considered the possibility of life beyond Earth, we have wondered about the dangers inherent in contact with aliens. At first these concerns stemmed from the possibility of violence: from the visitors' hostility or carnivorous tendencies to the consequences of our own. Science fiction has also explored the medical threats, from H. G. Wells's *War of the Worlds,* in which the common cold becomes a rapid and deadly plague to the visitors, to Michael Crichton's *The Andromeda Strain,* in which a virus from space invades Earth's mankind. But what is the likelihood of spreading diseases between creatures so foreign they occupy another world? What precautions should we take if a flying saucer lands in our backyard?

To answer these questions, we need a basic understanding of contagious diseases and how they spread. All infectious diseases are caused by tiny living creatures called microbes. Scientists call the ones responsible for diseases *pathogens* because those particular microbes cause pathology (disease), and because scientists need an unpronounceable Latin word for everything. (I'll let you in on a little secret. If your doctor tells you, for example, that you have idiopathic dermatitis, it means you have a skin condition and he doesn't know what it is. Like I said, we have a Latin word for *everything*.) Regular people call pathogens *germs*.

Now, by definition all disease-causing germs are parasites, which means they lack something that allows them to live and/or reproduce independently and must therefore survive on or in a *host* (e.g., you). The vast majority die if they are exposed to air for any length of time, which is why you can't catch AIDS from a doorknob. The "smartest" (most highly evolved) germs, such as the bacteria in the human intestinal tract, have mutated to a form that is beneficial, even necessary, to the host's survival. This assures the parasite a relatively safe means of growing and reproducing. Conversely, a "stupid" germ that kills its host destroys its own means of survival, too. A germ this anti-survival evolves rarely. The disease it causes has a rapid and devastating course but is easily contained, and it ultimately self-destructs. Its effect on individuals may be great, but its effect on mankind as a species is minimal. The Ebola virus is an example of this. Most germs fall between these two extremes, causing the host discomfort while he or she spreads the germ, then leaving the host alive for future infestation (colds, strep throat, etc.).

Before turning to aliens, we must first examine the spread of germs between species on Earth. When one compares the practice of human medicine with that of veterinary medicine, there is less overlap than most would expect. Because individual germs are so short-lived, they evolve much more swiftly than higher animals. A germ colony using a dog as a host gears itself to the lifestyle of a dog and usually cannot survive on or in a human. People cannot catch feline rhinotracheitis (a cat "cold"), and cats cannot catch human rhinovirus (the source of most human "colds"). Parvoviruses cause minor symptoms in dogs but can be devastating to puppies. In humans, parvovirus almost never causes any symptoms, although it can, rarely, produce birth defects in a fetus. So, should pregnant women avoid dogs? The answer is no. There are human parvoviruses, and there are canine parvoviruses; and never the twain shall meet.

Even external parasites (fleas, lice, mites—your standard "cooties") prefer not to cross species. Dog mites cause mange and human mites scabies. Neither is passed to the opposite species. Even cat fleas, known to occasionally bite humans, will preferentially abandon a human host for a dog or a cat. The problems occur when the fleas are not controlled and become too numerous for the animal host or when the owner "throws that flea-bitten creature outside," leaving the fleas without a host. Then the fleas have nowhere to go, so they feast upon the owner. If we cannot share these common parasites with Earth creatures, who have similar evolution and common ancestors, it seems unlikely that we have anything to fear from spreading germs to or from aliens.

Now, being a scientist, I will proceed to contradict myself: Nature is rarely consistent. Although most germs are species-specific, some do cross-infect. They do this in many ways, a common one being the use of a "secondary host." Germs that operate in this manner are spread through contact with other species who harbor, but bear no or few ill effects from, the germs. The immature germs are taken from the host, are deposited into a second host or vector, mature there, then are returned to the original host. This evolutionary survival mechanism allows the germ to "hide" in the secondary host, safe from anti-infectives (antibiotics and newer antiviral agents) and the host's natural immune system. Diseases that fall into this category include malaria. Mosquitoes suck out malarial gametes (sperms and eggs) from the blood of infected humans. The malarial sexual cycle occurs in the mosquito, then sporozoites (baby malaria) from mosquito saliva are injected into other humans.

This particular mode of transmission of germs from humans to space aliens or the reverse seems implausible to the point of impossibility. An arrangement of this sort would require years of parallel evolution between two species with high survivability. The continuation of malaria as a disease hinges not only on humans' survival but on mosquitoes' as well. If either link in the cycle was broken, malaria would have to adapt swiftly or, more likely, cease to exist. Until the aliens lived among us, or us among them, for many generations, no evolutionary system could possibly exist for aliens and humans to share a germ's life cycle.

Germs that are shared by different Earth species include rabies, kuru, tularemia, typhus, Rocky Mountain spotted fever, Q fever, yellow fever, and some others. None of these is a particularly common illness, although there have been one or two notable exceptions through history (e.g., the plague). Many species are susceptible to rabies, which is usually acquired through a bite wound or from infected transplanted nerve tissue (e.g., corneal transplant). Kuru can only be acquired from a transplant of nerve tissue or the ingestion of undercooked simian or human brains (cannibalism). Humans acquire tularemia by prolonged contact with rabbits, hares, and muskrats, such as occurs after skinning, intensive handling, or eating undercooked meat. Though less common, ticks can also spread the infection. Some forms of typhus and Rocky Mountain spotted fever are spread from rodents to humans by ticks, mites, and fleas. Q fever is spread by prolonged contact with livestock, such as occurs in slaughterhouses and wool-processing plants. Rarely, cows can carry a chronic infection in the udder and transfer it in their milk. Mosquitoes spread yellow fever between monkeys and humans.

Most germs shared between species depend on prolonged contact with intimate body fluids (blood, feces, semen, milk, neurological tissue, or injected saliva). Presumably, a first contact with other intelligent life-forms would not result in biting, violence, sex, transplantation, or exchange of excreta. If it did, death from the violence itself would seem a far more pressing issue. Vector-borne infections, meaning those passed by mosquitoes, ticks, mites, lice, and fleas, could pose more of a threat assuming that beings from other planets, solar systems, or galaxies share even as much of our biology as Earth rodents do. Protecting ourselves from these infections would mean warding off the vectors (such as with bug repellent), not the aliens.

Which brings us to the building blocks of life and the effects of evolution. It is an easily proven fact that life on Earth is composed of the same basic elements: cells. The only currently known exceptions are viral particles, which contain only cell components but therefore exist only as parasites (they require a host to survive). Without host cells, viral particles could not replicate and would soon become extinct. To date, no scientific evidence of life has been found beyond our Earth. We have discovered nothing to indicate, or to disprove, that life can exist based on building blocks different from our own.

Science fiction writers, like but not including myself, have suggested the possibility of life-forms based on an element other than carbon. Because of carbon's location on the periodic table, speculation has turned toward silicon. This theory is based on the basic-chemistry observation that elements in the same column (also called family) of the periodic table share certain physical and chemical properties in common. It should be noted that, using this assumption, lead-based life-forms might also exist. However, the silicon theory ignores a more significant basic-chemistry observation, namely that the first member of each family on the periodic table exhibits marked differences from subsequent members of the family because of smaller size and, subsequently, greater electro-negativity (stability). Carbon is one of the strongest examples. It is the first element of its family, silicon the second. The differences between carbon and silicon are too immense to discuss in the context of this single article; but ultimately, silicon's bonding is comparatively unstable. The cells of a life-form based on silicon would constantly break apart and thus die.

It seems far more likely that noncarbon-based life-forms, if they exist, would be based on the more inert elements, the first in each family. If we discard the possibility of gaseous life-forms (I personally find it difficult to imagine an intelligent life-form that takes the shape of its container), we're left with lithium, beryllium, and boron. Regardless of the elemental composition, it seems astronomically unlikely that any germ inflicting an alien with an entirely different chemical structure would prove capable of adapting to us. Remember, even germs that evolved with us rarely infect more than one species with our same composition. Beryllium is toxic, but it seems doubtful that an organism composed of it would exude solid beryllium any more than we exude graphite or diamonds. Although we do exhale carbon dioxide, the differences in what we and beings with a different elemental composition breathe would force a meeting in an environment toxic to one, the other, or both. If noncarbon-based aliens came to your backyard, they would require specialized respiratory gear (space suits), and we would not have to worry about what they inhaled or exhaled. And if they wore protective suits for breathing reasons, an exchange of dangerous germs seems nearly impossible as well.

Some early science fiction writers postulated the possibility of aliens regularly using a radioactive chemical or a toxin, or of these things being a natural part of their skin. The former seems nonsensical. Radioactive substances are dangerous not only to carbon-based organisms but to other materials as well. The vast majority of other toxins would require ingestion or injection into the bloodstream. Again, this would require either a monumental act of personal stupidity or violence on the part of the aliens. Our few known contact poisons are manufactured or refined. The odds against something they use casually, or their skin itself, being a deadly contact poison are tremendous. Even if this was the case, it seems obvious that touching an unknown creature is a silly thing to do.

Ironically the more akin an alien's biology is to ours, the more threat we pose to one another in the form of infectious diseases and germs, just as we share many more illnesses with apes and monkeys than with pigs. I have touched upon the reasons for this earlier. Like all living things, germs change to suit their environment; in the case of parasites, to suit their host. Because evolution is rarely haphazard, over time they tend toward specialization. It is far simpler and more logical for a given germ to adapt to one host than to many. The changes required for a parasite to use mankind and apes as hosts are clearly fewer than those required to use mankind and octopi.

The likelihood that intelligent life from other parts of the universe share physical or biological characteristics with us is high. Whether or not other elements can result in life, carbon certainly can. Though we still have much to learn about the universe, it seems clear that nature has some consistency to it. It is very unlikely that we were the single exception. Similar heavenly bodies are composed of similar chemicals, and all life-forms on Earth are made up of the same building blocks. It is probable that at least some other life in the universe is also composed of the same basic elements as life on Earth.

Just as likely, life on alien worlds little resembles us in physical appearance. The diversity of life on Earth alone is remarkable. Higher species reproduce sexually, meaning they combine genetic material from both parents in some fashion, because this allows for greater genetic diversity and strength for the species as a whole. When divided by a geographic barrier (such as an impassable mountain range or an ocean), species that reproduce in a sexual fashion undergo divergent evolution (they change in separate ways). Eventually, they become physiologically or behaviorally so different, they can no longer interbreed and another species is born. Throughout the history of the Earth, this has happened multiple times. Extrapolating, if Earth humans were placed on another planet and separated from Earth for hundreds of thousands of years, we should expect them to evolve so differently from those who remained behind, they could no longer interbreed with them. To expect a population with a completely parallel evolution and history to appear and to function biologically like ours is an absurdity. For their germs and ours to overlap is equally doubtful.

Which brings us to another salient point, though clearly off the topic. A huge contingent of people who claim to have been abducted by aliens suggest interbreeding as the reason. While this is an interesting (if somewhat warped) sexual fantasy, the likelihood of creatures from another planet, solar system, or galaxy being capable of breeding with humans is no better than the chances of you walking outside your home tomorrow morning and getting eaten by a *Tyrannosaurus rex.*

And speaking of precautions, which we weren't, let's look at history. The Soviets were heavily criticized for taking no microbial precautions on their first lunar landing. These seemed unnecessary given the hostilities of outer space. Scientists were later able to demonstrate that some spores can survive radiation, high temperatures, pressure, and vacuum. Consequently, the United States steam-cleaned *Viking* with temperatures in excess of 212 degrees Fahrenheit prior to the first Martian landing. While this sterilized the body of the rocket, it still left germs inside the enclosed areas of the ship.

The concern in this regard has not been for exposures our astronauts might receive or bring back to Earth but for germs left to breed in foreign places, thus endangering indigenous life or future missions of our own. After the United States' first lunar landing, the astronauts were kept in isolation for quite some time, as much to allay fears about "moon germs" as for any real concern about their safety. In truth, precautions of either type seem mostly unwarranted. Scientists, by training and thought, consider nothing impossible. However, the likelihood of a human germ existing where no human can is as remote as tossing a thousand pieces of a puzzle into the air and having them randomly land in their proper sequence. Possible, but only in the remotest sense of the word. Using current technology, ships can be sterilized but humans cannot. No matter how carefully we clean our tools, whatever humans contact they contaminate. Luckily, germs, being parasites, cannot exist without a host. So long as the humans return, the only organisms they can leave behind alive are harmless self-supporting ones. Without water and/or air, even these are desperately unlikely to survive. Sterilization procedures, while a good idea, are probably an unnecessary expense.

Now that we have explored the basics of microbiology, and history, we can finally conjecture about the precautions for a first-contact situation. Taken strictly on a medical basis, argument could be made for isolation of the visiting species and observation for changes in health during that time. Taking cultures of bodily fluids, as well as examination of the natural microbial flora and fauna of skin and gastrointestinal systems, would be ideal. Studying these germs would give us a much better idea of their infectivity and threat to us than the dissection that seems to form the threat of nearly every sci-fi movie based on alien contact, including *E.T.* and *Starman*. Surely, even the most devout biologist could see the greater value in interacting with a foreign species, especially an intelligent one, than in destroying it.

A species intelligent enough to travel through space would also certainly have at least as strong a command of its own body systems, germs, and diseases as we do of ours. They would have more information about these things than we could possibly discover by means of a few days or even years of isolation and examination. They would know, or at least have the technology to discover, whether or not one or more among them was ill. We could do the same for our people. Certainly, it would make sense for us to determine if our contact people were free of contagious diseases prior to the exchange, whether physical, inhalational, or simply verbal.

In a first-contact situation, cultural concerns would surely take priority over medical ones. Avoiding insult would seem prudent, and requesting isolation, decontamination, or submission for study could be considered offensive to them as well as to us. If we start an interstellar war, trading common illnesses would become the least of our worries. We should wear protective clothing, such as we might use in the room of a human with a contagious illness: Masks, gloves, gowns, and good hand washing seem appropriate and sufficient protection, assuming the environment of the contact does not necessitate additional gear simply for human survival. Once a full exchange of scientific and biological information occurs, those standard precautions could be abandoned as well—contingent upon the findings, of course.

In conclusion, it seems highly unlikely that visitors from other parts of the universe could exchange diseases with humans or animals of Earth. Using ambassadors free of contagious illnesses and the knowledge of the aliens about their own pathology and biology, we should be able to avoid passing disease to one another, even should such germs exist. Simple measures for containment of disease, such as those used in patient rooms today, should suffice until the information exchange occurs.

IIIIIIII

THE SOCORRO INCIDENT
by William R. Forstchen, Ph.D.

THIS IS YET ANOTHER incident involving a lone police officer, similar in some ways to the Schirmer Incident; however, here there were two backup witnesses.

On the afternoon of April 24, 1964, Officer Lon Zamora, a patrolman from Socorro, New Mexico, was chasing a speeding driver south of town when he noticed a descending "object" emitting flames settling to the ground. The object was several miles away and he turned to approach it. He lost sight of the object due to some intervening hills until he finally turned a corner on the road and was startled to find that he was almost on top of it. The object was in a gully by the side of the road, was egg-shaped, resting on legs that protruded from the bottom of the craft. Stopping his vehicle, he got out, at which point loud noises erupted from within the craft. Zamora sought shelter as the craft lifted off, ascended straight up, then darted off in a flat trajectory and quickly disappeared. Almost immediately after the vehicle departed, Sergeant Chavez, whom Zamora had called by radio while still approaching the craft, arrived. Zamora and Chavez examined the site where the craft had landed and both later reported that there were imprint marks and that a number of greasewood bushes were burning. A later investigation turned up an unidentified witness who came into the gas station in town and reported seeing a strange craft crossing the sky. The witness had also stated that he saw Zamora's vehicle approaching the downed craft.

ANALYSIS

This is yet again one of those troubling reports where we have a very reliable witness yet no real backup. The unidentified witness is a hearsay report; the only other corroboration is from Sergeant Chavez. Chavez stated that Zamora was a very reliable officer and not one who would ever have considered creating a hoax. Chavez also stated that when he first arrived on the scene, Zamora appeared deeply shaken and that together they examined the circular area of scorch marks and flaming bushes. Between the time Zamora called in with a report as to what he was seeing and Chavez's arrival, it would not have been possible for Zamora to have created the imprints himself nor to set out a precise circular pattern of scorch marks and flames. Furthermore, there were no human footprints anywhere near the landing site prior to the police officers' investigation.

There is little that Zamora could have done differently. He called for backup, he got out of his vehicle with the intention of approaching, then backed away as the vehicle lifted off. As in the Schirmer case, there was nothing to be gained by Zamora reporting such an incident, and everything to lose.

MODERN BIOLOGY
AND EXTRATERRESTRIALS

What will an alien look like? It is remarkable to
many people that almost all extraterrestrials
observed in connection with UFOs are
two-legged and generally resemble humans.
Here we see why that actually isn't so
remarkable. This article is a summary of a
detailed and scholarly presentation made to
the 1991 Mutual UFO Network [MUFON] Symposium.
It has been rewritten and presented here in
much simplified form with the kind permission
of the original author.

REVIEW OF BEGINNING CONCEPTS

An earlier article sketched out what we might expect an extraterrestrial
(ET) to look like. This article will further fill in that picture. I will
quickly summarize the starting points based upon frontier biology:

> • **Nature is uniform.** The physical and chemical processes at
> work in our solar system are at work in every solar system.
> • **The chemistry of life is everywhere the same.** Not only are the
> critical elements of life available in equal proportion everywhere,
> but the very amino acids and basic molecules of life may be found
> everywhere from gas clouds and planet cores to meteorites and
> comets.
> • **The forces that assemble proteins and DNA are everywhere
> available.** Volcanic heat, lightning, and ultraviolet radiation, which
> assembled our physical makeup, are commonplace on nascent
> earths.

• **The environments that produce life are very Earth-like.** We could likely walk, swim, and breathe on any world that would produce life. Other earths would have masses between one-half and two-and-a-half times that of Earth.

• **The same chemicals, acted upon by the same forces in similar environments will produce similar results.** The limited numbers of life-forming molecules create only limited numbers of larger molecules, the same ones that built our single-celled organisms, and all life on Earth.

The obvious question is, How similar? Some theorists, including myself, believe the results of such processes would be very similar in terms of large-scale biological design. Others claim that the products of other planets would be utterly different from anything we know on Earth.

Before I argue my position, let me address the alternative.

UTTERLY ALIEN ALIENS

Carl Sagan has said that humans will have more in common with petunias than with extraterrestrials. Other great thinkers, such as George Gaylord Simpson and Stephen Gould, have concurred. They believe in a Darwinian model of evolutionary change.

In this view, evolution is a totally random process, with no "guiding force." Thus, in a galaxy of tremendous diversity, with a biology of totally random change, any one form of creature is as likely as any other. There is, consequently, no chance that any two life-forms from different planets would look similar.

To put it bluntly, anyone who has seen little green men is a liar or a lunatic.

These are quite conclusive pronouncements. What do they arise from? Evidence? Argument? Experiment? Unfortunately, no. Sometimes a great thinker's own philosophy prevents him or her from even thinking about an issue. A philosophical bias can short-circuit scientific exploration, stopping it before it even gets started. That's just what happened with Sagan, Simpson, and Gould.

Each of these eminent thinkers had made up his mind about ET morphology before even weighing the evidence. The issue was, to them, a nonissue. They voluntarily stopped thinking, not because absolute diversity had been proven to them but because absolute diversity was mandated by their belief system.

How could such dogma have found its way into science?

Easily. Materialism is one of the fundamental tenets of Darwinian evolutionary science. The notion that evolution is absolute, undirected by any higher force, absolutely free and open-ended in its products, is not merely a matter of philosophy in Darwinian science but of actual methodology. The field's rituals of schooling and rites of passage program students with the dogma of random change. There can be no design or purpose in the universe. A thinker who has already accepted such a statement, whether consciously or not, cannot even imagine that ETs would show any similarity to humans.

In a way, it is an honest mistake, and therefore a forgivable one. Sagan, Simpson, and Gould have, after all, earned a little leeway.

Less forgivably, there are scientists with a practical bias against the idea that ETs might have humanlike forms. In the world of research, where government and philanthropic grants are the lifeblood of projects, a disdainful jab at competing projects can bring the money pouring in one's own direction. Public mockery can be profitable. Unfortunately, it can also squelch open-minded discussion and drag less-informed minds down with it.

Less-informed minds need no encouragement. The pedestrian observer often has his or her own ill-founded reasons to disdain human-looking ETs. Some are influenced not by Darwin but by Hollywood. It is much more appealing to think of completely alien aliens—like the shape-changing creatures you'd see in a big-budget F/X blockbuster—than of B-movie guys in rubber suits. The less human an alien looks, therefore, the more believable it is. The old aliens are just out of fashion. A similar bias comes from those interested in paranormal powers, mysterious nonmaterial creatures, extradimensional entities, and so forth. To such folk, "mundane" ETs, with structures similar to ours, are dull.

Science at its best rises above questions of fashion, fiction, and bias. We've given the naysayers their say. Now let's consider what similarities we might expect to see.

BEGINNING ARGUMENTS
FOR STRUCTURAL SIMILARITIES

What can be said to cut through such deep biases? Is it enough to point out that the emerging fields of biophysics and biomechanics have yet to rule conclusively on the basic polymers of life and the processes of evolutionary change? Would it be enough to say that the preliminary findings of such fields indicate that physics plays a powerful role in making structures turn out in limited varieties? Perhaps thousands of examples of convergent evolution might turn the tide.

Despite the dogma, evolution does not produce every possible form. Its products are limited to what works.

Perhaps a couple of intuitive analogies would help.

There are only so many ways to join Tinkertoys. The sticks don't connect to other sticks, only to wheels, and vice versa. The sticks and wheels connect like spokes or axles. There are a limited number of basic constructs: the lollypop, the microphone, the microphone with stand, the barbells, the spectacles, the spokes. Then come combinations built of those basic forms: the various triangles, quadrilaterals, pentagons, hexagons, septagons, octagons, and so forth. Next come combinations built from those secondary forms: the trihedron, the cube, and the other regular solids. Anything built from Tinkertoys will, therefore, be built of combinations of these basic forms.

At this point, some would say that despite a limited set of basic Tinkertoy structures, the possible combinations of this basic alphabet are limitless. Anything at all can be built of Tinkertoys. You could build a full-scale Sears Tower.

The reply is, "Not on Earth, you couldn't." The strength of the sticks and the friction bonds between sticks and wheels make a full-scale Tinkertoy Sears Tower impossible on Earth. It would collapse under its own weight, be dismantled by winds, sway and snap, separate, and burn away when struck by lightning. In other words, the physical forces at work on Earth make a full-scale Tinkertoy Sears Tower, and many other Tinkertoy structures, impossible.

Besides, we're not talking about possibility; we're talking about practicality. Biology doesn't create weird beasts just because it can. It creates them because they function well in their environment. So, too, the Tinkertoy structures we build need to function well, need to be capable of certain things. They need to be durable. They need to be mobile. They need to be repairable, reproducible, and adaptable. They need to be able to steal Tinkertoy parts from other, less well-constructed Tinkertoy structures, and to prevent others from stealing parts from them. In other words, they need to be competitive. Given all these restrictions, our hypothesized full-scale Tinkertoy Sears Tower now seems not only impossible but laughably impracticable.

Our Tinkertoy analogy is breaking down under these macroscopic design considerations. Let's shift gears, literally, to another analogy that will make large-scale limitations clear.

MIT conducts a famous contest in mechanical design: Student teams are given identical piles of junk and are instructed to design and build a machine that performs a certain task (usually gathering Ping-Pong balls from a tabletop). Once the machines are built, they compete in an elimination tournament to determine the best model.

Though many, many different designs are created, the machines all look surprisingly similar: They use the same starting materials in the same quantities, they must operate in the same environment (a tabletop), and they will attempt to perform the same task. Despite hundreds of entrant teams, each working separately and even secretively, the same dozen designs keep appearing. Of those dozen only a handful prove competitive, and the rest are quickly extinct.

Some things work. Others do not.

Interestingly, some of the most successful designs are constructed not simply to gather Ping-Pong balls but also to debilitate other machines trying to gather them. These designs are predators. Some predatory designs work poorly, and they are eliminated. But those that do work well dominate, and they, like the nonpredators, exemplify a very few successful strategies and structures. A clear and natural dominance chain is established, in which more able models rise to the top.

Imagine, now, if some machines could not only debilitate other machines but dismantle them, taking spare parts for their own use. They would be extraordinarily adaptive, "devouring" the competition and becoming stronger in the process.

In creating a contest to teach mechanical design, MIT has devised an exact paradigm for biological design and competition. The continual conclusion, from both arenas of study, is that, given certain parameters, only a few designs are competitive, and they will be evolved separately many, many times over.

Similarly, biology, which begins from the same "pile of junk" (which can only be joined in certain ways, like our Tinkertoys) and must perform the same task in the same environment, will produce a limited number of successful designs.

Aficionados of science fiction like to point out that things could evolve from different "piles of junk"—that is, be built from sulfur or silicon (methane, ammonia, etc.) instead of carbon. Returning to the MIT analogy, if the machines were built to run on gasoline or even nuclear fission instead of electricity, the products would be very different from those built currently by the students.

True enough. But it is hard to imagine a gasoline engine functioning very well at gathering Ping-Pong balls from a tabletop. Gasoline power is overkill for that task and that environment—as well as being expensive and stinky. In other words, gasoline engines are inefficient. And if gasoline is Ping-Pong ball overkill, imagine nuclear fission!

Similarly, energy calculations that have been made on alternate metabolisms of sulfur, silicon, and their ilk are not encouraging. Such creatures' energy systems would be inefficient, underproducing power (unlike gasoline and fission systems). Therefore such creatures would be sluglike poor cousins to waterbag creatures such as us, and once we arrived on the scene, they'd become museum pieces.

Most, if not all, ET life-forms would share an extremely similar biochemistry to us, with water as its solvent. To put it perversely, if we met creatures from space, we could probably eat them, and they eat us, much like the predatory MIT machines. Microscopically speaking, we have interchangeable parts.

In conclusion, creatures that evolve from the same materials (identical piles of junk), use the same metabolism (electricity), and compete for the same resources (Ping-Pong balls) in the same environment (tabletop) will eventually exhibit only those few structures and behaviors that work.

Put simply, ETs will look very much like us.

LOOKS CAN BE DECEIVING

Though ETs will look similar to us, and we could probably eat them, we absolutely could not produce offspring with them. We are not genetically compatible. We could not interbreed. We are not their children.

To state this in terms of popular culture, even if there are Sareks (Vulcans), there could never be Spocks (human-Vulcan hybrids).

Why the sudden pessimism?

Like it or not, biology mandates it.

Even if sex were manageable with an extraterrestrial (a none-too-pleasant prospect), the combination of sex cells into a zygote would be impossible. A human sperm and egg each carry twenty-three chromosomes, half of the human complement of forty-six. These twenty-three chromosomes aren't just floating around; they are stitched together in a line, like half of a zipper. Each nub of the zipper has a specific meaning, and the nubs have to line up exactly to be able to connect. When the male half and the female half zip together, a new human is designed.

Here's where the problem comes in. An ET would have to have

exactly the same DNA code words that we do (even on Earth there's a little variability) and have them stitched together in exactly the same order as our own. The odds against that coincidence are astronomical. Even here on Earth our closest genetic cousins, chimpanzees, have incompatible DNA stacks. About the nearest cross-species match is the horse and donkey, and the offspring of such a combination (a mule) is, itself, sterile.

The odds of an independently evolved ET having identical genetic strings are nil.

Some who feel they must defend the notion of human-alien hybridization say that through biological supertechnology, ETs could make even incompatible genetic stacks compatible. The problem with such arguments is that if ETs could so easily shuffle and stack the DNA deck, they would have no reason to crudely harvest human eggs and sperm—or any genetic material, for that matter. Such supergeneticists and molecular architects could make whatever they wanted from scratch right in the lab, rather than traveling hundreds of light-years in hopes of bringing back a few live cells.

Another attempted rebuttal of human-alien incompatibility is that ETs might not have been independently evolved. Perhaps we came from the same stock as they, our space brothers and sisters—or perhaps we are even their children?

Such rationalizations don't hold up. Our genes are 99 percent identical to those of chimps and gorillas. If we are the brothers or children of ETs, so are the great apes. Well, maybe they are, too. It would be pretty arrogant to think we are the only intelligent life-forms worth depositing on Earth. But the great apes share 99 percent of their material with gibbons, and they share with monkeys, and they with lemurs . . . with tarsiers . . . tree shrews . . . rodents . . . In the end, all creatures in the tree of Earth's life are connected by such stepwise graduations. If ETs deposited humans here, they deposited every last microbe. If so, this was the most patient project ever undertaken: four billion years of gradual forced biological development for the purpose of re-creating their own genetic codes so that they could abduct us and interbreed. The motives and means behind so extensive a project beggar the imagination.

The bottom line is that biology mandates that we aren't compatible with ETs and that they aren't interbreeding with us.

Does this mean that anyone who reports an abduction experience in which genetic materials are harvested is lying? Absolutely not. Just because hybrids are impossible doesn't mean ETs would have no reason to collect genetic samples. Human zoologists take tissue samples of, say, alligators, not to produce alligator-men; they just want to look at alligator tissue.

But enough nay-saying. The point is made.

THE MACRO STRUCTURE OF ETI

Having given time to the detractors and done a bit of detracting ourselves, let's stop talking about what intelligent ETs would not be and start talking about what they would be. A list of attributes from my previous article will start things off nicely.

According to previous arguments, we could reasonably expect intelligent extraterrestrials to

- Belong to the animal kingdom
- Dwell on land
- Be relatively large in size
- Have a tube-shaped, one-way digestive tract
- Have a two-way gas-exchange system
- Have a head with a mouth and major sense organs
- Have a large brain, protected by a skull
- Have an internal skeleton
- Have eyes and ears
- Have four limbs, two of which are manipulative appendages

One caveat applies: Such structures will be apparent only in ETs that have resulted from evolution. Obviously, if an ET results from genetic engineering, all bets are off as to the type and position of physical structures. On the other hand, it should be noted that many of the wilder creatures we have created through genetic engineering—fruit flies with legs where their eyes should be and three additional sets of wings—are absolutely maladaptive. Venturing too far afield from the valuable lessons of evolution does not produce superbeings but freakish monstrosities that will not survive. The reason such creatures do not exist in nature is simply that they cannot.

With that caveat in mind, let's get more specific about expected structures, considering both similarities to and differences from our own physical makeup. Neither of the following lists is complete.

Similarities:

- The head end would contain a food-intake orifice, two light sensors, a secondary air intake, odor sensors, and bilateral sound sensors, all in close proximity to the brain.
- The major sensory structures would be above the mouth so as not to hinder sensory processing while feeding.
- The auxiliary air intake would be close to the mouth so that one tube could serve both systems and so that food could be checked before eating (the olfactory sense is crucial for finding food and determining its edibility).
- The light sensors would be positioned forward and would be focusable.
- The sound sensors would be positioned laterally.
- A branching system of scaled tubes would use pumped water to bear nutrients from the food-processing system to the cells and would use a separate set of tubes to bring wastes from the cells back to the system.
- A large torso would contain the food-processing system and other maintenance organs.
- The internal skeleton would be strong, flexible, mobile, and positioned in a generally upright posture, to allow freedom to manually dexterous appendages.
- There would be two genders.

Differences:

- The sizes and shapes of various body parts would vary (e.g., bone length; body height; stockiness; size and shape of facial features, head, torso, and limbs).
- Pigmentations and textures of eyes, skin, horns, hair, nails, hooves, and so forth would reflect radiation conditions and body-part functions.
- Mouth parts—teeth, mandibles, bony plates, beaks, grinders, and so forth—would relate to diet.
- The number of digits on fore appendages would likely be between three and five, and those on hind appendages would vary more greatly down to none.
- The number of small bones, joints, and muscles would vary, along with joint angles, but there would be limited variability in the number of major joints and levering designs.

• Reproductive organs would differ in shape and size, though they would remain on the torso. Species might show a wide range of sexual dimorphism (outward differences between genders), from none to marked levels.

• Internal organs would vary in structure and placement according to the requirements of diet, gas exchange, and so forth.

What is the logic behind this particular list of similarities and differences? The logic is, in fact, bio-logic. As we have established in this paper and the last, extraterrestrial life will evolve most often (if not always) on Earth-like worlds orbiting Sun-like stars. Given that the evolutionary history of Earth represents billions of test cases, the creatures we see all around us every day (as well as we ourselves among them) are quintessential examples of what works on an Earth-like world. The preceding lists are most quickly and easily derived from taking inventory of our own planet's advanced life-forms. The first list tells the sorts of things that are consistent, species to species, and the second tells the sorts of things that aren't.

Each of the successful designs we see among Earth's fauna has a long, obviously nonrandom history. The general influences of physics as well as specific influences such as diet, habitat, and local competition are written all over the bodies of these creatures. There is nothing random about their design.

For some thinkers, such simple observations are enough. Do you want to see what extraterrestrial life will look like? Go to the zoo. Do you want to see what intelligent extraterrestrial life will look like? Go to the mirror.

There is much more that could be said to establish the likelihood of these similarities and differences between our own physiology and that of extraterrestrials—certainly much more than I have room to say here.

For the sake of illustration, let me present a brief case for the often-criticized characteristic of bilateral symmetry. Why would ETs be likely to have any symmetry at all? And if they did, why not radial symmetry?

Symmetry, like all other aspects of animal physiology, is subject to the effects of environment. The simplest animal forms, single-celled organisms, have complete symmetry—they are spheres. However you cut them in half, the halves are the same. When life becomes multicellular, specific cells gain specific tasks, and the sphere becomes a tube—a digestive tract. One direction of symmetry is lost. When that tube begins to seek food, moving forward, more symmetry is broken. It gains a front and a back, a mouth and an anus. Once the creature is large enough to be affected by gravity, another symmetry goes. Now our critter has a top and a bottom.

All that is left is bilateral symmetry.

Such beasties—the predatory worms in their earliest incarnations on our planet—did away with many other unfit flourishes of evolution. It was from them that all bilaterally symmetrical creatures, from caterpillars to carpenters, inherited their symmetry.

It is hard to imagine an Earth-like world where these processes would not lead to similar creatures.

Whether on sea or land, as animals become larger, quicker, and brainier, the head end must develop elaborately. The mouth defines this end, so it is already here. Anything needed to make sure the mouth gets plenty of food and the right kind of food needs to be here as well. Eyes are of utmost importance. The inevitable development of eyes in any environment with light is assured. Light conveys more detailed information over long distances than any other medium.

Why two eyes? That's a reasonable enough query. Let's consider this particular case.

WHERE'D YOU GET THOSE PEEPERS?

The reason for two eyes begins with bilateral symmetry. This final symmetry is valuable to keep. It provides the animal with focus and stability and makes forward movement possible. Imagine a fish with more fins on one side than the other. Imagine a turtle with three legs on one side and two on the other. Such creatures would be lucky if they ever went straight. For that matter, a predator that maintains a level body orientation can focus on its prey better than a creature that must roll over and over about an axis.

Furthermore, by maintaining bilateral symmetry, a creature can conserve genetic code—"the right side is the same as the left, only reversed." It's the old two-for-the-price-of-one situation. As long as you've genetically purchased one eye, you can get the second for free. So, too, other features such as arms and legs and nostrils come in twos.

Why not four or six? This discussion appeared in greater depth in the former article. The main reason is a balance of costs. Every additional feature requires an extra commitment of genes, brains, and nutrients and is a potential site of injury or illness. If the third eye does not provide a sufficient benefit to make these costs worthwhile, it will not exist. For nature, too many of a good thing is in fact too many.

Whatever the reason, on Earth, evolution decided very early that one eye wasn't enough and three was too many, and it's been that way ever since.

Now that we've settled on two eyes, let's decide where they go, relative to the mouth. Because the mouth is the beginning of the digestive tube, it will lie across the central line of the creature. The eyes will align symmetrically somewhere. But where? As far as evolution on Earth is concerned, the eyes are above the mouth, every time. Why? Let's consider what it would be like to have your eyes below your mouth:

• You're a herbivore chewing on a stalk of grass. Too bad you can't see that carnivore coming up ahead of you.

• You're a carnivore chomping on a herbivore that didn't see you coming. It decides to claw, and scratches your eyes out.

• You're a carnivore chewing on a herbivore. Juicy. The stuff is running down your chin and into your eyes.

• You're a mud-grubbing fish. How nice to have your eyes scraping the ground as you swim.

You get the idea. There are many other reasons why the eyes belong above the mouth of the food tunnel. What about eyes to the sides of the mouth? It's possible, though it rules out binocular vision and therefore makes for a pretty poor predator.

THE FACE, AND CONCLUSIONS ABOUT ET APPEARANCE

Now that we have a creature with a centered mouth and nose, eyes above them and forward, ears high and lateral, a skull-protected brain, and a pivoting neck, we have a face—the face that nature has given to all of Earth's advanced creatures. Is this really just a fluke of our planet? In my opinion, not a chance. Nature has had tens of millions of years to develop better or equal designs, but hasn't done so. Nature has made all manner of drastic structural changes in animals (remember that whales and dolphins once walked the Earth as land mammals), but did not change this face.

Regardless of the stature of the dissenters and the unfashionability of this view, two facts remain undeniable:

- The contrary theorists have no evidence for their view.
- The convergent theorists have an entire world for theirs.

When biology, biophysics, and biomechanics are brought to the discussion of ETI physiology—as well as the evidence of historical and convergent evolution—one cannot help concluding that ETs would share many structural similarities with humans. More than that, the similarities and differences we have predicted are precisely those reported by many who claim to have had sightings of ETs.

That singular fact behooves any reasonable, thinking person—let alone any scientist—to take such reports seriously and accord them the same level of open-minded critical attention given to any other eyewitness account of any other extraordinary event.

IIIIIII

THE CISCO GROVE INCIDENT
by William R. Forstchen, Ph.D.

September 6, 1964

THE CISCO GROVE INCIDENT has a rather strange quality to it that at times almost borders on the comic or absurd . . . as long as you were not Mr. S——, who experienced it.

Mr. S——, on September 6, 1964, went bow-hunting with two friends in Cisco Grove, California, which is a mountainous region a couple of hours west of Sacramento, up toward Lake Tahoe. As evening approached, Mr. S—— attempted to rendezvous with his friends only to realize he had wandered farther from their base camp than planned. Accepting the fact that he'd have to wait till dawn to get back, he prepared to spend the night out alone. Approximately two hours after dark he noticed a bright hovering light, which "looked just like a flashlight, or a lantern, at first, bobbing up and down, and I thought maybe it's a helicopter from a ranger station." The light was moving along the next ridge line.

He then lit three fires (a standard distress signal) to draw attention to himself. The light closed in and stopped, hovering approximately fifty to sixty yards away. Mr. S—— stated later, "That's what scared me, I didn't hear any noise at all." He couldn't see anything behind the light and at first he thought it was some sort of tiny object. The thought that it might be a flying saucer finally settled in and he fled, climbing a tree where he hoped he might not be noticed.

The light made a broad, sweeping turn around Mr. S——, moving over to a nearby canyon. In the moonlight Mr. S—— was finally able to discern the size and shape of the object. "Then it really scared me," he said. He saw something emerge from the ship and drop to the ground. A short time later he heard something moving through the bushes below. Mr. S—— stated that a humanoid-looking individual appeared, approximately five feet six inches tall, dressed in a "silver or whitish-looking uniform. . . . It seemed to have a helmet or hood. . . . Its face was dark."

Moments later it was joined by a companion, and the two approached the tree he was sitting in, stopped at the base, and looked up at him. He stated he could hear a "cooing" or "hooting" type sound and similar sounds coming from the ship.

A third creature appeared on the scene, and Mr. S—— described this one as looking like a robot, with a hinged jaw. Now starts the truly bizarre part of this event. The two humanoids attempted to climb the tree, which was devoid of branches for the first twelve feet. At one point one of them attempted to boost the other one up. The robot then opened its mouth and a white gas came out. Mr. S—— reported that he then passed out, but did not fall out of the tree because he fell across his bow. He awoke after what he thought was several minutes and finally scrambled farther up the tree and hooked himself to the trunk with his belt. He then fired the three arrows in his possession at the robot. The arrows struck the robot's chest and skidded off in a shower of sparks. Mr. S—— later stated that he did not fire at the humanoids because they were not directly attacking him, whereas he felt that the robot was.

The siege was now under way. There were repeated attempts at gassing him, and Mr. S—— responded by lighting a pack of matches and throwing it down. The creatures drew back. Hoping that the fire would scare them away, he started to tear off articles of clothing, set them on fire, and fling them down until finally all he had left were his pants, boots, and T-shirt. In desperation he even flung his bow at them.

A second robot appeared, and shortly before dawn a final attempt was made to bring him down, with both robots pouring out a stream of gas, which flooded the area. He passed out, and when he finally awoke, they were gone. Climbing out of the tree, he retrieved his bow and arrows, then made his way back to the base camp.

Mr. S—— did not seek any attention or report the incident. It finally started to gain notice when a family member contacted a former professor at a nearby college, who in turn contacted the air force. A captain from the air force interviewed Mr. S—— and took one of the arrows so that the head could be examined for metal filings. Later statements from the air force suggested that Mr. S—— might have suffered from hallucinations, then suggested that military maneuvers might have been going on in the area, or that he had been tormented by teenage pranksters dressed up as aliens, or even stranger, that he was attacked by "Japanese."

Mr. S—— later returned to the site of the incident and reported that it had been "swept clean," except for a few cigarette and cigar butts.

ANALYSIS

This is most certainly one of the more bizarre cases, with aliens fumbling to get up a tree, robots emitting gases, and a beleaguered man strapped to the top of a tree, retaliating by burning his clothes and shooting arrows.

Yet it should be noted that one of his companions also reported seeing lights while back at the base camp. It's also interesting that Mr. S—— did not seek to file a report—public attention only came when the story eventually filtered out through family members to a professor, and from there to authorities in the air force. The hypotheses put forward by the air force go beyond the simply bizarre into the absurd. Later checking showed that there were no maneuvers going on in the area, and if indeed military personnel had played a role in this, it certainly would have been a rather sadistic act on their part. Regarding the teenagers, Mr. S—— points out that the area where the incident occurred was remote, so it would have been more than unlikely that a group of kids would go hiking deep into the mountains dressed as aliens with the intent of waylaying and frightening a lone hunter (not to mention the fact that hunters tend to be armed). Even stranger is the notion that the "Japanese" could have done it. This relates to rumors of Japanese infiltration into the mountains of California during World War II, though for what purpose is not known.

This is a case where we'll essentially have to take Mr. S——'s word for it. What could he, or should he, have done differently? If the aliens had really intended to harm him, trying to "smoke" him out of the tree would have just been the first step. It almost seems as if they were simply curious about him, wanted a close-up look, but didn't really want to harm him. Trying to shoot the robot with the arrows was not necessarily a wise move since it could have provoked a serious response. Fortunately he made a clear decision not to take a shot at the humanoids and confined his defensive efforts to what he believed was a machine. Perhaps the thing he might have done differently would have been to simply climb down from the tree and find out what they wanted. Of course, that's easy to say when you are not alone in a remote wilderness in the middle of the night with two robots trying to gas you and two aliens below you trying to figure out how to climb the tree that seems to represent your only safety.

XENOLOGY

by David Brin. Ph.D.

Starting with the Drake Formula. explained
earlier. noted scientist and Hugo Award winner
David Brin takes a look at what alien civilizations
might be like. He then goes on to answer the
question of why if astronomers are now
finding Earth-like planets. or at least the fact
that such planets may be relatively common.
extraterrestrials are not.

In the early 1960s, while the world was entranced by the spectacle of human beings hurled into "outer space" in rocket ships, a series of philosophical earthquakes shook the sedate field of astronomy. Just when the skies were beginning to seem known and familiar, all at once things changed. Stellar astronomers suddenly faced unsettling data from new classes of objects called "quasars" and "radio galaxies." There were disturbing theories about so-called "black holes." Even those who had long studied planets now found their comfortable domains invaded by geologists and meteorologists, who weren't at all shy about moving into the new territory.

It was no coincidence that all of this happened just as the Space Race was getting under way. New instruments and techniques often lead to upheavals in a science.

Still, the greatest intellectual challenge to the worldview of modern astronomers came in the early sixties, not because of new space probes, telescopes, and computers but because of an idea.

Starting in 1959, with a classic paper by Cocconi and Morrison, a series of articles and books were published with titles like *Interstellar Communication, Habitable Planets for Man* and, in 1966, a major work entitled *Intelligent Life in the Universe* by Iosef Shmuelovich Shklovskii and Carl Sagan. With these studies astronomers began to concern themselves with life itself.

The early sixties were pivotal for the field of "exo-biology"—extraterrestrial biology—and especially the sub-branch that dealt with intelligent life, "xenology." For the first time it was legitimate for leading scientists to publicly consider the possibility of contact with intelligent species off of the planet Earth.

Of course a lot of thought had gone into the subject previously, on the pages of science fiction novels and magazines. Many of the private discussions between authors such as Sagan, radio astronomer Frank Drake, and Rand Corporation scientist Stephen Dole grew out of ideas germinated by the likes of Clarke, Asimov, and Clement during the thirties and forties. But prior to the publication of *Intelligent Life in the Universe*, the number of "respectable" papers on the subject printed in the West could be counted on one's fingers and toes.

In the Soviet Union extraterrestrial intelligence was not only considered possible but was required by Leninist dogma. (It was assumed dialectically impossible that any advanced intelligence could be anything but socialist, of course.) When scientist I. S. Shklovskii wrote "Universe, Life, Mind" in 1962, his thoughts were widely popularized, and extracts were reprinted in major Soviet scientific journals.

In the West it took more time for scientific speculation about the distribution of life in the cosmos to become acceptable. A tradition of skepticism and rigor kept Western science relatively safe from scientioreligions such as Lysenkoism, which caused so much harm in Russia. But the same attitudes made it hard for those interested in the possibility of alien life-forms to bring up the subject in scientific gatherings without being criticized for "playing with science fiction."

The older scientists who dished out the ridicule shouldn't be blamed too harshly. In squelching early discussions of exobiology, they may have been overreacting to the the excesses of earlier enthusiasts, such as Percival Lowell, the astronomer who convinced millions that there were living Martians and "networks of canals" on the red planet.

But with the arrival of the space age, resistance to "science fictional" ideas was dealt a fatal blow. Those who had declared that "spaceships" belonged only in comic books were caught flat-footed. A new generation of scientists brought exobiological speculation out of the fringes and onto the pages of respectable journals. These men and women, who had proven their scientific credentials with solid research, came from an age group that didn't consider "science fiction" a dirty word. Most of them had cut their teeth on the stuff.

The first time I witnessed the subject of extraterrestrial intelligence brought up at a scientific seminar was at a Wednesday Cal Tech colloquium in 1968. The speaker remarked on the remote possibility that pulsars might be beacons of an advanced civilization. They were, after all, several thousand times more regular in their repetitive "beepings" than any other astronomical radio source ever discovered.

The speaker was only partly serious, but sides were quickly taken, and it was soon very clear that most of those with tenure didn't like this kind of talk at all.

Attitudes were changing very rapidly during those years. A few years later some of those who were the angriest in 1968 applauded the loudest when Carl Sagan unveiled the gold plaque that was to be placed upon *Pioneer 10,* the first human artifact to be launched on a trajectory out of the solar system.

Today that plaque is famous. It, and those that followed on *Pioneer 11* and the *Voyagers*, depict the nude figures of a woman and a man, an arm raised in greeting, a schematic of the planets of our system, and a rayed pattern of lines and binary dots representing the most prominent pulsars detectable from Earth. The pulsar map should enable any distant beings who recover the spacecraft to trace its point of origin within a light-year in space, and its launch date to within six months.

Shortly thereafter respectable scientists were discussing not whether extraterrestrial intelligences exist but how to go about listening for signals from our nearest neighbors! Small (very small) amounts of public money were allocated to adapting radio telescopes for the search.

If the first revolution in the nascent field of xenology came on the pages of science fiction pulps of the thirties and forties, the Second Xenological Revolution took place in the sixties, when scientists in large numbers began asking, "Where are they?"

Anyone interested in the possibilities of life outside the Earth should certainly read *Intelligent Life in the Universe*. Although some of its science is dated, it remains the classic in the field. Still, to a veteran reader of SF, *Intelligent Life . . .* may seem overly tame and conservative. For instance, the authors barely mentioned the possibility of *travel* between the stars. To investigators of that time, it seemed pointless to discuss interstellar colonization.

Science fiction has long used, as furniture, ships that bypass relativity. But to early xenologists it was dangerous enough talking about alien life-forms, without risking one's scientific reputation talking about "hyperspace warpdrive" and the like. Shortcuts may lend SF a lot of pizzazz and spawn stories about galactic empires, but Einstein's speed limit dominates serious talk about life in the universe.

The gulfs separating the stars are vast. And during the sixties it seemed unlikely that even the modest velocities allowed under Einstein's edicts could ever be reached economically.

Thus the first era of modern scientific xenology (from 1959 to about 1972) dealt with the possibility of intelligent life springing up in isolation—here and there on fertile planets scattered across the sky—islands of intelligence separated from one another by vast distances and for all time.

THE AGE OF INNOCENCE

What could early students of this new science say about extraterrestrial life-forms? No matter how daring, they were faced with one major limitation: a near total lack of data. The only known case of intelligent life is here on Earth. Until the *Viking* mission, some held on to Percival Lowell's dreams for Mars. Now the evidence seems to weigh against finding even microbes there. Putting aside, for the moment, speculations about dolphins, whales, and gorillas, it's pretty hard to extrapolate a graph from only one data point.

Still, three scientific discoveries and one useful philosophical tool gave researchers the courage to make crude estimates about the distribution of life among the stars.

The first discovery came when it was found almost ridiculously easy to make amino acids, and other precursors to living matter, from abundant molecules such as methane, ammonia, and cyanogen. Stanley Miller subjected a water solution of these substances to electrical discharge and ultraviolet radiation and got an organic "soup" in short order. Leslie Orgel of the Salk Institute accomplished the same thing by a freezing process. The high pressures of ice formation not only gave up amino acids but the purine adenine as well. (Adenine is one of the four building blocks of DNA, and is the core of ATP, adenosine tri-phosphate, which controls the energy economy of the living cell.)

So many mechanisms have been found that can change crude precursors into "biological" molecules that today organic activity seems almost an automatic consequence of the distribution of chemical elements in the universe.

The second major discovery supports this point of view. During the last two decades, radio astronomers—listening to narrow emission lines from interstellar space—have discovered great clouds of complex molecules: ethylene, formaldehyde, ethyl alcohol; some even claim evidence for—you guessed it—adenine.

(Astronomer and science fiction author Sir Fred Hoyle, looking at starlight scattered from interstellar dust, thinks that the dust itself may actually be something akin to bacteria . . . living cells about a micron in size, in diffuse colonies spanning light-years and outmassing suns. It's an extravagant speculation, but fun to think about.)

It's clear, then, from basic chemistry and radio astronomy, that the basic materials for life are out there. What about the right environments? We have to assume, until we have reason to think otherwise, that complex life must grow and evolve to intelligence on planets orbiting stable stars. Are there other "nursery worlds" like the Earth?

There are plenty of stable, long-lived, G-type dwarf stars like the Sun out there . . . about 6 percent of the galaxy's several hundred billion stars. Are there planets circling many of them?

The data are still poor. It's hoped that the Space Telescope will tell us more about the companions of nearby stars. Some scientists think there is good evidence that at least one of our neighbors, Barnard's star, has possibly two dark companions a bit more massive than Jupiter.

We do know that F-, K-, and G-type dwarf stars rotate much more slowly than larger, hotter stars. The Sun contains 99.9 percent of the matter in the solar system, yet it has only 0.5 percent of the angular momentum. The rest is distributed among the planets of the solar system, especially Jupiter. Most astronomers believe that those slowly rotating stars that aren't members of multiple-star systems have to possess dark companions that were used to "dump off" excess angular momentum early during star formation. Recent models of gas-cloud condensation tend to support this belief.

We've covered three discoveries, then, that help us believe that it's reasonable to talk about life outside the Earth. What is that "philosophical tool" we mentioned that caps the legitimacy of xenology? It is sometimes called the cosmological principle, or the assumption of mediocrity.

Since Copernicus, astronomy has been a series of lessons in humility, all leading to the conclusion that "there is nothing special about where and when we are." First the Earth was displaced from the center of the solar system, then the Sun became a nondescript traveler in orbit about the rim of the galaxy. The galaxy became merely one island universe among billions, and the universe seems to have no "middle" at all.

The cosmological principle tells us we should avoid the temptation to think that there's anything unique about the Earth in space, time, or situation. It is the major philosophical underpinning for the new study of xenology. It forces even the most cantankerously conservative astronomer to admit that someone, somewhere, might be peering up at HIS stars, among which insignificant motes is our own Sun.

If xenology has some justification, then, where did the first generation of scientific xenologists get their numbers? How did they estimate the population of our galaxy . . . or the probable distance to our nearest neighbors?

The Drake Equation is the most popular way to guess at the possible distribution of technological species. It was invented by Frank Drake when he was at the Arecibo National Radio Observatory. It remains the most widely accepted tool for xenological speculation.

Let N = the current number of technological civilizations in the galaxy. Then,

$$N = R \; P \; n(e) \; f(l) \; f(i) \; f(c) \; L$$

Here R is the average rate of production of suitable stars since the formation of the galaxy, approximately one per year. (The current rate is slower. R is an average that includes the burst of star creation early in the galaxy's history.) P is the fraction of stars that are accompanied by stably orbiting planets. Factor $n(e)$ is the average number of planets per system that have the requisite conditions to support life.

The other factors include $f(l)$, the fraction of these congenial planets on which life actually occurs; $f(i)$, the fraction of these on which "intelligence" appears; $f(c)$, the fraction of intelligent species that attain technological civilizations, and L, the average life span of such a species.

For what then seemed fairly good reasons, Sagan and others chose to assign P and $n(e)$ each values near 1. These guesses, within an order of magnitude, don't seem to conflict with what we now know about planets.

For purposes of discussion it was assumed that congenial planets normally develop life, $[f(l) = 1]$, that about a tenth of the planets with life evolve intelligence $[f(i) = 0.1]$, and that about a tenth of the latter will see technological civilizations [$f(c)$ = 0.1]. In other words, a likely planet will contribute roughly 0.01 technological races during its history.

A complete discussion of the Drake Equation can be found in books and in many recent technical articles. (Some references for the interested reader are given at the end of this article.) There are reasons to believe that the equation is, in fact, short about three factors. But suffice it here to say that the best guesses, with plenty of up-and-down leeway in every parameter, led Sagan and others a decade ago to a rough estimate,

$$N = 0.01 \; L$$

This meant the average life span of technological races would determine the number present in the galaxy at any time. If self-destruction is the common fate of "civilized" species, then there might be no more than a handful of them in the Milky Way at a given moment, separated by vast tracts of silent starscape. If, on the other hand, a reasonable fraction of races live a long time, the galaxy might be teeming with life.

Cameron, von Hoerner, Shklovskii, and Sagan all guessed at L, allowing for various ways in which a culture might end. Generally, their results suggested that the number of civilizations in the galaxy might be on the order of one million, most of them long-lived and patient species. The numbers giving rise to this estimate were a bit arbitrary, but not unreasonable.

If the planets of a million stars held sophont races, then about 0.001 percent of all eligible stars in the galaxy would be inhabited by thinking beings. The average distance separating these islands of technology would be on the order of several hundred light-years—a gap that seemed unbridgeable corporeally, but easily crossed by radio waves.

This was the state of affairs in the early seventies. With interstellar travel virtually ruled out, the accepted model depicted isolated motes of intelligence separated by sterile tracts of space.

These speculations led to CYCLOPS, OZMA, SETI, and CETI. The search for extraterrestrial life was born. The radio astronomers who slapped together borrowed time and equipment to scan the sky were hopeful, and numerous articles about their endeavors came out on the pages of magazines.

We could take up several articles just talking about SETI. The early arguments over search strategy are fascinating reading. What kinds of antennae would be best suited for the job? Would extraterrestrial intelligent species (ETIS) transmit in the "water hole" frequencies? Should we transmit our own messages, or just wait and listen? If we wait, should we let our nearest neighbors get their first impressions of us from DEW-line radar and *I Love Lucy?*

Extraterrestrials might not use radio for long-range communication. If lasers carried their traffic, we might not be able to eavesdrop on interstellar conversations.

Even if we can't tap long-distance calls, though, we might still listen for leakage from a planet's commercial radio network . . . or search for a beacon . . . a signal *meant* to be picked up by new radio-using species like ourselves.

Many papers came out during the early seventies suggesting that advanced extrasolar sophonts would likely broadcast the interstellar equivalent of *Sesame Street,* to help younger species (like us) pass over their initial dilemma of survival or self-destruction. The reasoning went that it would be in the older species' interest to help its younger neighbors live long enough to get a decent conversation going.

The first formal search for extraterrestrial intelligence came when Frank Drake and his associates looked at the two nearest candidates, the two Sun-like stars that lie within twelve light-years and are not members of multiple-star systems. Drake's team found nothing but star noise coming from the K2 dwarf, epsilon Eridani. Then they turned their telescope to the star Tau Ceti.

And lo! They heard something! For a brief instant they felt a thrill, as modulated signals came down the cable, obviously of intelligent origin! But then, as the telescope settled down, the "signal" faded away, never to return. They soon concluded that the signal was indeed coded noise from the nearest civilization—some commercial traffic in nearby Milford, Massachusetts!

Undaunted, Drake and others expanded the search. The telescopes turned and scanned. Nothing was found. The Russians joined the search, enthusiastically. They reported only negative results.

No problem, astronomers suggested. Any advanced species wouldn't waste energy broadcasting over the entire bandwidth of, say, the hydrogen 21-centimeter line. To conserve power, and to attain a high signal-to-noise ratio, they would modulate over a very narrow band. Just wait, they suggested, until we can develop fineband simultaneous multichannel analyzers!

Yet the second and third generations of eavesdropping devices have come up with nothing.

True, still better instruments are planned. The money and time spent in the search has been insignificant compared with the potential rewards, which might include clues to the very survival of the human race. (There is a battle under way as this is being written, to restore the piddling two-million-dollar appropriation for SETI, which recently was proxmired to death.)

Still, just one decade ago some of the radio-xenologists were talking as if they expected to be cracking codes in short order.

Now a few even glumly propose that no one is "out there" after all ... at least, not in our vicinity.

How can this be? If we've been at the search for less than fifteen years, using spare time and borrowed equipment, how could anyone expect success so soon? Sure, it'd be nice to find neighbors twelve or twenty light-years away; you could hold a "conversation" within one person's life span, for example. But according to most calculations using the Drake formula, the average distance between technological civilizations might be a few hundred light-years. There are well over a million stars in a sphere a hundred parsecs across. It would take some time to search even the most likely of these, choosing only those radio bands we guess to be the best (not knowing whether our idea of "best" is universal).

Two hundred light-years makes "conversation" a little more difficult. But a *Sesame Street* beacon would be just as useful as ever at that range. Just knowing extraterrestrials *existed* might profoundly boost *Homo sap*'s sagging morale.

It seems like we are presenting an argument to restore that appropriation from Congress, not laying out a case for doom and gloom. It only appears to be a matter of time and effort. Success, in the long run, seems assured to the persistent.

What has changed, then? What has caused this spreading anxiety?

It's not the sort of thing one would expect to be a cause for pessimism. At first hearing it sounds like very good news.

Starships are possible—

THE THIRD ERA OF XENOLOGY

The Third Xenological Revolution began sometime in the mid-seventies, when several prominent scientists challenged the conventional wisdom that intelligent life arises upon isolated islands, forever separated by the wide gulfs of interstellar space. Sanger, Bracewell, Forward, Bussard, and others demonstrated that it's possible to build spaceships to cross the emptiness between the stars. No "magic" is needed. It isn't necessary to repudiate Einstein. Whether by lightsail or by antimatter rocket, humanity may be launching starships within a few centuries.

These "starships" would be nothing like the good old *Enterprise*. Limited to possibly a tenth of the speed of light, they could not travel terribly far by interstellar standards. But clearly they could carry people, possibly living several generations in transit. The "slow-boat" generation-ship of science fiction fame has been mathematically vindicated.

This is bad news?

Of course not. But the possibility of starships places a new and awesome burden on xenology. It presents us with a paradox that is very difficult to overcome.

What would *we* do if we had starships? If both history and literature tell us anything, we would look around for nice real estate and start colonizing. In fact, we wouldn't even need to find nice planets; stable stars with asteroid belts would do. Our own "belters" might by then prefer such virgin territory to "dirty planets," anyway.

Once the new colonies reached a high level of industry, say in a few hundred years or so, what would they do? Why, they'd send out more colony ships, of course. It seems obvious to almost anyone holding a book like this one.

Imagine a sphere of human settlement slowly expanding through space. How long would it take for colonies to be planted three hundred light-years from Earth? Even limiting ship speed to a tenth of the speed of light, and allowing each colony plenty of time to industrialize? Ten thousand years? Thirty thousand years?

Mankind has hardly changed at all, physically, in the last thirty thousand years. If we make a few social advances and avoid self-destruction, we should be able to fulfill the above scenario.

And why shouldn't anyone else? If this sort of expansion can occur once, why not for each of the million sophont races we calculated earlier? In well under 100,000 years the 200 light-year "average spacing" between races would be filled up!

Recent calculations by Eric Jones of Los Alamos Laboratories indicate that the scenario we have just described, of a slowly expanding sphere of settled solar systems, could fill the entire galaxy within sixty million years. It's not unreasonable to imagine at least one out of a million civilized races living that long. So why do we see no signs that the Earth has been colonized in the last sixty million years?

Why have we picked up no radio signals, when the stars should be humming with information and commerce?

Where are they?

This question marks the first traumatic awakening of the new science of xenology. It marks the end of a very short period of innocence. Starting around 1975 and building toward the present, the Third Xenological Revolution commenced. The dust has not yet settled, but one thing is clear. Some of our assumptions are wrong. The universe might turn out to be considerably more complicated than the scientist optimists of the late sixties had at first thought.

Of course, science fiction writers and readers could have told them that all along.

THE GREAT SILENCE

The Third Revolution in Xenology came with the realization that space *should* be filled with intelligent life. There appears to be no excuse any longer for the failure of SETI.

Indeed, why hasn't the Earth itself been colonized! The question, Where are they? might better be put, Why aren't they *here*? The quandary can be called the Mystery of the Great Silence.

We see no evidence for ancient alien cities in the Earth's crust. Venus and Mars apparently never were terraformed, though many now think we could tackle the job in a few centuries. The asteroids of the solar system appear to be untouched.

Most significantly, the Earth, until less than a billion years ago, was populated for two billion years by only primitive prokaryotic organisms. A visiting starship need not have landed colonists. All they'd have had to do was be careless with their garbage or latrine and the history of the Earth would be totally different.

It certainly looks as though we've been alone a very long time.

There have been several imaginative suggestions to explain the Great Silence. At the end of this article we'll compile a partial list.

Dr. Eric Jones, Dr. Frank Tipler, and Dr. Michael Hart all think it means that the earlier calculations of the probabilities of intelligent life were greatly overoptimistic. They suggest that the apparent absence of ETIs simply means that this part of the galaxy is uninhabited . . . that no race has got out there ahead of us to make an impact by colonization. Their Uniqueness Hypothesis implies that some or all of the factors $f(l,i,c)$ in the Drake Equation are really very small. For instance, some contend that intelligence such as ours is an evolutionary fluke.

Dr. Thomas Kuiper of JPL has presented strong arguments in refutation, showing that convergent evolution has happened frequently on Earth and might well occur elsewhere.

Dr. John Ball has dredged up the science fictional idea that the Earth is a "zoo" or wildlife preserve, and that extraterrestrials are already here, observing us. There are many variants to this concept, including "quarantine" (ETIs awaiting humanity's social maturity), a noninterference "Prime Directive," and many others. All imply we should add to the Drake Equation a factor to account for ETIs purposely avoiding contact.

Contact optimists, such as William Newman of Princeton and Carl Sagan of Cornell, have tried to make excuses for the extraterrestrials. In a recent paper Newman and Sagan suggested that truly advanced cultures would practice zero population growth and thus feel less pressure to expand into virgin territory. The rate of "galaxy-filling" calculated under their extremely conservative assumptions is slow enough to make it barely possible that the nearest expanding space-faring race simply has not reached us yet.

Sagan and Newman further propose that techniques of life extension—immortality—would make individuals of a race very conservative. If a passion for risk-avoidance took hold, a species' rate of expansion, V, could drop to nil.

Might a race naturally graduate to other interests after a certain amount of time? Science fiction is filled with possibilities, from extra dimensions to realms of the mind far more attractive than drifting through space and clearing land on some new world. Such "maturity stages" would affect L in the Drake Equation, as well as the velocity of expansion.

Our assumptions for $f(1)$ might be too high. Although the precursors of life—sugars, amino acids, nucleic acids—seem likely to be about as common as stardust, it's possible that the next steps to life might be much, much harder to reach, requiring some rare catalyst to set the process off.

From physics and SF comes the dreadful idea of "deadly probes." Saberhagen's "Berserkers" might make life rare if some technological civilization accidentally let loose something so monstrous. Gregory Benford's variant on the idea is hardly more optimistic. A particularly paranoid advanced species might not want any potential competition to rise up elsewhere. Self-replicating autonomous probes might be sent out to reproduce and fill the galaxy. Whenever new radio traffic indicates that new sentients are loose, these preprogrammed probes would home in on the signals with powerful bombs and stop the infection before it spreads.

It's already too late to call back the spherical wave of *I Love Lucy,* etc., that's already spreading through nearby space.

All of the hypotheses given above have their problems. Some seem to contradict the best knowledge we have in the field. Others, like the "zoo" theory, are almost innately untestable.

What we hope to do is to compile a list of these possibilities. I will start things off by talking about a few hypotheses that the xenologist speculators have mostly passed up. Some are a bit frightening. See also "Just How Dangerous Is the Galaxy?" on page 268.

THE FATE OF "NURSERY WORLDS"

In the Drake Equation the combined factor $f(i,c)$—the fraction of life-planets on which intelligence and technology eventually evolve—is generally assigned a value of about 1 in 100. The xenologists who put forward the "one percent" argument support it by citing the apparent fact that it took four billion years for the Earth to give rise to merely one technological race. This is almost half the viable life span of the planet. Intelligent life would seem to be a rare and wonderful thing.

But is this assumption tenable? It appears to be the weakest link in the chain of logic.

Let's consider the life cycle of a "Nursery World," a planet with a stable biosphere in which the slow evolution to intelligence can take place.

Evolution appears to have proceeded gradually at first and then at an accelerating pace for over three billion years. Except for (maybe) the introduction of sex, and later of flowering plants, there is no evidence in the fossil record to support the idea that the Earth was ever suddenly invaded by extraterrestrials who, "with kith and kine," introduced advanced flora and fauna. The Great Silence seems, at first glance, to have stretched through the entire Paleozoic.

If we assume the Earth lay untampered with until at least the time of the Jurassic, we can guess that it takes about three billion years for life on a Nursery World to evolve to a level of complexity that makes intelligence feasible.

What if humanity suddenly vanished? Would it take another three billion years for intelligence once again to arise on Earth? If so, it's reasonable to accept the guess that the number of technological species to erupt per habitable planet is of order less than one.

But *Homo sapiens* is not the only species to have benefited from three billion years of evolution. Today's German cockroach may look a lot like his distant ancestors, but he has accumulated many little tricks his cousins in the Triassic never heard of. The size of genome of the raccoon and wolf is hardly smaller than that of man.

Consider what's happened since the Cretaceous-Tertiary Catastrophe approximately sixty-five million years ago—the disaster that wiped out, over a period of a few hundred thousand years, almost every species of land animal whose adults massed more than forty kilos.

The creatures whose descendants went on to dominate the planet were small mammals: the early equivalents of mice, lemurs, and tree shrews. These humble animals expanded and diversified to fill all of the ecological niches left vacant by the demise of the large reptiles. We are among their descendants.

In spite of the present arms race, man still lacks the ability to exterminate mice, although he will probably soon be able to do an efficient job on himself. The sudden demise of this star system's current technological race would not finish off the Earth as a nursery. If "mice" did it once, they could probably do it again.

We are led to suggest that suitable worlds must pass through long initial "fallow" periods before attaining a level of biological sophistication ripe for intelligence. Afterward such planets should be able to produce sophont species at fairly short intervals, *depending upon the time needed to recover from the damage done by the previous sentient race.*

The interval between the Cretaceous Catastrophe and the present is a reasonable estimate for the time it takes to build a civilized race, once small and sturdy creatures have reached a high level of sophistication.

COLONIZATION ECO-DISASTERS

Let's go back to that expanding spacefaring species we were talking about earlier. Remember, calculations show that it might take as little as sixty million years for such a race to fill the galaxy. A question seldom asked by science fiction authors who write about colonization is, What happens to the colonized planets?

Unless the settlers leave large parts of their worlds fallow in wilderness preserves, or engage in "Uplift" bioengineering of local higher animals, their mere presence is likely to prevent the appearance of local sentient species. The cycle of production of intelligent species on a planet is probably delayed indefinitely by an active technological settlement. A world is not likely to serve as a useful nursery of intelligence so long as it is occupied by a spacefaring race.

When the tenants finally do vacate (or die off), the recovery time required before another generation of tool users evolves will depend on the way the settlers treated their adopted world. The more savage the exploitation of a colony planet, the more severe will be the thinning of the local biosphere. Our own technological civilization has markedly simplified ecological networks on Earth even where efforts have been made to preserve wilderness. In general, higher life-forms, more delicate and dependent upon complex environments than smaller creatures, go first.

When settlers finally do step aside—by attrition, disaster, exodus, or whatever—ecological recycling can resume, but recovery and regeneration of intelligence will take much more time, the longer a technological race occupied the planet.

EXPANSION SHELLS

It is generally assumed that a spacefaring race will expand into the galaxy either because of raw curiosity or population pressure. Either way, it's clear that the expansion soon becomes spherelike, with only the most recently settled worlds having much opportunity to seek new planets. For a race limited to slowboat technology, colonization will take place only in a thin shell surrounding an older, settled region within.

If population pressure is the primary motive for expansion, we have to wonder at the fate of the long-occupied worlds in the interior of the settled sphere, especially those near Home planet. The words *population pressure* themselves suggest the likely fate of these worlds.

Consider the settlement of Polynesia from roughly 1500 B.C. to about A.D. 800. The island-hopping analogy with interstellar exploration and colonization is apt up to a point. Jones borrowed growth and emigration rates for his model of interstellar settlement from Polynesian history. The intrepid Polynesian example is used as testimony to the likely success and viability of "star-hopping" colonization ventures.

Polynesia may, indeed, be representative of interstellar settlement, but not in a pleasant sense. The Hollywood image of island life is paradisical, but Polynesian cultures were subject to regular cycles of extreme overpopulation controlled by bloody culling of the adult male population, in war or ritual. There are many stories of islands whose men were almost wiped out, sometimes by internal strife, sometimes by invading males from other islands far away.

Meanwhile, introduction of domestic animals disrupted island ecosystems. Many native species were wiped out.

The most severe example is the island of Rapa Nui, also called Isla de Pasqua, or Easter Island. Isolated thousands of miles from its nearest neighbors, it was as much like an interstellar colony as any place in human history, when it was settled around A.D. 800. Mankind may devoutly hope to do better when finally embarked to the stars.

The Pasquans utterly destroyed the virgin ecosystem of Rapa Nui in a few generations, ravaging the forest until only banana trees were left. When no wood remained for houses or boats, they had to abandon the sea and its resources, along with all possibility of escape or trade. What remained was native rock—which they carved into hauntingly desolate images—and warfare.

When Europeans arrived, the natives of Rapa Nui had just about destroyed themselves.

Assume a settled sphere of expansion by an extraterrestrial intelligent species. What of the inner systems, *within* the sphere? The Polynesian example suggests a dismal image of increasing competition for dwindling resources with no escape valve for excess population, since all surrounding systems are in similar straits.

What happens to these inner worlds? They probably don't go looking to conquer their neighbors. Interstellar warfare seems to be a frightfully expensive proposition. Conflict arising from population pressure is far more likely to be local, consisting of struggles for resources within each planetary system.

In an old settled system all available asteroids would long have been turned into habitats. Safe inner orbits with unhindered access to solar power would be at a premium.

Even the most efficient space structures will require frequent replenishment of volatile substances—gases such as oxygen, hydrogen, and nitrogen. Comets might supply part of this need, but terrestroid planets would be closer and rich in the desired light elements.

One might expect to see a profound cultural split between those living on planetary surfaces and those in space. Competition and misunderstandings might tempt the space-dwellers to take advantage of their superior position to dominate their planet-bound cousins. It would be simple to bombard the cities on a planet's surface with redirected asteroids until civilization there was obliterated. Factor L clearly falls in such a case.

(The space-born, long divorced from any attachment to planetary life, might even see a terrestroid planet as a likely source of building materials! It wouldn't be beyond their ability to pulverize a world such as the Earth by arranging planetary collisions. This would certainly affect not only L but also *n(e)*, the number of *planets* on which life can evolve!) In any event, the innocent higher animals suffer in the crossfire.

ANOTHER EXPLANATION FOR THE CRETACEOUS CATASTROPHE

Let's return briefly to the episode about sixty-five million years ago known as the Cretaceous-Tertiary Catastrophe. There were, at that time, many advanced species of reptiles. The best candidate among these for a species possibly ripe for development toward tool-using might have been *Saurornithoides,* a midsized bipedal carnivore with the highest brain-to-body mass ratio of any reptile, approximately matching that of modern baboons. While there is no reason to think that this creature was particularly intelligent, he filled an ecological niche that might have been rigorous enough to encourage his glimmering abilities.

But *Saurornithoides* died out along with virtually all of the other great reptiles during a relatively brief period by geological standards.

If the demise of the dinosaurs puzzles paleontologists, the problem has been even worse for the marine biologists. The dinosaurs, at least, took as long as a few million years to die out. The tiny sea microorganisms experienced a greater catastrophe. Over half of the species of phytoplankton went extinct within about one year!

The latter mystery, at least, now appears solved. Recent deep-core drillings have uncovered thin layers of clay rich in exotic elements, including iridium (up to 25 times normal abundance of some isotopes), at sedimentary levels associated with the end of the Cretaceous. Discoveries in locations as diverse as Italy and New Mexico all seem to correlate a sudden invasion of strange dust with the equally sudden disappearance of many classes of oceanic microorganisms. Scientists now conclude that a major meteorite impact kicked up a great pall of dust that severely altered weather patterns, resulting in mass extinction by starvation when photosynthesis was interrupted.

For the marine creatures this seems sufficient, but don't forget that the dinosaurs were *already* dying out before this bombardment, starting with the greatest behemoths and so on down to the smaller herd animals. Their die-back was a lot like what we see happening today to the wild animals of Africa at the hands of white and black "intelligent" beings. The meteorite seems to have been only one of the last straws for the great reptiles.

Might the demise of the dinosaurs, then, be part of a hidden pattern? Is it possible that an alien colony began a process of extinction that was by the meteorite (or meteorites) only finished?

A natural planetfall can't be distinguished from one targeted against ground settlements of a technological species. Is it possible that the dinosaurs were innocent bystanders in a genocidal war among alien settlers in the solar system?

The bombardment might only have been the last act in a more gradual ecological catastrophe that began half a million years before, when settlement of the planet resulted in extinction of species after species.

The introduction, about this time, of flowering plants, is another environmental perturbation that had profound ecological effects. It's not absurd to imagine this fitting into an overall pattern of outside intervention.

The settlement of Earth by a spacefaring race about seventy million years ago, then, offers one more (admittedly tenuous) explanation for the destruction of the higher terrestrial life-forms over a brief period.

If we make this hypothesis, however, where are the traces of this earlier technological occupancy? Over sixty million years of oxidation will destroy many artifacts, but certainly some might survive.

Who can say? The cities we look for may lie beneath astroblemes. A look at a geological map of the Earth shows that continental plate boundaries have proved to be choice living sites. These plate-edge regions have suffered pronounced geological changes that could have erased most traces of alien settlement.

The final test of this hypothesis would be found among the planetoids of the solar system. The asteroids might hold remnants of visits to our star by extraterrestrials . . . perhaps whole cities, the leftovers of great populations: killed off, perhaps, by biological warfare in desperate retaliation by the Earthbound cousins they had annihilated.

CYCLES OF RECOVERY AND EXPANSION

This hypothetical explanation for the Cretaceous Mystery merely should take its place in a catalog of possibilities, perhaps near the bottom. Still, it's interesting to note that the period since that catastrophe—an interval that culminated in the development of *Homo sapiens*—is the same sixty million years suggested by Jones and others for an optimum minimal galaxy-filling time by a technological race.

The Cretaceous-Tertiary event was not the only one of its kind. At least four other mass extinctions are found in the sedimentary record, including one at the end of the Devonian and another at the Permian-Triassic boundary, approximately 225 million years ago. These events are less well understood and may have taken place over longer periods than that of the Cretaceous, but we may compare the rough 10- to 500-million-year intervals seen with those suggested by Newman and Sagan for galaxy filling by space-traveling species.

If the ecological holocaust of the Cretaceous was a local manifestation of the death spasm of a prior spacefaring race, whose overpopulated sphere of settlement spoiled and self-destructed as the shell of colonization passed outward, then we humans may have come into being almost too late. Any longer, and the next wave—the expanding shell of still another spreading technological race—might have washed over Earth before we had the ability to assert property rights . . . assuming we have that ability now.

We may wonder if the Earth is the first Nursery World to have recovered sufficiently, since the last wave of "civilization" passed this way, to develop a species with intelligence. Whether or not the end of the Cretaceous corresponded to the agony of dying starfarers, it may well be that colonizing cultures inevitably leave behind them wastelands empty of intelligence and living voices.

If we humans initiate an era of interstellar travel of our own, we may find all around us the blasted remains of an earlier epoch. Would we then learn a lesson? Perhaps. But with the ever-present opportunities for expansion, those humans who exercise self-restraint and environmental sensitivity toward their adopted worlds will not be able to force this tradition upon those who travel far away to establish newer colonies. A nucleus of selfishness is likely to expand more rapidly than a center of more rational colonization. While there may be zones where settlers preserve and protect the local ecospheres, cognizant of their long-range potential, others may be rapacious.

Certainly our environmental record here on Earth is a test. The list of extinct species, some of which might one day have become starfarers, is long and growing longer.

The Great Silence may be the sound of sands drifting up against monuments. It may be quiet testament to the fate of species which allow "population pressure" to be their motivation for the stars.

MORE IDEAS

We'll begin a "morphological" analysis of the Great Silence by presenting the following list of possibilities:

1. *Solitude*—We are unique in evolving technological intelligence.

This hypothesis implies something is very wrong with current use of the Drake Equation. Habitable planets may be rare, or some "spark" may be needed to initiate life out of a prebiotic soup.

The final step to intelligence may require some software miracle that makes it far more improbable than currently thought.

Alternatively, the last term in the Drake Equation—the average life span of technological species—may be on the order of decades. This might be due to some "inevitability" of self-destruction, or due to the "Deadly Probes" of Saberhagen and Benford.

2. *"Magical" Technology*

It may be that technological species soon discover techniques that make radio and even colonization irrelevant. We may be on the verge of such discoveries right now, though it's hard to imagine any race totally abandoning the electromagnetic spectrum, whatever its other options.

3. *"Quarantine"*—The hypothesis of purposeful avoidance of contact.

This is an idea long popular in science fiction. It explains the Great Silence by suggesting that the solar system is kept as a "zoo." Or benevolent species might want to let Nursery Worlds lie fallow for long periods, to nurture new sentience.

Related ideas are that observers are awaiting mankind's social maturity or have quarantined us as dangerous, perhaps infected.

Kuiper and Morris have also suggested that members of a galactic radio club would not contact "beginners" because this would wreck our usefulness as members of the network. Making us information consumers too early would spoil us as information *providers,* whose unique experience would add richness to galactic culture.

ETIs may visit the solar system for reasons having nothing to do with us.

A problem with "Quarantine" is the galaxy's differential rotation. Our neighbors don't remain our neighbors. If during one epoch we live near environmentalists, ten million years later our sun could enter the domain of a less scrupulous race. The quarantine hypothesis appears to call for some degree of cultural uniformity in the galaxy . . . hard to accomplish in a relativistic universe.

4. *Macrolife*—The abandonment of planet-dwelling as a lifestyle.

Expansion will generally come from those colony worlds most recently settled. There might be a great selective process favoring those individuals suited to living in starships. One can imagine the pioneers eventually deciding that planet-bound existence is filthy and degrading. This might result in either of two different behaviors, each compatible with the Great Silence. Truly space-borne sophonts might greedily fragment terrestroid planets for building material and volatiles, leading to disastrous versions of "solitude" or "low rent" (see below), or they might cherish Nursery Worlds for what they are and protect them as in option "quarantine," without any conflict of interest or desire to use high-gravity real estate.

5. *"Seniors Only"*—More alternate lifestyles.

It's often suggested that spacefaring sophonts might "graduate" to other interests after a reasonable time. This would set a limit to the period of expansion, though not, perhaps, to exploration.

Discovery of immortality could tend to promote conservatism, and an aversion to the dangers of spaceflight.

6. *"Low Rent"*—Earth is inaccessible or undesirable.

Spacefaring sophonts that otherwise had the means might choose to bypass Earth. A few possibilities to consider are the following.

a) The one technique for travel faster than light (FTL) which has drawn some support from the physics community has been "geometro-dynamic"—via controlled entry into the zone of influence of a black hole and traversing space-time through hyperdimensional shortcuts. If such a version of FTL travel were possible, convenient, and efficient, one might expect galactic civilization to cluster around entry and exit points. Long-range slowboat technology would languish.

The fact, then, that astronomers have observed no nearby black holes may be a manifestation of the so-called Anthropic Principle. If a "usable" black hole were closer, the Earth would have already been settled, an ecological holocaust would have ensued, and we would not exist to observe the black hole. Thus the fact that we are here is consistent with a failure to observe nearby black holes.

b) Another systematic effect that might make for periods of inaccessibility is the migration of the Sun around the center of the galaxy. We are currently on our way out of a gas-and-dust-rich spiral arm. In a few million years the Sun will be in an "open" area, where there are few bright, younger stars. Spiral arms are home to the dense interstellar hydrogen clouds. These are thought required to run Bussard ramscoops, but today that particular type of vehicle is falling into some disrepute. Besides, the clouds might also be hazards to other forms of travel.

c) Earth life-forms rely almost totally on the left-handed isomers of complex organic proteins and amino acids. This might not be the case elsewhere. Should "dextro-" life dominate everywhere else, we might find Earth systematically avoided because there would be nothing here for prospective settlers to eat!

These are just a few examples of an endless supply.

7. *Migration Holocaust*

This category has received the most attention in this article. Transient occupation of a Nursery World by a techno-culture might cause extinction of local higher life-forms, delaying the local upsurge of intelligence and resulting in a neighborhood so depleted that we are the first to recover in the nearby area.

CONCLUSION

The quandary of the Great Silence gives the infant study of xenology its first traumatic struggle: between those who seek optimistic excuses for the apparent absence of sentient neighbors and those who enthusiastically accept the silence as evidence for humanity's isolation in an open frontier.

As humanity grows up, we're finding out just how complicated the universe can be. We've seen that "Galactic Empires" have implications far beyond anything considered even by the science fiction of the past. The universe has many more ways of being nasty, if it so chooses, than we had thought.

Opportunities do not, however, have to be taken up. While the author doesn't accept that elder species will necessarily be wiser and more restrained than contemporary humanity, he does suggest, and hope, that such noble races *do* crop up from time to time. If such a culture lived long, and retained much of the strength and vigor of youth, it might have taught a tradition of respect for the hidden potential of Life to all subsequent spacefaring species.

It might turn out that the Great Silence we're experiencing is like that of a child's nursery, wherein adults speak softly, lest they disturb the infant's extravagant and colorful time of dreaming.

REFERENCES

On Interstellar Travel Technology

Bracewell, R. N. *Nature* (London) 186 (1960): 670.

Forward, Robert. "Interstellar Flight Systems." AIAA Paper No. 80-0823 (1980).

Martin, A. R. "Project Daedalus—Final Report of the British Interplanetary Society Starship Study." BIS. A. R. Martin, ed. (1978).

O'Neill, Gerard K. *Physics Today* 27 (1976): 32.

On Possible Dispersal of Intelligent Life

Ball, John A. *Icarus* 19 (1973): 347.

Billingham, John, ed. *Life in the Universe.* Cambridge, MA: MIT Press, 1981.

Cameron, A.G.W., ed. *Interstellar Communications.* New York: W. A. Benjamin Inc., 1963, 1970.

Hart, Michael, *Q.J.R.A.S.* 16 (1975): 128.

Jones, Eric. *Icarus* 46 1981: 328.

Kuiper, T.B.H., and M. Morris. *Science* 196 (1977): 616.

Newman, William I., Carl Sagan. *Icarus* 46 (1981): 293.

Shklovskii, I. S., and C. Sagan. *Intelligent Life in the Universe.* San Francisco: Holden Day, 1966.

On the Cretaceous Catastrophe

Alvarez, L. W., W. Alvarez, F. Asaro, and H. V. Michel. *Science* 208 (1980): 1095.

SECTION FOUR

GUIDELINES
OF INTERPLANETARY
CONTACT

FIRST CONTACT

by William R. Forstchen, Ph.D.

So where are they? If it is scientifically
probable that we are sharing the universe
with other intelligent species, why haven't
they contacted us? Dr. Forstchen, a professor
of history, reflects here on the hazards
we've seen in the past when two societies
with different levels of technology meet.
The history of our planet may well give some
insight into the causes of the elusive nature
of contact with extraterrestrials, or the
concerns of those people in the government
who are dealing with this situation.

A conquistador, during the conquest of Mexico, found himself in a rather difficult predicament, but he was convinced that his superior grasp of celestial mechanics would save the day. Having been captured by some locals, who seemed to be less than pleased with his arrival, he surmised that they were preparing to do him in, using some grisly pagan custom. Fortunately one of his captors knew a little Spanish, and the conquistador quickly explained that his god was vastly superior to their gods. This argument seemed to have no effect. He then pulled out all the stops. The well-read conquistador, who had been studying the six-teenth century version of an almanac, announced that his god was an-noyed at one of his servants being detained, and to show his ire, the sun would grow dark. The conquistador went on to describe, in lurid detail, how his god would continue to devour the sun until his un-friendly hosts agreed to release him.

The locals, upon hearing this pronouncement, looked at him with wide-eyed wonder and gathered around for a quick council meeting, with occasional glances over their shoulders. The conquistador, confident of his ploy, would point at the sky to reinforce his threat.

At last the council meeting broke up, and the CEO of the committee approached the alien who threatened to darken their world. Shaking his head, the CEO began to speak . . .

"We have heard and considered your threat to darken the sky. There seems to be a misunderstanding here. We never had any intention of doing you harm."

The conquistador smiled, nodding gravely now that he believed himself to be in the superior position and most likely contemplating hitting them up for all their gold as an appropriate "friendship" offering to help smooth things over.

"But," the chief suddenly continued, "you have insulted us beyond all ability to bear. Just who the hell do you think you are? Do you take us for a bunch of idiots? We'd like you to know that our calendar has been calculated out to a degree far superior to your own. Of course we knew a partial eclipse of the sun was due to start this afternoon at three-thirty-two P.M., Aztec Central Time."

The chief fixed the conquistador with an icy gaze. "Partial, not total. Such a childish trick might have worked with our Pueblo neighbors to the north, but around here it just isn't going to wash. Therefore, we've changed our minds and we've decided that you will be the entertainment for tonight. . . ."

Such a heart-rending end based upon an assumption of superiority in the realm of science and technology is usually quite rare. Though the one conquistador was definitely a loser in the clash between vastly different societal systems, the overall result of this confrontation was all but preordained. Native American culture was about to lose, as has any society when confronted by another that in some key area, usually military, has a technological edge.

In this unfortunate age of political-correctness thought police, perhaps some definitions are in order before exploring the topic of what happens when a "superior" culture meets an "inferior" one. The words *superior* and *inferior* do not necessarily imply that one society is intrinsically better than the other or that one society is, in an ultimate sense, right while the other is wrong. (Though this male of European descent does tend to side with the Spanish against cultures that ripped out human hearts, sautéed their victims' livers for dinner, and caponed captive children to fatten them up for the pot.)

The bottom line historically, whether one likes it or not, is that any society that is more technologically advanced will indeed come to dominate one that is inferior, and unless there is a Galactic Bureau of Multicultural Sensitivity that is armed with the quotas for the preservation of inferior cultures, chances are that humanity's first contact will result in a cultural subordination and collapse.

Let us consider several historical examples to support this view. The classic one is the rapid move on the part of Europe to dominate the rest of the world in the sixteenth and seventeenth centuries. Most of the ingredients that went into giving Europe the tools for this feat can be directly traced to a remarkable R and D program, undertaken by the Portuguese in the fifteenth century.

Portugal is a country blessed with next to nothing except rocky soil. The great trade routes of the fourteenth and fifteenth centuries, which were dominated by Italy, flowed from the Italian Peninsula to the Middle East, North Africa, and Constantinople and from there across Asia. The Italian trading states maintained a hammerlock hold on nearly all goods passing from the eastern to the western Mediterranean, with Portugal at the short end of the stick when it came to obtaining precious goods at affordable prices.

In the early fifteenth century Prince Henry the Navigator of Portugal established what could only be defined as a research lab and think tank to break the Italian monopoly to the east. The goal was to round Africa, a task they knew they could accomplish due to records of a Phoenician expedition that had circumnavigated Africa in the sixth century B.C. Nearly seventy years after starting the project, the first Portuguese ship rounded the Cape of Good Hope and crossed into the Indian Ocean. In that seventy-year interval of R and D, the Portuguese redesigned sailing ships, from vessels that were only capable of short-distance hops between coastal ports to ships capable of ranging for eight weeks or more without docking (the upper limit at this time being the question of vitamin C deficiency, which after sixty to seventy days results in scurvy). Perhaps the most important design factor was the efficient placement of broadside firing artillery, enabling the Portuguese, and the Spanish, English, French, and Dutch conquerors that followed, to shatter any seaborne opposition that might contest their arrival.

Here is the classic example of the impact of high- versus low-tech. One hundred to two hundred men aboard a caravel could venture ten thousand miles, project power, face thousands, and at times tens of thousands, in opposition, and still triumph. Granted there were minor reversals, the loss of ships to storms and local resistance, but the result was inevitable. The jump in technological levels between the Aztecs, the Incas, and the Carib as opposed to the Portuguese and the Spanish was of a magnitude comparable to the one between ourselves and a spacefaring society capable of transstellar travel at sub–light-speed.

My argument goes way beyond the simple point of impact in such a struggle: the moment when a conquistador wearing a breastplate, helmet, and armed with a fine Toledo sword, backed up with harquebuses and cannon, meets an Aztec warrior bearing a wooden or leather shield and wielding a club tipped with flint. Some might argue that this is no clear demonstration of superiority and wander off into a deconstructionist historical view that one weapon system is actually not all that superior to the other (an easy enough point to debate until your own life depends upon the choice of weapons). Amateur theorists might glibly announce that the whole game would have been evened up if only the Aztecs had been given a fair chance to fight with equal weapons, therefore showing that European society was not really so superior.

Let's imagine that this absurd idea were to be tried out. In a sudden show of good sportsmanship Cortés decides to give his opponents some modern weapons and even train them in how to use them (a philosophy of foreign affairs that seems all too prevalent at the State Department). After this training and a few handshakes the opponents withdraw to opposite ends of the field . . . and the Spanish still, to put it politely, kick their butts. For mere possession of high-tech weapons does not in any sense imply the potential for an even match. The reason is that the Spanish come from the society and mind-set that created both these weapons and the elaborate infrastructure, economic and social, that engendered them whereas the Aztecs are locked in a paradigm that is obsolete and doomed to extinction.

Tactical applications such as the tercio (firing by file, then countermarching to the rear, reloading, and coming forward to fire again) are ingrained in Spanish thinking. The Aztecs, even with such modern weapons, would not have any of the basic political, psychological, and physical infrastructure to support their continued use beyond one or two engagements. Nor could the type of social system that would support a modern war be cobbled on to the old Aztec methods; it would require a fundamental reordering beyond their ability. The high-tech weapons of the Spanish implied a modern system of organization, command, and control, logistical support, and even a different definition of war. Aztec society was simply incapable of mounting any type of effective resistance against high-tech warfare sixteenth-century style; it was beyond their ability to shape any type of effective reply.

Another argument for why the Aztecs failed to resist effectively is that their societal reasons for fighting a war were not suited to the type of war needed to be fought against their high-tech invaders. After initially securing their land by conquest, most of the campaigns fought by the Aztecs during the half century prior to the invasion were for the purpose of securing "messengers" for their gods. Campaigns were launched to harvest prisoners, and as a result stunning an opponent was far preferable to killing him. However, a mere stunning blow against an armored Spaniard tended to elicit a steel blade in the chest or a musket ball in the head as a reply.

Only one non-European society was ever able to mount an effective reply to the European expansion, and that was Japan. Portuguese explorers and missionaries reached Japan early in the sixteenth century, and within fifty years had established a thriving enclave centered in Nagasaki. In the last decades of the sixteenth century and early into the seventeenth, Japan was convulsed by a protracted civil war for control of the shogunate, a period that is the backdrop for most samurai films and for James Clavell's novel *Shogun*. A modern arms race developed between the rival factions, and the Portuguese followed the standard practice of supplying arms and technical expertise to any and all who could pay. By the time the Tokugawa faction had successfully wrested control from their rivals, clan armies of ten to twenty thousand musketmen, supported by artillery and siege trains, were in the field. A home-grown industry to supply guns, powder, and all the accouterments thrived within Japanese territory. The armies were so well trained that some believe Japan would have been fully capable of projecting its power outward, perhaps even to directly confront Spanish and Portuguese encroachments into Western Pacific waters. It is amusing to speculate that if the Hapsburgs had been able to hire the Tokugawas' battalions and ship them back to Europe, they might very well have shattered Gustavus Adolphus at Brentenfeld, and, given the Tokugawas' mastery of intrigue, might have moved from there to control of central Europe.

If the Portuguese, however, had even sensed the remotest possibility of a Japanese counterinsurgence using high-tech weapons, it is fairly safe to assume the pipeline would have been cut. The interesting conclusion to this particular issue, though, is the famous decision by the Tokugawas to revert back to an earlier status quo once the civil war was won. The Portuguese were expelled, all contact with the Western world was forbidden, and the precious artillery and muskets upon which Europe had built its empires were banned, thus allowing the continued dominance of the traditional samurai class.

The eventual conquest was, however, merely postponed.

In the post-Vietnam era it has become somewhat chic to argue that high-tech is ultimately a trap and that given certain circumstances the low-tech approach can indeed win. Examples such as our own Vietnam experience or the Soviet invasion of Afghanistan are the favorite examples. This argument is without merit. In both cases, the low-tech society was the proxy of a high-tech state and as such received a continual supply of high-tech weapons. North Vietnam had jet aircraft, a very sophisticated radar network, the latest SAMs, and open-ended logistical and financial support from a number of other sympathetic nations, such as China, Sweden, and certain areas of Hollywood.

The high-tech solution could have worked, for the argument that we fought with "one hand tied behind our backs" does have merit. The December 1972 bombing offensive clearly proves this point. After initial heavy loses, full air superiority was achieved over North Vietnam, whereupon they immediately went back to the only means by which they could win a victory, which was at the negotiating table.

This viewpoint might not sit well with those who have enshrined the antiwar movement and the memory of the heroic "people's struggle," but it is the cold reality. And it highlights one final point in the high-tech versus low-tech argument, one that must be considered in view of the potential of a First Contact. The high-tech answer to winning the war in Vietnam was very simple: Nuke 'em till they glow.

We had 'em and they didn't: Thirty or forty well-placed one-megaton warheads would have made the rice paddies bounce, and the war would have been over. Granted there might have been certain political ramifications, but those need not be considered here. Chances are that given enough bitter resolve, we might very well have bluffed the rest of the world into accepting our solution. Some readers might at this moment be convinced that I am a historian in need of therapy for such a suggestion. However, all I am saying is that we may have to accept the possibility of a universe without any fundamental sense of morality. The morality we humans have slowly evolved, in spite of such counterexamples as Rwanda, Auschwitz, and the Gulag, at least prevents most governments from incinerating children in a nuclear fire, even if they are "enemy" children. It is this "worldview" that thankfully prevented us from doing the Big One in Vietnam, though if Saddam Hussein had used poison gas in the Gulf War, the American public might very well have supported the popping of a nuke in reply (yet even with that provocation it is impossible to imagine President Bush authorizing such a vengeance shot against downtown Baghdad).

A fundamental point to realize in this discussion is that we are considering the application of high-tech versus low-tech in a human-versus-human setting. For the potential for darkness in a human-versus-alien contact we might look to history. John Keegan, in his seminal work *The Face of Battle,* noted that at Agincourt and Waterloo soldiers tended to more readily display compassion for their enemies who were of the same branch of service or social ranking than for those who were either above or below them. Cavalrymen tended to treat a wounded rival from the same branch of service as worth sparing, but would unmercifully slaughter fleeing infantry, even when they had cast aside their weapons and were incapable of resisting. Infantrymen, in turn, would bayonet a wounded cavalryman with relish while stepping past a wounded infantryman to get at the horseman. The same stood true of knights and yeomen at Agincourt, and tankers versus infantry at St.-Lô and the Bulge. At sea there has evolved a generally accepted tradition of rescuing fellow seamen once their ship goes down, and in the air the act of machine-gunning a man in a parachute is considered beneath contempt, except for one key exception: when a conflict has racial overtones.

The German-Soviet conflict from 1941 to 1945 stands completely apart from the struggle Germany waged against the Allies. The war on the Eastern Front was fought with an implacable fury because by both sides it was viewed as a racial conflict. German units that had fought on the Eastern Front, when transferred to the Western Front, often had difficulty "adjusting" to the more circumspect ways of fighting and dealing with enemy wounded and prisoners.

The war in the Pacific is an even more telling example. Japan clearly billed its offensive in the Pacific as a racial conflict to purge the region of the white invaders. The racial overtones were evident in our response as well. Such a simple thing as cartoons from the war period show the Japanese cast in the worst of racial stereotypes, while their German allies tend to be shown as mindless machines serving an authoritarian state. A famous *Life* magazine photograph from 1943 actually shows a young woman writing her Marine boyfriend a thank-you letter for the Jap skull he had sent to her as a souvenir. It's doubtful whether the story would have been run if the skull were German, or worse yet, the skull of an Italian, who at best was only half enemy, and a rather comical one at that.

Even the particular weapons deployed indicate the difference. Napalm was first used in the Pacific war and, due to ethical concerns, rarely in Europe. Indiscriminate firebombing was accepted practice for the U.S. Air Force flying over Japan, and yes, there were even some arguments regarding the greater ease of using atomic weapons on Nagasaki rather than on Düsseldorf. The war on both sides took on such an implacable character because it was extremely easy to dehumanize the opponent. And such an opponent is far easier to kill than one whose humanity you accept and can thus empathize with. This is the most disturbing point to consider when contemplating the reality of First Contact—for after all, dehumanizing aliens will be the easiest thing in the world for the most obvious of reasons. And from their perspective dehumanizing us, or dealienizing us, if you prefer, will be easy as well.

The shifting perceptions of First Contact as portrayed in popular culture have been interesting to follow over the past fifty years. The golden age of pulp fiction tended to dwell on BEMs (bug-eyed monsters), who came in search of conquest or with the clear intent of stealing women with Jane Russell physiques. Films of the forties and fifties were almost universal in their fearful vision of the results of First Contact, except for a few exceptions, such as *The Day the Earth Stood Still.* Two dominant themes were clearly visible: Either the aliens were here to conquer Earth or they would come as parental guardians, at best to save us from ourselves.

This trend was shattered with Steven Spielberg's two great classics, *Close Encounters of the Third Kind* and *E.T.* In both films Spielberg designed the physiology of the aliens to appeal to our own parental instincts. The aliens were friendly, visiting us either for the most altruistic of reasons or, even better, because they needed to be protected. Ever since, the dominant theme concerning First Contact has been either one of beneficence or, at worst, one in which occasional kidnappings occur for purposes of experimentation.

Literature in the field is mixed, ranging from Pournelle and Niven's *Footfall,* which deals with an enemy who should have won hands down but doesn't (because that is not how attempted best-sellers are made) to Carl Sagan's altruistic aliens of *First Contact.* Few, however, have truly examined the full implications and concerns a genuine First Contact will actually create.

Let us build a scenario with a number of variables in order to examine the potential outcome of this First Contact, assuming the date were to occur sometime within the next five years.

The first absolute given is that whoever contacts us will have a superior technology. Harry Turtledove, in a brilliant series of stories, created an alternate picture of aliens arriving with a sixteenth-century tech level, but the chance of such an event is all but impossible. The ability for interstellar travel, be it by direct propulsion, wormholing, warping, hyperdriving, or simply good old-fashioned multigenerational ark ships, implies a tech level centuries, perhaps millennia ahead of our own. They will be a superior civilization, whether we like it or not.

There can be but three basic attitudes these aliens will possess when they encounter us: They will be either hostile, friendly, or neutral with the capacity to go either way at some future date.

The "universal view" of the Roddenberry, Spielberg, and liberal wing of science fiction postulates that if a civilization has survived long enough to arrive at a tech level capable of supporting interstellar flight, it must have learned to transcend the random and organized acts of violence in which humanity indulges. The reasoning is that failure to master this trait would otherwise have resulted in self-annihilation due to the potency of weapons high technology can create. It is a comforting assumption, for it implies that whoever we meet will therefore be peaceful and will show us the path as well. It is an argument that is fundamental to the "universe" of *Star Trek* with its Federation rules of noninterference, a premise that therefore explains why there hasn't been a true First Contact yet: We are simply not ready for the honor and privilege of joining the friendly galactic club.

It is a warm thought to go to sleep with at night, dreaming that the universe is a friendly place and that when we grow up, we can play too. But any civilization that sleeps with that dream is just waiting to get clubbed— simply ask the rest of the world about maintaining such a view in the sixteenth and seventeenth centuries when European "transcontinental" ships spread their sails and swept across the universe of Earth.

One standard argument against this scenario is that if an aggressive civilization is out there, why haven't they bumped us off already. This is false logic, the second step of the process being that since we haven't been bumped off yet, this stands as proof that there is nothing bad out there. This is as absurd as an Aztec or Maori being granted the realization of other continents in the fourteenth century and then arguing that since they haven't been invaded, there is therefore nothing to worry about.

By way of analogy, comets have been colliding with planets for billions of years, but up until recently such an event had never been witnessed, and many said it was absurd to worry about when compared with far more pressing problems here on Earth. In the summer of 1995 this argument was laid to rest. The problem is that if it had been us rather than Jupiter that was hit, a fair portion of humanity might have been finished. When it comes to cosmic encounters, hindsight tends to be useless after the fact.

But if there are bad guys cruising around the universe, why haven't we been hit yet? There are a wide number of possible responses. Maybe they don't know about us; maybe we don't have anything they want; or maybe they just haven't gotten around to it yet. If we accept the premise that UFO contacts are real, then the question of whether the folks out there know about us or not is moot—we are on the map.

So why no invasion or direct contact? An analogy might very well be found in the exploration of the Pacific by European navies and merchant ships. The South Pacific is dotted with thousands of islands. Certain islands that were found to be rich in resources or were located along certain strategic routes were quickly explored, outposts were established, and these islands were later overrun by missionaries, settlers, and French artists. There were hundreds of other islands that were barely touched. The locals might see an occasional ship sail by on the horizon, in much the same way we report seeing the occasional UFO, but none bothered to stop, for there was nothing there worth exploiting, or perhaps a better harbor was to be found at the next island over the horizon.

With this analogy in mind, it's interesting to remember that these islands became one of the battlegrounds for World War II. Overnight millions of soldiers from both sides flooded into the Pacific, vast fleets roamed the seas, and armadas of silver-winged gods crisscrossed the skies. Yet except for certain key strategic points, many of the islands were barely touched by the war and the native populations were left alone. Along these lines it is disturbing to consider that the occasional UFO could be a kind of PT boat or P-38 Lightning recon flight just checking up on this forgotten atoll to make sure the enemy is not lurking about. If so, let's hope we don't wake up one morning to discover that we're the next Tarawa or Guadalcanal in a war we know nothing about and have no stake in other than the fact that we're the beachhead about to get softened up, our casualties defined simply as "unavoidable noncombatant damage."

So if there is a civilization out there with the intent to do us harm eventually, there remains the question, Why haven't we been hit yet? The ultimate answer is that it doesn't really matter why. It could be that there is no reason to do so yet, there are questions of strategic necessity, or that some petty princeling has yet to wake up with an upset stomach and the need to vent his spleen (if he indeed has a spleen). In a broader historical sense the timing of it doesn't matter, only the ultimate end result: annihilation.

And annihilation or enslavement would be the only possible end result, all fantasies of *War of the Worlds* and *V* aside (besides, no high-tech civilization would be stupid enough to invade without considering the possible biological hazards, and as for invading Earth to steal our water, that's even dumber than coming here to steal overly endowed women wearing Wonderbras). It's amazing how many inferior SF stories and films involving an invasion have the bad guys arrive with their fleet and then swoop down to peashoot us to death, chasing people up and down the streets in a game of laser tag. Pournelle and Niven at least touched on what would really happen in *Footfall:* An attacker holding the high ground of space would simply stone us to death.

If our enemies are at the lower end of the high-tech scale—in other words, they arrive here aboard sub-light ark ships—all they would need to do is to pick up a few dozen rocks the size of the Astrodome, boost them up to twenty clicks a second, and let them hit. The impact of a few million tons of mass hitting at twenty kilometers per second would be rather impressive. Once the firestorms had died down, the rest would be easy: no elaborate battles, no gallant human heroes rising up to do battle in hurriedly constructed X-40 transatmospheric fighters—the show would be over, and those survivalists hiding in Idaho could fight it out with their M-16s and finally with spears.

If our asocial neighbors were to arrive here and possess a higher tech level with the capability of going translight, the game would indeed be over. Try calculating out the resulting explosion from one kamikaze ship of a thousand tons' mass impacting into our precious world at 0.9 light-speed. I'm sorry to report that all the elaborate preparations of *Star Wars*' Empire in building not one but two Death Stars was a boondoggle worthy of our own Congress, and almost as absurd as a B-2 bomber. The same effect on Princess Leia's planet could have been achieved by taking an antiquated star cruiser, pointing it at her world, and hitting the full-speed-ahead button.

End result of any war delivered from space: We lose.

There is one version of this scenario that should be considered, though, which is the thesis that within the next fifty to seventy-five years we may achieve a high enough tech level to prepare ourselves for such an attack. This enlightened approach could be the result of a sudden global awareness that all our eggs are in one basket and that a one-percent investment of global GNP to ensure that our genetic pool will still be around a millennium from now just might be worth it. At the very least it could mean that we don't experience here what must have occurred on Jupiter when the shock waves from the comet rippled through its atmosphere. Another motivater might be a warning of some sort, either from a less than belligerent visitor or by picking up some info, either from SETI or the next generation of deep-space telescopes, that indicates a war is going on out there. An analogy might be that of a New Guinea native in 1940 somehow cobbling together a crystal radio and tuning in to Edward R. Morrow's broadcasts.

If we were therefore to prepare, chances are that in the end we'd still be listening to *Götterdämmerung* while putting on 100 sunblock and waiting for the shock wave to hit. Our definition of a forward defense, even as far out as the Moon or Mars, does not in the slightest mean we've matched technologies. The leap from orbital defense to trans-stellar flight is as profound as going from a couple of coastal galleys rowing back and forth outside the harbor to a sixteenth-century broad-side-firing galleon. To draw on the historical example again, the only way the Aztecs could have prevented the Spanish conquest was to have comparable ships standing off the Leeward Islands and the Bahamas ready to nail any Spanish ship before it could ever land and thus establish a base. Better yet, the Aztecs could have landed in Cádiz and Lisbon and torched the shipyards, thus further ensuring their own survival. Matching tech for tech and the forward projection of power are the only true solutions to the problems of dealing with aggressive neighbors. The Mahanian Doctrine undoubtedly applies to the seas of space as it did to the oceans of this world.

Forward projection of Earth's defenses into low or high orbit against a possible incursion would most likely not be effective against any type of organized attack, though it might help fend off the occasional free-booter. Our opponents could hang out in the asteroid belt and play "dump the rock down the gravity well," with us waiting at the bottom. The only true defense in the long run against a belligerent neighbor is forward projection to the edge of our system and beyond, to make sure that a true First Contact occurs where we would have some hope of meeting as equals, while at the same time the process of creating this forward projection would elevate our own tech level to a potential match with whoever is out there.

A question might be raised here as to why an alien race would even be interested in conquering and killing us. The most cynical of answers could be, Why not? History is filled with examples of one society or group attacking another for no better reason than the simple fun of it. Native American cultures, counter to what their p.c. defenders say, took immense delight in waging war on their neighbors in order to prove their machismo, to count coup, and to round up an occasional guest for a late-night torture session. Nearly every preindustrial society viewed warfare as a means of testing one's manhood, gaining stature and honor, and of course picking up a little loot on the side. Actually, nationalistic and ideological goals are a fairly recent development for most of the world. It would be dangerous to assume that there are no civilizations out there that do not view warfare in such a light.

Such an attack might not even be an organized act by a state. Many a community of natives in the Caribbean was raped and slaughtered by freebooters who had nothing better to do that day. Or we might find ourselves caught up in a Kiplingesque story involving a couple of discharged alien soldiers who decide they want to be king.

What is even more frightening is the thought of an alien sociopath running amok on our world. There could very well be a Jeffrey Dahmer or Ted Bundy out there right now, licking his three sets of lips and looking for a race to trash since "there's nothing else to do tonight." If his ship were to pack trans-light-speed capability, the task would be simple, again through the act of accelerating up a couple of rocks. We might someday wind up as an article on page seven of the galactic newspapers alongside accounts of worlds getting swallowed by wandering black holes (the front page, of course, would be devoted to the latest marital difficulties of the galaxy's imperial family). An alien agent would obtain the film rights, an alien Geraldo might devote a talk-show hour to how the sociopath was actually the victim driven to his act by a cruel universe, and the alien Bundy would eventually write a best-selling book ... while we, dear reader, would be no more.

What else might they want besides our heads? There are some valid speculations that for a higher technology, civilized planets are worthless pieces of real estate. Why bother to go down into a gravity well when all the resources needed for life can be garnered from asteroids and low-gravity moons and when limitless energy streams by from the stars? If this scenario is true, then perhaps there is an explanation for the absence of organized contact. We could very well be like the tribes that live at the bottom of Copper Canyon in Mexico and the Grand Canyon. The mile-and-a-half hike straight down to tangle with someone simply isn't worth the bother, especially when they don't have any unique resources that are not just as easily obtainable up on the plateaus. Again this logic has a certain flaw to it, since we are dealing with all our eggs in one basket. One misassumption can result in annihilation, not to mention the fact that just because it hasn't happened yet doesn't mean it won't.

Perhaps there might be certain scarce resources here. Maybe they like the view or want to open up a vacation theme park. We could very well be a Midway Island or Tinian, our position suddenly having great strategic significance. Or, on an even darker note, we could be a vast potential labor pool.

Most speculations about high-tech societies postulate the eventual creation of cornucopia machines, automated devices capable of making whatever we desire. But suppose this is not necessarily true. A society pressed by war needs significant raw resources and the labor to manufacture the tools they desire. One of the more amusing details of the *Star Wars* trilogy I often wondered about was where the rebel forces kept the massive logistical and industrial support required for their resistance movement. In World War II, both Germany and Japan saw their conquests not only in terms of the precious natural resources they gained but also the hundreds of millions of slaves they subjugated who could then be used to off set the numerical advantages of their opponents.

Slavery might not be dead out there after all. Would we cooperate? Absolutely ... especially if they held the high ground and could wipe us clean in a single strike. The Mongols used such a system to rule most of Russia for a hundred and fifty years. There was no need for an occupation, just a clear understanding that as long as the tribute flowed, the local princes would be left to their own devices; if the tribute failed, total destruction was the result. Again, such an act might not be a policy by an organized state. We could see ourselves facing the alien equivalent of the East India Company, or Walker's filibusters in Nicaragua, or the equivalent of the Free Corps units that wandered the Ukraine immediately after World War I.

One final argument against all of this might be that a destructive war would damage a fragile ecosystem that in and of itself might be the most precious resource in the universe. Fine, then simply spread a genetically engineered Ebola that is airborne and dropped like cluster bombs around the world. Who knows? Maybe all the alleged medical experiments conducted on abductees are leading straight to this point.

With all this speculation about an overtly hostile attack, some attention should nevertheless be devoted to the fantasy that maybe, just maybe, they're nice and friendly out there, that they're sort of just like Americans or at least how Americans would like themselves to be seen. They'll come down the gangplank of their cruise ships smiling indulgently at our quaint native customs, speak platitudes about the beauties of galactic multiculturalism, and offer to set up a galactic New Deal or Great Society program to end poverty. If they should ever arrive in this manner, like a bunch of Washington consultants from the Department of Alien Resources and the Equal Galactic Opportunities Commission, my recommendation is to lock the door.

Tied in to this fantasy is the belief that such visitors would arrive with a host of panaceas, such as a cure for cancer, a means for ending war, limitless energy, and the elimination of daytime television talk shows. Let's consider but one of these "gifts," a universal cure for cancer. How could something like that not be greeted with resounding joy? Personally, I've lost friends to the disease, had a bad scare with my dad some years ago, and fear the rotten thing might come someday to get me as well. Who in their right mind would not be overjoyed with such a gift from our loving neighbors?

What about the medical industry devoted to cancer, which in the United States alone receives hundreds of billions of dollars a year in income, along with the tens of billions of dollars in capital investments? If such an improvement were offered, one of the largest industries in America would be shut down within twenty-four hours and hundreds of thousands of highly trained professionals would be out on the street. The shock wave would then reverberate through the pharmaceutical industry and into the myriad support services, ranging from hospital food services (perhaps worth destroying anyhow) to coffin makers. The tens of billions going into the training of new personnel and R and D would dry up overnight. A thriving import industry of tens of thousands of patients coming from around the world for treatment would stop, and the export industry of what used to be high-tech medical equipment would cease as well, thereby further disrupting the United States' balance of trade. The stock market would be in turmoil as investors in any area, or subrelated area, of the medical industry would dump out. And what about Social Security? The actuarial tables used to project what we will need in the year 2015 to keep Social Security afloat are finely tuned calculations. Millions of baby boomers who would have fallen victim to the Big C and thus never make it to retirement will now be standing with hands outstretched, waiting for their fair share. FICA taxes might very well have to double, thereby further increasing the tax burden and affecting the money supply available to deal with paying off the deficit. A simple solution might be to raise the retirement age to seventy-five, but any politician who even dares to suggest this will be lynched by the AARP.

Reverberations continue to spread. The population curve would climb even higher, placing additional strains on natural resources. And what about disease envy? Though cancer would be gone, wouldn't those people dealing with heart disease, TB, pneumonia, Parkinson's, Lou Geh-rig's, and so forth now turn to our benefactors and scream, "Hey, what about us?" If, by this point, our friends were becoming increasingly disgusted with the whining triggered off by the cancer cure and decided to withhold additional cures, what might the reaction be then? Or sup-pose the only trick they had in their bag was cancer; they might say so, but would we believe them? And finally, suppose they did offer all those cures. The reverberations created by the cure for cancer would be magnified a hundredfold.

Now apply this scenario to an ending of war. There would be almost universal praise, followed by massive layoffs and dislocations, and our friends would be burdened with the additional task of wearing blue hel-mets and going into "friendly" places like the Balkans, Central Africa, and Los Angeles to keep the peace, since people would still go after one another with knives or whatever other weapons they could contrive.

One rather amusing speculation applies to the area of religion. Let's imagine that our friendly aliens are a truthful lot and have been hanging around above us for some time. Now they admit that religion X (think of a belief system you don't agree with) is false, that Prophet So-and-so never lived, or that he or she got the story wrong, or, worst of all, that the guy ascending into heaven was actually the result of a teenage-alien prank played on the gullible natives. Chaos, absolute chaos, would be the result. I can think of a rather fanatical branch of one religion that would go truly ballistic, denounce the aliens as the Greatest Satan, and murder them on sight. Then what?

Concerning other aspects of technology, let us say they were to offer us limitless energy and the ability to travel to the stars, what then? Historically examples of cultural dislocation triggered by the impact of a high-technological society on a low-technological one are in general rather depressing if you are on the low end. Traditional industries, social organizations, community structures, and systems of government are thrown into turmoil. Such instances include the Portuguese, French, and British impact on India; the British, French, and American whaling industry in the South Pacific; Russian expansion into Central Asia; and of course the relentless American expansion across the continent.

Even if we were dealing with an alien contact in which information was the sole item exchanged, Earth's society would be thrown into tur-moil. The path of technological advancement is strewn with dislocation and rebirth. As each new advance in technology takes place, it inevitably produces a traumatic impact on some group, at times on an entire so-ciety. Someone loses so that others may win. The demonstration of the full interchangeability of parts by the gun manufacturer Colt at the Crystal Palace Exposition of 1852 is a classic example. During the period of the Napoleonic Wars interchangeability of parts had been crudely introduced with the standardization of the production of pulley blocks for the Royal Navy as well as for Eli Whitney's system of producing muskets. However, the true interchangeability of parts without the need for any additional milling was not clearly demonstrated until Colt opened up a booth in the American Pavilion at the World's Fair in London. Colt stole the show and at the same time triggered a panic in the European arms market. The British Parliament actually sent an investigative committee to America to find out what was going on; it returned with the pessimistic report that Great Britain was about to lose its dominant position as leader of the Industrial Revolution.

What about other negative impacts? Colt's system of automation in the making of parts for his revolvers employed leading-edge machinery—and semiskilled labor. The skilled artisans who had been needed to carve out musket stocks and do the fine-tooling of forged gun parts were now finished. Thousands of highly skilled workers in the worldwide gun industry were out of work within a decade. An impact some don't even realize is that the British government wound up contracting with Springfield to purchase the new high-tech systems for the making of Enfield rifles. By 1861 the new system was on line, just in time to supply the Confederate government with hundreds of thousands of quickly mass-produced precision muskets. Rather ironically this supply enabled the Confederacy to arm itself and, in some cases, go into the field during the first year of the war with equipment superior to that of the Union troops. Without this new high-tech mass production the South would not have been properly armed and might very well have fallen far earlier than it did.

The same type of unforeseen impacts were true with Ford's system, which made the automobile affordable to the middle class. Hundreds of thousands who worked in the older transportation industry—wheelwrights, harness makers, blacksmiths, feed suppliers, and city street sweepers—were soon out of work. Granted, the upside of these changes is that those who are dislocated will eventually reenter the marketplace working at a higher tech level. We can see this ourselves in our own family histories. Our parents and, even more likely, our grandparents tended to work as manual laborers. Now that technology has eliminated those jobs, later generations accept the change as a normal part of existence.

The problem with a friendly alien exchange is that the technological changes we ourselves might have evolved over a hundred, five hundred, or five thousand years will be compressed into an intense few months. There will be little if any time lag, no transitional technological paths, no multigenerational process of change. It will happen all at once, with the potential that in short order a major part of the global economy might very well be dislocated. Hundreds of millions who labor, identify themselves through their work, and take pride in what they do will find that their products have become worthless. Europe did this to the rest of the world during the Industrial Revolution, but even at its worst the impact was spread out across decades and enveloped the world in a wave movement rather than crashing into the entire global population in one overnight explosion.

As an SF writer I must say that my very first reaction upon hearing of a "friendly" First Contact would be one of both wonderment and elation. However, it's the more sober thinking that comes after the contact that is troubling. Perhaps few of us realize just how far-reaching the implications might be. I'm a history professor and author; the potential impacts: My services as a professor might very well be obsolete, at least in the classroom. Consider a true AI teaching computer, a 3CPO professor with infinite patience, programmed with the teaching skills of a true master, capable of full-interactive display, armed with actual holo films of all the major events since the Egyptians—my presence in the classroom would be, as they say, history. The author side? I might still have a chance, but suppose all our literary forms are turned upside down by the literature of our friends. The whole field of SF might be dead, or else require a massive reeducation of our authors. The entire publishing industry might go belly-up as well if traditional forms of information transfer were to be rendered obsolete.

Multiply this phenomenon across nearly every aspect of our society and within six months of the aliens' arrival the welcome mat might very well be replaced with hundreds of thousands of protesters outside their embassy, screaming, "Aliens, go home!" (Sounds familiar, and when considered from this perspective, perhaps it is now a bit easier to understand why American influence is sometimes viewed with such intense hostility.)

Yet, once they are here, they will in a sense never be able to truly go home again. We might try the Japanese method of sealing the borders and kicking them out, but their influence will still be there: the fundamental realization that we are not alone and must now deal with the rest of the universe. Old paradigms will be shattered, with no time to adjust to the new. Societal trauma will be the inevitable result.

One of the limitations of many historians, both liberal and conservative, is their ability to identify the profound societal shifts that ensue from invasions, plagues, wars, and collapse but lose sight of the individual traumas such events generate. We can evaluate a particular occurrence as being ultimately good for the progress of humanity, yet forget that it usually entails profound loss for millions of innocents. It is easy to be detached because, after all, these people have been gone for hundreds, often thousands, of years and thus are more abstract than real. We might marvel at the beauty of St. Petersburg, but we tend to forget that it was built on the bodies of a hundred thousand slave laborers. Or we might agree upon the benefits of turning the Great Plains into the food basin of the world, but only if we don't feel a personal connection with the original inhabitants. Great historical events often have wonderful results, so long as it's not your generation who is going through it.

Perhaps, in a long-term sense, a friendly First Contact experience might be beneficial for humanity. It might save us from ourselves, it might open up the universe to us, we all might live to a hundred and fifty. On the other side, especially in regard to short-term upheaval, there would be massive economic collapses, severe social turmoil, the disintegration of comfortable norms, and a form of global traumatic stress syndrome. Maybe our great-grandchildren might appreciate the effects of a friendly contact in this present time, but for those who'd experience it now, the incredible sense of wonder it would engender would be tempered by all that would follow.

We've been lucky so far. We might very well avoid contact until after we are "out there," when the consequences would be minimal. If, by chance, you are the one who is contacted while out for a ride on some country road, enjoy the experience, then do us all a favor—tell them to go home until we're ready; otherwise we might all find ourselves experiencing that wonderful Oriental curse, "May you live in interesting times."

IIIIIIII

THE ARAÇARIGUAMA INCIDENT
by William R. Forstchen, Ph.D.

OF THE VARIOUS INCIDENTS reviewed in this book the Araçariguama Incident is perhaps the most terrifying. There have been reports of fatal consequences caused by encounters with UFOs, but if this one is true, the manner of death is perhaps the most disturbing on record.

The incident occurred on March 5, 1946, in Araçariguama, a small, isolated village in the Brazilian interior. Strange lights had been observed in the sky before March, moving about in an irregular fashion over the forests and mountains. March 5 was Shrove Tuesday, a festival day, and Joao Prestes Filho of Araçariguama had spent the day fishing with a friend. Joao's friend later testified that Joao had seemed in the best of health and there had been no indications of any problems, either physical or emotional.

Joao left his friend at approximately seven in the evening to return home. An hour later Joao burst into his sister's house, shouting that when he had opened the window of his own house after arriving home, he had been struck by an intense beam of light; stunned, he had fallen to the ground, then had got up and fled.

Neighbors of his sister came over, and Joao kept repeating his story. One of the witnesses was Aracy Gomide, thirty-nine years old, a fiscal inspector for the prefecture of São Roque and also a local medic or EMT. Gomide testified that at first the only evidence that something unusual had occurred was the terror displayed by Joao, but then strange and frightening symptoms began to appear.

Joao's skin turned colors, looking as if he had been boiled—and then it literally started to fall off his body in large hunks. Joao's flesh began to drop off from his jaws, chest, arms, hands, legs, and feet. His bones were clearly visible, with only small pieces of flesh clinging to the tendons. Next his ears and nose slid off his body. Amazingly Joao at first did not seem to feel any real pain. He tried to talk, but the only sounds that came from him were meaningless gurgles and cries.

He was loaded into a cart, and Gomide and other members of the community tried to rush him to the nearest hospital, which was hours away, but he died before getting there. The death certificate simply read that Joao had died from generalized burns.

Subsequent investigations revealed nothing unusual or out of place regarding Joao's house. There were no witnesses to the actual event and no other deaths reported, but for months afterward there were continued reports of lights bobbing and weaving in the night sky.

ANALYSIS

Joao's death reads like a script from a horror movie. One can only imagine the terror of watching someone literally disintegrate while still alive, the symptoms similar to having been boiled to death or exposed to high-pressure steam for a prolonged period. However, the amount of time it would have taken for boiling water or steam to lift flesh from bones would have killed Joao outright, and the witnesses claim that when Joao first arrived at his sister's house, the only evidence that something was amiss was his obvious terror. Also, Joao did not say he was in pain, though anyone who has been injured by boiling water or steam knows that it is a very painful experience.

There's no known pathogen that could create Joao's symptoms, in spite of some of the overwritten prose regarding Ebola and other diseases. True, some things can break down a person's body, but they do not cause a person to disintegrate piece by piece in a matter of minutes.

What happened? We simply don't know. None of the flesh was preserved for later evaluation, there were no other witnesses, and all we have is a report from a very reliable witness, that someone in Araçariguama died a horrible death from an unknown cause. If we accept the UFO theory, it is interesting to note two facts: (a) there are no other documented cases of such a terrible death (though there are numerous reports of skin discoloration, burns, and symptoms that seem to indicate exposure to radiation or intense electromagnetic fields); and (b) the date of the event is a couple of years before what we could define as the modern outbreak of UFO sightings. One could speculate that Joao was the unfortunate victim of an early contact and that subsequent visitors have taken the precaution of not exposing people to whatever it was that killed Joao. This idea at least offers the comfort that Joao's death was accidental, because if it was by design, the implication is indeed troubling and makes one wonder when it might happen again.

JUST HOW DANGEROUS
IS THE GALAXY?

by David Brin, Ph.D.

There may be another reason why we
haven't been contacted by extraterrestrials,
several in fact. These all relate to the fact
that life as part of an interstellar community
may be rougher than that in any neighborhood
on the earth. Dr. Brin also speculates on the
serious question of what we can do if the
pilots of the UFOs are as far above us in
intelligence as we are the animals.

"The Universe has many more ways of being nasty, if it so chooses, than we had thought."

This was one conclusion we arrived at in my article titled "Xenology" (see page 221). That article began straightforwardly enough, as an overview of the "Great Silence": the strange and apparently longstanding absence of extraterrestrial intelligent life. However, by the time it was over, it seemed to lead us ever closer to a stark realization.

Something strange and perhaps very dangerous may be going on out there.

Put simply, we should not have been alone this long. In fact, it seems we shouldn't even exist!

By all of the logic of contemporary science, the Milky Way should be teeming with commerce and conversation and the noise of millions of intelligent life-forms—just as depicted in so many SF tales. Interstellar travel is not trivial, but it *is* quite feasible, according to many leading scientists. And even the simple starships that appear within a century's reach of our own crude technology should enable an expanding civilization to fill the galaxy in under a hundred million years, one percent of the age of the Milky Way.

The Earth should have been settled, not once but many times, over the last three billion years. The traces of past occupation of the solar system should be visible in the rocks and sky. And yet they are not.

Oh, there were fables aplenty, back when Europeans started exploring and conquering. But every "lost civilization" turned out to be one of our own—human. In tilling and excavating our planet, miners and builders haven't stumbled over the crumbled ruins of alien cities. They find no odd ores that are inexplicable by natural processes. Notwithstanding silly films about Easter Island and the Nazca Plain, there is simply no good evidence that the Earth has ever been visited at all.

All it would have taken was a sandwich wrapper, dropped by a visiting alien during the pre-Cambrian Period, to have set off changes we could read today in rocks all over the Earth. For during that two-billion-year epoch nearly any invasion by outsider microbes might have overwhelmed our primitive ancestors and left unmistakable traces. Obviously pre-Cambrian visitors were either very tidy or else they never existed.

All this is strange, but the disturbing evidence of absence continues as we look upward.

Venus and Mars show no signs of ever having been terraformed, nor do the asteroids appear to have been moved or altered in any way—activities our great-grandchildren will presumably think are everyday.

Finally, we haven't met any wise old alien star robots, as Frank Tipler of Tulane University calculates we should have by now. According to some fairly strong logic, such "Von Neumann probes" should have arrived long ago, and would have been waiting ever since for the Earth to evolve someone smart enough to talk to.

Well, we've got radio and space travel now. But no friendly robot has said hello yet.

Where *is* everybody? Does this really mean we are alone?

Debate over this issue has come as a shock to believers in SETI (the Search for Extraterrestrial Intelligence). Just when they seemed to have won acceptance, suddenly they had to contend with jokes that exobiology was "the only scientific field without a subject matter."

The argument has raged in some of the most prestigious astronomical journals, featuring a philosophical war of sorts between those who might be called the "Contact Optimists," led by Carl Sagan and Frank Drake of Cornell University, and the "Uniqueness" proponents, spearheaded by Drs. Frank Tipler, Eric Jones, and Michael Hart. The discussions have been heated, at times even peevish-sounding.

Tipler, for instance, has claimed that Sagan's obsession with aliens arises out of some sort of innate human fear of loneliness, which one rises above only with courage to face the emptiness that we will fill.

Sagan declares, in turn, that Tipler and his companions suffer from their own "innate human fear," that of the alien and the unknown. Of course it is only with courage that one rises above this fear to face...

...You see how the logic goes.

Here we'll try to summarize the issue as it stands today, and go on to look over some of the letters readers sent in, in response to the original periodical publication of "Xenology." We will see if some of them have offered up any new ideas.

THE RETREAT OF THE CONTACT OPTIMISTS

In June 1984, a new subunit of the International Astronomical Union gathered in Boston, devoted solely to discussing the question of extraterrestrial intelligence. At that meeting the trend of several years has continued. The Contact Optimists—those who have fought the hardest to believe we have neighbors in space—continued to beat an organized retreat. They have dug in behind fortress hypotheses—offering excuses for the tardy, laggard extraterrestrials—struggling to explain their strange failure to appear.

In so doing, the Contact forces have begun to sound downright gloomy. Indeed they hardly deserve the appellation "optimists" anymore!

Starships are impossible, some of them declare.

The ETs kill themselves off before they get very far, others say.

Or extraterrestrials are pinchpennies, who would shrink back from the challenge of the stars.

All this from the scientists who once carried the science-fictional banner. Strangely, it is their opponents, the Uniqueness crowd, who now cluster in excited circles at these conferences, chattering about starships and galactic colonization... colonization to be done by our descendants in a frontier galaxy.

Just who are the "conservatives" in an argument like that? We certainly do live in fascinating times.

In response to "Xenology," we received readers' reactions to the problem posed by the Great Silence. Before we get to those suggestions, however, it might be a good idea to review the problem, briefly.

Many will recall our discussion of the Drake Equation, for decades the main tool in thinking about possible distribution of technological species in the galaxy.

If N is the current number of technological civilizations in the galaxy, then

$$N = Rf(p)n(e)f(l)f(i)f(c)L$$

where R is the average rate of star formation; $f(p)$ is the fraction of stars that are calm and long-lived and accompanied by stably orbiting planets; and $n(e)$ is the average number of planets per star system that have the requisite conditions to support life.

The other factors include $f(l)$, the fraction of these congenial planets on which life independently appears; $f(i)$, the fraction of *these* on which "intelligence" spontaneously develops; $f(c)$, the fraction of those intelligent species that attain technological civilizations, and L, the average life span of such species after attaining technology.

For what still seem fairly good reasons, Contact people assign rather high values to most of these factors. For instance, most astronomers tend toward the belief that good, "candidate" planets circling favorable stars should be fairly common.

Similarly, modern biologists mostly seem to accept odds for life and intelligence that aren't fantastically small.

According to the old SETI logic, a likely planet will contribute roughly 0.01 technological races during its history. Multiplied by several billion candidate systems, this results in an expectation that there could be anywhere around a million advanced species in the galaxy at this very moment.

Before 1975, when most scientists still thought interstellar travel was impossible, these numbers sounded just fine. A million scattered races, all living on the planets where they evolved, meant a mean separation of a few hundred light-years between civilizations—perfect for a network of radio communications among patient, wise peoples. The SETI forces figured that once their multichannel analyzers were finished and they got enough radio telescope time, they would stand a fair chance of tuning in on this galactic web of chatter and friendly advice within a generation or so.

And then the excitement would begin. Once contact was made, the quiet assumption went, mankind would never be the same again.

As we have seen, the lovely logic fell apart under the realization that one form of starship or another really ought to be possible. With the introduction of travel, visitation, colonization, it becomes clear that an average separation of a few hundred light-years is trivial. Not only is the Drake Equation no longer complete. We see that it doesn't even predict anything anymore!

When we introduce star travel, we suddenly need three *new* factors:

> • *v*, representing the velocity with which an interstellar culture grows into space, pausing to settle likely solar systems and rebuild necessary industry before continuing its expansion again.
>
> • *L2*, which is the lifetime of a zone of colonization into which a species has expanded, after which the settled region becomes "fallow" once again.
>
> • *A* an "approach/avoidance" factor, different for each culture, representing a "cross-section for discovery" by contemporary human civilization. (In other words, how likely is it we would even notice them? For example, a culture with a preference for settling only comets would likely never even have visited the Earth and might exist even now in our solar system without our having discovered them.)

By including these factors in the appropriate formulas one can put together an algorithm to try to predict *C*—the probability of contact between human beings and extraterrestrials. (Alas, we cannot go into a detailed discussion of the mathematics here. Interested readers are referred to paper (1), cited at the end of this article. However, one requirement is that all the equations must reduce back to the Drake Equation again if starships turn out to be impossible. The equations do.)

We now have a "morphological" way of looking at the problem. The seven factors of the old equation, plus the three new ones, give us a "space" within which to sort out our ideas, an organizational aid that was missing until now.

The ten probability terms are vital. It turns out the differences of opinion between the Contact and Uniqueness forces divide precisely according to *which* of these factors each uses to explain the absence of prior settlement of the Earth!

Contact proponents admit that visits to Earth have been sparse, if they have happened at all. They merely choose different explanations (or excuses) for the fact that we have observed no beings from other stars.

Uniqueness advocates tend to concentrate on the left and middle of the Drake Equation. For instance, some claim that planets are rarer than has been popularly believed, or that many Earth-like worlds get trapped into Venus-type runaway greenhouse effects, destroying any chance of developing life.

Other Uniqueness savants bitterly dispute this. Planets are plentiful, men such as Michael Hart say, but the odds of *life* developing are far smaller than people tend to believe. Life *will* appear on all those worlds, Hart insists, but only after our descendants bring it there with them.

Still others, such as Eric Jones of Los Alamos, claim that it is the step to *intelligence* that was a fluke here on Earth. It is unlikely to be repeated elsewhere.

Those on the Contact side disagree, of course. They believe the factors leading to technological civilization ought to be quite large. Technic societies should crop up all over the place. How, then, do the Contact forces account for the apparent absence?

Some, such as Frank Drake, still hang on to a belief that star travel cannot happen. Factor v does have its attackers, then, in the face of a tide of popular and inventive starship designs.

And hypotheses abound as to why extraterrestrials might *choose* to make themselves invisible: to avoid contacting us, or to abjure star travel even if it is possible, or to have neglected to settle our solar system in the more than three billion years that it has been prime real estate.

(The relevant "approach/avoidance" factor—A—was popular among those readers who wrote in. A number of diverse reasons were offered for why ETs might have refrained from colonizing—or even visiting—the Earth. The range of ideas was enthralling and a tribute to the breadth of human imagination.

(But that's just the point! Any of those explanations might work for one or two alien races—maybe for a dozen. But if any ETs were as diverse as men and women, the excuses run into trouble. Can the Contact people seriously contend that out of millions of races, *some* would not behave as humans do in so many SF novels, setting forth in their space conestogas to settle and alter their new homes?

(True, aliens "might think differently than we do." But if there are enough of them, ought not a *few* to behave like us?)

As always, the most entertaining of the Contact Optimists was Carl Sagan. Anxious to find an excuse for the missing aliens, and too smart to disdain starships, he has come up with the most fascinating explanation of them all. And in so doing he and his colleagues have quite possibly done mankind a very great service.

NUCLEAR WINTERS

In the Christmas 1983 issue of *Science,* the prestigious journal of the American Association for the Advancement of Science, there appeared an article entitled "Nuclear Winter: Global Consequences of Multiple Nuclear Explosions." It has come to be referred to as "TTAPS"—after the initials of its authors, R. P. Turco, O. B. Toon, T. P. Ackerman, J. B. Pollack, and C. Sagan. In many ways this historic document has shaken up all prior thought over the potential consequences of modern major warfare.

If the models presented by the TTAPS authors are correct even within two orders of magnitude, one can only conclude that the present nuclear arms race between the great powers is a pointless waste of time and money. If they are correct, even a small, "limited" nuclear war will devastate the Northern Hemisphere and leave it barren of civilization, nearly denuded of life.

It would not be the awesome blasts, nor even the lingering radiation, those demons we have feared for so long. There is reason to believe some fragment of America or Russia might survive those effects.

Rather, it would be the cold and dark of a long, long winter that brought the great killing. Dust kicked up into the sky by as few as a hundred nuclear ground bursts, or soot launched into the stratosphere by airburst-ignited fires would, the scientists say, shut the world down into a frigid, years-long night which very little would survive.

Far short of an effective "first strike," any party trying to launch a sneak attack would doom its own citizens to starvation, even if the other side never retaliated at all!

At least that is the contention of the authors of the TTAPS paper. In the months following the *Science* article there have been numerous reported follow-up studies, but the scientific grapevine has yet to tell of anyone who has successfully disputed the article's overall conclusions.

Very interesting—and perhaps vital for us to think about—but what has all this to do with extraterrestrials?

Well, there is reason to believe that the nuclear-winter scenario had its birth in a struggle to find excuses for the absence of starfaring aliens!

In order to trace this kinked chain of logic, consider the position Contact proponents such as Sagan found themselves in, in recent years. Unable to convince themselves that starships are impossible, they had to come up with some universal mechanism to explain how both the *numbers* of extraterrestrial species and their *rate* of *colonization* and *expansion* could be small enough to explain the Great Silence.

Sagan's answer has been to propose the following:

Assume that two types of species achieve technology—the peaceful and the aggressive. Peaceful races will presumably not have the same assertive, greedy drives that have caused men and women to seize every opportunity to conquer and spread here on Earth. These quiet civilizations will expand into neighboring star systems only slowly, if at all. So slowly, in fact, that we can excuse their absence by saying, simply, "They just haven't arrived here yet!"

Only aggressive types would push ever outward, filling the galaxy as fast as the models of Jones and Hart and Tipler contend they would. And those species must first pass through a dangerous phase—that period between the discovery of nuclear weapons and the development of viable star travel.

Sagan maintains that there are only two ways of getting through this extremely awkward and hazardous period. Warlike species must either cure themselves of their aggressive tendencies (in effect becoming "peaceful") or they must die.

In other words, the "optimists" in this quandary are now suggesting that the galaxy is sparsely occupied by long-lived pacifists—who drive their starships only on Sundays, presumably—and by the ice-covered planetary tombs of all the rest . . . species who could not learn to control themselves.

But for this rationale to work, there had to be an easily triggered mechanism for destroying civilizations. It must be more powerful even than blasts and radiation, so compelling that one could envision it happening again and again, to every warlike race that failed to make the transition to a calmer mode of life.

The nuclear winter appears to offer Sagan's brand of Contact aficionado just such a mechanism.

Did the TTAPS paper—so topical and hotly debated today—arise originally out of a desire to explain the absence of extraterrestrials? I do not know for certain, but it is an intriguing possibility. If that is the way the thought processes worked, it would have to be one of the most fascinating quirks in intellectual history.

THE CHART OF EXPLANATIONS

Why do we seem to be alone?

All of the explanations offered have a quality in common. Each suggests a way to suppress one or more of the "factors" described above, in order to make the overall contact number fit the sparse (nil) observations. In an attempt to organize them for comparison, these theories have been arranged in a chart (see page 278).

Uniqueness proponents say that technological civilizations rarely develop and that some of the first four factors on the chart must be extremely small. Contact Optimists prefer to attack one or more of the four on the right, suggesting that there might be many alien races out there, but that they are short-lived, or slow to travel, or reluctant to make contact.

Many of these theories were discussed in the "Xenology" article on the Great Silence. We will go over them lightly here in review, and concentrate on those that got the biggest response from the readers.

EXPLANATIONS FOR THE GREAT SILENCE

As we've seen, the favorite explanations of the Uniqueness proponents have to do with ways in which the probability of spontaneous intelligence is suppressed.

Category One: *Solitude*

1. Habitable planets may be rarer than astronomers now believe. (Suppresses factor $n(e)$.)

2. Some unexpected "spark" may be needed to initiate life out of prebiotic compounds. (Suppresses $f(l)$.)

3. The final step to intelligence may require some "software miracle" that makes it far more improbable than currently expected. (Suppresses $f(i)$.)

The problem with these ideas is that they seem to go against the grain of most accepted modern science. But if they are right, we may simply be the first tool users ever to come along. We are the "Elder Race."

Does this stretch our credulity too far? Not according to some of our readers. A. J. Dunlop, S. Hervais, and Kathryn Drennan each wrote in to propose that the proper conditions for developing intelligent life might only have come about lately in galactic history. Each referred to the famed Russian scientist V. S. Troitskii's idea that until a few billion years ago conditions in the galaxy just weren't right yet.

Is it possible things simply weren't "ripe" until now? Certainly life had to wait until supernovas had spewed out enough heavy elements to make rocky worlds and organic chemistry possible. But those conditions were met long, long before the Earth was formed, and we are still left with the awkward question, Why us?

Still, the stew just might now have reached the point of simmering, and we could simply be the first to hop out of the pot.

4. Insatiable curiosity and manipulativeness, such as humans display, may be rare among intelligent species. (This effect would obviously suppress factor *f(c)*, the frequency of appearance of high technology.)

Three readers wrote in suggesting this alternative. Poul Anderson said, "The puzzle is why we're as bright as we are. Pithecanthropus was doing all right." He proposes that intraspecies selection, especially sexual, became fierce in protohumans, leading to a strange animal that is uniquely clever and capable of fitting itself to live in a vacuum or the bottom of the sea.

Kathryn Drennan of Glendale, California, and John Bowling of Troy, Alabama, suggested separately that most *Human* civilizations have been too conservative ever to have developed starships. To quote from Bowling's letter, ". . . Hero's steam engine . . . Roman aqueducts . . . Egyptian astronomy . . . What happened to the spaceship? The modern West did produce [them] . . . but is the modern West typical of [even] our one technological species?"

In other words, maybe the key was a not-too-likely cultural shift. Julian Jaynes, in his famous book *The Origin of Consciousness in the Breakdown of the Bicameral Mind,* proposed that such changes in the human being's software/firmware can be as important as all of the hardware development that went on as our brains grew.

There is one more variant on hypothesis four, called "Water Worlds," which the author holds in reserve for the end of this article.

Category Two: *Graduation*

5. It may be that technological species sooner or later discover *advanced techniques* that make radio and even colonization irrelevant (as suggested in numerous SF stories). Conceivable as this idea seems, it is

CHART OF POSSIBILITIES

	n_e	f_l	f_i	f_c	L	L_c	v	A_v
SOLITUDE								
1) Habitable planets are rare [1, 3]	[-]							
2) "Spark" of life rare [4, 5]		[-]						
3) "Spark" of intelligence rare [4]			[-]					
4) Few intelligences ambitious				[-]				
GRADUATION								
5) Undetectable technologies [2]								[-]
6) New Realms are beyond our ken [SF]							[-]	[-]
TIMIDITY								
7) Aversion to risk [2]							[-]	[-]
8) Self-cure against "aggressive tendencies" [2]							[-]	[-]
QUARANTINE								
9) "Zoo"								[-]
10) Fallow preserve [1]								[-]
11) Awaiting our maturity [SF]								[-]
12) Covert contact [SF]								[-]
13) Low rent								[-]
14) Friendly probes [3, 6]								±?
MACROLIFE								
15) Greedy planetary breakup [1]	[-]							
16) No contact with Nursery Worlds [1]								[-]
DANGEROUS NATURAL FORCES								
17) Galactic spiral arms [7]			-?	-?	-?		-?	
18) Falling rocks [7]			-?	-?	-?		-?	
19) Black holes, jets, and "deadly things" [1, 7]			-?	-?	-?		-?	
DANGEROUS "UNNATURAL" FORCES								
20) Migrational holocausts [1]				[-]	[-]			
21) Planetary breakup [1]	[-]							
22) Inevitable self-destruction [2, 8, 9]						[-]		
23) Deadly Probes [SF]						[-]		
OPTIMISM								
24) Water worlds [1]				[-]			[-]	[-]

[-] means the effect is expected to be negative on one of the factors
[+] indicates where it may be positive

Numbers in parentheses after listings are references to the list at the end of this article.

Column key:
- n_e: number of useful planets per star
- f_l: percentage that develop life
- f_i: percentage of f_l that gain intelligence
- f_c: percentage of f_i that attain technology
- L: span of isolated ETI
- L_c: characteristic ETI colony life span
- v: effective settlement expansion velocity
- A_v: approach/avoidance factor

hard to believe any race would totally abandon the electromagnetic spectrum, whatever its other options.

6. It has been suggested that spacefaring sophonts might "graduate" to *other realms* or unimaginable endeavors, coming to look on planets and starships as mere toys. This would set a limit to the period of expansion, though not, perhaps, to exploration.

Either of these scenarios would lower our expected contact cross-section, *A*, with such a civilization. They might also tend to reduce *v*. As reader Bob Ardler of England put it, advanced sentients have so often been depicted as more powerful Londoners or New Yorkers, "stupid, quarrelsome sex maniacs who happen to fly and read minds." But truly advanced sentients could be quite different.

Category Three: *Timidity*

7. There might be reasons races develop an *aversion to spaceflight*. Discovery of immortality, for instance, might make individuals reluctant to take even the slightest risk. (Suppresses *v* and/or *A*.)

8. Those species who do not destroy themselves may, as Sagan proposes, "cure" themselves of aggressiveness, and so become *slow starfarers*. (Suppresses *v* and/or *A*, but increases *L* and *L2*.)

Chris Rohr of Petaluma, California, wrote in to suggest that intelligent species might all develop a form of telepathy, through mind-computer links, which would make their lives far richer than existence as mere individuals. If this happened, then people might be reluctant to venture too many light-days from the center of their civilization in order to avoid, in effect, lobotomizing themselves.

It is a clever idea. Still, it is hard to say it would apply in *all* cases, which is what we need from an overall explanation—one that works convincingly.

Category Four: *Quarantine*

9. One venerable SF idea explains the Great Silence by suggesting that the solar system is kept as a sort of "*zoo*."

10. Or benevolent species have a tradition of letting "Nursery Worlds" lie *fallow* for long periods, allowing new sentience to nurture on likely planets.

11. Observers might be *awaiting* mankind's social *maturity*, or may have quarantined us as dangerous. A galactic radio club might avoid too early contact with beginners like us in order to allow us to develop our own unique culture to contribute to the galactic mix.

12. A listing would not be complete without including the farfetched idea that aliens are already in *covert contact* with governments and groups on the Earth. There is a charming Poul Anderson story about this concept, in which the Earth's sole "member of the Federation" was an obscure tribe of Southwest American Indians . . .

13. The *low rent* explanation suggests that the Earth has been simply too unattractive to be settled, or perhaps even visited by aliens. This idea was discussed in some detail in "Xenology." For various reasons it would seem unlikely.

14. Finally, it is possible that Frank Tipler's famous "probes"—those variants on John Von Neumann's self-replicating robots that should make star exploration cheap and easy for even the timid—might behave just a little differently than Tipler has imagined. Perhaps there are scores or hundreds of these friendly probes just sitting around in the solar system patiently waiting for us. It is conceivable that they do not consider mere access to radio sufficient proof that we are intelligent enough to talk to! Perhaps it is required that we prove our ability actually to go out there in person before they will deign to say hello.

Any of these ideas, if true, would dramatically affect the contact cross-section, factor *A*.

There is a problem with nearly all of the quarantine scenarios unfortunately. They all appear to call for some degree of cultural uniformity in the Milky Way, some mechanism by which the pattern can have been enforced not just recently but for billions of years in a galaxy of constantly shifting neighborhoods and star formations. Such a rigid pattern would seem well nigh impossible to accomplish in a relativistic universe.

Our readers seemed to understand this. Few letters even referred in passing to quarantine.

Category Five: *Macrolife*

It is possible to imagine another set of reasons why the Earth was never colonized. Perhaps waves of interstellar wayfarers *have* passed this way. If they had to take millions of years along the way, living in vast "slow-boat" starships, there might have been strong pressures selecting for the sorts of people who *like* living in space. It is conceivable they might come to abandon planet-dwelling as a lifestyle. This could lead to either of two different behaviors.

15. Truly spaceborne sophonts might greedily *fragment* terrestroid *planets* for building material and volatiles, having a terrible effect on factor *n(e)*.

16. Alternatively, they might have a tradition of *cherishing "Nursery Worlds,"* protecting them without any conflict of interest or desire to use high-gravity real estate.

Alas, there is a problem with *"macrolife,"* as well. We have looked over our asteroid belts carefully in recent years. These are the same small bodies that such starfarers would covet—which our own grandchildren may be melting and re-forming in a century or so.

Current analyses appear to indicate that they have been untouched since the beginning of the solar system. No one, it appears, has ever disturbed them.

You will recall we began this article with the statement that "The universe has more ways of being nasty, if it so chooses, than we had thought." This conclusion is particularly striking when we take note that *none* of the explanations offered to this point really seem to explain the Great Silence in a truly convincing way.

What is needed is a *universal* mechanism, one that acts impartially and over extremely long time scales, which would keep the numbers of extraterrestrial species small or suppress their rates of expansion among the stars.

A few ideas have been proposed that seem to fit these criteria. The reader is warned that some of them might be unsettling.

If it is any consolation, I will try to finish this article with an *optimistic* scenario, one that satisfies all of the above criteria without being nasty. In the meantime, however, let us proceed to the long list of ways in which the universe could be mean.

Category Six: *Dangerous Natural Forces*

Might there be aspects to the physical nature of the galaxy that make conditions hazardous to life or intelligence? Perhaps, as K. Arondee of Florida wrote in to suggest, the Earth is exceptional because it is among the few worlds lucky enough to have escaped some truly major natural disaster.

We have already mentioned the possibility that the Earth was lucky not to have fallen into the "Venus Trap"—the runaway greenhouse effect that killed our sister world—nor the perpetually frozen tundra of the "Martian Trap."

Here are some other "natural" hazards. Any of them could have disastrous effects on factors $f(l)$, $f(i)$, $f(c)$ or L.

17. *Spiral arms* are dangerous. In its 230-million-year orbit around the galaxy, our solar system is currently passing out of a gas- and dust-rich "spiral arm." We cross these regions of shocked gas clouds and hot young stars every hundred million years or so. Passages through the thick portions of the galactic plane come about three times as often.

These can be dangerous events. Spiral arms are where dense interstellar hydrogen clouds are compressed to form new stars and where supergiants flash through their tempestuous evolution to end their quick lives in supernova explosions.

It is not currently thought that these intermittent passages are so hazardous that life-bearing worlds are in perpetual danger of being sterilized; however, the possibility is serious enough to merit consideration. Dr. David Criswell of La Jolla, California, and A. J. Dunlop of London have each proposed that advanced cultures would eventually tire of playing galactic roulette and leave the spiral arms for good—setting up shop out in the Milky Way's "halo" of stars that drift in long, lazy orbits out of potential harm's way. That could, they say, explain why we don't see anybody flying around this part of the galaxy.

Those who can leave, do.

18. *Falling rocks.* In "Xenology," we covered some of the reasons why many scientists now believe the dinosaurs were killed off by a giant meteorite impact. Indeed, as many as ten major ecological catastrophes can be read in the Earth's crust, when large numbers of species went extinct virtually overnight. The assumption today seems to be that the Earth, from time to time, suffers the equivalent of a "nuclear winter," caused by random impacts with drifting asteroids.

Are the collisions random, though? Papers have abounded, just in the last year, with hypotheses about cycles of destruction—rhythms of comet or asteroid infall driven by some hidden mechanism.

It has been suggested that a dark, small companion of the sun, called Nemesis or Shiva, orbits far beyond the comet belt, dipping in every 26 million years or so to perturb icy and rocky debris into the inner solar system. Alternatively, interactions with the galactic plane, or spiral arms, might trigger such events.

In any case, one possible explanation for the Great Silence is that other solar systems are in even worse shape than we are, that other worlds are routinely and repeatedly smashed by cosmic debris, leaving us the first to climb up far enough to look around.

19. *Black holes, jets, and "deadly things."* Elsewhere I have discussed one other disturbing possibility: that our Milky Way contains an object or objects far more dangerous than mere shock fronts and falling comets. Radio astronomy has recently demonstrated that many galaxies contain powerful and dangerous "things" such as gigantic jets of relativistic particles. Modern theories suggest these beams of destruction are caused by huge black holes at the galaxies' cores. We have no idea if we share this galaxy with such frightful items, only that there is an upper limit to their size and energy. That still leaves a lot of room for small but still dreadful terrors. (In fact, there is strong evidence for a "small" black hole, of a few hundred solar masses, near the center of the Milky Way.)

How does all this relate to the Great Silence? Well, let's imagine there *are* one or more such devils and that we just happen to be on a rare orbit that avoids our galaxy's energetic monsters? If that were so, it would certainly explain how we would be the first to survive long enough to reach the stars.

Category Seven: *Dangerous "Unnatural" Forces*

Nature could be malign, as we have seen. But there are other dangers as well, dangers that might arise from life itself.

20. *Migrational holocausts.* A question covered in detail in "Xenology" was, What happens to planets that are colonized by an expanding interstellar civilization? In that article we saw that unless the settlers leave large parts of their worlds fallow in wilderness preserves, or engage in "Uplift" bioengineering of local higher animals, their mere presence is likely to prevent the appearance of local sentient species. A world is not likely to serve as a useful nursery of intelligence so long as it is occupied by a spacefaring race.

When the interstellar tenants finally vacate or die off, it may be a long time before a local species of tool users evolves. The worse the interstellar colonists treated their temporary colony planet, the more severe will be the effects on the delicate higher life-forms, the very ones that would be expected to grow up to be the next generation of starfarers.

By this scenario, the Earth might be the first Nursery World to have recovered sufficiently—since the last wave of "civilization" passed this way—to develop a species with intelligence. That would explain the apparent loneliness.

(In response to "Xenology," David Rubin of Staten Island wrote in to suggest a new factor for the Drake Equator: $M(d)$. The M stands for "massacre" and the d for "dinosaur.")

This scenario would have dramatic effects on factors $f(i)$, and $f(c)$, and possibly on L and $L2$ as well. The problem with the hypothesis, though, is that it suggests we should see signs of past colonization on the Earth. We do not.

21. Breakup of Nursery Worlds by starfarers hungry for building materials was an idea discussed earlier, under the category called *macrolife*. Planets might die before they ever get a chance to produce intelligent species. This would certainly affect L and $n(e)$, the number of planets on which life can evolve. It is also chillingly consistent with the Great Silence. Earth could be the only Nursery World in the area to have been missed. If so, no wonder we have no neighbors!

22. *Inevitable self-destruction* is another cheery theme we spoke of earlier. The TTAPS nuclear winter scenario tells us that many alien races, indeed, might have found themselves where we now stand, on the teetering precipice between self-ruin and self-control. The factors influenced here are clearly L, v, and A.

23. *Deadly probes* takes the concept of Von Neumann self-replicating probes a step farther, turning it into an idea familiar to SF readers. Both Saberhagen's "Berserkers" and the more sophisticated version discussed in the SF of Gregory Benford reflect the possible dangers of unleashing machine probes onto the galaxy without lots of forethought.

Suppose a thousand races sent out friendly robot emissaries, just like Frank Tipler has proposed. Now imagine only *one* instead dispatched monster machines whose sole task was to home in on sources of modulated radio and destroy them before the newly fledged competitors could spread out into the galaxy. It is a disturbing thought. *The Honeymooners* has passed Tau Ceti, by now. And it's too late to call back *I Love Lucy*.

This scenario, severely affecting $f(c)$, L, and v, is completely consistent with the universe as we observe it. It need only have happened once for it to have become the status quo, keeping the galaxy silent and empty for billions of years. The possibility is quite chilling.

Category Eight: A *Grasp* at Optimism

The great debate seems to be a war among scientists all of whom grew up reading science fiction. The Contact folk—Sagan, Drake, etc.—emphasize their dream of meeting other minds. Uniqueness people, such as Jones and Hart, openly state their preference for an empty galaxy in which our descendants can spread and prosper without competition from older, more advanced species.

In their attempts to explain the Great Silence, each side has tried to suppress one or more of the ten factors. The explanations have ranged from the patently absurd to the frighteningly compelling. And we've seen that the most convincing hypotheses appear to be the most disconcerting as well.

Is there any *friendly* explanation for the Great Silence? Isn't there any way the universe could look the way it does and still let *both* sides get their dream—a galaxy with other minds to talk to and yet still wide open for our great-grandchildren to have adventures in?

I have managed to come up with one. You tell me if it works.

24. The *water world scenario.* We have spoken of the possibility of a "Venus Trap" and of a "Mars Trap" that might pull Earth-like worlds in downward spirals toward conditions where life can't exist. Indeed, there are equations that indicate that both runaway greenhouse effects and permanent ice ages are potential "syndromes" for a vast variety of terrestroid worlds.

This leaves us with the impression that Terra miraculously found itself on a narrow fence between two death scenarios, and that might be true.

On the other hand, it might not. Some scientists believe that there is a deep valley, a cusp, between the Mars and Venus catastrophes. Within this valley there is another "trap," pulling all planets within its reach. It is the pleasant trap of the water world.

The existence of life on Earth has had powerful repercussions. It has pulled most of the carbon out of the atmosphere and regulated the planet's temperature so that it varies less than the heat output of the Sun itself. Most of all, it has featured the preservation of vast oceans.

If this turned out to be a common phenomenon, let us consider the possibility that *the Earth is unusually dry for a water world.* In other words, what if the vast majority of this kind of planet has far less dry land than the Earth?

Geneticists now know that species diversity and rates of evolution depend on the *size* of the environment involved. It is unlikely that land creatures would develop to the complexity they have on Earth on a world with only island archipelagos and tiny continents.

That does not necessarily mean that intelligence per se is impossible on such planets. After all, dolphins and whales are already pretty bright. But it does imply that there would be very few places where "hands and fire" beings would develop the technology and basic outlook on life necessary in order to take to the stars.

There might be millions of intelligent races out there, ignorant and uncaring about starships, preoccupied with their own oceanic adventures. The factor affected by this scenario is $f(c)$, the likelihood of developing technical civilization.

The result? Envision our descendants setting forth, as Jones and others anticipate. They will find no other starfarers, and at first it will seem that they are all alone. At last, though, they will discover other minds— minds that pose no threat, no danger.

Intelligent whales, or squid, or octopus—why should they refuse the roving humans' request to make use of local asteroids upon which to build their cities and factories? If the strange-looking bipeds are willing to bring down exciting toys and machines, why not invite them to come take their vacations on the shores of the "useless" little islands, to splash and play and exchange philosophy lazily under the balmy sunshine?

Humans could be the voyageurs—the transporteers—carrying mail and slow philosophical discussion among the water sapients, who will only be grateful for the service, of course, never jealous. Our great-to-the-nth grandchildren will have their adventures, and in so doing serve to tie the galaxy together.

It sounds like a way to give both sides in our great debate what they want, without having to have a dangerous, malign universe that's apparently out to get us.

I promised to end on a note of optimism, and I cannot do any better than that.

Now, if only it were true.

REFERENCES

Articles cited in the chart

(1) G. D. Brin. *Quarterly J. of the Royal Astronomical Society* 24 (1983): 283.

(2) William I. Newman and Carl Sagan. *Icarus* 46 (1981): 293.

(3) F. Tipler. *Physics Today* 34 (1981): 5.

(4) A.G.W. Cameron, ed. *Interstellar Communications*. New York: W. A. Benjamin Inc., 1963, 1970.

(5) S. Dole. *Habitable Planets for Man*. Elsevier, 1970.

(6) R. N. Bracewell. *Nature* 186 (1960): 670.

(7) D. Brin. "The Deadly Thing at 2.4 Kiloparsecs." *Analog,* May 1984.

(8) R. P. Turco et al. "Nuclear Winter: The Global Consequences of Multiple Nuclear Explosions." *Science* 222 (December 23, 1983): 1283.

(9) P. R. Ehrlich et al. "Long Term Biological Consequences of Nuclear War." *Science* 222 (December 23, 1983): 1293.

General
(10) John Billingham, ed. *Life in the Universe.* Cambridge, MA: MIT Press, 1981.
(11) T.B.H. Kuiper and M. Morris. *Science* 196 (1977): 616.

IIIIIII

THE SECOND BRAZILIAN INCIDENT
by William R. Forstchen, Ph.D.

THIS SECOND INCIDENT IN Brazil might have passed unnoticed except for the fact of whom it happened to—Professor Joao Guimaraes, a well-respected and highly educated professor of Roman law at Santos' Catholic University. Yet again this is a case of someone who had everything to lose and nothing to gain by making a public report of what happened.

Professor Guimaraes claimed that he was lounging on the beach near São Sebastião in July 1956 when a sixty-foot-wide saucer descended and landed near him. Two tall "men" emerged; both were blond with green eyes. He attempted to converse with them in English, French, Spanish, and Italian but got no response until he became aware that they were talking to him telepathically. He was invited aboard the spaceship, and after he went inside, the ship lifted off and was soon out of the atmosphere. Guimaraes provided no other details, stating that some of the things he learned he preferred to keep to himself. He did admit later on that the aliens talked with him about Earth, their concern about the environmental impact of nuclear testing, and a desire to someday help us along. An hour after the flight began, they touched back down on the beach, he left the ship, it took off and disappeared.

ANALYSIS
This is yet another case of someone having everything to lose and nothing to gain by reporting his or her experience with a UFO. Professor Guimaraes was a highly respected professor teaching at a conservative religious college in a conservative community. Reports of taking trips in a UFO are not necessarily the best career-enhancing moves for someone in academia, so this case should draw some serious consideration.

Professor Guimaraes's report has no sensationalistic aspects to it. He readily admitted that he kept it quiet for more than a year before finally deciding to go public, and even then there were certain aspects of the experience that he simply preferred to keep quiet. The whole thing sounds like nothing more than a friendly ride around the stellar neighborhood.

THE ROSWELL EVENTS

by Kevin Randle

Many people are familiar with the
Roswell Incident. It has given rise to
references in movies and on TV and was
featured in the box-office hit *Independence
Day*. Here Kevin Randle, perhaps the most
noted expert on the event, looks at what
happened in a completely new light. He asks
not *what* happened but *why*.

Roswell, New Mexico—July 4, 1947

The events that took place outside of Roswell, New Mexico, in July 1947 shaped the UFO phenomenon for the next fifty years, though most of us didn't realize it. In the last few years, there has been a campaign by the federal government to convince us that nothing extraordinary happened at Roswell. The debris recovered, according to air force officers, government officials, and the skeptical community was nothing more spectacular than the remains of a weather balloon and a rawin target, now claimed to be part of the then top-secret Project Mogul.

However, according to those who were stationed in Roswell in 1947, weather balloons, no matter what the source or classification, were not responsible for the incident. The balloons used in the experiments were nothing unusual, but were common weather-observation devices and rawin radar reflectors that had been in use for a number of years. They had not been changed or modified in any fashion that would have concealed their identity from the officers and men at Roswell. In fact, according to the air force, several civilians recognized the balloons as such. It was only the highly trained men of the 509th Bomb Group who couldn't recognize the balloons as balloons.

The events, which now comprise the Roswell story, actually began about July 1, when radars at various installations in New Mexico picked up an object "flitting through the sky." It would flash from one point to another and then disappear for several hours. If this testimony is reliable, it effectively rules out any balloon explanation. While it is true that the radar reflectors used as part of Project Mogul would certainly be visible to radar, the target wouldn't "flit through the sky," nor would it disappear for hours to return periodically.

Because of the radar sightings, a watch was established at the White Sands Proving Grounds (later the White Sands Missile Range) near Las Cruces, New Mexico. Although a number of men, including some sent from the Roswell Army Air Field (later Walker Air Force Base) kept a constant watch, nothing spectacular happened. After twenty-four hours, the watch was suspended, and the men returned to their regular duties.

Late on the evening of July 4, 1947, the object reappeared on the various radar screens in central and southern New Mexico. In the skies over Roswell a number of people saw something flare brightly and then disappear. William Woody, a boy working outdoors with his father, saw the side of their house brighten. He turned in time to see a white object with red streaks in it fall toward the ground. Woody said that it was in sight for ten or eleven seconds before disappearing.

There were others who saw something in the sky that same night. Catholic nuns at Saint Mary's Hospital recorded an object above Roswell. They made note of its passing in the nightly log of their observations.

On the base itself, Corporal E. L. Pyles was walking across the parade ground when he looked up to see what he thought was a shooting star. It moved across the sky and then arced downward. There seemed to be an orange glow around it and a halo near the front of it. Under questioning later it seemed that the event took place in the early part of July 1947, only days before Pyles read about the balloon explanation for the Roswell events in the local newspaper. That helped investigators establish a time frame for Pyles's observation.

So, we have a number of people, in widely separated locations in southern New Mexico, reporting a light in the night sky. There is nothing that links these reports to the crash of the alien spacecraft that same night. None of the witnesses saw the object, or light that might have had an object behind it, hit the ground. Each reported the light in a location that indicated it may have fallen north of town. Woody and his father traveled north out of Roswell a day or two later to find the object. That act becomes important later as the information is examined. If the light is not related to the object that fell, it is an amazing coincidence, especially when Woody's actions are considered.

Outside of Roswell that same night, in the high desert, Jim Ragsdale was hiding out with a married lady friend he identified as Trudy Truelove (who died about a year later in an unrelated traffic accident). According to him, in a taped interview conducted in January 1993, the night was rough, filled with strong winds, lightning flashes, and bursts of rain that hammered at the dry ground. About 11:30 P.M., there was a brilliant, blinding, flaring light overhead. The blue-white light was so bright that it hurt their eyes and reminded Ragsdale of the flame on a welder's torch.

The object roared overhead and slammed into the ground about a mile or so from where Ragsdale was parked. Although the woman was reluctant to investigate, Ragsdale insisted. Using a flashlight with weak batteries, Ragsdale walked to near where the object had crashed. With the little light available, he couldn't see much. He could tell that something strange had crashed, but he had been drinking heavily and he wasn't supposed to be where he was. He decided that he could wait until morning before he explored further.

The next morning, before the military arrived on the scene, Ragsdale managed to get a closer look. He found an object stuck in the ground, near a short cliff. During a taped interview, Ragsdale said, "You could tell where it hit. . . . One part was buried in the ground, and part of it was sticking out of the ground."

But more important than the craft were the bodies of the flight crew visible on the ground near the object. Ragsdale said, "[There were] bodies or something laying there. They looked like bodies. They weren't very long . . . four or five foot long at the most."

Wreckage was scattered around the site, and Ragsdale picked up some of it before the military arrived on the scene. There were sheets of broken metal. Ragsdale said that some of it could be crumbled into a ball and, when released, would unfold itself. Other metal would hold whatever shape it was bent into. Some of it reminded him of carbon paper, meaning that it was thin, lightweight, and dark. It was, however, much stronger than any carbon paper he had ever seen. Ragsdale said that he had seen nothing like it.

Before he could get a good look at the damaged craft, the alien bodies, or metallic debris, the military arrived, driving across the high desert. They announced themselves with a siren and a cloud of swirling dust. Ragsdale said that he saw a county sheriff's Ford that held a number of MPs. From the distance, Ragsdale watched as the convoy of trucks spread out around the ship as if to screen it from view.

Ragsdale slipped away, keeping low and out of the view of the military police, who were scrambling up the hills to form the cordon. He was afraid that he had stumbled across the wreckage of a secret military craft. The bodies, clearly not human, were "dummies," or something like that, according to Ragsdale. At least that was what he believed for a few minutes until he had a chance to think about it.

As Ragsdale retreated, unseen by the military police, the soldiers were fanning out across the impact site. Major Edwin Easley, the provost marshal of the 509th Bomb Group, ordered that the trucks that had followed the cars screen the downed craft. Frank Kaufmann, and a group of intelligence specialists who had ridden in with the military police, stood back, smoking cigarettes and watching as one man, dressed in a protective suit, moved forward. He was searching for signs of radiation. When he found nothing dangerous, the others advanced, studying the craft, and looking at the bodies of the dead flight crew.

Easley's MPs rounded up the only civilians that were left on the impact site. These were a group of anthropological students and their instructor, Dr. W. Curry Holden. Ragsdale said nothing to me about Holden's group, and Holden was apparently never in a position to see Ragsdale, who had been working very hard to stay out of sight.

When I interviewed Holden in November 1992, he told me that he had been on the site and seen it all. Although we didn't discuss the case at length, given Holden's advanced age, he did confirm the site north of Roswell, that there had been bodies that were clearly not human, and that the craft looked like nothing he had ever seen before. Holden's opinion about the bodies is important because, as an anthropologist, he was familiar with apes and monkeys.

Holden and the students were questioned at the site and then escorted into Roswell for a complete debriefing. They were told that what they had seen was a matter of national security and if they ever spoke about it, funding from various government grants would disappear and they would never work in their chosen fields again.

It should be noted that neither Holden's wife nor his daughter had ever heard the story before I interviewed him. Both believed that because of his advanced age he was confused about the topic. However, during the interview, I was careful in my questioning, trying not to lead him nor to provide him with any clues as to what I wanted. I tried to frame my questions in the negative so that he would respond in the negative if he were picking up cues from me. If he was responding specifically to my questions, then he should have answered in the negative.

With all the civilians off the site, the task of cleaning up the area began. Kaufmann later said that all the creatures were dead when the military arrived. Easley never discussed with me the conditions of the flight crew. In fact, he rarely said anything about them, though he did refer to "the creatures" in front of family members and his doctor just prior to his death in Fort Worth.

According to Kaufmann, two of the creatures were outside the craft, one sitting next to a cliff looking as if he had sat down for a nap. Kaufmann said that the creature looked to be at peace. The other was partially inside the object, draped over the edge of a hole ripped in the side. Three others were found later, hidden inside the craft.

The creatures were smaller than humans, with heads that were larger than humans'. The eyes were big but not the black orbs reported by abductees. They were bald, with grayish skin, the color compared to Data of *Star Trek: The Next Generation*. The creatures, according to the men who were there, do not match the descriptions of aliens provided by abductees.

The craft, according to Kaufmann, Lewis Rickett (the counterintelligence agent at Roswell), and others, was heel-shaped. Both Kaufmann and Rickett used that term. Interestingly, a photograph taken two days later, over Phoenix, Arizona, showed a craft that is similar in shape to that reported down at Roswell. The air force, not surprisingly, has classified the photograph as a hoax.

The bodies were put into lead-lined body bags (or at the very least, some kind of special bags), transported to the base, and later flown out. There are reports that a preliminary autopsy was started in Roswell but the work was not completed. The bodies were flown out on two separate aircraft, one of them traveling to Washington, D.C., and later on to Wright Field outside of Dayton, Ohio.

The second aircraft, according to sources, flew directly on to Wright Field. Brigadier General Arthur Exon was stationed at Wright Field in July 1947. According to taped interviews with him, he learned from friends that both debris from the crash and the bodies of the flight crew were brought into Ohio. While he saw nothing there, he was told about some of the activities that took place in the attempt to identify the wreckage. He said that his friends told him they have never seen anything like it. They were unable to identify the metallic components that they had been given. It was the opinion of those to whom Exon spoke that the debris was from a spacecraft.

Later, according to Exon, he flew over both the impact site where the craft was found and the debris field, where there was only scattered metallic wreckage. Under questioning, Exon said, "[It was] part of the same accident, but [there were] two distinct sites. One, assuming that the thing, as I understand it, as I remember flying the area later, that the damage to the vehicle seemed to be coming from the southeast to the northwest, but it could have been going in the opposite direction, but it doesn't seem likely. So the farther-northwest pieces found on the ranch, those pieces were mostly metal."

In other words, General Exon had just confirmed that two sites had been found, one by rancher Mac Brazel and another, closer to Roswell. That was the same as the information I would develop over a number of years and that would corroborate part of the story told by Frank Kaufmann.

Exon, when asked about the bodies of the dead flight crew, said, "There was another location where . . . apparently the main part of the spacecraft was . . . where they did say there were bodies."

Clearly, Exon did not see the bodies himself, but did confirm their existence in his statements. While assigned to Wright Field in 1947, he was in a position to learn the truth about the crash. Rather than reject the notion of an alien spacecraft crash, Exon discussed it from his perspective as a military officer on the scene in Ohio at the time the material and bodies arrived at the base.

By the end of Saturday, July 5, the bodies had been removed and the craft and debris cleaned up. There was little to be seen in the field, and, according to one source, experts in camouflage were brought in to hide the marks on the ground. The military wanted nothing left behind that would identify the site for the curious.

That was the part of the story that had remained hidden, even after some of the case had been uncovered. Misdirection by the military and the government had kept some researchers looking in the wrong place and at the wrong time. Originally, it was believed that the wreckage was not recovered by the military until July 8. As the information developed it became clear that a significant portion of it had been missed during the first investigations. This would cause some confusion for those unfamiliar with the report.

It was the next day that the conventional story began. As reported by so many others, W. W. "Mac" Brazel, the ranch manager living to the northwest of Roswell, appeared in town. He had a story of strange metallic debris scattered in one of the pastures south of the ranch headquarters. He told Sheriff George Wilcox about it. He also told KGFL radio announcer and reporter Frank Joyce.

It's unclear who suggested that Brazel call the air base. Joyce said that he told Brazel to do it. That doesn't really matter now. Brazel or the sheriff called the base and spoke to Major Jesse A. Marcel, the air intelligence officer.

Marcel listened to the story and reported it to his boss, Colonel William Blanchard, who ordered him to check it out. He suggested that Marcel use one of the counterintelligence agents assigned to the base. Captain Sheridan Cavitt has been identified as the man who accompanied Marcel to the debris field. This is a fact confirmed, more or less, by Cavitt in an interview conducted with him by the air force in the spring of 1994.

On Monday, July 7, after spending what had to be an uncomfortable night at a shack about three miles north of the debris field, Marcel and Cavitt accompanied Brazel out. According to Jesse Marcel, interviewed more than thirty years later by Bob Pratt, "[You could tell] which direction it came from and which direction it was heading. It was in that pattern. . . . I could tell it was thicker where we first started looking and it was thinning out as we went southwest."

Marcel then performed what might be the critical experiment in the field. He told Pratt, "I wanted to see some of the stuff burn, but all I had was a cigarette lighter. . . . I lit the cigarette lighter to some of this stuff and it didn't burn."

Marcel and Cavitt spent the day on the field, according to the Pratt interview of Marcel, collecting the debris. About dusk, Marcel sent Cavitt back to town in the jeep, while he stayed a while longer. When he left, there was still considerable debris left on the field. He had been able to collect very little of it. According to Marcel, "We picked up a very minor portion of it."

On his way into the base, Marcel stopped at his house. He wanted both his wife and young son to see the debris. Marcel would later say that he knew it was something extraordinary and he wanted to show it to them before it became classified. While looking at it, Viaud Marcel spotted some writing on a small I-beam. Jesse Marcel Jr. describes the writing as purplish, a violet not unlike that from an old-fashioned mimeograph machine, and made of geometric figures—squares, circles, and triangles, among other shapes.

Marcel then collected the debris, put it back in the car, and drove it on to the base, where he would meet with Colonel Blanchard. Later that morning, July 8, Marcel was ordered, by Blanchard, to fly, with some of the debris, to Eighth Air Force Headquarters in Fort Worth, where Brigadier General Roger Ramey waited.

It was also on the morning of July 8 that First Lieutenant Walter Haut, the base public relations officer, was ordered by Blanchard to issue a press statement. According to Haut, he received the information over the telephone (or might have received a written statement), wrote the release, and then hand-carried it into Roswell. The statement, which went out over the teletype wires that day, claimed that officers at the Roswell Army Air Field had captured, with the help of a local rancher, one of the mysterious flying saucers. The craft was being taken to Fort Worth by Major Marcel.

Within hours, however, General Ramey had issued his own press statement claiming that the excitement in Roswell hadn't been justified. The debris was nothing more spectacular than the remains of a rather common weather balloon and a rawin radar target device. Photographs taken at Eighth Air Force Headquarters in Fort Worth by Major Charles A. Cashon and newspaper reporter-photographer J. Bond Johnson seemed to bear this out. The seven pictures all showed the unmistakable remains of a neoprene balloon and aluminum-foil radar target. An Eighth Air Force weather officer, Warrant Officer Irving Newton, identified it easily. Marcel, however, later told reporter Johnny Mann that those pictures were staged and didn't contain the debris he'd brought from Roswell. Besides, his cigarette lighter would have had some effect on the debris from a rawin target, if that was actually what it had been.

That was the end of the story until Len Stringfield and Stanton Friedman interviewed Marcel Sr. in 1978. Marcel told both researchers that he had recovered pieces of a flying saucer while in Roswell, and provided the clues to crack the story. Several books and dozens of magazine articles, documentaries, and even a feature-length film resulted from those early interviews.

After the initial reports in July 1947, the federal government in general, and the air force in particular, refused to comment on the case for decades. If anyone managed to get a comment from an official spokesman, it was always that the air force stood behind their original answer: The crash at Roswell was nothing more than a weather balloon and rawin target, and the air force didn't have any little bodies on ice or hidden away from the public.

However, in September 1994, the air force issued a report on the Roswell case. They had reexamined the event, interviewed five people, and determined that the Roswell case was not a weather balloon as they had originally reported. They had told a lie in 1947. It was actually . . . a weather balloon. The difference was that now they could release the information that the balloon belonged to the then (1947) top-secret Project Mogul. Same balloon, same radar reflector, just a new name and the cloak of a secret project. That answer made no more sense today than it did in 1947.

The air force report claimed that Mogul Flight 4, launched on June 4, 1947, was the culprit. The air force and the media all accepted this as the end to the Roswell case. It was the end of the controversy, with everyone satisfied now that the project had been declassified.

The only documentation for Flight No. 4, however, was the diary kept by Dr. Albert Crary, the leader of the project. The entry for June 4 reads, "Out to Tularosa Range and fired charges between 00 and 06 this A.M. No balloon flight again on account of clouds. Flew regular sonobuoy mike up in cluster of balloons and had good luck on receiver on ground but poor on plane. Out with Thompson P.M. Shot charges from 1800 to 2400."

The next day, June 5, Crary wrote, "Up at 4 to shoot 2 charges for balloon flight. Whole assembly of constant altitude balloons sent up at 0500. . . ." The flight of that balloon was well documented, and the path eliminates it as a possible culprit. In fact, only Flight No. 4, because of the limited documentation available, could be counted as a candidate.

But Flight No. 4 was only a sonobuoy and a cluster of balloons. Crary mentions nothing about the array train that would have contained the rawin targets. If there were no targets, then the debris found by Brazel could not have come from Project Mogul, and the air force explanation fails. There is no reason to assume a full array train because Crary is quite specific on that point. He mentions that Flight No. 4 was canceled on the morning of June 4. The only flight made contained a sonobuoy lifted by a cluster of balloons. The documentation, then, suggests no array train. This is a fact that skeptics, reporters, and the air force conveniently forget. The only documentation available argues against the air force explanation.

Eyewitness testimony, gathered by a number of investigators, also argues against the balloon explanation. Joe Stefula, a researcher living in New Jersey, located one of the military police officers involved. According to the testimony of that officer, there was evidence that the object had "skipped" across the ground, leaving three deep gouges in the tough terrain. The officer also said that he saw evidence of an "overburning." It was the officer's opinion, based on his firsthand observations, that an aircraft had crashed. It was impossible for a balloon, even a cluster of them that hauled an array train aloft, to have caused the physical damage he saw. He was quite sure of that.

The air force, in their investigation and my research, failed to find any documentation that an aircraft had crashed in the right location at the right time. In other words, the documentation available eliminated an aircraft accident as an explanation. The air force was quite clear on that point.

The Roswell case, then, according to many of the witnesses who were there, was the crash of an alien spacecraft. Major Edwin Easley, the provost marshal who was responsible for security at the impact site, told me that it was an extraterrestrial craft. Dr. W. Curry Holden, the long-lost archaeologist, told me he had seen the craft and the bodies of the alien flight crew. Frank Kaufmann, one of the men responsible for clearing the field, said that it was extraterrestrial. Jim Ragsdale provided a description of the bodies that clearly suggested something from another planet.

Others, such as the officer found by Stefula, provided us with clues to eliminate the balloon explanation. Lewis "Bill" Rickett described debris that clearly was not part of a balloon project. There are, on record now, nearly fifty people who say they handled some of the debris. Almost none of the descriptions can be classified as parts of a balloon and array.

And remember that Jesse Marcel Sr., while on the debris field, tried to burn some of the debris. Although he used only his cigarette lighter, he was unable to burn it. A neoprene balloon, such as that used by Project Mogul, was so fragile that exposure to sunlight caused it to blacken. The supports for the rawin target were made of balsa wood, which would have burned easily. Skeptics and the air force suggest that the supports in the Mogul balloons had been dipped in glue for strength. This, according to them, prevented the balsa from burning. Of course, such a suggestion is ridiculous on its face, but they are all satisfied with it. The Roswell case has been explained to their satisfaction. That is, if they ignore all the testimony from a large number of men and women who can prove they were in Roswell in July 1947, the event has been solved.

The Roswell case, then, given its nature, didn't provide much in the way of two-party communication with the alien race that flew the ship. The limited communication spoke very loud, but the message was very brief. They, the aliens, were telling us, apparently unintentionally, that another intelligent race inhabited the universe with us. We were being told that we are not alone. It is an important message, one that was quickly obscured by the government and the military, and one that was the result of the accident.

It also raises a question that I find interesting. What if they had crashed the ship on purpose? What if it wasn't an accident? Oh, not that they flew a ship into the ground and killed the crew intentionally, but that, as they moved through space, traveling toward Earth, crew members died. Maybe it was by natural causes, the result of accidents on the ship, or by illness. When they arrived here, five of them had already died. To announce their presence in the most nonthreatening way possible, they arranged the crash, complete with the dead flight crew.

Beginning in late June 1947 stories of flying saucers had begun to fill the newspapers. Speculation was rampant. No one was suggesting an invasion from space, but all were suggesting explanations for the sightings. These ran from late cases of war nerves, to hallucinations, to spots in front of the eyes, to experimental aircraft. A few suggested an extraterrestrial hypothesis, but most believed the answer would be found on Earth, in secret laboratories and in secret experiments.

An alien race that landed on Earth in the summer of 1947 would have found a population ill prepared to deal with the reality of intelligent life outside the solar system. If confronted with the sudden knowledge that we were not alone, panic could result. The war that had ended less than two years earlier could have been reignited with new antagonists. It presented a real problem for the aliens if they were observant. How to tell us that they existed without causing various social, religious, and economic problems?

However, if the announcement was made by a dead flight crew in a ruined ship, the situation would be somewhat different. Now, instead of seeing a superior race that had mastered interplanetary, and probably interstellar, travel, we see a vulnerable race that makes mistakes. We don't see creatures who are superior to us, because they obviously make the same mistakes we do. How else to explain the crashed ship and dead crew?

And what better place to stage the crash than in New Mexico? Atomic research that had resulted in the atomic bomb had been conducted in New Mexico in the years before. The first atomic explosion had taken place in central New Mexico. The first tiny steps that would lead the human race into space had been taken by Dr. Robert H. Goddard near Roswell, New Mexico, and were continuing at the White Sands Proving Grounds about a hundred miles away. The scientific talent to understand the situation and to appreciate the significance of an extraterrestrial presence was already assembled throughout New Mexico. It was the perfect place to stage such an announcement, if that was their plan.

The announcement of alien intelligence was made on the evening of July 4. The craft and bodies were recovered by the military all during the day of July 5. And then the plan failed because the government decided that the news was too big to be released to the general public. Science, or rather some of the top scientists in the country, were aware of what had happened. The military, at least those at the very top, knew what had happened. And, of course, the leaders of the government had been briefed by those who had been on the scene.

Their decision, apparently, was to bury the truth, release a false but believable story, and announce that flying saucers were nothing more than an illusion. On July 9, 1947, their plan was put into effect when both army and navy officials began a concentrated effort to suppress the stories of alien spacecraft.

Yes, it was a calculated risk. If it could happen once, it could easily happen again, and the government might not be able to hide the truth a second time. They had no control over such a situation, but they could control the media.

Secrets and the military mind come into play when trying to understand why they would take such a chance. As a former intelligence officer I was taught that those who did not have the proper clearances were not to be exposed to classified information. It didn't matter how compromised the information already was, how much my questioners already knew, or how much had been published in the media or broadcast on radio and television. If the topic was classified by my superiors, I was to deny all knowledge of it, regardless of the circumstances, unless the questioner had the proper clearance, granted by those same superiors.

For example, while I was serving on active duty at Richards-Gebaur Air Force Base, a situation developed in the Middle East. Classified messages were transmitted from the area to all intelligence functions around the world. I read many of them, just as I was supposed to. However, I received a telephone call from a newspaper reporter wanting to know more about the situation. He claimed to be a former officer himself and understood the restrictions I faced; he just wanted to confirm, from another source, the information he had. I, of course, denied all knowledge of it. He suggested that I didn't know my job, I was incompetent, and besides, the whole story was already in *Time* magazine. I told him I was sorry, but I didn't know anything that would help him at that time. And I told him that I hadn't had a chance to read the latest issue of *Time*.

The point is that even with the information out, published in the public arena, even with a reporter who had as many sources as I did and who had good, solid information, I was forced by regulations to deny all knowledge of the event. It made no real sense, but it was what was required by regulation.

So we have a situation in New Mexico that answers the questions of alien presence. A form of communication has been established, though it is a one-way discourse. We can study the craft, we can dissect the bodies, but what we can learn is limited and a dialogue can't be initiated. There seems to be an opportunity to step back and examine the situation, but only if there is no pressure from legislative representatives, the various news media, and the general public. The air force took a calculated risk and buried the information, telling everyone that flying saucers were nothing more than an illusion. Yet all the time they were working to learn more from the remains of the craft picked up outside of Roswell.

The communication that had been started with the Roswell crash was terminated as it began. We made no response that could be observed by them other than to pretend it didn't happen. When time passed, the situation changed, and our jet fighters met their spaceships, often we would shoot at them. Without ever uttering a word, without any sort of face-to-face, direct confrontation, communication between us would have been established: We are hostile. We know they are vulnerable. Unfortunately neither message allows for the establishment of a meaningful dialogue. It only allows us to react to the situation.

This is, of course, rank speculation. There was nothing found on the impact site to suggest the crash had been intentional. There is nothing to suggest that the crash had been planned to announce, in a nonthreatening way, that aliens had arrived here. In fact, the question that needs to be asked is, If the first attempt failed, as it did, why not select a new site and try it all over again?

Again the answer is highly speculative. It might be that they monitored the radio reports and realized the turmoil the sightings of their craft were causing around the world. Maybe they realized that the human race was not mature enough to handle the information that we are not alone in the universe. Maybe their strategy was to provide just one opportunity, and if it was not seized, they retreated for a period of time. Maybe they believed we weren't smart enough to figure out what had happened.

I have no answer here. All I know is that a ship crashed and was recovered. The only message that I know was received is that we are not alone in the universe, and that message could easily be a by-product of an accident. It could be that no communication with the human race was desired then or now and that that explains the lack of attempts to establish further communication with us.

There is, however, another possibility here. It was reported by a couple of the Roswell witnesses that one of the aliens survived the crash for a period of time. When the military arrived on the scene, the being was sitting with the bodies of its dead companions. It seemed to be in mourning. If true, that fact would have opened up a different area of communication. For if we could have learned its language or it could have learned ours, then a direct, specific dialogue could have been established. It would be one that would answer many of the questions we have, questions that couldn't have been answered by a wrecked spaceship and the bodies of a flight crew.

Again, it must be stressed that there are only two firsthand witnesses who claim there was a survivor. There are other, second- and third-hand sources, who also suggest that one of the beings might have survived the crash. The best information available at this point is that all were killed in the crash, or died in a matter of hours after it, before the military arrived. Forgetting that for a moment, we can speculate further.

If one of the aliens did survive, there would have been some kind of communication. That couldn't have been helped. If nothing else, our government would have tried to learn if the alien represented a threat to us. Our government would surely have worked from that assumption, because that seems to be the one we, as a race, always make. Besides, military and government officials would have known that every time a technologically superior civilization comes into contact with a technologically inferior one, the latter ceases to exist. That doesn't mean the inferior civilization is conquered, or invaded, or that there is even conflict, but that the introduction of the technology changes it profoundly. "Communication" in this case might have been nothing more than a demonstration of their technology. Once humans learn that something can be done, they do it. Once we see an invention, a dozen people begin adding to the idea, adding it to our society. And as we advance technologically, we change our civilization. Think of how the personal computer and the Internet have changed communications in the last few years. I can now send mail with the speed of light and expect a response in a matter of minutes rather than days or weeks or months.

A good example of the technological destruction of a civilization is the introduction of the horse into the Western Hemisphere. Once the horse spread to the Plains Indians, the Indian way of life there changed radically. The Plains Indians became more nomadic, ranging over a much larger area and coming into contact with so many other Indian societies. It wasn't a conquest that caused the change but the introduction of a technology, even if that introduction was only of the horse. Eventually the technological superiority of European society overwhelmed the Indians, but only after it became easy to move troops and supplies a great distance rapidly. That was only after the invention of the revolver, the locomotive, and the telegraph. It was only after the technology advanced to a point where the human factor was outweighed by the inventions.

The government officials, and the military at Roswell, if they had found a survivor, would have wanted to communicate so that they could exploit that new technology. The alien could have made understanding the technology so much easier. Toys, machines, and computers are much simpler to use if there is an instruction booklet.

Even if there had been no alien to assist in understanding the technology, if our government and scientists could have figured out how it worked, we could still have gained a huge lead over our enemies in the Cold War. Without any more communication with the race that built the craft, without the necessary instruction booklet, the aliens could still have radically altered the way of life on this planet.

If one of the beings had survived the crash, our government would have worked to teach it our language or to learn its language. Indeed, I have a military source who told me, on the condition that I don't reveal his name, that that is exactly what happened. The alien being learned how to speak English easily and told something of its history to military officers appointed to exploit the creature. It was also asked questions about the craft, interstellar flight, and its own history.

I also heard a single story from a man who claims to have been in contact with the survivor in the early 1950s. He said that the alien easily learned English while in captivity and that a dialogue was established with it. He insists that it told him and other officials a great deal about its society, its technology, and the operation of the craft.

This tale sounds suspiciously like those told by "Falcon" and "Condor," two men who also claim to have had communication with alien beings and whose stories are still unsubstantiated, two men who were interviewed a number of times by UFO researchers.

The problem with all these tales, whether they are from "Falcon" and "Condor" or from my single source, is that we have been unable to corroborate any of them. They are told by men who claim to have had high-level security clearances. The information is so highly classified, they say, that those of us who are outside that specific intelligence community and the various government offices are unable to verify a word of it. If the stories are true, we would certainly expect to be able to substantiate the level of security classification claimed by them. And if the stories are true, we would indeed be unable to corroborate them through normal research channels because of that high level of classification. If in fact the events at Roswell took place, then it would be easier to believe that some kind of communication with the aliens would have taken place after the events than it would be if there was no event in 1947. It makes it easier for us to believe in the tales of "Falcon" and "Condor" and of my unnamed source. Once the question of alien existence has been answered, everything else follows.

Indeed, we can't accept these stories on faith alone. We must have some sort of independent evidence. The credentials offered by "Falcon" and "Condor" were checked by others and were said to be perfect. They are who they claim to be, according to those who examined the credentials—but then, those making the claim had a financial motive in making it. It made for better television if "Falcon" and "Condor" were real government agents. No proof has been offered to us in the general public, and no disinterested third party has had the opportunity to examine those credentials. The claim remains useless to us as researchers.

The stories of "Falcon" and "Condor" have been well reported in the past by others. Both claimed to have studied the aliens as part of their intelligence jobs, and both learned that the aliens had been involved in genetic manipulations of the human race, had given us our religions, and enjoyed strawberry ice cream. They claimed long and profitable communication with an alien being. Their tales were featured for the first time on the *UFO Cover-up Live* broadcast in October 1988.

Other UFO researchers attempted to learn who "Falcon" and "Condor" were. According to those researchers, "Falcon" was an air force sergeant named Richard Doty, who had at one time been assigned to the Air Force Office of Special Investigation. "Condor" was an air force captain named Collins. Neither seemed to have the credentials that would have put them into contact with an alien creature. Both did have military credentials, but many of us could provide the same kind of credentials. Nothing was proven. Of course Doty and the captain have denied they are "Falcon" and "Condor." Those who have endorsed the "Falcon and Condor" stories have denied that either man has been accurately identified by independent researchers.

In fact, one of the things that has harmed the UFO field in general and the Roswell case in particular are the stories told by "Falcon" and "Condor." Their stories were widely reported and then ridiculed. It has been suggested that they were agents of disinformation who were ordered to tell the wild tales to undermine the growing interest in the Roswell case. If their stories were weird enough, the general public wouldn't believe it because of how weird they were. Interest in the Roswell case, and in UFOs, would be ended. The secrets would be safe.

In other words, communication between the people of Earth and the alien races has been inhibited by the actions of the United States government. They have worked long and hard to prevent any sort of communication because once that communication is started, it will be impossible to stop. Once the truth is learned, it will be impossible to erase that truth from the public mind. The ramifications for our society, according to these theories, would be disastrous for us all.

Once again, it's not that we have been communicating with an alien race, or that they have an interest in destroying our civilization. Those sorts of ramifications would be a by-product of any communication. Our own history and anthropology are filled with examples of the destruction of one culture through mere contact with another. Communication didn't even have to take place.

Anthropologists are supposed to be well aware of the pitfalls of introducing new elements into a primitive culture. They are taught a "prime directive": Don't interfere with the society you are observing. Sometimes, however, even the most innocent of acts results in disaster.

For example, one anthropologist went to study a primitive tribe that possessed few stone axes. If someone needed an ax, he or she had to follow a prescribed ritual in order to borrow one from a societal leader who owned it. Their particular social structure encouraged communication between the commoners and those few leaders who had an ax. This established highly defined relationships among the people and facilitated communication.

The anthropologist who arrived, to encourage the natives to cooperate with him, provided steel axes. A steel ax is far superior to a stone ax. It cuts deeper, better, and holds a better edge. The people soon learned that a visit to the anthropologist would result in the gift of a steel ax. By handing out the axes, the anthropologist had unwittingly destroyed part of the social structure of the village. The ritual for borrowing a stone ax was no longer needed because a steel ax could be obtained by speaking with the anthropologist.

The mere act of introducing the steel axes was enough to radically alter the social and hierarchical structure of the village. The importance of the leaders was diminished because one of the symbols of their authority had been replaced by a better object. Why go through the ritual to obtain the stone ax when a steel ax is readily available? The leaders' power base was eroded by the simple introduction of the steel ax, a technologically superior object. Naturally, the anthropologist didn't intend for his gifts to the people to harm the society, but that was the outcome. And it wasn't even the result of communication but of the mere act of supplying a superior device.

It is certainly possible that our own leaders, having seen the lessons of the past, are afraid of what the simple act of communication with aliens will do to their power base. That idea isn't as farfetched as it might sound. In fact, in the early 1960s, the question was posed to experts in various scientific and religious disciplines What would happen if there was communication between people of Earth and an alien race? Of the fifteen disciplines queried—anthropologists, sociologists, economists, and theologians, among others—fourteen said the contact would be disastrous for our civilization. They weren't even talking about a face-to-face confrontation envisioned in science fiction films, but only one in which an intelligent message is received from space. What if the SETI program produced indisputable results?

Once again, we're not even talking about a two-way dialogue but the mere discovery of a signal. Any response would take years. If, for example, the source of the signal were any of the star systems more than thirty light-years from Earth, then it would still be sixty years before any two-way communication would be completed—if they could even detect and translate ours, and if they felt like responding to it, and if their civilization hadn't already collapsed for some reason.

Of course, if we increase those numbers, then the time between discovery, response, and answer to the response increases. If the system were fifty light-years from Earth, it would take more than one hundred years before the return message could arrive. More than a human being's lifetime. If we learned of them today and didn't hear back for a century or more, would we even still be interested in the answer when it came?

Yet even with the uncertainty of a message from space and with the possibility that a lifetime could pass before a second message could be received, the negative effect on our society could be widespread, many of the thinkers said. Speculation ran from a collapse of our civilization due to the simple knowledge that someone else exists in the universe to a shutdown of some industries as people come to realize that better answers to our questions may exist.

Even if the speculations from the 1960s study prove to be inaccurate, it is clear that the government officials who requested the report took it seriously.

One example of the kind of havoc that can be wreaked in a society is what happened during the infamous Orson Welles 1938 radio drama *War of the Worlds*. The broadcast suggested that an invasion was taking place and that the "Martians" were now in New Jersey; however, listeners were informed four times during the broadcast that it was a *radio drama*. Nonetheless millions of people panicked, convinced that alien invaders had landed and were attacking the towns of New Jersey. They believed it was only a matter of time before the whole world would become consumed in the conflict.

The lesson might have been improperly understood. The conclusion is clear: Even when presented with all the information needed to understand the situation, the general public is likely to react to such news with uncontrollable fear. Therefore, it would seem that telling them the truth about an alien-spacecraft crash in New Mexico, even though it was clear there would be no follow-up attack by the aliens and that an invasion was not imminent, could result in panic.

When the events took place in Roswell, the *War of the Worlds* broadcast was only nine years old. It had been big news in 1938, and it is reasonable to assume that those setting policy in 1947 knew that.

Thus, Roswell presented a real problem for those in power. What should they tell the public? Flying saucers had been reported for about two weeks before the crash took place, but there was no solid evidence that they were anything more than illusions. Yes, there had been good sightings by pilots, police, and other authorities, and there was also a great deal of speculation about them. But no one really knew what was happening. And, more importantly, there was no hard physical evidence. When all else failed, those in power could always demand, "Where is the evidence?" Without it they could, and often did, suggest there was nothing to the reports of flying saucers.

A study of the newspapers of the period supports this conclusion. As mentioned, the speculation ranged from illusion and hoax to extraterrestrial craft. However, the tone of the articles seems to suggest that the majority of the reporters, and probably a majority of the people, suspected that the flying saucers were American secret experiments. After all, less than two years earlier the entire world had been stunned by the existence and deployment of atomic bombs. If science could produce, in complete secret, a single bomb that could level a city, couldn't it also produce a craft, in complete secret, that operated on the fringes of science just as the flying saucers do? Wasn't it reasonable to believe that the craft were American secrets? Who else had the technology or the capability?

This may be the reason there was no resulting panic this time. People weren't talking in terms of spacecraft and alien existence, except in a limited fashion. It certainly was one subject of speculation, but not one that was taken seriously by many. This other explanation was attracting more public attention, despite denials of any secret experiments at the highest levels.

The Roswell crash removed all doubt among military and government authorities about the sources of the sightings. Suddenly, in one instant, they must have realized what was actually going on. The flying saucers were craft from another planet; no other conclusion could be drawn. They had the hard evidence in hand, and if they had ever suspected a human enemy, such as the Soviets, the bodies of the flight crew must have ended that speculation. The dead pilots were clearly not Soviets; they were clearly not beings who had been born on this planet at all.

Their first question, then, would have been, What would the impact be of an announcement that a spacecraft had crashed in New Mexico? Clearly those in power believed disaster would result. They couldn't afford to let anything out until they had more and better information about the nature of the phenomenon. They couldn't allow the public to know the truth until they had some answers.

Think of it this way: Some sort of communication had once and for all been established. It was an announcement by the aliens of their existence, whether intentional or not. Nothing more could be known except after long and careful study by Earth-based scientists. We couldn't learn whence they had come without some help. We couldn't learn anything more about them without some additional information. We couldn't read their manuals, if any were found. We couldn't understand their charts unless some clue were provided. Jesse Marcel's description of symbols on the I-beam suggests they had a written language, but we had no way of deciphering it.

In fact, Steve Lytle told me that his father, a mathematician, had been given one of the I-beams from the crash with the instruction to try to decode the strange markings. The problem is that it wasn't a secret code but a foreign and unknown language. There had to be some sort of key, a Rosetta Stone, to understand the language, yet none had been provided.

The only message from the aliens, then, would be the fact of their presence. "We are here." But that was all that we were able to learn. To announce their existence would be to invite questions to which there were no answers, and that would be to invite mass panic. At least those in power believed that to be the result.

The communication was one-way with no chance to ask questions or to learn more. Thus there was nothing to do except bury the report. It wouldn't have been good policy to say that a flying saucer had crashed but we don't know anything more about it.

The question that should be asked now is, How should it have been handled? Naturally, we have the benefit of twenty-twenty hindsight. Much has happened in the UFO field over the ensuing fifty years. Society has become more sophisticated, there is currently a vast communications system in place, and we are all more aware of our surroundings. We have access to all sorts of information on our personal computers that would have been impossible to imagine even five years ago.

I believe that initially the government had no choice in the situation. They were as confused as the rest of us when they were presented with the physical evidence that we are not alone. We must also remember that they were unprepared because there was no historical precedent for such an occurrence. Sure, we could look at the appearance of the Spanish at the doors of the Aztec empire, but that was still humans contacting humans. And, they, meaning the governmental officials, could see that it didn't turn out particularly well for the Aztecs. Conquest did take place. The Aztec Empire ceased to exist.

So the government actively suppressed the information until they had a chance to evaluate it. They were fortunate the crash took place where it did. The military could silence the local media, for with all the secret projects under way in New Mexico it wouldn't have been hard to convince them of their civic duty. If that failed, a few threats would be enough to put an end to any independent thought.

But once the situation stabilized, as it eventually did, a controlled release of the data might have been useful. The only problem is that once the cat was out of the bag, even partially, it wouldn't easily have lent itself to being stuffed back in.

It is instructive to reflect on what happened to subsequent UFO stories over the following few years. On July 9, 1947, both the army and the navy began actively to suppress reports of flying saucers. This is evident from newspaper accounts of the period. By the end of the month, the public had forgotten about flying saucers, though it is clear that neither the government nor the military had. However, with few or no sightings being reported, they could claim it had been nothing more than a summer fad. Nonetheless they continued to investigate the few reports still being filed, regularly concluding that there was nothing to them.

In 1949 the air force announced that Project Sign, the official investigation of UFOs, was being closed. They had carefully examined two hundred or so reports, they said, and had found explanations for all but a few, which in turn might have been explained if all the important information had been related by the witnesses. There had simply been insufficient data to allow for a proper investigation in these instances.

Of course, they didn't close the project, but merely changed the name of it to Project Grudge and kept right on investigating. To the general public the situation was over and there was officially nothing to the phenomenon. After all, no one had found any hard physical evidence, as far as the general public knew.

In the summer of 1952, the situation changed as thousands of sightings were made, and saucers were reported over Washington, D.C., on two successive Saturday nights. When the wave ended, in the fall of 1952, hundreds of reporters were phoning Project Blue Book and the Pentagon demanding explanations. Congress wanted to know what was happening. The general public was very interested in flying saucers, suspecting that they were not being told the truth.

What is important, however, is that the proof positive was supposedly never found. Even though there were photographs, movie footage, radar reports, air intercepts, and eyewitness testimony, everything could always be explained away if the man providing the explanation appeared sincere enough. Which is to say that the calculated risk taken in July 1947 to bury the Roswell case had paid off. The truth hadn't been learned by the public and the real proof hadn't surfaced to contradict the official spokesmen.

That fact may have persuaded those who actually did hold the answers to keep them from the public. There was no compelling reason to tell the truth in 1952 because the solid evidence had never surfaced. For more than five years the authorities had been sitting on the answer. Why rock the boat now?

Of course, there is a good answer to that: At any moment the entire situation might be exposed. Although the information proving the Roswell case is still held by those who have controlled it from the beginning, they do not control the pilots of the alien spacecraft. If one lands at the Pentagon or the United Nations tomorrow, the news media will be there to cover it. Then the answer will be out, for there would be no way of hiding it anymore. We will all know the truth.

And what will the result be? Scientists, sociologists, anthropologists, and others continue to argue about that. Some believe that unprecedented panic will be unleashed once the truth is known. Others believe that we are now sufficiently sophisticated to take the revelation in stride. After all, most of us have been raised on astronaut landings on the moon, shuttle space flights that are now so routine that the media no longer cover the launchings live, and the thousands of science fiction stories that speak of alien races and interstellar flight as if they are established fact.

I believe that if authorities were to announce now that the Roswell crash of fifty years ago actually occurred, the potential danger of a negative mass reaction could be easily defused. People might react strongly at first, but they would also have to realize that although the reality of extraterrestrials has been known about for five decades, our actual lives have not been affected. Society has not changed radically. The information has been known for half a century, yet nothing has changed.

But such a cushion would not exist if a spaceship were to land at the United Nations tomorrow. All we would know is that an alien race had found the Earth. We couldn't think in terms of this half-century of knowledge. We would have to deal with the situation immediately, and a great many people would be franticly imagining an invasion fleet orbiting Earth, ready to land.

So, had I been in charge in 1947, I too, might have tried to cover up the Roswell Incident until I had understood what was going on. I would have learned as much as I could about the alien ship, but eventually I would have released the information into the mainstream. Maybe authorities reasoned that since the situation had stabilized, there was no need to tell the truth. After all, it might have been a fluke, never to happen again, or at least not again for centuries. Why rock the boat now that the ocean was calm?

Carl Sagan has suggested that we could expect one visitation every ten thousand years. If he is right, and we had that visit in July 1947, it might be millennia before it happens again. By that time human beings should be more mature and better able to handle the information.

Maybe by that time, it will be us in the spacecraft, it will be we who have discovered life on another world, perhaps another civilization themselves on the verge of interstellar flight.

Or maybe this time, if it happens here again, those in charge will realize that it is something to be shared. Maybe they won't bury the report, pretending that it didn't happen.

However, now that we have begun to unravel the Roswell Incident, the continued suppression of it by the government only adds to our distrust of them. It has become just another example of an all-too-common event: A story leaks out to the public, it gets denied by those in charge, but it turns out to have been true all along. This is why we are becoming more jaded. We are finding that we have less and less reason to believe what our leaders, both civilian and military, are telling us.

Roswell might not have been an example of dialogue between two separate kinds of beings, but it *is* an example of communication among ourselves.

IIIIIII

THE UPSTATE NEW YORK INCIDENTS
by William R. Forstchen, Ph.D.

DURING THE SPRING AND summer of 1964 there was a rash of sightings in the upstate New York area focused around Binghamton. The first major sighting was claimed by Gary Wilcox, a farmer in the Newark Valley area. Wilcox claimed that on April 24, 1964, while he was working in his fields, a bright flash of light that seemed to emanate from a hill on his property caught his attention. Wilcox drove his tractor up to investigate, and when he approached to within a hundred to a hundred and fifty feet, an egg-shaped craft became visible. His first thought was that it was a wing, tank, or some other object that had fallen from a plane, but then he saw that it was actually hovering about four feet off the ground. Getting off his tractor, he approached the object and touched it.

Two humanoid "men" came out from under the craft. They were

approximately four feet tall and wore one-piece silver-colored coveralls, their heads concealed under what appeared to be helmets. One of them approached Wilcox and in clear English said, "We have talked to people before."

Wilcox claimed that a two-hour conversation now ensued, with the humanoids asking most of the questions, which centered on farming techniques. The visitors claimed they were from Mars and visited Earth a couple of times a year to collect "samples." They expressed interest in the type of commercial fertilizer Wilcox used, so the former offered to fetch a bag. The beings finally reboarded their ship, which departed at a remarkable rate of speed and after traveling a short distance seemed to disappear. Wilcox went back to his barn, took a bag of fertilizer, and hauled it up to the field where the encounter had happened. The following morning it was gone.

Wilcox said that throughout the whole incident he thought someone might be playing a joke on him, wondering if he was on *Candid Camera*, a popular television show of the sixties where ordinary citizens were "stung" by unusual jokes or scams while the entire event was secretly filmed.

At first Wilcox was reluctant to discuss the event, sharing it only with his parents. A week later the incident regarding Officer Zamora out in New Mexico hit the press, and eventually Wilcox talked with the local sheriff, who came up to the farm to examine the site. The air force and the FBI were contacted, but there do not seem to be any records of Wilcox being interviewed by either agency, though there was a soil sample taken by a local civil defense official, who stated that there was a significant level of radiation still present around the site.

This seemed to be the start of a continued series of sightings in the region throughout the rest of the year. A number of sightings of lights in the sky were reported in the Binghamton area late in July. The most interesting one was a report by Louis Daubert on July 27, 1964. He was approximately fifty miles northeast of Binghamton, heading to a Girl Scout camp to visit his daughter, who worked as a counselor. Daubert reported that he saw an elliptical-shaped object hovering in a field near the road. He estimated that the object was twenty-five feet in diameter and roughly seventy-five yards from his car. He claims to have watched the object for five to ten minutes, stating that it was metallic and "shined with an iridescent glow around the outer edge like a fluorescent light." Just before departure it shot three beams of light at his car, then took off at high speed.

What is significant about this sighting is that Daubert was close enough to the scout camp that at least ten counselors working there saw the object as well. One of the counselors stated that shortly after taps she felt a wave of heat and the leaves in the trees begin to stir. Then she saw a streak of light head straight up across the sky; it disappeared after several seconds.

The following night a bright, shining object that appeared elliptical in shape was reported over Binghamton by at least twenty witnesses. A number of other sightings were reported into early August. The incidents finally tapered off, but there were renewed sightings over Tioga County, to the west of Binghamton, early the following year.

ANALYSIS

Taken on its own, the Wilcox incident might very well be dismissed. After all, it doesn't seem likely that a farmer would spend two hours standing beside a hovering spacecraft discussing crops, farming, and fertilizer with two visitors, as if they were all hanging around at the local general store. Yet Wilcox was only one of dozens who reported sightings in the tri-county area around Binghamton during that summer.

There are, however, several points to consider in Wilcox's favor. Like witnesses in so many incidents, Wilcox did not seek out any attention. At first he only shared it with his family, then word leaked out, at which point he finally went public. Everyone who has interviewed Wilcox or who knew him before the incident describe him as laconic, hard-working, sober, and not prone to imaginative flights of fancy.

The second point is the fact that there was a high level of radiation in the area where Wilcox reported the sighting.

Third is an interesting coincidence that few people have linked together: Wilcox's description of the ship is rather similar to the one provided by Officer Zamora out in New Mexico the week before. One could perhaps see a correlation here and even suggest that they might have been one and the same.

On the surface the Wilcox encounter might seem laughable, especially the discussion of fertilizer, but if the visitors were from a planet where agriculture was a difficult pursuit, one might see some logic behind it all. For that matter the visitors might just have felt friendly and wanted to chat. This reviewer's wife has worked as a translator for visiting Russian agricultural specialists coming to America to examine our farming techniques and confirms that the conversations between farmers from the two different systems are always detailed, intense, and last for hours, with both sides extremely curious about how the other side works.

A key additional point here is the fact of numerous sightings that erupted in the area even before Wilcox went public, with many people reporting objects that looked similar to Wilcox's.

There really doesn't seem to be anything different that Wilcox could have done while the encounter was going on. He approached the craft in a friendly manner, chatted for two hours, offered help if needed, and even jokingly suggested they take him for a ride. Perhaps the only thing he could have done differently after the event was to take notes immediately regarding what had happened. Wilcox did state that there seemed to be a jellylike substance on the ground where the craft had touched down, but he never attempted to take and preserve a sample for later analysis. In general, though, his attitude and approach can actually serve as a rather good model of how to carry on a conversation with visitors. If there is a regret, it is that Wilcox didn't have a stronger background in the hard sciences so that he could have picked up more concrete information from his chatty friends.

ALIEN FIRST AID

by Mickey Zucker Reichert, M.D.

One of the most compelling images in the
Roswell Incident is that of a dazed or injured
alien sitting next to one that was even
more severely hurt. Considering how today
we are constantly warned not to move
crash victims for fear of making their injuries
worse, the problems of dealing with an alien
whose physiology is completely different
are imposing. If you were the first person
to come upon the site of a crashed UFO,
what should you do?

Believers in the Roswell Incident maintain that two injured humanoid creatures were discovered at the site, one in shock, the other unconscious and leaking a fluid that appeared to be blood. This raises intriguing possibilities and interesting questions. If, instead of landing, a spaceship were to crash into your backyard, what should you do?

The practice of medicine is the logical extension of centuries of studying human anatomy and response to various procedures and drugs. It's not an exact science. Individuals vary markedly in their responses to pain, injury, and illness as well as their reactions to medications and operations. One man's antidote is another's poison; the penicillin that cures your pneumonia might kill someone allergic to it. A remedy cheered by all as a savior today might constitute malpractice tomorrow. Given the variability among humans alone, and the long course of study it has taken to reach this stage of modern medicine, the idea that we have anything to offer wounded aliens seems ludicrous. However, if, as in the Roswell example, we are dealing with humanoid creatures, it seems likely that they followed a similar evolutionary track. If they kind of look like us, it's conceivable that they share much of what makes us tick. The constituent parts of astronomical bodies are, to the best of our knowledge, consistent. Life might prove equally invariable.

All right, then. Since speculation about the constitution, function, and appearance of space visitors is infinite, but medical science is not, let's assume for the moment that the creatures in the spaceship share similar biology. Let's start with a logical earth comparison: Instead of a spaceship, let's say that an airplane has plummeted from the sky and slammed into your children's sandbox. What would you do then? I hope you answered, "Call for help. This is more than I can handle."

Naturally, you would probably first remove yourself and family from danger. This would include making sure that none of you has become trapped beneath the wreckage and removing yourself, your spouse, and your children from the hazards of present or future explosions. Your next prudent step would be to call for professional help. Unless you have emergency medical and surgical training, as well as the supplies and personnel of a hospital at your disposal, you cannot handle the injuries likely sustained in an accident of such magnitude. As a physician, by the way, I would do exactly the same things. I don't carry an operating room in my pocket; and all the knowledge in the world, if I had it, doesn't increase the number of my hands.

If a spaceship crashed in your backyard, you should do nothing different, so far, than if it were an airplane: Ensure your safety and phone for assistance.

Portrayals of evil scientists and doctors in B-grade sci-fi flicks to the contrary, we are not involved in some weird, organized conspiracy to hide anything "different." Like me, the vast majority of doctors chose the profession because they care about people and want to do everything they can to help. It is ridiculous to think that we suffer through eight years of schooling that costs a lifetime to repay and a minimum of three years of residency (read: slave labor), and spend what seems like twenty-eight hours a day working or on-call because we have some driving need to cover up alien encounters or because we may someday have the chance to dissect visitors from distant planets. Heck, I refused the dog lab at medical school. I've stuck my hands inside bleeding car-crash victims who wouldn't survive long enough for me to glove. If I'd risk my life for some stranger unlikely to survive with or without my help, how could I not extend that compassion to intelligent extraterrestrial visitors?

Lecture over. Let's assume you've made the call. Remain as calm as possible. A hysterical person babbling about a UFO is unlikely to accomplish more than placing his or her own sanity in doubt. Describe the location of the accident. Explain that some sort of vehicle has crashed and that immediate medical help is needed.

When our dispatcher receives a call from a person professing to have discovered a spaceship filled with wounded aliens in his backyard, he assumes several things. Quite honestly, it never occurs to him (or me) that the caller actually discovered a spaceship filled with wounded aliens in his backyard. However, depending on the demeanor of the caller, he usually dispatches paramedics to the scene in the belief that the caller has misidentified a small aircraft, a balloon, or even a motor vehicle. In most cases, he is right. So far, in the others, we've found nothing but psychoses or duplicity.

With that understanding, if you ever really do find a spaceship, please allow understandable doubts based on past experience. Just tell the person answering the call that there's been a terrible accident. Let the paramedics discover their patients are visitors from outer space. Seeing the ship and its nonhuman occupants should speak louder than any telephone description you might give.

You've made the call. Now what do you do while waiting for the paramedics to arrive? Let's assume you can assist the injured parties without placing self, neighbors, or family at risk from fire or explosion damage. Do not assume you are out of danger. Let's use the Roswell example and say you tried to assist the bleeder. Imagine what the other being might assume if it awakened to find some terran poking and prodding at its companion. Consider the danger inherent in such a situation before you make the decision to approach and attend. Remember that the chances of communicating your altruism will approach nil, and do not assume the other will not simply kill you and hold the rest of us responsible for your "hostility."

But let's assume you've judged the risks and found them acceptable. You've decided to proceed despite the danger. The majority of people don't know basic first aid for humans and creatures of Earth, let alone visitors from other planets. Medical technology, our knowledge of human anatomy, and our observations of responses to therapy, trauma, and illness improve daily. It makes sense to start with basic therapies for humans, watch their effects, and modify treatment based on the response we received. When we have so much science and study behind us, random guessing seems silly as well as an injustice to those we are hoping to save.

Unless evolution turns out to be a stable process from world to world, the probability that a creature with a completely parallel origin shares our anatomy seems remote. If the victim, or its companions, are alert, allow them to handle the problem. Surely even the least intelligent spacefarer would have more knowledge of how to care for their own wounded than we would. Stand by to assist in case such a request is made, assuming any communication is possible. However, such a situation should not wholly supplant a call to 911.

Let's return to Roswell, where we're dealing with humanoid creatures. You're waiting for the paramedics to arrive, and you want to administer essential first aid. Initial assessment should include the following: First, decide if it is absolutely necessary to move the patient for purposes of safety. For example, if the ship landed in your pool and the occupants might sink, removing them may be necessary. The same holds true for creatures trapped inside a burning vehicle. If you must move the trauma victim immediately, do so. But be aware of your own safety! Ascertain that the risks are acceptable to you before proceeding. I cannot emphasize this enough. Don't leap into the pool if you can't swim. Realize that a burning vehicle could kill you also. These warnings may seem obvious, but many lives have been lost to stupid heroism. And, of course, risk to innocent bystanders is never acceptable.

If movement is not definitively necessary and the victims are "breathing" and not actively "bleeding," watch them in place until professional help arrives. If movement is necessary for safety or to administer urgently needed first aid, attempt to stabilize the victim's neck before moving. Do not bend, twist, move, or otherwise maneuver the neck. You will do more harm than good. Using an unyielding surface, perhaps a chunk of the wreckage, immobilize the neck and spine with caution. Try to get a feel from the logical anatomy of the creature so that your stabilization efforts do not cause the damage you're trying to avoid. For example, if all of the creatures have hunched backs, don't try to force the spine to conform to a flat board. Attempt to keep it in the natural anatomic position and in as straight a line as possible. Integrity of back and neck should be preserved, assuming the creature has a spinal cord. The idea is not to damage the neurological system such that you permanently paralyze the victim. The neck is most important, at least in humans. Damage there may guarantee that the patient can never breathe without assistance again.

By the way, in most states, you are not legally bound to assist; but once you start basic life support, you have committed yourself. Do not quit until either help arrives, you are endangered, or you have become too exhausted to continue. Not only is it the law but it is the only moral and honorable thing to do. If you don't trust yourself to help without causing more damage, do nothing other than prepare to point the way and follow directions.

Now, let's say you feel confident of your ability to help and of the necessity for immediate intervention. You now have your patient lying on its back, assuming it has one; and you're both free from any additional danger. It's time for the primary survey. First priority in humans is the airway; second, breathing; third, circulation and control of bleeding; fourth, disability; and last, a thorough examination.

Does the creature breathe? Is it, or are any of its companions, conscious or unconscious, inhaling and expiring air from any orifice? If so, does it appear comfortable or is it desperately gasping? If the creature is not "breathing," this could be because creatures of its ilk don't "breathe" as we do, or it could mean it will die if it is not resuscitated. Seek clues from others, if any exist. If you can identify a breathing orifice, ascertain that it is not plugged. Imagine the course of the airway, and carefully position the opening to allow air to properly enter it. Search for obstructions, inhaled foreign material (such as bits of wreckage), or the equivalent of the human tongue. Remove impediments if this can be done safely, especially without lodging them deeper, or experiment with positioning. Throughout, be conscious of the need to keep the "neck" and "back" steady. In humans, especially children, simple repositioning of the airway can mean the difference between life and death.

Once the orifice is open, check to see if breathing occurs spontaneously. If not, and the creature is distinctly mammalian, attempt to blow air into the orifice. Recognize the danger inherent in contact, such as infection, acid saliva, or the exhalation of a dangerous substance. A CPR mask, if you own one, seems prudent. However, if the visitor cannot tolerate our atmosphere, cardiopulmonary resuscitation (CPR) is doomed to failure. Tanks of whatever substance they breathe might not resemble ours, and the risks inherent in playing with otherworld gases are too high to warrant an attempt at resuscitation with anything other than Earth air or oxygen.

Feel for a pulse at many sites. Without knowledge of anatomy, you cannot begin to guess where the arteries might lie; and studies have shown that, in an emergency, most laymen cannot find pulses in humans. A space creature may or may not even have a circulatory system. If you cannot find a pulse, pressure on the blood pump or pumps (heart or hearts) may help, but only if you can locate it. Look for sights of obvious hemorrhage (bleeding). Wrap any such areas with a cloth, making sure to locate the exact site of injury. Place firm pressure directly over the wound with your hands for as long as possible, without letting go even for a moment. Any creature with a circulatory system will have some method of clotting. Large losses of fluid, no matter the type, will result in irreversible shock.

The neurologic assessment should include whether the creature is conscious or not. If it is, it must be "breathing" and its "heart" pumping. The only assistance it might need from you is to stop bleeding or help with movement. Compare its color with others of its kind. If it has eyes and pupils, note their reaction to light.

Reassess the patient at least every five minutes. Is it still conscious? Still breathing? Is the pulse you found still there? Is the color changing? Is the "bleeding" staunched? Is it arousing or lapsing into a deeper state of sleep? If it has obvious eyes, are the pupils' responsiveness changing? Deterioration requires immediate attention. The sooner the assistance, the more likely a successful resuscitation.

One point I want to beat into the ground. Although CPR has saved some human lives, the chances for survival increase dramatically the sooner the patient is transferred to a hospital and into the care of medical professionals with proper equipment. The success rate for general-first-aid measures performed on alien creatures would be expected to be much lower. The kindest and most appropriate thing to do in a situation where injuries need tending is to call for professional help as swiftly as possible.

Because of the Roswell descriptions, I'd like to say a few words about shock. There's a general misconception that it's akin to being stunned and that time will bring the victim around. Nothing could be farther from the truth. Shock occurs when the body is unable to supply the perfusion (blood flow, including oxygen and nutrients) necessary for vital organs. Compensated shock means that other processes of the body are able to maintain perfusion to vital organs. For example, the blood vessels in the fingers and toes may clamp down, decreasing their blood flow to allow more to go to essential organs, such as the kidneys, heart, and brain. At this stage, shock can usually be reversed. Untreated compensated shock often progresses to uncompensated shock, in which the processes fail. Death ensues.

The unconscious, bleeding alien described by the Roswell Incident advocates would almost certainly also be "in shock." Hypovolemia (decreased blood in the veins) is the most common type of shock in accident victims. It is treated by stopping the bleeding and running appropriate fluids (usually blood) into the veins to replace what was lost. The other alien, if not also bleeding, likely suffered from obstructive shock. This means it suffered from a process that inhibits the heart from pumping. In other words, there's enough blood/fluid but it's not getting properly distributed. In humans, this is most often secondary to cardiac tamponade (fluid, usually blood, that has leaked into the membrane around the heart), tension pneumothorax (air trapped in the pleural cavity, which allows pressure in the chest to build to higher-than-atmospheric pressure), or pulmonary embolus (a blood clot in the lungs). Distributive shock, loss of neurologic tone of the blood vessels, can be due to spinal shock and would also be a possibility. None of these can be treated without expertise and/or specialized equipment.

Let's run through one possible scenario, assuming the alleged crash at Roswell occurred in your own backyard. You and two friends, John and Ruth, arrive first upon the scene. You see two humanoid creatures. One was thrown from the wreckage (apparently not wearing his seat belt!) and appears to be leaking blood. The other still sits in the vehicle, unmoving. John brought his trusty cellular phone. He calls 911, explaining that he's come upon the scene of an accident. He gives the address and requests immediate help.

Meanwhile, you and Ruth approach the victims. Both are grayish in color. They appear similar to humans, with childlike proportions: The head occupies a larger relative body surface area and the neck is shorter and fatter. Let's say the one still in the ship appears to be breathing comfortably, its chest moving in and out. The eyes are closed. The ship is quiet, and you see no smoke. You judge that the vehicle is unlikely to explode or catch fire, and all three of you decide it's worth risking your lives to save these extraterrestrial visitors.

For now, the one in the ship is in less need of immediate attention because, though unconscious, it is breathing "normally." You move to the one thrown clear. Unlike its companion, its chest is still. Its skin is paler, and a pink substance is pouring from a wound in its thigh. It's lying on its side.

John finishes his call and goes to assist the other alien. Ruth scrambles to your side to help, bringing a boardlike piece of the wreckage. Together, you stabilize the creature's neck and back, rolling it onto the fragment in a supine (on the back) position. You determine from its appearance that the creature's relaxed jaw allows its square tongue to fall back into its airway. You pull the jaw outward without disturbing neck position. This frees the airway of the tongue, but spontaneous breathing does not occur. You see nothing else blocking the airway. Remembering your CPR training, you deliver two breaths.

While you are assessing, Ruth has wrapped a tight dressing around the thigh wound. She holds it tightly with one hand, searching for a pulse with the other. She doesn't find one. You quickly check the neck and arms, without success. The chest appears similar to your own, so you attempt one-man CPR with chest compressions and breathing. After a few rounds, Ruth tells you she can feel only a tiny, weak pulse accompanying your thrusts. She thinks it felt stronger the one time your hand slipped and you pressed lower on the chest wall. You shift the position of your CPR efforts, and Ruth tells you she now feels a good pulse with each stroke.

The bandage on the creature's leg is soaked, so Ruth abandons her pulse search to check the wound. The "blood" had disguised its position. It's nearer the groin area than she remembered. With that in mind, she rewraps the bandage and applies pressure to the proper location with both hands. Within ten minutes, the bleeding is contained. The creature's color improves. You continue your efforts. As the wound clots, Ruth shifts around to check the creature's eyes, which respond to her key-chain flashlight but not as much as she expects. She shouts to John to check his charge.

John calls back that the other creature is swaying, still breathing, its color unchanged. He thinks it's only stunned, not in shock. He checks its eyes, and the reaction he describes is very similar. Its skin is ice-cold, and he covers it with his coat. He asks for Ruth's as well, and she rushes it over to him.

By now, you are tiring and ask Ruth to replace you at giving CPR. She works into a two-man CPR mode, and you continue to assist the creature to breathe. Nothing has changed, but it does not seem to be getting worse. You glance over in time to see the other creature's eyes flicker open. You call a careful warning to John and Ruth. You all watch the creature. It stares back, glassy-eyed, gaze weaving from you to its companion. It shakes its head, apparently clearing it.

Ruth takes over the CPR while John attempts communication with the creature. Apparently, it reads your gestures as nonthreatening. It climbs from the wreckage, carrying something that could be a weapon, and heads toward its companion. John and Ruth move aside. The creature straps the device over its companion's face.

At that point, help arrives. Assuring the creature in the best nonverbal manner possible that these people will help it, you allow the paramedics to work. After they get over their initial surprise, they radio back a description of the aliens. The hospital prepares for their arrival. They ask you to describe what you've done so far and tell you you probably saved the creatures' lives.

Everybody hopes that's a good thing.

||||||||

THE HOPKINSVILLE, KENTUCKY, INCIDENT
by William R. Forstchen, Ph.D.

THIS INCIDENT, WHICH OCCURRED on August 21, 1955, can be taken either as an event boarding on the absurd, or one that was a tragic misunderstanding that could have had grave results.

A gathering of friends was taking place at the rural farmhouse of Cecil "Lucky" Sutton after having attended a "Holy Roller" church service. According to Cecil's mother, the meeting had been emotionally charged and that everyone was still "worked up." Cecil's father was walking through the house when he looked out the back door and saw a bright silver object, which he stated was about two and a half feet tall and appeared to be round. Another man at the house reported going outside to get a bucket of water and saw a flying saucer come over the trees and land several hundred feet away. Shortly afterward the group saw upward of a dozen "little men" with huge eyes, with hands and arms out of proportion to their body size, approaching. One of them had his arms up over his head as he approached the house, a gesture that was described by one of the witnesses as looking like he was expecting to be robbed.

The armory was broken out as, according to a local paper report, "the men got their guns." One of the little men came up to the house, pressed his face against the window, and was greeted with a shotgun blast.

The men decided to go outside to see if they had bagged one of the aliens. As they emerged from the house, one of them was grabbed by an alien perched on the roof, but he managed to shake himself free, and the group retreated back into the house, Sutton knocking another one down with a shotgun blast.

The aliens were reported to have been hit a number of times, the sound of the bullets striking the aliens reminding one of the witnesses of the noise heard when gravel strikes a bucket. The impacts, however, didn't seem to do any damage; the aliens simply flipped over, then seemed to float up off the ground and flee, only to sneak back again a few minutes later.

When the group saw their chance, they fled the house in two cars and went to the police for help. A number of police and even some military police went to the scene. No little men were seen, though there was evidence of gunfire as reported. The police stayed for two hours, then left. Shortly afterward, according to those in the house, the aliens returned. One of the women reported that she saw an alien peeping in the window at her, its hands raised over its head. She called for the others, and one came in with a shotgun and shot the alien in the face. Again there was a replay of the events earlier in the evening, with the aliens finally leaving just before dawn.

ANALYSIS

This case certainly has a strange quality to it, and almost has the feel of a bad sci-fi movie from the fifties with backwoods folks holding off the aliens with rifles and shotguns. The additional elements that could cause one to doubt was the admission by one of the group that they had returned from a Holy Roller church meeting and were emotionally charged up. There had also been earlier discussion of flying saucers, and one of them had a photograph of a supposed alien, which was actually a monkey spray-painted silver.

Police reported that there was no sign of tracks from the aliens, no imprint of a craft where it supposedly landed, the only evidence being the damage from the gunfire. The police did report, however, that there was no evidence of drinking, and one of the officers publicly stated that he saw no reason to disbelieve what was reported. This reviewer recently talked with a resident of Hopkinsville, Kentucky, who still remembers the incident. He stated that the witnesses to the event never changed their story regarding what happened and even years afterward stood by the validity of their report.

So let us, at least for argument's sake, accept the report as genuine. What went wrong? Obviously the aliens picked the wrong house to drop in on. What is significant is that the alien approaching the house did so with arms raised. As in the Papua Incident, this is an interesting human gesture usually meant to display that one is unarmed and/or intends no harm, though the interpretation of one of the witness was that the alien held its arms over its head as if it expected to get robbed.

It didn't get robbed, but it did get a shotgun blast in the face at close range.

The witnesses reported that when hit, the aliens would flip over, then get up and scurry away, the bullets obviously having no effect. There were no reports of return fire and no one on the human side was hurt in the fusillade. If there is a conclusion to be drawn from this incident about what could have been done differently, it applies primarily to the aliens. Don't approach a house on planet Earth with arms raised over your head and then peek in the window.

CROP CIRCLES

by Chris Talaraski

Late in July 1980, a news item in southwestern England's *Wiltshire Times* regarding unusual circular depressions found in an oatfield caught the eye of Ian Mrzyglod, a ufologist with the British UFO Research Association (BUFORA). With several colleagues, he arrived the following day at John Scull's farm to determine if these circular, swirled markings were UFO-related or the result of a more terrestrial origin. Suspecting a meteorological explanation, he contacted local meteorologist G. Terrence Meaden, who would eventually propose the plasma vortex theory, which involves a naturally occurring atmospheric phenomenon.

Since the early crop circles encountered were simple in design without the later elaborate rings and assorted appendages, initial theories were confined mainly to hoaxes, helicopter damage, whirlwinds, and UFO landing sites. Mrzygold's handful of investigators took soil and plant samples, looking for traces of radioactive particles in the event that aliens were landing in the Wiltshire fields. Unfortunately, the test results obtained from Bristol University did not contain any anomalous data, but this did not deter others from dismissing the extraterrestrial hypothesis.

One year later a retired electromechanical engineer, Pat Delgado, was informed of a series of circles appearing at Cheesefoot Head in Hampshire. His fascination with the enigmatic circles would result in several written reports that found their way into *Flying Saucer Review,* thus opening the door to wider speculation regarding an ET origin.

While some researchers were considering an ET origin for the annular circles, others were being more conservative and critical in their analyses. Jenny Randles and Paul Fuller of BUFORA, in their 1990 book *Crop Circles: A Mystery Solved,* were supporting Meaden's plasma vortex theory while also searching for historical evidence of pre-1980 circles.

Meaden's theory was based on an as yet unrecognized energy vortex that was dependent on topographical obstructions. This hypothetical vortex is a "rotating ball of electrically charged air," according to Meaden, that "consists of tiny molecules of air that have lost negatively charged electrons, thus resulting in a positively charged cloud of ionized gas." Meaden observed that a fair number of circles were formed downwind of the abundant chalk hills in the area of Wiltshire. He believed the vortices of rotating electrically charged air were being generated by the flow of air over these sloping chalk hills, leaving the circular impressions in their wake. Meaden's data purportedly could also account for other UFO sightings that had plagued the area.

Between 1980 and 1983 the majority of the circles investigated were relatively simple in design. Ranging from multiple groupings to solitary formations with accompanying rings, most could be explained by something akin to Meaden's vortex. By 1983 some quintuplet sets of circles had Meaden revising his theory to allow for the peculiar groupings and attributing them to breakdowns in the descending vortices. Inevitably Pat Delgado and Colin Andrews, who had worked alongside Meaden, would reject his theories, crediting the rise in frequency of observed circles and their growing complexity to a nonhuman intelligence.

In the hope of witnessing circle formation, a number of attempts were made to capture this elusive event. Operation White Crow, an eight-day project in June 1989 mounted by Colin Andrews, used an assortment of video and infrared cameras to try to record a genuine event, to no avail.

With the arrival of the pictograms in the 1990s—huge formations featuring connecting corridors, keylike attachments, claws, and accompanying satellite additions—it was becoming apparent that something more intricate than whirlwinds was involved. For better or for worse the phenomenon was gaining worldwide attention. An extraterrestrial agent was looking more plausible with each discovered design. The Alton Barnes double pictogram found on the morning of July 11, 1990, on Tim and Polly Carson's farm stretched to a length of approximately four hundred feet and drew hundreds of visitors along with throngs of media.

Other pictograms studded the Vale of Pewsey in Wiltshire, appearing in close proximity to archaeological sites such as Silbury Hill, the stone circle of Avebury, and Stonehenge.

Gerald Hawkins, an astronomer who concluded that Stonehenge was an astronomical observatory, found intriguing evidence that some crop-circle patterns were exhibiting unusual mathematical and musical properties. In eleven of eighteen crop formations, Hawkins encountered ratios of small whole numbers that matched the ratios that characterize the diatonic scale. Surprisingly, the ratios would yield the eight tones of an octave in the musical scale that coincide with the white keys of a piano. Hawkins would delve further into the circles mystery by looking for geometrical associations in the placement of the circles. A group of three circles arranged in a triangle found in June 1988 at Cheesefoot Head would prompt Hawkins to look for geometric theorems originating from the ratios of the circles' areas. Ultimately he would derive five theorems that were not to be discovered in any of Euclid's works. If hoaxers were responsible for these annular circles, their work was displaying an intelligence and foresight that did not seem likely of pranksters out to befuddle the swelling numbers of crop-circle researchers and devotees.

Throughout Great Britain local circle-watching groups and full-scale organizations blossomed. The Center for Crop Circle Studies, formed in the summer of 1990, functioned as a hub for communications between all researchers and for the collation of data. The CCCS publishes *The Cereologist,* which invites all viewpoints on the subject, including ufologists, dowsers who claim the circles have dowsable properties, New Age advocates, and supporters of James Lovelock's Gaia theory, who feel the circles were efforts of an ailing Earth to communicate its distress. Paul Fuller's *The Crop Watcher* continues to look at rational explanations for the circles.

The summer of 1991 proved to be pivotal to the cereological community. Elaborate designs continued and were at the same time causing investigators to look closer at the hoaxing aspect of the phenomenon. At Ickleton, near Cambridge University, a formation appeared that clearly depicted a Mandelbrot set, representative of equations found in chaos theory. Some cereologists were convinced that this was yet another indication of communication by some form of intelligence. The proximity of the school leads others to doubt the formation's authenticity. Branding circles authentic is becoming risky business. Meaden proclaimed a simple circle as genuine only to find out it was made by the Wessex Skeptics, a local group that derided the phenomenon. The season ended with Doug Bower and Dave Chorley's admissions that they had been responsible for a large number of circles for a period of thirteen years. The two elderly gentlemen had also duped Pat Delgado into heralding one of their formations at Sevenoaks as genuine. Still, the large quantity of circles reported made it difficult to accept that all circles were the product of hoaxers. It should be noted that southwest England does not have a monopoly on unusual circular markings in their cereal crops. The United States, Germany, Belgium, and more impressively Canada were displaying similar swirled depressions, though not on such a grand or numerous scale.

After 1991 many people discounted the circles phenomenon as hoaxes; yet without fail the circles continued into 1992. Not daunted by the realization that the subject was losing credibility, several investigators proceeded with a series of scientific and pseudoscientific ventures.

Project Argus, a joint U.S. and British 1992 study of the circles, brought a much-needed objective look at the phenomenon. Differing from the aforementioned crop studies, Argus focused on detailed analyses of soil and plant samples after crop-circle formation had occurred. Maintaining a base of operations at Alton Barnes from July 8 through August 28, 1992, Argus's members investigated more than twenty formations. The project conducted tests ranging from electron microscopy, which examined plant cell-wall structure, to gamma spectroscopy, which looked for short-lived radioactive isotopes in soil. The project did not find an absolute way of determining whether some circles were the product of human design. There was no evidence of aberrant radiation or DNA degradation in the tested formations. However, plants inside the circles showed a larger number of microscopic blisters than outside control samples; also the soil displayed a higher incidence of magnetic-flux intensity. This magnetic anomaly did not appear in a tested known hoax.

While Project Argus was conducting its fieldwork in late July 1992, another project was setting up shop in Alton Barnes. Project Starlight led by Dr. Stephen Greer of CSETI (Center for the Search for Extraterrestrial Intelligence), a U.S.-based UFO organization, was getting ready to establish contact with the aliens that were surely creating the splendid designs in the fields. Greer, an emergency room physician from Asheville, North Carolina, founded CSETI in 1990 in hope that a more interactive approach with the aliens will lead to full contact. Greer and his CSETI members would descend on areas of high UFO activity trying to achieve a CE-5 (Close Encounter of the Fifth Kind, a human-initiated contact). Unlike SETI, which uses an array of radio telescopes to listen for possible signals of alien origin from the stars, Greer uses a variety of apparatus more suited to communicate with the aliens that are, in his opinion, already in our local vicinity. High-intensity military spotlights, video, still cameras, and a number of highly motivated individuals are his preferred methods of investigation.

Greer has included operations at Gulf Breeze, Florida, an area of questionable UFO activity, and Mexico City, site of a prolonged wave of UFO sightings in 1993. The link with crop circles and UFO activity is tenuous at best. Hard evidence supporting an association between the two phenomena has been limited to a small number of eyewitness reports and inconclusive video. Nevertheless, the summer of 1992 brought a fair contingent of UFO investigators to southwest England to witness firsthand and report on the suspicious markings.

Woodborough Hill at Alton Barnes presented an excellent location for Greer to conduct Project Starlight. Overlooking a wide area of Tim and Polly Carson's farmland, one had a panoramic view of the Vale of Pewsey and the neighboring Golden Ball and Milk Hills. One night late in July a rather significant gathering of cropwatchers, cereologists, and several curious Argus team members, including the author, arrived to participate and otherwise politely observe CSETI's efforts. The sun had set just after ten P.M. that evening and not long thereafter the jewel-like band of the Milky Way spread across the sky. As the crowd grew accustomed to the darkness, various sources of lights were attracting the attention of some eager participants. Spotlights from an apparent shopping area due south of the hill striking a cloud bank had some excited viewers commenting rather erroneously on a possible UFO sighting.

Transport planes and helicopters from the Upavon Military Base were passing close to Woodborough Hill that night, flying without lights and prompting discussion on the military's role in the phenomenon. Several people also spotted a short-lived orange glow near the base of Milk Hill. Close to midnight Greer brought out his powerful spotlight and began to intermittently flash it at the night sky. Some CSETI members broke off from the large number of attendees and engaged in New Ageish exercises to enhance the climate for an alien contact. Unfortunately, that night inevitably offered little in the way of a human and alien liaison. Subsequent outings later that week would provide Greer with more chances for a possible interaction. Robert Irving reports in the January– February 1993 *Crop Watcher* that after midnight one night as Greer was packing up his equipment, several witnesses claimed to see a long strip of revolving lights that changed from red to green to white south of Woodborough Hill. Greer estimated the craft to be a hundred feet in diameter and roughly a quarter mile away. After a few minutes of viewing the object Greer flashed his spotlight twice, a number of times, and received the same signal back. This exchange continued for some time, but the alleged craft did not land. Pranksters or maybe misidentification of military aircraft were most likely responsible for the display, but Greer was convinced a nonterrestrial craft had been the source.

Curiously, the previously mentioned orange glow near Milk Hill may have generated a crop formation. The day following Greer's exercise,

Project Argus members received a call from pilot Busty Taylor, who has photographed and investigated scores of circles over the years, with news of a circle adjacent to Milk Hill. Upon locating the formation, which resembled a large comma or phone-receiver shape, team members were assembled to gather samples and data. The formation, which would be dubbed "God's Telephone," was unusual in that it was discovered on a field that had sustained storm damage known as lodging, an irregular flattening of the crop by wind and rain. A fair portion of the circle was placed directly on the damaged wheat, leaving a sporadic area of partially erect clumps of crop standing. It appeared as though whatever force was used in the formation of the circle had had difficulty when encountering the lodging. The circle had a windswept quality in its overall construction and featured the common trait of unbroken, flattened stalks bent just above the soil line along with familiar patterns in stalk placement that have been observed with crop circles. One would question why hoaxers would choose this location for their artwork considering the irregular terrain. Also, why would they leave these areas of standing crop in the circle?

In 1990, close to this same field, an extremely small silver object, less than a foot in diameter, was videotaped weaving in and out of the crops for several minutes before disappearing above an adjoining hill all during daylight hours. As with most UFO video and photographic evidence, nothing conclusive could be ascertained by analysis as to the exact nature of the object.

The majority of witnesses to UFOs in crop-circle country do not relate observing structured crafts, and those few who see circles as they form tell of whirlwinds or unusual wind-driven mists that descend on the fields. The historical evidence of pre-1980 circles is abundant enough to negate a hoax theory for all documented crop formations.

The "Mowing Devil" incident in Hertfordshire in 1678 contains an unmistakable account of a series of circles found one August morning. Circle proponents have repeatedly stressed that the phenomenon began in the early 1980s while ignoring historical references, thus bolstering their claims of alien intervention. If aliens are the culprit behind the phenomenon, they have been toiling in the fields for almost three hundred years, for altogether unfathomable reasons.

It has been suggested that there may be elements of hoaxing, meteorological disturbances, and an intelligence behind the circles all mixed together. This could explain some of the more confounding aspects of the enigma. Every year circles occur despite the declining media interest and the prevailing conclusion that hoaxing is the answer. While a large quantity of formations can be attributed to hoaxes, there is no question that something unique is happening in cereal crops on an annual basis in England.

Two years after Project Argus and Starlight, an unnerving incident took place on July 21, 1992, near Alton Barnes. Colin Andrews reports in his *Circles Phenomenon Research Newsletter* (Summer 1994) that he and eight colleagues were driving in a van during the middle of the day on a road overlooking a field that had a large circle resembling an eye. After stopping, two military helicopters buzzed Andrews and his colleagues. When they reentered the van and continued driving, the helicopters followed them; one copter then broke off and buzzed several researchers in the formation down below. Not long after this harassment, the other vehicle headed for Woodborough Hill, where it was observed to stop and slowly approach a small pulsing light. This light was similar to the one videotaped at Milk Hill in 1990. Andrews then recounts how the helicopter reached a point in front of the object, which was then seen to blink out and appear behind the helicopter. Fortunately this event was caught on videotape and shown to a large audience. Again, the object's nature cannot be determined, and the preceding episode is open to interpretation.

If the object is a bona fide nonterrestrial craft, one wonders who will make first contact—UFO researchers or members of the military? The elusive nature of UFOs throughout the last fifty years might signify that contact as we expect it may not happen at all, or else it has already transpired under the guiding hand of government and military agencies.

HOW TO GET ALONG
WITH AN EXTRATERRESTRIAL

by G. Harry Stine

Okay, you've helped make a successful
First Contact, and within a few years we
find ourselves part of a community of,
hopefully, friendly races among the stars.
Just how should we act? In an era when we
are struggling to deal with man at his worst in
Bosnia, Iraq, Iran, parts of Africa, and many
other of our so-called civilized states, is it
too early to begin asking how we should
treat extraterrestrial beings from other,
possibly very different, races? The answer to
this may be in the metalaws presented here.
They might do some good if applied on
Earth as well.

Question: What are you going to do and how are you going to act
when you first meet Zork Aarrggh, an inhabitant of Beta Lycris A-3?

Answer: You are going to be very, very careful. You are going to try
to understand him. And you are going to religiously follow the principles of metalaw.

Not only are we engaged today in the first steps outward to the stars,
but we are also diligently searching for evidence of both extraterrestrial
life and extraterrestrial intelligence. If we do happen to find extraterrestrial intelligent life, and if we happen to recognize it as such, we will
attempt to communicate with it.

While this search is getting under way, a very small number of people
are beginning to think about what to do if and when we finally make
contact. In some ways, the situation is rather like a dog chasing a car
and managing to clamp his teeth on the bumper; what is he going to

do with it once he's got it? This is why this small number of people have, over the past thirty years, been thinking about possible rules of conduct and action when dealing with extraterrestrial intelligent beings. They have given birth to the new field of metalaw.

Metalaw is just what the word implies: *meta* is a prefix denoting "above" or "beyond." Law is a system of rules of conduct and action governing the relationships between entities, rules that have been classified, reduced to order, put into the form of rules, and mutually agreed upon. Metalaw is therefore a system of law dealing with all frames of existence and with intelligent entities of all kinds.

However, succinct as the definitions of both law and metalaw are, the rules of conduct and action that are created, classified, ordered, formed, and agreed upon involve "intelligent beings." So, perhaps we'd better take a cut at defining what we mean by an "intelligent being."

Dictionaries say one thing. Biologists say something else. And psychologists may or may not agree with either. But the discussion can be initiated by defining an intelligent being or entity as a system having *all* of the following characteristics:

1. Self-awareness
2. Possession of a time-binding sense—that is, the ability to consider optional future actions and to act upon these considerations
3. Creativity, which author Arthur Koestler defines as the ability to make bi-sociative syntheses of random matrices to produce new ideas or things
4. Adaptive behavior, the capability to override the preprogrammed behavior of instinct and adapt behavior patterns to perceived present or potential future circumstances
5. Empathy, the ability to make imaginative identification with another intelligent entity
6. Communicativity, the ability to transmit information to another intelligent being in a meaningful manner

This list may not be complete. But as it stands, it is a start at defining an intelligent entity. An intelligent entity must have *all* of these characteristics, and it may have more. If the entity does not have every one of them, we could not consider it to be intelligent.

Many animals, especially the higher mammals, may possess some of these characteristics ... but not *all* of them. Dogs may be self-aware, may have a short-range time-binding sense, are highly empathic, can communicate reasonably well but not completely, but fall short in creativity and perhaps in adaptive behavior. The Great Apes have some of these characteristics, but not all of them. Dolphins may, but the work that showed so much speculative promise a decade ago has gotten very quiet lately.

We have now built some machines that have some of these characteristics, but not all of them . . . yet. We may be able to build machines having all the characteristics of an intelligent entity, and we may be closer to doing that than many people believe. If we do create an intelligent machine, we must be ready to treat it as an intelligent entity under our rules of law. Which means we had better have metalaw well worked out very quickly.

Most human beings, regardless of the culture in which they have been born and raised, have all six of these characteristics. Not all humans possess all of the characteristics to the same degree. Some may have very little of a given characteristic, and this could be due to genetic inheritance, prenatal nutrition, or cultural training and environment. Save for those unfortunate human beings who are retarded or otherwise suffer from neurological or psychological trauma, we can generally state that every human being has all six characteristics of an intelligent entity, whether he/she be an Einstein or an aborigine. And it can generally be said that one can take any normal, average newborn human being from any place in the world and, with well-understood methods of training and education, turn that human being into a person who would meet every test of an "intelligent entity."

However, we or our progeny stand a very good chance of running headlong into the problem of recognizing an intelligent extraterrestrial entity when and if contact is ever made. It makes little difference whether we are the contactors or the contactees.

One of the major problems is: How do we act and how do we react toward an intelligent extraterrestrial being? How do we apply our rules and codes to the situation?

As a matter of fact, we could use an answer to that question with respect to interpersonal relationships and even international diplomacy between human beings whom we already know and recognize as being intelligent beings! How can we expect to make friendly and useful contact with an extraterrestrial intelligence if we cannot do the same among ourselves?

The human race is a singularly successful terrestrial species. It is also made up of individuals who are mean, nasty, vicious, deadly, covetous, greedy, deceitful, distrustful, and violent killers . . . of their own species. But our single most important invention may not lie in the province of our material technology but in the increasingly sophisticated means that we have developed to keep from killing one another some of the time. In contrast to warriors who apply physical force, we have developed specialists in human conflict called lawyers. These professional people of law not only codify, define, and write the laws under which we live, but they also interpret them and enforce them—using the services of warriors if the need arises.

However, we now have a welter of different—and often conflicting—sets of rules, regulations, codes, and laws under which we live. The rules differ from city to city, state to state, nation to nation, and even culture to culture. The code Napoleon differs greatly from English common law, which in turn is quite different from the laws of Arabic countries or the nations of the Orient. International law only scratches the surface in attempting to cross-connect between legal systems. And international law is also highly compartmented.

With all the different systems of law on Planet Earth, which one is optimized for use when Zork Aarrggh comes into the picture? Which code of conduct and action will be used to govern the relationships between Tommy Dort and the alien "Buck"? Between Kip Russell and The Mother Thing? Or even between Shor Nun and Seun?

At first glance, it appears to boil down to two choices:

(a) Kill!
(b) Apply the Golden Rule

The former is obviously wrong unless you are under direct attack from the extraterrestrial entity with no options for either negotiations or retreat.

But the latter is also wrong ... very wrong! And perhaps as deadly as the first alternative mentioned!

The Golden Rule derives from a Judeo-Christian cultural ethic: "Do unto others as you would have them do unto you."

When dealing with an extraterrestrial intelligent entity that perhaps has different biochemistry, genetic inheritance, and cultural bias, the Golden Rule could turn out to be the most deadly way to approach the problem! Something as simple as giving the alien a wiff of our twenty-one percent oxygen atmosphere at sea-level pressure could kill him outright; he may come from a different atmosphere. Triple-distilled water could poison him. And even the "universal" human gesture of peace and goodwill, the upraised hand, could be understood to be a threat to strike with that very hand.

The Golden Rule won't work. As a matter of fact, it really doesn't work too well among human beings of different cultural backgrounds.

This was realized by the founder of the field of metalaw, Andrew Gallagher Haley (1904–1966). Haley was a Washington, D.C., attorney specializing in international law, especially that dealing with radio communications. When the great Hungarian-American fluid dynamics scientist Dr. Theodore von Karman needed somebody to set up a company to make the solid propellant rocket takeoff boosters for airplanes called JATO (Jet Assisted Take Off) that had been developed by Dr. von Karman and his associates at Cal Tech in 1942, he called upon Andy Haley who formed and became the first president of Aerojet Engineering Corporation. After the war, Haley went back to practicing law in Washington, but also became more deeply involved in astronautics. He became the president of the old American Rocket Society and was one of the founders of the International Astronautical Federation (IAF) in 1949. During one of the IAF meetings in Brussels, Belgium, Haley began discussing the sorts of things we are discussing here with Dr. Frank J. Malina, one of his former Aerojet JATO colleagues. Haley presented the first paper on metalaw at the 8th IAF Congress on September 19, 1956.

In this initial paper, Haley recognized the shortcoming of the Golden Rule. He replaced it with the First Principle of Metalaw, hereafter named Haley's Rule:

Do unto others as they would have you do unto them.

Haley's Rule may be one of the prime philosophical and ethical statements of the twentieth century. It is pregnant with implications. The more one thinks about Haley's Rule, the deeper one gets into one's own ethical outlook on the world. It is a loaded statement.

It is not only the *only* way to treat an extraterrestrial intelligent entity, but it is also the only way to treat other human beings.

If you are to do unto others as they would have you do unto them, it means that you are going to have to understand them and to empathize with them. It demands a respect for them as individuals and a respect for their cultural background.

And, yes, it is also the truth in the jocular statement "A sadist is one who is kind to a masochist." But this very statement indicates that there must be some qualifiers to Haley's Rule. Obviously, there must be, because we called it the First Principle of Metalaw.

The other principles of metalaw have their roots not only in classical philosophy and ethics but in the thinking and writing of people such as Dr. Isaac Asimov, Dr. Jack Williamson, Lewis Padgett, and a host of other science fiction writers. You will find disturbing echoes of the Three Laws of Robotics here. You will find the echo of Gene Roddenberry's "Prime Directive" of *Star Trek*. And you will even find some of the principles set forth in historic documents such as the Declaration of Independence of the United States of America.

Robert A. Freitas Jr. discussed some of the preceding material in a different manner in the April 1977 issue of *Analog* ("The Legal Rights of Extraterrestrials"). He calls the First Principle of Metalaw the Great Rule rather than Haley's Rule. In the tradition of scientific inquiry, permit me the idiosyncrasy of naming the First Principle after the man who is responsible for it. Additional principles of metalaw have been proposed by Dr. Ernst Fasan, an Austrian jurist, who lists eleven principles. Fasan's wording may have suffered in the translation; be that as it may, Fasan's principles are often ambiguous and somewhat slippery. At the risk of being compared with the hypothetical critic of Moses ("But can they remember all ten? Wouldn't it be better to start with a couple at a time?"), I have tried to wrap it all up in six general principles of metalaw. At one time, I believed there were seven, but I discovered that one was redundant. All six of them are presented together here because one must always consider them together as a system, which is what metalaw is.

First Principle (Haley's Rule): Do unto others as they would have you do unto them.

Second Principle: The First Principle of metalaw must not be followed if, by so doing, the destruction of an intelligent being would be the result.

Third Principle (Rule of Self-defense): Any intelligent being may suspend adherence to the first two principles of metalaw in his own self-defense to prevent other entities from restricting his freedom of choice.

Fourth Principle (Rule of Survival): An intelligent being must not affect the freedom of choice of another intelligent being and must not, by inaction, permit the destruction of another intelligent being.

Fifth Principle (Rule of Free Choice): Any intelligent being has the right to a free choice of living style, living location, and socioeconomic-cultural system consistent with the principles of metalaw.

Sixth Principle (Rule of Free Movement): Any intelligent being may move about at will in a fashion unrestricted by any other intelligent being provided he does not breach the Zone of Sensitivity of another intelligent being without permission of that being to do so.

To wrap this system up, a new definition is needed, and the definition itself probably needs additional massaging. The Zone of Sensitivity is another metalaw concept. It is a volume of space about an intelligent being that extends out to the individual's thresholds of natural sensory detection *and* to the thresholds of his socio-economic-cultural system. This is probably yet imprecise, but perhaps we should leave something for the lawyers to argue. In any event, it is highly likely that *all* of the principles of metalaw will cause controversy. At this point in time, this is healthy and necessary if we are to work out a usable, viable system. As Dr. Theodore von Karman once said, "How can we progress without controversy?"

The principles of metalaw are the principles of freedom because it is patently impossible to consider any system of law dealing with all frames of existence and with intelligent beings of all kinds without this structure of freedom. Is there any other way to treat Zork Aarrggh? If you treat him as the Spanish treated the Aztecs or the Incas, as the Europeans in general treated the Amerindians, or as colonials of all sorts have treated the indigenous natives throughout history, you may be in very big trouble. Zork may not be the noble savage, if that is the initial impression he presents; that strange device he holds may be a disintegrator, or a communicator that controls a planet-buster.

Human beings are going to have a tremendous amount of trouble learning to adhere to *any* of the principles of metalaw, let alone all six of them. For at least the last ten thousand years since the beginning of the Neolithic Age when people began living in villages, the human race has been following a widely variant code of ethics or rules of behavior. Every culture on Planet Earth today runs on the basis of this Neolithic Ethic that was first put into words by Dr. Carleton S. Coon, the anthropologist: "You stay in your village, and I will stay in mine. If your sheep or cattle come to eat our grass, we will kill you. However, if we want some of your grass for our sheep and cattle, we will come and get it. Anybody who makes us try to change our ways is a witch, and we will kill him. Stay out of our village!"

Since most of the world today operates with this Neolithic Ethic, knowledge of it helps one make some sense of international affairs, especially in the Middle East. The Neolithic Ethic was wildly successful because it did succeed; it permitted the stabilization of the village system that grew into the city government that became the nation-state. It was a viable defensive mechanism in a world where there wasn't enough to go around, a peasant economy where everyone had a little bit of everything but nobody really had very much of anything. It was a viable ethic when, if you wanted it, you had to take it from somebody who had it.

But the world has changed in the last two hundred years because of the development of technology and the industrial market system wherein if you don't have it, you make it instead of taking it.

Out of this new industrial market system is growing the capability for us to move at will around our own planet and out into space as well. The industrial lifestyle requires the "marketing concept," which states that one must produce what customers want to buy lest he go belly-up in bankruptcy in the competitive free market system or, in the centrally directed economy, lest he end up with ten million butter churns that nobody wants because everybody already has two of them. The modern marketing concept of the industrial culture is totally in harmony with the principles of metalaw.

But aren't we now in a postindustrial culture? Perhaps parts of the United States, Canada, Western Europe, and Japan are getting there, but we are not really there yet. The world is still a long way from the postindustrial culture, in spite of the pronouncements of Herman Kahn, William Irwin Thompson, and others. How can it be otherwise when nearly half the human race on this planet cannot read or write its own native language, let alone another language? How can we be in a postindustrial world when human beings are starving by the millions and still breeding by the millions while striving against incredible odds to become part of the new industrial culture? How can we possibly be in the postindustrial era when politicians, economists, and even some corporate managers continue to tinker with the new system using old concepts? How can we be postindustrial when we are just beginning to develop the codes of the industrial culture and when most of the world still operates on the Neolithic Ethic?

The Neolithic Ethic right now is holding us back in our development as a species, and it will have to be replaced as rapidly as possible with something like metalaw.

Yes, there are inconsistencies within the six principles of metalaw and the basic definitions that accompany them. It is yet an imperfect system because it is very new and very revolutionary to our traditional ways of thinking. These inconsistencies should not be reasons to hold back from giving them a try, because the legal profession will expand and evolve to handle the inconsistencies in metalaw just as they do today in common law, corporate law, criminal law, and bureaucratic law, among others. There will always be individual cases to adjudicate in metalaw, cases that hinge on the fine points of the inconsistencies in the rules and the interpretations of those rules. Metalawyers and metalaw judges will evolve to make the rule interpretations and to judge each separate, individual case of inconsistency.

As seen through the eyes of the metalawyer, the human race still has a very long way to go before the great change replaces the old Neolithic Ethic with something like metalaw.

And we may very well not be given the opportunity to complete this evolutionary change before we are suddenly confronted by the fact that "we are not alone."

If the reports of close encounters of the third kind are true, it may well be that we have already been contacted but, because of our lack of an ethic such as metalaw, we have been put on "hold" until we do come up with it. Put yourself in the shoes of an extraterrestrial with an ethic of metalaw that controls his actions and relationships with his colleagues; under those conditions, would you want to bring the present members of the human race into your interstellar club?

If history is any reliable indicator of future trends, however, it is most likely that we will get caught with our ethics down. Contact is likely to happen before we develop a culture based on metalaw. If this does happen, it may be a very expensive learning process for us.

And there are still problems of conflict even if we do possess the ethic of metalaw. The failure of metalaw to resolve conflicts in the interstellar arena (and even on our home world, to some extent) could result in one of two alternatives: (a) there would be open conflict known as war, the use of physical force to coerce and to resolve the conflict in the old, tried-and-true traditions of the hunter that still reside in each of us to a greater or lesser degree because they represent the tried-and-true survival instincts of millions of years of evolution; or (b) disengagement and/or mutual retreat to separate territories, perhaps following ritual combat just to show "we're not afraid to fight if we really have to," in a manner that many mammalian species on Planet Earth resolve their conflicts. However, the latter alternative implies a surplus of turf and an endless frontier, which, in turn, brings up an interesting speculation: If we had the final frontier of space in which to disengage in a conflict, would this lead to a lessening of warfare on Planet Earth?

We will not know whether the former or the latter alternative is going to be "the easy way out" that all life-forms on Earth follow as a natural law until we learn how crowded the universe is and how difficult it is to move around in it. If the universe is empty of intelligent life-forms except ourselves, we will be able to disengage ourselves from our own conflicts, and we will still need the new ethic of metalaw just to improve the means with which we get along together. If the universe is teeming with intelligent life-forms, it's another story . . . and it's back to the Paleolithic of Planet Earth where the human race evolved in a world of scarcity, limited turf, and limited resources. We will be entering a universe where others already exist . . . and we'd better have something like metalaw for certain in that situation!

So, how do you act toward Zork Aarrggh of Beta Lycris A-3? You'd better have some sort of understanding of him first, particularly if you are the contactor. You'd better study him closely, study his culture carefully, and figure out what he would like done unto him. Otherwise, you stand a very good chance of making him very unhappy at the least. And if he becomes unhappy, he may be meaner and nastier than you are when you are unhappy.

If, on the other hand, you are the contactee, you'd better hope that Zork Aarrggh knows and understands the principles of metalaw!

APPENDIX A. Solar and Terrestrial Maps

Following are unmarked maps of the solar system (Earth is the third orbit out, fifth planet from the left) and Earth's major continents. These may assist you in discussing location, or at least in demonstrating a knowledge of solar and terrestrial geography with an extraterrestrial you may meet.

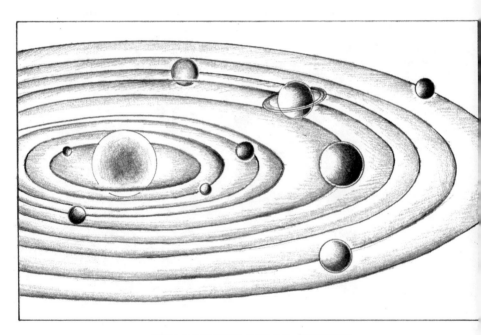

THE EARTH'S SOLAR SYSTEM

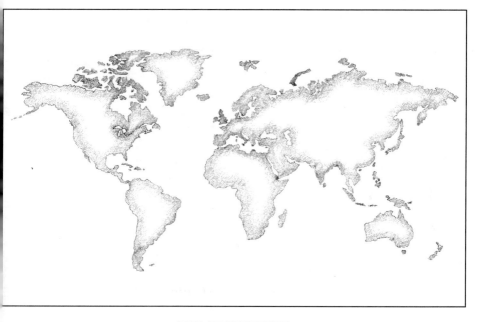

THE CONTINENTS

NORTH AND SOUTH AMERICA

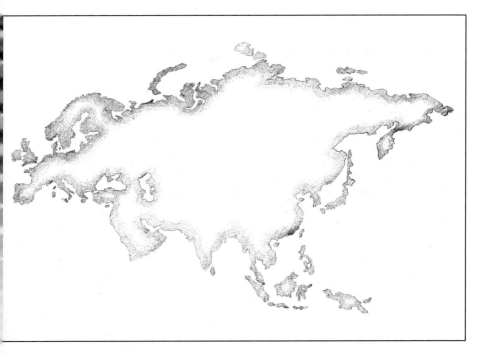

EUROPE AND ASIA

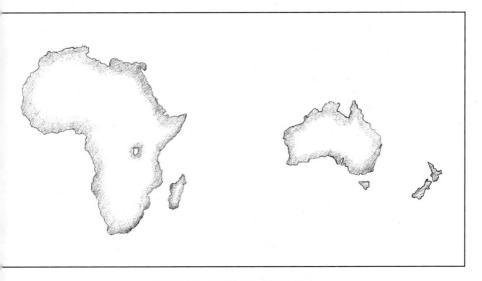

AFRICA AND AUSTRALIA

APPENDIX B. Naming Objects

Presented here as communication aids are the images and names of objects you are likely to have to present in a contact situation. These are divided into three groups: body parts, natural objects, and man-made objects. They may at least assist you in explaining the relationship between our spoken and written languages.

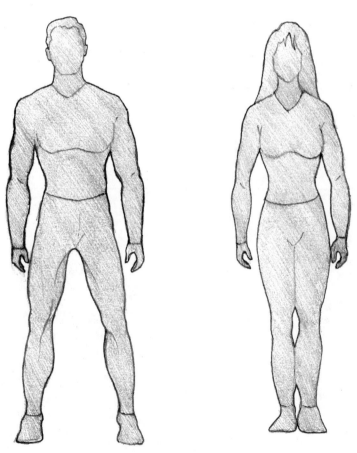

MAN AND WOMAN

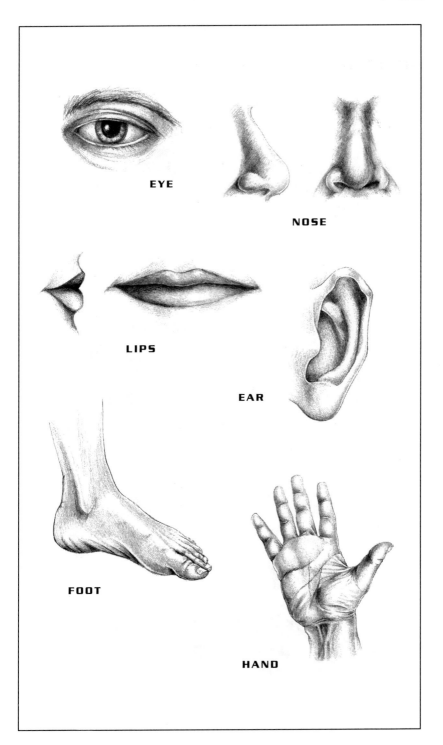

EYE

NOSE

LIPS

EAR

FOOT

HAND

ROCK

WATER

FIRE

TREE

GRASS

FLOWERS

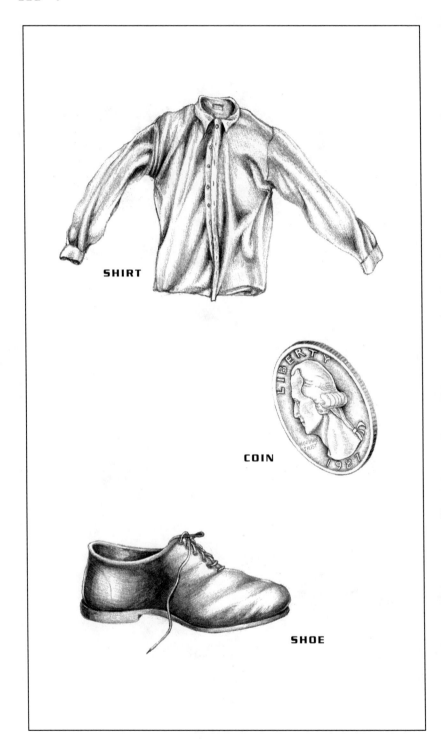

SHIRT

COIN

SHOE

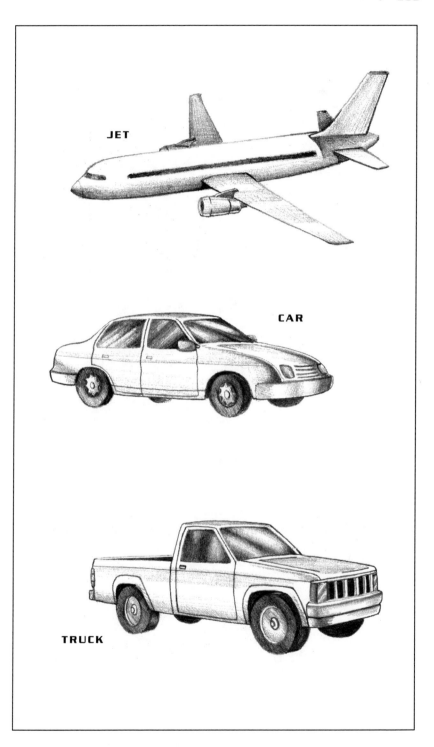

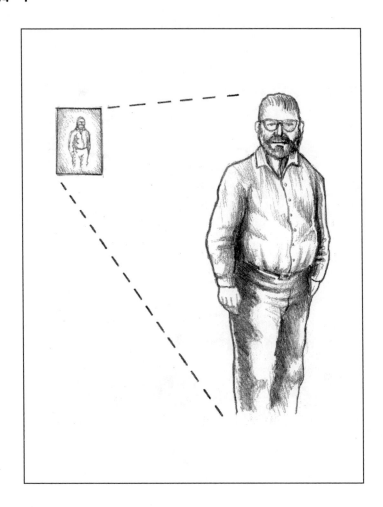

PHOTO
(May be used to explain your attempts to take a photo.)

APPENDIX C. Declaration of Principles Following the Detection of Extraterrestrial Intelligence
(The "Postdetection Protocol")

We, the institutions and individuals participating in the search for extraterrestrial intelligence,

Recognizing that the search for extraterrestrial intelligence is an integral part of space exploration and is being undertaken for peaceful purposes and for the common interest of all mankind,

Inspired by the profound significance for mankind of detecting evidence of extraterrestrial intelligence, even though the probability of detection may be low,

Recalling the Treaty on Principles Governing the Activities of States in the Exploration and Use of Outer Space, Including the Moon and Other Celestial Bodies, which commits States Parties to that Treaty to "inform the Secretary General of the United Nations as well as the public and international scientific community, to the greatest extent feasible and practicable, of the nature, conduct, locations and results" of their space exploration activities (Article XI),

Recognizing that any initial detection may be incomplete or ambiguous and thus require careful examination as well as confirmation, and that it is essential to maintain the highest standards of scientific responsibility and credibility,

Agree to observe the following principles for disseminating information about the detection of extraterrestrial intelligence:

1. Any individual, public or private research institution, or government agency that believes it has detected a signal from or other evidence of extraterrestrial intelligence (the discoverer) should seek to verify that the most plausible explanation for the evidence is the existence of extraterrestrial intelligence rather than some other natural phenomenon or anthropogenic phenomenon before making any public announcement. If the evidence cannot be confirmed as indicating the existence of extraterrestrial intelligence, the discoverer may disseminate the information as appropriate to the discovery of any unknown phenomenon.

2. Prior to making a public announcement that the evidence of extraterrestrial intelligence has been detected, the discoverer should promptly inform all other observers or research organizations that are parties to this declaration, so that those other parties may seek to confirm the discovery by independent observations at other sites and so that a network can be established to enable continuous monitoring of the signal or phenomenon. Parties to this declaration should not make any public announcement of this information until it is determined whether this information is or is not credible evidence of the existence of extraterrestrial intelligence. The discoverer should inform his/her or its relevant national authorities.

3. After concluding that the discovery appears to be credible evidence of extraterrestrial intelligence, and after informing other parties to this declaration, the discoverer should inform observers throughout the world through the Central Bureau for Astronomical Telegrams of the International Astronomical Union, and should inform the Secretary General of the United Nations in accordance with Article XI of the Treaty on Principles Governing the Activities of States in the Exploration and Use of Outer Space, Including the Moon and Other Celestial Bodies. Because of their demonstrated interest in and expertise concerning the existence of extraterrestrial intelligence, the discoverer should simultaneously inform the following international institutions of the discovery and should provide them with all pertinent data and recorded information concerning the evidence: The International Telecommunications Union, the Committee on Space Research of the International Council of Scientific Unions, the International Astronautical Federation, the International Academy of Astronautics, the International Institute of Space Law, Commission 51 of the International Astronomical Union and Commission J of the International Radio Science Union.

4. A confirmed detection of extraterrestrial intelligence should be disseminated promptly, openly, and widely through scientific channels and public media, observing the procedures in this declaration. The discoverer shall have the privilege of making the first public announcement.

5. All data necessary for the confirmation of detection should be made available to the international scientific community through publications, meetings, conferences, and other appropriate means.

6. The discovery should be confirmed and monitored and any data bearing on the evidence of extraterrestrial intelligence should

be recorded and stored permanently to the greatest extent feasible and practicable, in a form that will make it available for further analysis and interpretation. These recordings should be made available to the international institutions listed above and to members of the scientific community for further objective analysis and interpretation.

7. If the evidence of detection is in the form of electromagnetic signals, the parties to this declaration should seek international agreement to protect the appropriate frequencies by exercising the extraordinary procedures established within the World Administrative Radio Council of the International Telecommunication Union.

8. No response to a signal or other evidence of extraterrestrial intelligence should be sent until appropriate international consultations have taken place. The procedures for such consultations will be the subject of a separate agreement, declaration or arrangement.

9. The SETI Committee of the International Academy of Astronautics, in coordination with Commission 51 of the International Astronomical Union, will conduct a continuing review of the procedures for the detection of extraterrestrial intelligence and the subsequent handling of the data. Should credible evidence of extraterrestrial intelligence be discovered, an international committee of scientists and other experts should be established to serve as a focal point for continuing analysis of all observational evidence collected in the aftermath of the discovery, and also to provide advice on the release of information to the public. The committee should be constituted from representatives of each of the international institutions listed above and such other members as the committee may deem necessary. To facilitate the convocation of such a committee at some unknown time in the future, the SETI Committee of the International Academy of Astronautics should initiate and maintain a current list of willing representatives from each of the institutions listed above, as well as other individuals with relevant skills, and should make that list continuously available through the Secretariat of the International Academy of Astronautics. The International Academy of Astronautics will act as the Depository for this declaration and will annually provide a current list of parties to all the parties to this declaration.

(Endorsed April 1989 by the Board of Trustees of the International Academy of Astronautics and the Board of Directors of the International Institute of Space Law.)

APPENDIX D. People to Contact for First Contact

The following organization *wants* you to contact it first, even though it is not included in the SETI Postdetection Protocol: Mutual UFO Network, 103 Oldtowne Road, Seguin, TX 78155. The Mutual UFO Network (MUFON) is one of the oldest and largest UFO groups, with members in every state, who collect data and investigate claims.

The remaining references have not necessarily *asked* to be contacted, but represent other types of authority and expertise beyond ufology as such and should be seriously considered on a high-priority basis:

1. The top Signal Intelligence (SIGINT) officers of

- the National Security Agency. I do not have permission to give you their phone number, but you may be able to get it through an emergency request to the operator.
- Department of Defense Advanced Research Projects Agency (ARPA). The same applies here as with NSA.
- Central Intelligence Agency (CIA). Again, in an emergency, the phone company is supposed to help you.

2. The top mathematical linguists from Cal Tech and MIT, plus Noam Chomsky if MIT doesn't volunteer him

- Frederick Thompson, Cal Tech, (818) 354-6230, fbt@csvax. caltech.edu
- Noam Chomsky, Department of Linguistics, MIT, Cambridge, MA 02319, (617) 253-1541, fax (617) 258-8226

3. The presidents of the following organizations:

- Science Fiction and Fantasy Writers of America, Michael Capobianco, 14005 Robey Drive, Hughesville, MD 20637, (301) 274-9489, fax (301) 870-9181; Genie—M.CAPOBIANCO; Compuserve—70713,44
- The American Association for the Advancement of Science, Executive Director Dr. Richard S. Nicholson, 1333 H Street, NW, Washington, DC 20005, (202) 326-6400, fax (202) 289-4021

- The American Astronautical Society, Executive Director Carolyn F. Brown, 6352 Rolling Mill Place, Ste. 102, Springfield, VA 22152, (703) 866-0020, fax (703) 866-3526
- The American Astronomical Society, Dr. Peter B. Boyce, 1630 Connecticut Avenue, NW, Washington, DC 20009, (202) 328-2010, fax (202) 234-2560
- The American Institute of Aeronautics and Astronautics, Executive Director Cort Durocher, 370 L'Enfant Promenade, SW, Washington, DC 20024, (202) 646-7400, fax (202) 646-7508
- The International Astronomical Union, General Secretary Dr. J. Bergeron, 98 bis, blvd. Arago, 75014 Paris, France; phone: 1-43258385, fax: 1-40512100
- The National Science Foundation, Director Walter Massey, 1800 G Street, NW, Room 520, Washington, DC 20550, (202) 357-9498
- The National Research Council of the National Academy of Sciences, Executive Officer Philip M. Smith, 2101 Constitution Avenue, NW, Washington, DC 20418, (202) 334-2000, fax (202) 334-2158
- The RAND Corporation, 1700 Main Street, P.O. Box 2138, Santa Monica, CA 90407, (310) 393-6411, fax (310) 393-4818
- The Hudson Institute, Chappaqua, NY

4. The following key NASA personnel:

- NASA Administrator
- JPL Director Dr. Edward C. Stone, (818) 354-3405
- Chief of the Extraterrestrial Research Division of NASA Ames, John Billingham

5. DR. THOMAS MCDONOUGH, the SETI Director of the Planetary Society, 65 North Catalina Avenue, Pasadena, CA, (818) 793-5100

6. The following heads of these linguistic and anthropological organizations:

- Laboratory for Computational Linguistics, Carnegie Mellon University, Department of Philosophy, Pittsburgh, PA 15213; Director David A. Evans, (412) 268-5085, fax (412) 268-1440
- Linguistics Research Center, University of Texas, University Station, Austin, TX 78713-7247, Director Dr. Winfred P. Lehman, (512) 471-4566, fax (512) 471-6084

7. The following individuals:

- DAVID BALTIMORE, Nobel Laureate in Medicine and Physiology, Rockefeller University, 1230 York Avenue, New York, NY 10021-6399, (212) 327-7600, fax (212) 327-7949
- RICHARD BERENDZEN, President, American University, Physics Department, American University, Washington, DC 20016, (202) 885-1400, fax (202) 885-1428
- ELEANOR MARGARET BURBIDGE, former President of the American Astronomical Society, Professor of Astronomy, Department of Physics, C-011, University of California at San Diego, La Jolla, CA 92093-0111
- MELVIN CALVIN, Nobel Laureate in Chemistry, University Professor of Chemistry, University of California at Berkeley, Berkeley, CA 94720
- ALASTAIR G. W. CAMERON, former Chairman of the Space Science Board of the National Research Council, Professor of Astronomy, Harvard University, Harvard College Observatory, 60 Garden Street, Cambridge, MA 02138
- M. S. CHADHA, Senior Researcher, Phabha Atomic Research Center, Bombay, India
- FRANCIS CRICK, Nobel Laureate in Medicine and Physiology, Distinguished Research Professor, Salk Institute of Biological Studies, 10010 North Torrey Pines Road, La Jolla, CA 92037, (619) 453-4100, fax (619) 453-3105
- DAVID RUSSELL CRISWELL, Institute of Space Systems Operations, University of Houston, Houston, TX 77204-5502
- ROBERT S. DIXON, Assistant Director, Ohio State University Radio Observatory
- I. M. DONOHUE, former Chairman of the Space Sciences Board of the National Research Council, Profesor of Atmospheric Sciences, University of Michigan, Ann Arbor, MI
- FRANK D. DRAKE, former Director of the National Astronomy and Ionosphere Center, Goldwin Smith Professor of Astronomy, Cornell University, University of California, 413 Natural Science Building II, Santa Cruz, CA 95064
- FREEMAN J. DYSON, Professor of Physics, Institute for Advanced Study, Princeton, Olden Lane, Princeton, NJ 08540, (609) 734-8000, fax (609) 734-8399
- MANFRED EIGEN, Nobel Laureate in Chemistry, Max Planck

Institute for Biophysical Chemistry, Gottingen 37077, Germany; phone: (0551) 201432

- THOMAS EISNER, Jacob Gould Schurman Professor of Biology, NB&B, 347 Mudd Building, Cornell University, Ithaca, NY 14853
- JAMES L. ELLIOT, Associate Professor of Astronomy and Physics and Director of the George R. Wallace Astrophysical Observatory, MIT, 77 Massachusetts Avenue, Building 54-422A, Cambridge, MA 02139, (617) 253-6315, fax (617) 253-6208
- GEORGE B. FIELD, Senior Scientist, Smithsonian Astrophysical Observatory, and Professor of Astronomy, Harvard University, 60 Garden Street, Cambridge, MA 02138, (617) 495-7461, fax (617) 495-7326
- VITALY L. GINZBURG, Lenin Peace Prize Laureate, Senior Staff Member, Lebedev Physical Institute, Leninskiy Prospekt 53, Moscow 117924, Russia; phone: 1354264; fax: 1358533
- THOMAS GOLD, former Director of the Center for Radiophysics and Space Research, John L. Wetherill Professor of Astronomy, Cornell University, 7 Pleasant Grove, Ithaca, NY 14850, (607) 255-4341, fax (607) 255-8544
- LEO GOLDBERG, past President of the International Astronomical Union, former Director of the Kitt Peak National Observatory, 950 North Cherry Avenue, Tucson, AZ 85719, (602) 327-5511, fax (602) 325-9360
- PETER GOLDREICH, Lee A. DuBridge Professor of Astrophysics, 176 S. Bridge, California Institute of Technology, 1201 East California Boulevard, Pasadena, CA 91125, (818) 354-6193
- J. RICHARD GOTT III, Associate Professor of Astrophysics, Princeton University, Princeton, NJ 08544
- STEPHEN J. GOULD, Professor of Geology and Alexander Agassiz Professor of Zoology, Harvard University, Museum of Comparative Zoology, Oxford Street, Cambridge, MA 02138, (617) 495-2463, fax (617) 495-5667
- TOR HAGFORS, former Professor of Electrical Engineering at the University of Trondheim in Norway, Director of the National Astronomy and Ionosphere Center, Cornell University, Max Planck Institute of Aeronomy, Post Fach 20 D-3411, Katlenburg-Lindan, Germany
- STEPHEN W. HAWKING, Lucasian Professor of Mathematics, Cambridge University, Cambridge CB3 9EW, England
- DAVID S. HEESCHEN, Senior Scientist and former Director of the

National Radio Astronomy Observatory, 520 Edgemont Road, Charlottesville, VA 22903-2475, (804) 296-0211, fax (804) 296-0278
* JEAN HEIDMANN, Chief Astronomer, Observatoire de Paris (Paris Observatory), F-92195 Meudon, France
* GERHARD HERTZBERG, Nobel Laureate in Chemistry, Distinguished Research Scientist, National Research Council of Canada, (613) 993-9101, fax (613) 952-9696
* REV. THEODORE HESBURGH, President, University of Notre Dame, P.O. Box Q, Notre Dame, IN 46556, (219) 631-5303, fax (219) 239-6927
* PAUL M. HOROWITZ, Professor of Physics, Harvard University, Cambridge, MA
* SIR FRED HOYLE, former Professor of Astronomy and Experimental Philosophy, former Director of the Institute of Astronomy, Cambridge University, England, c/o the Royal Society, 6 Carleton House Terrace, London SWIY 5AG, England
* ERIC M. JONES, Staff Member, Los Alamos Scientific Laboratory, MSF 665, P.O. Box 1663, Los Alamos, NM 87545, (505) 667-7000, fax (505) 665-3910
* JUN JUGAKU, Research Institute of Civilization, Tokai University, Hiratsuka, Kanagawa 259-12, Japan
* N. S. KARDASHEV, Director of the Samarkand Radio Observatory Institute for Cosmic Research, Russian Academy of Sciences & Astrospace Center, Moscow, Russia
* KENNETH I. KELLERMAN, Senior Scientist, National Radio Astronomy Observatory, 520 Edgemont Road, Charlottesville, VA 22903-2475, (804) 296-0211, fax (804) 296-0278
* MICHAEL J. KLEIN, Senior Scientist, NASA Jet Propulsion Laboratory, Pasadena, CA, (818) 354-7132
* RICHARD B. LEE, Professor of Anthropology, University of Toronto, Toronto, Canada
* PER-OLAF LINDBLAD, Professor of Astronomy and Director of the Stockholm Observatory, S-133 00 Saltsjobeden, Sweden; phone: 8-7170380; fax: 8-7174719
* PAUL D. MACLEAN, Chief of the Laboratory of Brain Evolution and Behavior, National Institute of Mental Health, 9916 Logan Drive, Potomac, MD 20854, (301) 496-1371, fax (301) 480-1668
* MIKHAIL YA. MAROV, Department Chief, M. V. Keldesh Institute of Applied Mathematics, Russian Academy of Sciences, Moscow, and Professor of Planetary Physics, Moscow State University,

Miuskaya Ploshchad 4, Moscow 125047, Russia; phone: 95-9723714

- MATTHEWS MESELSON, Thomas Dudley Cabot Professor of the Natural Sciences and Professor of Biochemistry and Molecular Biology, Harvard University, 7 Divinity Avenue, Cambridge, MA 02138
- MARVIN L. MINSKY, Donner Professor of Science, former Director of the Artificial Intelligence Laboratory, MIT, Media Laboratory, MIT, 20 Ames Street, Cambridge, MA 02139, (617) 253-0338, fax (617) 258-6264
- MASAKI MORIMOTO, Director, Nobeyama Radio Observatory, Tokyo, Japan
- PHILIP MORRISON, Institute Professor, MIT, Boston, MA
- BRUCE C. MURRAY, former Director of the NASA Jet Propulsion Laboratory, Professor of Geological and Planetary Science, 159 S. Mudd, California Institute of Technology, Pasadena, CA, bcm@earth1.gps.caltech.edu
- WILLIAM L. NEWMAN, Assistant Professor of Planetary Physics and Astronomy, Dept. of Earth and Space Science, University of California at Los Angeles, Westwood, CA 90024-1567, (310) 206-0686, fax (310) 206-5673
- JAN H. OORT, former President of the International Astronomical Union, Professor of Astronomy, Leiden University, Leiden, Netherlands
- ERNST J. OPIK, Senior Scientist, Armagh University, Northern Ireland
- LESLIE E. ORGEL, Research Professor, the Salk Institute, Adjunct Professor of Chemistry, University of California at San Diego, P.O. Box 85800, San Diego, CA 92186-5800, (619) 453-4100
- FRANCO PACINI, Director, Arcetri Observatory, Largo E. Fermi 5, Firenze 50125 Italy; phone: (055) 2752232; fax: (055) 220039
- MICHAEL D. PAPAGIANNIS, President of the Commission on the Search for Extraterrestrial Life of the International Astronomical Union, Chairman, Department of Astronomy, Boston University, Boston, 1105 Lexington Street, No. 5-10, Waltham, MA 02154, (617) 353-3081, fax (617) 353-6488
- RUDOLF PESEK, Chairman on Astronautics of the Czechoslovak Academy of Sciences, Czech Technical University, Prague
- W. H. PICKERING, National Medal of Science Laureate, former Director of the NASA Jet Propulsion Laboratory, Lignetics, Inc.,

1150 Foothill Boulevard, Suite E, La Canada, CA 91011, fax (818) 952-5009

- CYRIL PONNAMPERUNA, Professor of Chemistry and Director of the Laboratory of Chemical Evolution, University of Maryland, College Park, MD 20742, (301) 405-1897, fax (301) 405-9375
- JONATHAN VOS POST, jpost@earthlink.net, http://www.magic-dragon.com
- EDWARD M. PURCELL, Nobel Laureate in Physics, Gade University Professor Emeritus, Lyman Laboratory, Harvard University, Cambridge, MA 02138
- DAVID M. RAUP, Chairman, Department of Geophysical Sciences, University of Chicago, 5757 Woodlawn, Chicago, IL 60673, (312) 702-2163, fax (312) 702-2166
- GROTE REBER, Inventor of the Radiotelescope, Tasmania, Australia
- MARTIN J. REES, Phurman Professor of Astronomy and Director of the Institute of Astronomy, Madingly Road, Cambridge University, Cambridge CB3 OHA, England; phone: 337548, fax 337523
- DALE A. RUSSELL, Chief of the Paleontology Division, National Museums of Canada, Ottawa, Canada
- ROALD J. SAGDEEV, former Director of the Institute for Cosmic Research, Soviet Academy of Sciences, Moscow, Russia, now at the Physics Department, University of Maryland
- CLAUDE E. SHANNON, Inventor of Communication Theory, National Medal of Science, Donner Professor of Science Emeritis, MIT, 5 Cambridge Street, Winchester, MA 01890
- JILL TARTER, Research Astronomer, University of California at Berkeley, NASA Ames Research Center, MS TR-002, Moffett Field, CA 94035
- KIP S. THORNE, Richard P. Feynman Professor of Theoretical Physics, 151 West Bridge Annex, California Institute of Technology, Pasadena, CA, kip@tapir.caltech.edu
- V. S. TROITSKY, Scientific Director, Radiophysics Research Institute, Gorky, Russia
- J. P. VALLEE, Hertzberg Institute of Astrophysics, Edinburgh, Scotland, UK
- SEBASTIAN VON HOERNER, Senior Staff Member, National Radio Astronomy Observatory, Krumenacker-Str. 186, Esslingen 73733 Germany

- EDWARD O. WILSON, National Medal of Science laureate, Baird Professor of Science and Professor of Biology, Harvard University, Museum of Comparative Zoology, Oxford Street, Cambridge, MA 02138, (617) 495-2463, fax (617) 495-5667
- BENJAMIN ZUCKERMAN, Professor of Astronomy, University of California at Los Angeles, 405 Hilgard Avenue, Los Angeles, CA 90024

APPENDIX E. Encounter Equipment

For an encounter of any kind, you will need:

1. This handbook.
2. A friend or buddy who can corroborate what you see and assist you if you are injured. It is strongly advised that you do not go alone. Unsupported sightings are generally less credible.
3. A bright flashlight by night and/or a laser. The brightest flashlights are made for scuba diving and these can be very bright. Check the King Pelican brand at your local scuba diving shop. Be very careful with a laser. The beam can blind you or someone around you. The small pointer ruby lasers are no more powerful than a flashlight and of little additional use.
4. Two still photo cameras: One should be a point-and-shoot auto-focus and auto advance. The second should be a 35mm camera with a powerful telephoto lens. For daytime, use 400-speed film in the auto-focus and 100 speed (for the greatest detail) in the 35mm. At night use 1000-speed film in the auto-focus camera and 400 in the 35mm. The higher the speed, the coarser the grain in the film and the less detail recorded.
5. Warm clothes, a hat, hiking boots, and suitable water or other rations needed for both comfort and safety.
6. Several pencils and paper.
7. A magnetic compass. This not only will help provide location but can also record anomalous magnetic effects during a sighting.
8. A topographical map. Be sure to mark your route and the estimated location of any encounter before moving on.
9. Powerful binoculars. Binoculars are easier to sight a moving object in, but a powerful telephoto lens on a camera can serve the same purpose.
10. A small mirror, preferably 2 to 3 inches across with beveled edges to allow it to be handled easily.
11. A cell phone if you will be in range of a node and the phone numbers of local police, air force, and UFO organizations.
12. A pocket tape recorder. The type used to dictate memos will be the easiest to carry. This may not function during an encounter,

but will serve to record your detailed impressions immediately after the encounter.

Be sure to notify someone you trust of where you are going. If you disappear or are injured, this will both provide a corroborated record of the lost time and help to ensure your safety.

APPENDIX F. Possible Locations for Encounters of the First Kind

NOTE: There is no way to be sure of seeing a UFO. Even the most devoted expert can spend years without having an encounter. The appearance of UFOs seems to be cyclical and often recurs in the same area several times, followed by no further encounters.

Locations:

1. Near Area 51 in New Mexico. A lot of people are seeing something, but *what* is open to often heated debate. Do try to avoid the restricted areas, as it is a criminal offense to enter them.

2. Mexico City, Mexico, has a record of regular appearances of UFOs. In 1996 this was one of the most dependable locations for sightings.

3. Southwestern England. These seem mostly connected to crop circles, which often also appear without any UFO sightings.

4. The Amazon Basin, very cyclical and erratic, but occasionally intense.

5. The western Canadian provinces, away from urban areas. Perhaps here the multitude of sightings result from the visibility given by the open areas. Again, the exact location changes, with multiple night sightings not uncommon.

The reality is that there is no way of predicting where or when an encounter might occur. There is no discernible pattern, nor is there any type of event or date that elicits a UFO response. The best approach is to be always ready, and always alert to the opportunity. Encounters can happen to anyone and are most likely to be recognized by those who are prepared—you.